D1520794

Home ➡ WORDS

Studies in Childhood and Family in Canada

Studies in Childhood and Family in Canada is a multidisciplinary series devoted to new perspectives on these subjects as they evolve. The series features studies that focus on the intersections of age, class, race, gender, and region as they contribute to a Canadian understanding of childhood and family, both historically and currently.

Series Editor
Cynthia Comacchio
Department of History
Wilfrid Laurier University

Manuscripts to be sent to
Brian Henderson, Director
Wilfrid Laurier University Press
75 University Avenue West
Waterloo, Ontario, Canada, N2L 3C5

Home ➡ WORDS

Discourses
of Children's
Literature
in Canada

Mavis Reimer,
editor

WLU

Wilfrid Laurier University Press

This book has been published with the help of a grant from the Canadian Federation for the Humanities and Social Sciences, through the Aid to Scholarly Publications Programme, using funds provided by the Social Sciences and Humanities Research Council of Canada. We acknowledge the support of the Canada Council for the Arts for our publishing program. We acknowledge the financial support of the Government of Canada through the Book Publishing Industry Development Program for our publishing activities.

Library and Archives Canada Cataloguing in Publication

Home words : discourses of children's literature in Canada / Mavis Reimer [editor].

(Studies in childhood and family in Canada)
Includes bibliographical references and index.
ISBN 978-1-55458-016-3

1. Home in literature. 2. Children's literature, Canadian—History and criticism. I. Reimer, Mavis, 1954–   II. Series.

PS8069.H65 2008   C810.8'0355   C2007-903604-X

Cover design by David Drummond. Text design by P. J. Woodland.

∞

This book is printed on Ancient Forest Friendly paper (100% post-consumer recycled).

Printed in Canada

Published by Wilfrid Laurier University Press
Waterloo, Ontario, Canada
www.wlupress.wlu.ca

CONTENTS

□ □ □

LIST OF FIGURES

Figures 1–16 appear in a section that begins facing page 124.

□

□ □ □

ACKNOWLEDGEMENTS

RESEARCH FOR THE ESSAYS IN THIS COLLECTION and the consultations and meetings of the researchers were supported by a multi-year grant for collaborative research from the Social Sciences and Humanities Research Council of Canada through its Research Development Initiatives program. Additional funding came from the University of Winnipeg; Grande Prairie Regional College, Alberta; the University of Victoria; Deakin University in Melbourne, Australia; and the Australasian Children's Literature Association for Research. This book, a major result of the research collaboration, has been published with the help of a grant from the Canadian Federation for the Humanities and Social Sciences, through the Aid to Scholarly Publications Programme, using funds provided by the Social Sciences and Humanities Council of Canada.

Behind the authors of the various chapters in the book stands a group of able research assistants. Over the four years of our research, these included Kelly Burns, Charlotte Fortier, Sara Harms, Laura Jakal, Robbie Richardson, Melanie Dennis Unrau, Matt Reimer, Andrea Siemens, Andrew Reimer, Andrea Hutchinson, Maria Reimer, Charlie Peters, Sophie Walker, Janice Banser, and James Nahachewsky. We were helped in our work by office and administrative staff members in all our institutions. Special thanks are due to Rebecca Stillwell, of the Department of Modern Languages and Literatures, at the University of Winnipeg, and Sophia Sherman, in the office of the School of Library and Information Studies at the University of Alberta, for going well beyond the call

ix

of duty. We were aided in the preparation of this manuscript by the careful work of Jayne Hildebrand, Honours English student at the University of Winnipeg, and by the incomparable Sharlee Reimer, Research Coordinator in the Centre for Research in Young People's Texts and Cultures at the University of Winnipeg, whose energy drove us through the last months and weeks of detailed work, checking, and rechecking required by such an undertaking.

Ongoing conversations with colleagues and administrators sustained many of us in our intellectual work. We thank, in particular, members of the Department of English and the Department of Modern Languages and Literatures at the University of Winnipeg. All of us were borne up, too, by the friends and families who are the wind beneath our wings.

The project was unique in the extent of the exchange of views and resources, reworking of drafts, and testing and challenging of ideas among the collaborators in what we called the Childplaces project, or, more simply, the Home project. This book is the result of the agreement of twelve people to work closely with one another over several years and is a testament to their passion, their patience, their tenacity, their sense of humour, and their goodwill.

□ □ □

INTRODUCTION ➡ **Discourses of Home
in Canadian Children's
Literature**

Mavis Reimer

Enter "home" as a search term in the online
version of the *Oxford English Dictionary* and your computer screen quickly
fills with a long list of possible sites to visit. Printed out, the entry for the
primary term yields more than thirty pages of definitions and examples
of the word, as noun, adjective, verb, and adverb. This listing is followed
by listings for more than seventy-five words, compounds, and phrases
beginning with "home": "home-coming," "home rule," "home run," "home
truth," "homework." The search engine for the dictionary doesn't easily
allow a compilation of all the words and phrases that include "home" in
another position, but even a cursory troll yields such intriguing entries as
"bring oneself home," an idiom for recouping financial losses, and "go
home," a euphemism for death. The many overlapping and sometimes contradictory meanings of the English word make it difficult to translate into
French, as Danielle Thaler and Anne Rusnak remark in their chapters in
this volume.

From the beginning of the multi-year project out of which this collection of essays developed, the collaborators agreed that we would not pre-
scribe particular ways of thinking about "home" for our study. In the first
place, while we are all scholars of literature, we do not share a specialism
within the discipline. Only one of us—Louise Saldanha—is trained as a
specialist in Canadian children's literature. Many of us—Perry Nodelman, Andrew O'Malley, Danielle Thaler, Anne Rusnak, Margaret Mackey,
Clare Bradford, and I—have focused most of our scholarly work on texts

for children, although in different periods, national literatures, and forms. Neil Besner and Doris Wolf specialize in Canadian (adult) literature. And two of our members approached the project with other interests that intersected with the aims of this research: Paul DePasquale studies writing by and about North American Aboriginal peoples and Deborah Schnitzer works as a semiotician to develop vocabularies for talking about verbal and visual intertexts. These differences in training, in theoretical commitments, and in the objects of our studies mean that each of us pays attention to different texts and to different aspects of texts. What we shared at the start of the project was little more than a suspicion that texts for children act as amplifiers for the simultaneously commonplace and resonant idea of home.

But our reasons for not restricting the ways in which we took up the question of home were not only pragmatic but also theoretical. It quickly became clear to us that the problem of the meanings of "home," like the keywords Raymond Williams discusses in his study of the vocabulary of culture and society, is "inextricably bound up" with the problems and possibilities the word is used to discuss (*Keywords* 15). As a result, we chose to begin by studying the languages of home in use in literary texts, and by trying to articulate the rules, beliefs, and values governing these uses; to articulate, in other words, the discourses of home circulated and interrogated in different Canadian children's texts. Among the texts studied in this volume are various groupings of award-winning fiction in English and French, historical fiction for young adults, texts by Aboriginal writers and writers of colour, a wide range of picture books, and Catherine Parr Traill's *Canadian Crusoes*, a book usually identified as the first English-Canadian novel for children.

We did not attempt to cover the field of Canadian children's texts or to represent all the possible theoretical approaches to the study of children's texts. In this sense, the project is an untidy, rather than a finished, one. Our hope is that the design and the outcomes of the project will open questions for further study—by scholars and teachers of Canadian children's literature, certainly, but also by scholars and teachers in such adjacent and overlapping fields as Canadian literature, international children's literary and cultural studies, and pedagogical and curriculum studies. Neil Besner, Clare Bradford, and Margaret Mackey—to whom we assigned the task of watching the progress of the primary research with a view to identifying the conjunctions and disjunctions between this work and ongoing work in Canadian (adult) literature, commenting on unacknowledged cultural and national ideologies, and developing practical applications of the research—suggest some of the directions that might be pursued by scholars in these related disciplines.

We met as a group for working meetings annually for three years and, between our symposia, exchanged recommendations for reading and sent drafts of papers through an electronic discussion board. While we did not reach a set of systematic conclusions about the ways in which discourses of home function in Canadian children's literature, our regular and ongoing communications with one another led us to see some senses of home as more resonant and some questions about home as more urgent than others for the study of this literature.

"Home" is an auratic term in children's texts generally.[1] The primary setting of children's books typically is the dwelling in which the protagonist lives, usually with members of her or his family. Narrative adventures and misadventures that take a child away from home often are resolved with the child's return to it, so that theorists of children's literature sometimes use "home" to describe the full narrative closure of conventional texts for children,[2] a sense analogous to its use in the language of games and computers.

Because home normally is the site of the satisfaction of the most basic human needs for shelter and food, the depiction of stable and safe housing in narratives for children can be read as the adult promise, or hope, that the world is a place in which children can not only survive, but also thrive. The understanding that an adequate home is a primary obligation of adults to children is shared much more widely than in children's literature, of course. The right to a standard of living adequate to health and well-being, specifically including "food, clothing, housing and medical care and necessary social services," is enshrined in article 25 of the United Nations' Universal Declaration of Human Rights, for example, and these rights are explicitly extended to children as "members of the human family" in the Convention on the Rights of the Child. A child inside a family home is a naturalized image clearly assumed by social service and child protection agencies across Canada and elsewhere: the presence of the child outside the home or inside an insufficient home is a primary trigger for the intervention of the state.[3] That children ought to be in safe and nurturing homes is a conviction so widely held that international and domestic aid organizations often feature homeless, hungry children in their appeals for donations, because they know that depictions of such lack will prompt public generosity.[4] Nancy Batty has demonstrated that, despite the acknowledgement of humanitarian agencies that there has been an over-reliance on images of starving children in their advertising, they continue to use what she calls the "obscene images" of "a virtual pornography of suffering" children because such images deliver the results they seek (27). These media texts reveal and produce a context from which literary texts featuring homeless young people or lost children or endangered children, like those in the recent Young Adult novels I discuss in my chapter, take their affective charge.

Homes as material places not only supply the physical necessities of survival, but also privacy, which the Supreme Court of Canada has maintained "is essential for the well-being of the individual" in an interpretation of the Charter of Rights and Freedoms (qtd. in Mosher 43). In other Charter judgements, the Court has linked bodies and homes as protected under the rights of privacy accorded Canadians and has held that such rights are grounded in exclusion, in the ability "to prevent others from transgressing these boundaries without consent" (Mosher 44). Indeed, Rosemary George has argued that "a pattern of select inclusions and exclusions" is "the basic organizing principle around which the notion of the 'home' is built" across discourses in English (2). Having a space to which one can control access is closely related to notions of ownership and property, notions that, as Perry Nodelman demonstrates in his discussion in this volume, can be encoded in, and decoded from, narrative technique.

Owning property is a mark of the successful middle-class consumer in Canadian society, as the real estate and business sections of newspapers repeatedly assure us, and the number of new housing starts a key indicator of the economic health of the nation.[5] In public discourse, middle-class home owners stereotypically are imagined as male; housekeepers and homemakers almost invariably are gendered female.[6] As house and home magazines make obvious, the maintenance and decoration of domestic space is not only an expression of female taste, but also an indicator of class and racial status.[7] The rooms featured in decorating magazines, furnished with beautiful objects but empty of the people "who make housework," function unambiguously as "an erotic vision of home," according to Kim Golombisky (1). Such a function is continuous with the domestic ideology being articulated in the nineteenth century in England, which, Nancy Armstrong argues, ascribed to the middle-class wife and mother the cultural tasks of wanting and then of putting in place "the objects that flooded in from the colonies" (*Desire* 34). Andrew O'Malley argues in his chapter in this volume that this domestic ideology was also transplanted to the colonies—as seen in the books written for children in the "home country" and in the young Canadian colony—and turned to the end of making invaders into settlers.

If homes are places from which people can be kept out, they can also keep people in their places. Anne Rusnak, discussing contemporary novels for children published in Quebec in her chapter in this collection, observes that these child protagonists rarely leave home for adventures. They are much more likely to invite adventure into their homes and to find that home expands to accommodate them. The deep sense of fitness and belonging connoted by being "at home" is the objective of many central characters of children's texts, not only in French Canada, and networks of family and communities are frequently shown to be essential to the realization of such a state of mind and heart. But the multivalency of the concept of home means that senses can be separated from one another and opposed, as well as conflated with one another. Louise Saldanha in her chapter notes the ways in which the structures of the family home and of the public space of the larger community often contradict rather than recapitulate one another in texts by writers of colour in Canada. While the rhetoric of official multiculturalism asserts that racially marked children are included in the home of the nation, and some of the writers work to verify this ideal, Saldanha finds that the narratives often also reveal the official discourse to be founded on strategies of exclusion and containment.

In its focus on *Canadian* children's texts, this collection of essays invokes and assumes the common usage in which "home" is understood as the nation, as it is in the first line of the national anthem in both official languages, in which home, nation, and territory are explicitly yoked together: "O Canada, / Our home and native land," "O Canada, / Terre de nos aïeux." The power of this linguistic and conceptual linkage has often been remarked by theorists of the nation and nationalism, and in postcolonial theory and criticism of the past decades. As Ghassan Hage observes, nationalist practices are enabled by the "structure of feeling" that constitutes the "homely imaginary," a structure built on "the key themes of familiarity, security and community" (*Paranoid* 40). Using some of the same terms, Benedict Anderson theorizes the production of the nation by focusing on the "institutions of power" through which colonialist states build the "imagined community" of the nation (*Imagined* 163).

The first of these institutions, according to Anderson, is the census, which provides the identity categories used to define a population. Clare Bradford, in her comparative reading of Australian and Canadian children's texts here, demonstrates the circularity of that definition: in both literatures, gendered identity categories work to construct the national citizens who can confidently claim the nation as home if they "conform to the will of the national imaginary" (192). The second institution of power is the map, which projects organized views of the national dominion and fixes its boundaries with other territories. W.H. New has proposed that the discursive construction of Canada is derived from "boundary rhetoric" in which Canada is imagined as "a place that *includes*, a place that *excludes*, as a place *divided*, as a place that *distributes* resources and power, and as a place that embraces some ongoing principle of *boundary negotiation*" (5). In her chapter in this volume, Deborah Schnitzer finds that windows in Canadian picture books are often the sites of such border practices, articulating and disarticulating the relations between here and there, inside and outside, now and then. The third institution of power in Anderson's analysis is the museum, which works to establish narratives of legitimate national ancestry. It is this function that many of the writers in this volume uncover in the Canadian texts they investigate, as, for example, in the historical fiction of Quebec, in which Thaler sees the figure of the *coureur des bois* used to propose the possibility of a mingling of Aboriginal and immigrant cultures as the basis of home. But, more often, the writers here find that the Canadian narratives of legitimate ancestry produced for young people are built on disavowals of the Aboriginal presence in the spaces claimed for the nation.

Disavowal, Elisabeth Bronfen observes, is always a double utterance, in which "something is affirmed in the same gesture that it is denied" (70). If this is so, then much of Canadian children's literature can be said to know, and to betray its anxiety about its knowledge of, the dispossession on which the home of the nation is founded. The centre of this volume properly is occupied by Doris Wolf and Paul DePasquale's study of picture books by Aboriginal authors in Canada. As Wolf and DePasquale demonstrate, contemporary Aboriginal writers in large numbers are producing fictions for children that challenge the dominant narratives of the nation. Working within and against a literary form that was shaped by the "heavy" history of colonialism and neo-colonialism, the Aboriginal authors for young people they discuss write home as intergenerational connectedness, access to land, and political protest.

Scholars of children's literature often remark on the peculiar fact that young people's texts are identified by their target audience rather than by their producers, many scholars building on the observation by Jacqueline Rose that children's fiction "rests ... openly on an acknowledged difference, a rupture almost, between writer and addressee" (2). As one of the foundational questions of the genre, the relation between the text and the reader is a question that informs much theoretical and critical work on children's texts, including several of the essays in this volume. In her chapter, Margaret Mackey explores the problem of what young readers can and should be told about the discourses of home circulating in Canadian children's literature. One of the traditional tasks of children's literature has been to produce its readers as good citizens, a task closely bound up with its imagining of home. Rosemary George argues that such an imagining should be understood as "a display of hegemonic power" and a setting-out of the markers of "a naturalized socialization process" (6); perhaps, then, it is not only difficult but impossible to translate scholarly discourses about children's texts for the readers addressed by those texts. Perhaps the translation of scholarly challenges to hegemonic displays of power—a challenge many of the critics in this volume hope their work undertakes—requires, first, that the very notion of "the child" is challenged and changed in the "real" world of which the academy is a part.

The image of Canada outside the country often is closely associated with its spectacular landscapes and extreme weather, an image manipulated by tourism boards at all levels.[8] The North, the garrison, forests, bogs, islands, blizzards, and violent thunderstorms—these iconic places and scenes have featured in much Canadian literature, including much Canadian literature for young people, and also appear in many of the books studied in this volume. But none of the writers here focuses on the representation of the natural world or assumes that there is an easy access to nature that does not pass through culture. There is a shared sense in all these essays that the natural has been overwritten by culture, that an understanding of home in Canadian children's literature must begin from an account of the social, political, and economic conditions that form places and place readers. As Edward Said observes, "It is in culture that we can seek out the range of meanings and ideas conveyed by the phrases *belonging to* or *in a* place, being *at home in a place*" (*The World, the Text, and the Critic* 8).

This emphasis on cultural meanings is consonant with current practices of literary criticism in general. But it was also overdetermined by the specific context in which our research and discussions have taken shape. The proposal for the project was finalized in the month following the events of September 11, 2001; the ways in which various notions of home have been deployed and contested in public discourse since then have entered many of our discussions. The auratic links between nation and home, and home and children clearly were assumed and exploited in the series of addresses to the nation made by President George W. Bush in the days and months following 9/11. Announcing the establishment of a cabinet position to coordinate the organizations that defend "the homeland" on September 20, 2001, for example, Bush ends with an appeal to Americans to "hug your children," implicitly equating the military defences and offensives of the nation with a family embrace. Keeping "American children calm and safe" was identified as a principal value in another of his speeches later that fall, even as the U.S. military was preparing its plans for its "shock and awe" bombing campaign against the homeland and the homes of Iraqi children and adults.[9]

William Walters has proposed the neologism "domopolitics" as "an analytic" that describes the contemporary "reconfiguring of the relations between citizenship, state, and territory" as seen, in particular, in the attempts to rationalize "a series of security measures in the name of a particular understanding of home" (241). Domopolitics includes the tactical juxtaposition of the "warm words" of home "with the danger words of a chaotic outside" (241), the "re-bordering" that has suspended the "expectation of a borderless world" (250), and the dispersal of the control functions of borders "into networks of information and surveillance" inside the national territory (251).[10] In Canada, governmental and media debates about participating in the American invasion of Iraq and, later, joining the American plan for continental missile defence revealed the different assumptions among Canadians about what constitutes home in a globalizing world. That such questions are not ones that will be decided only by Canadians has also become clear. As I write this introduction, passport offices across Canada are being swamped by citizens anxious to acquire the documents that will establish their identities as authorized travellers at American border controls.

Completing our research and writing within these political contexts confirmed what we only suspected when we began this project: learning to read "home" matters. Discourses of home concatenate the knowledge of self with territory, the desire for belonging with the ownership of property, the rights to privacy with gendered spaces, safety with nation. Disturbances to one of these senses of home can reverberate at any or all of the points along the chain of meaning. Learning to read "home" in children's texts matters. The homely imperatives adults direct to children through the texts designed for them proceed from determinate constructions of class, race, gender, and nation, and entail complicated understandings of the relation of self and other, kin and stranger, here and there. Learning to read "home" matters: it is, perhaps, the beginning of rewriting it.

□ □ □

Notes

1   I first saw the descriptor "auratic" attached to the idea of home in Rosemary George's book, *The Politics of Home* (2). The neologistic adjective form suggests the diffuse sense of mystical meaning that attends the idea.

2   For example, Jon Stott and Christine Francis maintain that all settings in children's literature can be categorized as "home" or "not-home" and that children's narratives typically proceed from "not home" to "home" (223–24). Christopher

Clausen observes that books widely acknowledged as books "for children" are those in which "home is clearly where the characters belong and where, after many vicissitudes, they return" (142). While Virginia Wolf outlines a range of plots in children's literature, she concludes that "home is the dominant place" in each of them (54) and that the "essential homelessness" explored in much modern literature for adults (66) is finally denied in children's literature. And Reuben Sánchez, in demonstrating that Chicana writer Sandra Cisnero creates a new myth for her community, nevertheless reveals that myth to be constructed in terms of the dialectic of home/homelessness and escape/return. Building on Clausen's and Wolf's observations, Perry Nodelman argued, in *The Pleasures of Children's Literature* (1992), that the narrative and thematic pattern he calls the home-away-home story is, in fact, the most important of the defining characteristics of children's literature as a genre (147), a claim reiterated in subsequent editions. Maria Nikolajeva argues, to the contrary, that there has been a generic shift in children's literature, which is now characterized by more open endings that question the value of a return home, and Eliza Dresang argues that, under the pressure of new technologies, texts for young people are "departing from the usual or traditional" patterns, such as the circular home-away-home story (4).

3   For example, in Manitoba's Child and Family Services Act, the child's right to a home is never stated explicitly, but the picture of the child in a family home clearly governs as the ideal. Indeed, many sections of the Act are not readable unless one assumes that the natural state of the child is to be safe in a family home. The clearest definition of what constitutes a "good-enough" home comes in the list of the rights and responsibilities of homemakers assigned by an authorized agency to care for a child temporarily "in the child's home." These include the presence of a caring adult, normal housekeeping, and maintenance of the home; the reasonable control and discipline of the child in the home; and the provision of necessary goods and services (art.13, sec. 3). The same Act includes provisions for apprehending children who abscond from "any premises where the child is lawfully placed" (art. 53, sec. 1).

4   See, for example, the *World Disasters Report 2003* on the home page of the International Federation of Red Cross and Red Crescent Societies, which features Iraqi children collecting jugs of water and Angolan children queuing for food. Other repeated shots in the video depict children against a background of damaged homes or confined in institutions. The first link on the page is to a "How to help" page, which outlines procedures for making donations to national societies belonging to the international federation, for online donations, and for bank transfers.

5   To take one instance, an article in the Weekend Report on Business in *The [Toronto] Globe and Mail* featured this warning: "Housing-fuelled consumer spending has been a major force in North American and global economic growth over the past several years—and poses a major threat if it dries up" (Leitch B8).

6   While most contemporary house and home magazines are careful not to use gendered pronouns in the texts of articles, the assumption that interested readers are likely to be female can be found everywhere. For example, in the May 2006 issue of *Domino*, one piece begins with a picture of a woman in designer-labelled

dress, coat, pumps, bag, and headband, and the question "Can this outfit be turned into a room?" (67), suggesting the metonymic correlation between woman and house. Most of the many advertisements in the magazines feature images of white women between the ages of 20 and 40 using the products being sold. Among the few men who appear in these magazines is a middle-aged white man in the May 2006 issue of *Traditional Home*, who stands behind and watches over his wife and three daughters, an image that accompanies a story about buying a house.

7 There are few women of colour depicted in the magazines; when they do appear, it is often in relation to articles about ethnic food, as, for example, in the May 2006 issue of *Martha Stewart Living* in which three generations of Vietnamese women—whose family story is said to be "all about food" (Gelder 151)—cook a "feast" for Mother's Day. An African-American couple who appear in an advertisement for a DIY store are depicted looking in amazement at a "$350,000 home built just for you," which the store is using as the "giveaway" for a promotional contest (*Domino* 105). African-Americans, apparently, cannot assume, and need rather to "win," a place in suburban American society.

8 British Columbia's longstanding, and now trademarked, campaign to promote its province as "Super, Natural British Columbia" is the most obvious, but not the only, example of this marketing strategy.

9 The speeches of Bush on the subject can be found on the website of the White House.

10 Diana Brydon first directed me to Walters's article.

CHAPTER 1	➡	**Homing and Unhoming:**

Homing and Unhoming: The Ideological Work of Canadian Children's Literature

Mavis Reimer

The most valued story in English-language Canadian children's literature is a narrative in which the central child character, pushed out of an originary home by the decisions or behaviour of powerful adults, journeys to an alien place and, after a series of vicissitudes that occupy most of the tale, chooses to claim the unfamiliar space as a new home. In this story, home is understood to be a product of human shaping and sharing, an understanding often signalled at the turn of the narrative by the exchange of a manufactured object between characters who have previously been in conflict with one another. The newly formed home is not constituted primarily through biological ties of filiation, but rather through affiliative bonds: the novels built on this pattern frequently end by celebrating a "family" comprising an assortment of people linked by their shared commitments to ideas, practices, and values.[1]

This narrative pattern is exemplified by the most decorated book in the history of Canadian children's literature, Janet Lunn's *Shadow in Hawthorn Bay*, which won five major juried awards in the years after its publication in 1986.[2] Set during the time of the Highland clearances in Scotland in the early nineteenth century, Lunn's story describes the solitary and perilous journey of fifteen-year-old Mary Urquhart from her ancestral home in Scotland to Upper Canada. The strangeness of the new country is emblematized by Mary's fear of the "low, dark woods" that fringe the Ontario farming community in which she settles (203) and by the community's fear of her preternatural "gift of the two sights" (6). Her story ends when she offers Luke, the suitor she has rejected

1

twice, a cloth she has woven for his wedding shirt. This gift consolidates her claim to membership in the "neighbourhood" that includes her adopted son, her students, and her employer: "Here where I have been so afraid and so sure I did not belong—teaching, working with Julia Colliver, living with Henry, being with you—I am more a part of your neighbourhood than I ever was of my own in my own hills" (214). A second gift, which Mary receives in a parcel from her father in Scotland, confirms her decision as a fitting one: the Urquhart cairngorm brooch he sends signals his belated acceptance of her decision to emigrate to Canada and marks her new, chosen family as the rightful heirs of the old family.

The movement of child subjects from given bonds of filiation to chosen bonds of affiliation appears to align Canadian children's texts with postmodern celebrations of mobile subjectivities. As many theorists and critics have observed, contemporary literature has embraced metaphorical homelessness as an ideal. The migrant, the exile, and the nomad are all figures through whom contemporary writers explore the illusory quest for fixed identity and the possibility of defying what John Durham Peters calls "settled power" (33). Indeed, Erin Manning has observed that "a certain territorial homelessness" attends the sense of "being Canadian": "'Being Canadian' has always presented itself to me as somewhat coterminous with homelessness, if one can gauge a nation by its incessant preoccupation with its own sense of elusive identity" (xvii). Canadian children's texts extend her personal observation to a more general experience of Canadianness. Not only is a mobile subject at the centre of many Canadian children's texts, but also the geographical and psychological separation of "home" and "away" typically is represented as impossible, since "home" and "not-home" are enacted on the same place.

But the trajectory of most Canadian children's texts, like children's texts generally, is to home the child subject, both the subject inside the book and the subject outside the book. And this homing is accomplished by building what Rosemary Marangoly George has called the "pattern of select inclusions and exclusions" that constitute "the basic organizing principle" of the notion of home (2). Focusing on the long middle of Lunn's *Shadow in Hawthorn Bay*, during which her central child figure is homeless, allows readers to make visible what Pierre Macherey calls "the conditions of the possibility" of this text's ideological achievement of home (91), "what the work is *compelled* to say in order to say what it *wants* to say" (94).

Refusing Homelessness

Danielle Thaler, writing about Québécois fiction for young people in her chapter in this volume, observes that historical novels "*tend[ent] à sacraliser*" the facts that become the founding myths of a nation (29). In her terms, the historical setting of Mary's story works to sanctify the narrative of immigration as the founding story of English Canada. But, not only does this exemplary text of Canadian children's literature issue the call to "make it home" to its readers, it does so in thematic terms that exclude the possibility of homelessness and the homeless. Mary's progress toward claiming a home in Hawthorn Bay can be charted through her encounters with homeless people and by her refusals of the various kinds of homelessness they represent.

The first homeless people Mary meets are vagrants, people, to use Toby Benis's definition of the term, who both "lack housing" and have "vexed relationships to the community" (12). When Mary reaches the harbour from which the ship is to sail to Canada, she stays in the same bed in a rooming house as the Macfeeter family, a mother and two daughters who represent themselves as immigrants to Canada, but who turn out to be itinerant and disreputable women who steal Mary's provisions for the journey and then vanish into the city without a trace. As in much contemporary discourse surrounding "street" women who are outside the enclosures of private homes, there is an insinuation of sexual impropriety in the textual descriptions of this fully female family, with "their dirty, unkempt hair and clothes" and "their never-ceasing talk of the soldiers at the fort and the fancy clothes they meant to buy" (29). When Mary sets out to find them and her property after she discovers she's been robbed, she herself becomes the object of "rude invitations of men in taverns" (31).

The narrator's description of Mary's response of "venomous" anger (31) to the Macfeeter women's misrepresentation of themselves seems, on the surface, excessive, since Mary also chooses to survive as a vagrant while she waits for the ship to sail, sleeping rough in the countryside and foraging for wild food. But the differences between Mary and the Macfeeters are also clear: these can be described by their attitudes to property and to sexuality. The Macfeeters have few possessions but want many, especially "fancy clothes"; after Mary re-provisions herself, she carefully hoards in a cave her foodstuffs for her voyage and thriftily decides to live off the land while she waits for orders to board ship. The Macfeeters eye the soldiers lasciviously; Mary spends her time in the country telling stories to children and indignantly refuses the offer of food from a man who wants a kiss as payment. The homeless Macfeeters are city dwellers, while Mary's unhoused condition is linked to the rural and the natural, the outside world in which she feels most at home, as we're told within the first few pages of the novel: "She felt as though she had been born out of [the] earth, that she was kin to the whin and broom and heather that grew so profusely over the hillsides, that there were tiny unseen roots growing along her body, reaching out for the land, drawing nourishment from it" (10–11). In other words, homelessness is *not* a condition of having "no permanent abode" in this passage, but rather the practice of not storing up goods, of promiscuity, in both sexual conduct and personal property. Mary's behaviour, by contrast, can be seen as what Andrew O'Malley calls a "display of the middle-class investment mentality" (46), a behaviour that is both privileged and naturalized in Lunn's text.

Throughout Lunn's novel, Mary's bodily purity and access to material goods is guaranteed by the presence of children. The fact that she attaches herself to children in her travels makes her unapproachable sexually, while her "natural" ability to communicate with them and to enthrall them with her stories secures from their parents many gifts she needs to survive—food, train tickets, a coach ride, and, eventually, a job as a school teacher in Hawthorn Bay. Children allow Mary to appear as both a proper and a propertied woman, despite her actual condition of homelessness, and it is the presence of children that allows the narrative to perform the close connection of these two terms.

Mary's second encounter with homelessness comes in her conversations on board the ship. Mary discovers that most of her fellow passengers on the *Andrew McBride* are exiles, forced from their lands by greedy landlords and clan chiefs. The place to which they are travelling, the backwoods of Upper Canada, is represented by the narrator immediately following the description of these conversations as settled by "refugees from the revolution in America" (37). The characterizations secure the sympathy of readers with both sets of homeless people and align the Highlanders and the Loyalists with each other. The reader is given a proleptic sense of the ending in this early scene: the exiles on the ship are travelling toward people like them, almost, it seems, going home.

Hamid Naficy has noted that, although there are a "variety of registers, experiences, and nuances of exilic conditions," "[e]xile is inexorably tied to homeland and to the possibility of return" (3). When Mary arrives in Hawthorn Bay, she soon learns that, among the exiled, there are those who do root themselves in their new place of residence—Mary's metaphor of belonging is literalized in this story about a farming community—and there are those who remain homeless, looking back longingly to the old country. In Lunn's novel, the homeless don't survive: Lydia Anderson, who cannot be consoled for the loss of her comfortable life in America, wanders into a snowstorm and dies; Mary's cousin Duncan, who cannot reconcile himself to the "low and dark" forests of Ontario (3), drowns himself; Zeke Hazen, a Vermont Loyalist, "got so homesick for his hills" that he "took a chance on being imprisoned or done to death, and he went back home—never been heard from again" (117–18). Mary's climactic choice to claim a place in the "neighbourhood" of Hawthorn Bay is a refusal to live her life as a perpetual exile. What Edward Said in *Cul-*

ture and Imperialism calls the "exilic energies" of boundary-breaking (332) is contained in Lunn's story by the immigrant project of homemaking.

Or, perhaps more accurately, the homemaking narrative is built on the exclusion of exilic energy. There is one self-banished exile at Hawthorn Bay, whose presence in the story complicates the story of immigration. This is Simeon Anderson, Luke's brother, who is a heavy drinker, cruel to children and animals, and sexually aggressive—three common markers of interdicted masculinity in contemporary children's literature, according to Rolf Romøren and John Stephens (220). In Lunn's novel, Simeon leaves the community after impregnating a young girl, a girl his widowed father subsequently marries. The transgressive energy of the outlaw son will be domesticated through this simultaneously natural and fostered fathering of his child, but the boundary-breaker himself is unhomeable within the terms of the immigrant narrative. In this subplot, it becomes clear that home is a gendered space, occupied by women and their children, and secured by good men who police the boundaries of that space.

Mary also encounters Aboriginal nomads. On the final stretch of her journey, as she sets out to walk the last hundred miles of backwoods Ontario, she is rescued from a swamp by a "dark man" who appears from nowhere and from whom she runs in terror (45), although he's never seen again in the text. Later in her story she befriends the Mohawks who invariably materialize silently and then "disappear into the trees" (131) in the text, a motif eliding Aboriginal presence with landscape that is common in settler literature.[3] The nomadic version of homelessness—what Peters calls "being homeless and home-full at once" (21), since home is at once nowhere and everywhere—makes visible a significantly different story at the edges of this narrative from the homemaking story at its centre, a different story in which home is a community of always-travelling kin. In Peters's view, the "conceptual raids on nomadic life" by recent social theorists celebrate the "stealth toward settled power" nomadism can involve (21). In *Shadow in Hawthorn Bay*, the narrator reports that Mary feels "easier with the Indians than she did with her white neighbours" (130–31). But, as we might expect from the other refusals of homelessness, Lunn's text shows the nomad both to depend on and to support the sedentary settlers: Mary first meets Owena when the Mohawk woman appears at her cabin to pick the mint Mary's aunt has planted there; when she asks Owena to teach her to use native plants for healing, the Mohawk woman immediately agrees. By having Owena later present Mary with a traditional dress, Lunn legitimates Mary's process of indigenization, making this conceptual raid on nomadic life a source, rather than a disturbance, of "settled power."

The attribution of second sight to Lunn's central character is the last of the ways in which homelessness, in the psychological sense of a manifestation of the unhomely,[4] is represented and resisted in Lunn's text. From childhood, Duncan and Mary have been described as "reflections of one another," as one another's "shades" (5). Mary's repeated experience of hearing Duncan calling her is an uncanny one: she both recognizes the familiar beloved voice and is terrified by its strange power to pull her toward danger. At the conclusion of the novel, Mary's decision to close the eyes of the shadowy figure of Duncan she sees beneath the surface of Hawthorn Bay, so to send his spirit to rest in peace, is a refusal to live with the presence of the *Unheimlich* in her new home. Proper, propertied, gendered, and settled, Mary asserts her right to a personal sense of the plenitude of being "at home." After quieting Duncan's voice, she walks into the "low, dark woods" she has always feared as full of malevolent spirits, pronounces that the woods are empty of "old ones," and knows that "this new land had reached out to her" (203). Her last words in the novel inaugurate a new age in a new land, the beginning of history in this place: "[I]t begins here now. We are the old ones here" (216). In seeking "to establish a nation," Alan Lawson has observed, the settler both "needs to become native and to write the epic of the nation's origin" (28). Mary, as her author demonstrates, is well on her way to accomplishing both of these tasks.

The conclusion of *Shadow in Hawthorn Bay* is a textbook example of the "syntax of forgetting" Homi Bhabha describes as the double, pedagogical and performative, discourse of the nation (*Location* 160). Using the form of a historical narrative, Lunn works to consolidate "an authority that is based on the pre-given or constituted historical origin *in the past*"; using the plural first-person pronoun for the celebration of the final achievement of home, Lunn conscripts her readers also to perform "that sign of the *present* through which national life is redeemed and iterated as a reproductive process" (*Location* 145). That the "minus in the origin" (*Location* 160) is the erasure of the presence of Aboriginal "old ones" already in the land is predictable. The assertion of *terra nullius* is "colonialism's most enabling fiction," according to Len Findlay (43).

But, even within the terms of Lunn's text, the will to constitute a new history is interrupted rather than triumphantly complete. Mary's premonitions have, throughout the novel, been evidence of her peculiar receptiveness to ways of knowing not recognized by the rest of the community, but which, nevertheless, allow her to foretell and forestall a number of disasters in the settlement. Lunn's text itself can be read other ways than it overtly asks to be read, most importantly in the paradigmatic link it forges between Mary's encounters with the "dark man" and with Duncan. The Aboriginal man who terrifies Mary by his unexplained appearance and then disappearance is separated in the temporal sequences of both story and discourse from Mary's drowned cousin Duncan, whose face appears in the dark shadow in Hawthorn Bay.

But the imagery of the scenes confirms that the two men are metaphorically related characters. Mary comes "face to face with a dark man looking down at her" through the boughs of a cedar tree when she almost drowns in the swamp in her night journey toward the settlement (45). At the end of the novel, she wades into the water of the bay, resigned to following the voice that has called her from Scotland, and sees a negative, mirror image of the dark man's face: "Duncan lying beneath the surface, his dead white face turned towards her, his black hair floating around him like the fronds of a fern. His eyes were open, his hands were outstretched, waiting" (199). She runs in fear from the outstretched, helping hand of the "dark man" in the swamp; she closes Duncan's eyes and evades his outstretched and waiting hands.

In other words, the text links Mary's escape from the dead gaze of her Scottish cousin to her escape from the presence of the indigenous inhabitants of the land, consigning both to a past that must be refused. Mary, however, chooses to read her refusal differently, by making another connection in which she substitutes settler Luke Anderson for Duncan: "I came to this place when Duncan called and now I know you were the one here waiting for me" (214). The story closes with the declaration with which Mary marks her marriage to Luke as genesis: "[I]t begins here now" (216). But the unconscious of the text is haunted by other memories and other histories she will not acknowledge.

Making It Home

The score of awards given to *Shadow in Hawthorn Bay* suggests that the ideology of home constructed in Lunn's book is one widely recognized and widely shared in Canada, or, at least, widely believed by Canadian adults to be important to share with young people. To use Pierre Bourdieu's term, Lunn's book carries "symbolic capital" in Canada (*Language* 128). In particular, Lunn's high valuation of the chosen home resonates with other Canadian award-winning fiction for children. Daniel Coleman has argued that the Canadian allegory of nation relies on a structure of "generative deferral," in which "[t]he immigrant is represented as a subject who must be constantly reinvented at the margins of the nation." Seen from this perspective, the dominant tradition of Canadian children's literature, in its representation of its central characters as immigrants, clearly reinscribes the allegory of the Canadian nation.

In *The World, the Text, and the Critic*, Edward Said distinguishes between two kinds of human ties—those of filiation and those of affiliation. Filiation, which Said defines as the presentation of "natural continuity between one generation and the next" (16), is insistently problematized in the theoretical texts of "high modernism" with which he is principally concerned in this study. In looking for other ways "to produce new and different ways of conceiving human relationships" (17), these writers develop the versions of social bonds he calls affiliation, "transpersonal" bonds that provide "a kind of compensatory order" (19). Using Said's terms, we might say that the dominant texts of English-language Canadian children's literature value relations of affiliation over filial relations.

The celebration of the chosen home and family with which these texts conclude is, in many ways, an appealing vision of a new way of conceiving human relationships. The critical choice of the central child character invariably is against solitude and for community. Community itself is not a homogeneous or kinship group, but a heterogeneous collection of people. In Michael Bedard's *Redwork*, for example, the final scene takes place in the public space of the movie theatre in which Cass works and ends as his "family" walks in the door to watch an old Charlie Chaplin film together: his family includes his mother, Alison; her boyfriend, Murray; Cass's friend Maddy; and Cass and Alison's elderly, disabled landlord, Mr. Magnus.[5] Many of the culminating scenes, in fact, resonate with the official ideal of multiculturalism in Canada as a chosen community of shared difference, a durable and cathected idea in Canadian society.

But the fact that children's literature is a literature written *by* adults *for* children complicates the meanings of these chosen affiliations. Among the many award-winning novels that use a narrative pattern in which an alien place is chosen as home by the protagonists are Jan Truss's *Jasmin* (1982), Bedard's *Redwork* (1990), Julie Johnston's *Adam and Eve and Pinch-Me* (1994), Don Aker's *Of Things Not Seen* (1995), and Tim Wynne-Jones's *The Maestro* (1995). These five novels not only privilege the child's choice in their plotting, but also thematize reading, writing, and artistic production as enabling the "free" choice of the "true" home. In their reflexivity, the texts make visible the ideological project of English-language Canadian children's literature: the conditions under which it is possible to "make it home" in this literature and the identity of those who can answer this call.[6]

Most of the central children in these five novels choose not to live with their "natural" families in their given homes at the conclusion of their stories; rather, they find or accept other bonds with adults and children with whom they feel "at home." *The Maestro* offers a clear example of this plot. The father-son relationship in the novel is predicated on rights and ownership: Cal Crow physically asserts his proprietary rights to every "real good thing" Burl discovers (181), and Burl retaliates for his father's brutality by finding his secret fishing hole and stealing his favourite baits. By the end of the novel, Burl has decided to accept the invitation of a sympathetic teacher and her husband to live with them. Burl's choice to relinquish connections with his "natural" parents is verified not only by its position at the end of the narrative, but by its narrative style. The passage of free indirect discourse in which Burl ruminates about solutions to his dilemma gives narrative authority to his judgement about what is possible and what is impossible: "He would write to his mother. But he couldn't go up to Dryden, no more than he could move in with Cal and Tanya" (222).

According to Said, "[A]ffiliation belongs exclusively to culture and society" (20). In these children's novels, the transpersonal bonds that the central characters choose are founded on "cultural" connections in the most obvious senses. In *Adam and Eve*, for example, Sara Moone first learns to value writing through working as a typist for a cultural historian (who speaks "with rounded vowels, like somebody on CBC Radio" [62]) and then uses her own writing to uncover her subconscious knowledge that her connections with her foster family are more profound than her feelings for the birth mother who arrives to claim her. In *Of Things Not Seen*, Ben Corbett's bonds with fellow writers Ann and Sadie give him the courage to leave his abusive stepfather's house for a shelter, where he is joined by his battered mother; in *Redwork*, Cass Parry knows that he has arrived at home when he agrees with Maddy to take up the alchemist's quest from Mr. Magnus, a quest that will commit them to years of textual and experiential research. These cultural communities are intensifications of the common motif in Canadian children's literature of the exchange of made objects.

Since the publication of Said's study in 1983, however, there has been much theoretical troubling of the categories of culture and nature. For example, Rosemary George, re-reading Said's concepts of filiation and affiliation, suggests that we might rather read "'filiations' as those bonds that are naturalized as 'natural' through the discourses that differentiate them from those bonds that are naturalized as 'artificial' or as 'affiliations'" (17). There is a significant investment in the idea of the natural in these texts, an idea that is often associated with the wilderness, which has been a conventional setting in Canadian children's literature since the nineteenth century. In *Jasmin*, for example, Jasmin Stalke runs away from a chaotic family home to the wilderness; it is while she is living in a cave abandoned by a coyote that she realizes her talent for sculpting; the sculptures that "grow as if by a sort of magic" in her hands (72) are of the "happy" animals (73) she observes in the landscape around her. When her idyll is disrupted by a sudden and violent thunderstorm, Jasmin finds her way to the isolated home of Jules and Hana, artists like herself, who have built a house that is a more adequate shelter than her den but which nevertheless "let[s] in the star-filled sky" (168). Burl in *The Maestro* runs away from his parents' house to the wilderness, where he finds a reclusive composer (reportedly based on pianist Glenn Gould) by following a song that "glide[s] out" to him "like a small boat on the green lake in the sun-drenched air" (34). The "cottage" the Maestro has built is dominated by a "huge sail of a window" that is "alive with stars" (59). What is most "natural" in these novels, in short, is artistic expression and the often unspoken connections forged between artists. To use George's terms, it is cultural bonds that are naturalized as filiations.

On the other hand, the discourse of natural parents is often associated with machines and the mechanical and marked as unintelligible. For example, Jasmin's crowded home is characterized by the sounds of a television that is never turned off, six squabbling siblings, and a father who passes his evenings in drunken and slurred stupor in his armchair. The violence of Ben's stepfather in *Of Things Not Seen* is usually fuelled by his drinking; the final beating Ben endures before he leaves home is described as a tearing, unending scream: "It shrilled and wailed, clamoured and clung to them, lifted them up out of themselves and flung them forward into darkness" (186). In *The Maestro*, Cal is "drunk, most likely" by the time he gets home from work (19) and, while Burl learns "to recognize the signs of a foul mood" in a too-noisy arrival—"the engine [of the car] revving too high, the car door slamming, footsteps too heavy on the porch" (25)—Cal's anger sometimes is signalled only by "a sullen kind of quiet like thunder a long way off" (7). When Burl walks away from his father for the last time, Cal is ranting wildly and "sobbing horribly" (209). The Woman's revelation to Sara that she is her birth mother and wants her back is followed by Sara succumbing to a feverish, three-day delirium.

The "'breaking of ties with family, home, class, country, and traditional beliefs'"—as Said, quoting Ian Watt, observes—is often presented as a necessary stage "'in the achievement of spiritual and intellectual freedom'" (19). This, indeed, seems to be the case in these novels. In each of these texts, the children's decision to break their ties with family promises to allow them to become more truly themselves. Burl in *The Maestro* sees his new home as one that allows for quiet with "no secrets hiding in it" (178); Jasmin is "going to get a private little room of her own" (192) within the family home; Ben in *Of Things Not Seen* is confident that his choice is the beginning of a journey, "a chance to start over on [his] own terms" (192), not unlike Mary's beginning at the end of *Shadow in Hawthorn Bay*. Mary's story, in fact, can be read as a performance of the moment when affiliation and filiation change places, the chosen bond of marriage promising the establishment of the natural continuity of generations, the choice naturalized by the blessing of the land itself. In its refusals of homelessness, Lunn's text conceals the conditions of its making, its exclusions of others, notably Aboriginal others, from the "true" home. Similar structures of displacement and concealment also operate in the metafictional novels of Truss, Johnston, Aker, and Wynne-Jones, but the inclusions and exclusions are cast in the terms of class rather than race.[7]

The repeated metaphor of unintelligibility in the novels of Truss, Aker, and Wynne-Jones—the drunken father—has a long literary history as a metonym of the feckless underclass, and, as Romøren and Stephens indicate, this figure is also a common sign of interdicted masculinity in contemporary children's literature. The discourse of the novels subordinates an analysis of material conditions to the celebration of artistic expression, but the markers of social status scattered throughout the texts make it clear that choosing home is a class project in these Canadian texts. Simply put, the homes the children reject are lower-class homes; the homes they choose are cultured, middle-class homes. The loaded descriptions of the children's originary homes require little explication. The Crow house in *The Maestro* is a "shack," "built of scraps of timber; greying chipboard and peeling tarpaper—stuff that Cal had begged, borrowed or, more likely, stolen" (18); the interior of the "shack" is unfinished (25); and the family car is an old Plymouth Burl dubs "the Turd-mobile" (18). Cal is a mill worker. In *Of Things Not Seen*, the house Jim Rankin has rented in Brookdale, with its "sagging roof, cracked chimney, and three colours of vinyl siding," is the sort of house "no burglar would give ... a second glance" (27). Rankin works in an elastic factory. His car, an "old LTD" (43), is given to breaking down on Commercial Drive, much to Ben's embarrassment. The Stalke house in *Jasmin* is "on the edge of civilisation," unfinished and without indoor plumbing and surrounded by "a junkyard of overturned cars and rusted farm machinery" (5). Bud Stalke is a subsistence farmer and junk dealer.

As these descriptions indicate, the lower class in these texts is marked by the careless treatment of things and by immobility or uncertain mobility; predictably, in the homes the children choose, material possessions are valued and ordered.[8] To give just one example, the description of David and Natalie Agnew's house, which Burl chooses as foster home, is filled with the details of its domestic comfort: there is a "finished basement," with a bathroom including a shower; Burl finds "clean pyjamas," his "[f]reshly laundered" clothes (175), and flannel sheets in the extra bedroom (174); the "spacious, cheery kitchen" (177) echoes with the comforting sounds of "cupboards opening and closing" (174) and boasts the comfortable presence of tea towels, napkins, and strawberries. The Agnews' car is compact, solid, and dependable.

More consequential is the outcome of these stories in which the children, by moving from their given family homes to their chosen family homes, earn the right to possession on a much larger scale. Imaginative possession and material possession are imbricated in the conclusions. Jasmin, for example, returns to her family home in the knowledge that Jules's and Hana's "golden house,"

with its "paint-smelling studio" (188) and its "clear view" of the whole valley (172), will be available to her regularly as a weekend and holiday refuge.
Burl sees the welcoming Agnew house as a concession to his need for safety,
but his story ends with the knowledge that he has an invitation to return to
Ghost Lake and, like the Maestro before him, to "mine some of [its] beauty"
(218). Sara's choice to remain on the Huddleston farm roots her "between
moon and sun, joined to the universe, part of the earth, connected to [her
foster] family" (178), giving her both something to write about and a property
to help improve and secure against creditors. Even Ben, whose story ends in
Lazarus House, a shelter for victims of domestic abuse, sees the books and
papers his mother is studying as the "bricks and mortar of the new life she and
Ben were building for themselves" (192). Three of the five novels image the
new home as a ship[9]: like latter-day colonists, these children are set to take
possession of the land before them.

Their right to do so, moreover, is enforced by the powers of institutions
and institutional representatives. Natalie Agnew, Burl's chosen foster mother
in *The Maestro*, is a teacher; his natural father Cal Crow is hospitalized at
the end of the story. A minister and a teacher help Ben to make his break with
his stepfather, while Jim Rankin is arrested and incarcerated by the police.
Jules and Hana negotiate a new relationship for Jasmin at school; Bud Stalke
is compelled to renovate his house by the social workers assigned to moni-
tor the family; and LeRoy, Jasmin's mentally deficient brother for whose care
she has been responsible, is sent to "a special home where he [can] get special attention and training" (191). There is a structure of disavowal evident
here. The sometimes violent attempts of natural fathers to restrict the children's movements and to assert their proprietary rights to their children are
repudiated in the novels, but then appropriated by the institutions of power
that support and maintain the class of culture and of property. Affiliation, while
a rejection of biological ties in the texts, re-presents authority in "validated
nonbiological social and cultural forms" (Said, *The World, the Text, and the
Critic* 23).

These five novels, like many texts of this consecrated pattern of English-
language Canadian children's literature, turn on the crisis of the child's choice.
The need for the child to choose home is represented in stark and urgent,
even melodramatic, terms. Failure to make the move from outside the "true"
home to inside it, central characters come to recognize, will result in death.
The emblematic scenes in which characters come to this knowledge often
feature extreme weather, either literally or metaphorically, linking these scenes
with the warnings about the fate of unrooted exiles in the homemaking story
of *Shadow in Hawthorn Bay*. In *Jasmin, Redwork, Of Things Not Seen*, and
The Maestro, the child faces the threat of physical death; in these four nov-

els, the child character also recognizes the imminence of spiritual or psychological death, as does Sara in *Adam and Eve*. Failure to make the right choice means not to be in the discourses of these novels. There is an ironic duplicity here: the child's choice is highly valued as formative of home but, at the same time, there is obviously only one right choice. The double terms fit precisely into the definitions of ideology from which most cultural and literary critics proceed. In postindustrial, democratic societies, as James Kavanagh observes, hegemonic ideology is constituted by individuals "freely" taking up the given terms of their subjectivity and their subjection (310). In their emphasis on choice, then, these award-winning Canadian children's novels enact and confirm a fundamental mechanism of our society.

Written as they are *by* adults, the emphasis on the child's choice suggests a recognition at several levels of the central importance of children to the reproduction of societal consensus. It is, of course, literally true that the consent of children will determine the replication of the terms of the dominant ideology into the future. The child's choice represented inside the book also replicates and secures the choice of the adult writing the book, or the adult promoting the book, particularly in these books about reading, writing, and artistic production. Jacqueline Rose has noted that, in children's fiction generally, the child functions as "something of a pioneer" who gives our world back to us "with a facility or directness which ensures that our own relationship to [it] is, finally, safe" (9). The child's "discovery" and then choice of the right home in these novels ensures that the adult construction of that home is verified, the "real" being, as Pierre Bourdieu has observed, that which is durably and collectively produced and then (mis)recognized (*Language* 170).

The stark terms of the child's choice inside the book also seem a potent tool for the manufacture of the consent of the child outside the book. For the reader, consent offers, in Catherine Belsey's terms, the "position from which the text is most readily intelligible" (67) by bringing the child reader into agreement with the child character and the narrator who focalizes the child character in these predominantly realist novels. In these texts that thematize reading and writing, consent is secured on another level as well, as the child reader outside the book enacts membership in an affiliative community like the one privileged inside the book, by agreeing with the adult author outside the book who guarantees the truth of the story. Response to the book, then, itself becomes a marker of the cultural place of the child outside the book. In this enunciative situation, meanings and practices are "reciprocally confirming," "constitutive and constituting," as Raymond Williams has noted about ideological systems in general (*Marxism* 110).

An Unhomely Home

The haunted text is an idea much explored in criticism of Canadian literature and often associated with the problematics of defining a home in Canada. For example, in her recent collection of essays on Canadian postcolonialism, titled *Unhomely States*, Cynthia Sugars begins her introduction by quoting poet Dennis Lee's 1973 observation that "'if you are Canadian, home is a place that is not home to you'" (xiii); and Alan Lawson lists "the *Unheimlichkeit* of home" as one of the recurrent tropes of anxiety in the texts of settler cultures (25). But the notion of the Freudian "uncanny" has acquired much wider cultural currency, being taken up by such notable theorists as Jacques Lacan, Hélène Cixous, Jacques Derrida, and Homi Bhabha. In her genealogy of the concept, Anneleen Masschelein suggests that one of its important functions in culture has been to signify "the return of the repressed that ... exposes the ideological closure of definitions and concepts" (62). Lunn's text can be understood within these terms: while she works for narrative and thematic closure by naming and claiming home, the metaphorical structures of her text align syntagmatically separated narrative moments and reveal the repression of the Aboriginal presence on which that claim rests.

In this sense, as Homi Bhabha has observed, the unhomely can be a political experience of "unfixing" or destabilization of such imperialist categories as centre and periphery. Any claim to pure identity is always disrupted by "the estranging sense of the relocation of the home and the world—the unhomeliness—that is the condition of extra-territorial and cross-cultural initiations" (*Location* 9). The work of recall and "unfixing" in a realistic text such as Lunn's, however, is the work of the reader. If realism offers the reader a "representation of a world of consistent subjects who are the origin of meaning, knowledge, and action" (Belsey 67), the resisting reader who links the paradigmatic events of Mary's encounters with the "dark man" and her dark cousin can unsettle the ideological closures of the text by seeing that Mary is not fully in control of her meanings, knowledges, and actions, which are generated elsewhere and performed through her. In Michael Bedard's *Redwork*, on the other hand, the narrative itself disrupts the possibility of a readerly position of confident understanding, both by staging in its form and by thematizing the irruption of the unhomely in the home.

Like the central characters in the novels of Truss, Johnston, Aker, and Wynne-Jones, Cass chooses home and constitutes a family through affiliative bonds; like these novels, too, Bedard's narrative represents Cass's choice as a critical one. But, unlike the other central child characters, Cass never identifies home as a dwelling that he can own or make his own. At the end of his story, he continues to live in a rented second-floor flat with his lone parent Alison. Even this flat, with its porous borders, is not an effective enclosure for a private domestic life. The windows of the sun porch from which Cass believes he is invisibly surveying his new neighbourhood in fact allow him to be fully available to the gaze of the people on the street. His bedroom admits the sounds of his landlord's radio from the bedroom below, and his dreams are infiltrated by Mr. Magnus's traumatic memories of his service in the trenches of World War I. As this plot detail indicates, fantastical events bleed into the realistic frame of the world of *Redwork*. Cass's choice to take up the alchemist's quest Mr. Magnus must abandon as old age and his war injuries overtake him is represented by the narrator as a "coming ... home" (229) for Cass, but "home" here is taking up the ancient search for the Philosopher's Stone, a quest that is acknowledged as "a dark way" and, likely, a way without an end (273). Cass not only chooses to live with the presence of the unhomely in his home, but to become a student of "the mystery" (275). The novel itself, divided into three books headed by enigmatic epigrams from William Blake, *Gloria Mundi*, and *Casablanca*, positions the reader with Cass as a seeker after truth and a student of mystery.

A popular version of Canadian political and military history is to represent World War I as the event that forged a nation from a colony. While Bedard's novel answers the question of the meaning of home differently than do the other novels I've discussed, it too can be seen as participating in the discourse in which home is linked to nation. The texts considered to this point, notably, were all produced in the two decades after the establishment of Canadian children's literature as an institution. With the growth of various popular nationalist movements during the 1970s aimed at countering or containing the overwhelming American influence on Canadian life, new attention and resources were directed to the writers and publishers of children's literature. A series of achievements during this decade is evidence of this new attention. In 1974, the Children's Book Store opened in Toronto; in 1975 the scholarly journal *Canadian Children's Literature/Littérature canadienne pour la jeunesse* was founded; in 1976, the Pacific Rim Conference on Children's Literature was held in Vancouver, the Canada Council established its prizes in children's literature, the National Library of Canada created the position of Children's Literature Librarian, and the International Board on Books for Young People opened the Children's Book Centre in Toronto; and, in 1977, the Book Centre inaugurated the annual Children's Book Festival. With support from the Canada Council and provincial arts councils, small alternative presses and regional presses with imprints specializing in children's texts began to publish during the decade, among them Kids Can Press, Annick Press, The Women's Press, Tree Frog Press, and Groundwood. One measure of the success of these initiatives was the rapid increase in the production of Canadian material for young readers, from ten books a year in 1950 to 200 in the late 1980s (*cf.* Egoff and Saltman 306, 309). That many of these narratives centre on the project of homemaking seems consistent with the historical context of their production.

Since the late 1990s, however, an increasing number of narratives for young readers have been published in Canada that, in their preoccupation with the unhomed and the homeless, appear to challenge the terms of earlier children's literature. Several of these novels have won or been nominated for major literary awards.[10] In two of them—Deborah Ellis's *Looking for X* (1999) and Elizabeth Wennick's *Changing Jareth* (1999)—encounters with homeless characters are not refused but sought out by the central child characters. While Khyber and Jareth ultimately choose or make new homes, thereby recapitulating the privileged plot of English-Canadian children's texts, the unhomed they befriend mark possibilities for both young people of resisting the diagnoses and enclosures of institutions. Two other novels—David Poulsen's *Last Sam's Cage* (2004) and Martine Leavitt's *Heck Superhero* (2004)—follow young male protagonists who live on the streets for much of their stories and whose return home to battered and sick mothers at the end of the narratives is represented as contingent and inconclusive. In Barbara Haworth-Attard's *Theories of Relativity* (2003) and Martine Leavitt's *Tom Finder* (2003), similarly, the central characters are homeless young men, Dylan in Haworth-Attard's novel a "throwaway" and Tom in Leavitt's novel a "runaway" from abusive homes. The middles of both narratives document their protagonists' struggles to find shelter, food, personal safety, and networks of relationships on the streets of major cities. The crisis scenes of these novels resonate with the emblematic scenes of violent weather in the earlier Canadian children's novels, during which characters acknowledge that they must move inside or come undone, but neither of these novels re-homes its central character in its conclusion. Each ends, rather, with the central character out on the streets, having rejected the possibility of returning home.

Operation Go Homeless

Peter Hollindale, in a well-known article on the ideology of children's books, maintains that the social, political, and moral beliefs a writer wants to recommend to children might be considered the "surface" or overt ideology of a text. It is at this level, he suggests, that "fiction carries new ideas, non-conformist or revolutionary attitudes, and efforts to change imaginative awareness in line with contemporary social criticism" (28). It is because children's literature often seeks to make overt social, political, and moral recommendations to its readers that scholars in the past have often dismissed it as didactic and, therefore, as unworthy of serious consideration as literature.

That the recent Canadian novels are didactic in this sense becomes obvious when they are read beside the proliferating literature on homeless young people in Canada. Contemporary sociological discourse has developed complex categorizations of street kids: a literature review in a 2002 Canadian Housing and Renewal Association study finds, among others, distinctions made between "throwaways" and "runaways," a category further divided into "runners" and "in and outers"; and between "curbsiders" and "entrenched street youth" among "street-involved youth" (Novac 8). The novels repeat these and other distinctions, as, for example, in the scene of Tom Finder's education in identity by "entrenched street youth" Pepsi:

> "Burb kids come to the streets because they think the world is only as bad as their daddy. Come to think of it, you've been here too long to be a burb kid. Maybe you're a freep. Are you a freep?... Everyone's here for a reason. You've got your punch kids, and your diddle kids. Those ones are the runaways. Then you've got your throwaways.... So, what are you?" (Leavitt 53)

According to the 2002 study, the literature indicates that young women on the street are likely to act out "conventional sex roles—locating new squats, nursing others and helping them through hard times" (Novac 19). Dylan in Haworth-Attard's novel is saved by women several times, bandaged by Gladdy and sheltered in an abandoned warehouse by Amber after he has been beaten by a local pimp and pusher, while Janice and Pam introduce Tom to the "family" of young people who squat in the abandoned Old Spaghetti Factory in Leavitt's novel. Both pregnant Amber in *Theories* and Janice in *Tom Finder*, who has relinquished her child to adoption, "had been in public care when younger," as the sociological studies suggest is likely (Novac 20).

The writers also share an orientation to this knowledge, seeking, as Hollindale predicts, "to change imaginative awareness in line with contemporary social criticism." Street kids in public, media discourses are typically portrayed either as victims or as victimizers, either, as law professor Dianne Martin notes, disenfranchised and estranged or "demonized and criminalized" (98), and the enactments of laws such as Alberta's Protection of Children Involved in Prostitution Act (1998) and Ontario's Safe Streets Act (1999) both assume and reify such identities. By contrast, more progressive legal and sociological discourse seeks to find ways to attend to what Lucie White calls "the moral agency, the political saavy [*sic*]—the human particularity—of the living communities of people who find themselves poor," often by listening to "what those who live in poverty say about what it means" (307). Recent social criticism is filled with such attempts to pay attention, from the many articles based on interviews with street kids and on their responses to questionnaires[11] to a study such as the 2003 *Voices from the Margins: Experiences of Street-Involved Youth in Winnipeg*, supported by the Winnipeg Inner-City Research Alliance, which not only records the stories of homeless young people as they told them, but also involved street kids as community researchers (Higgitt, Wingert, and Ristock 7–9). Both Haworth-Attard's and Leavitt's novels could be read as continuous with this progressive discursive strategy, furnishing the street kids at the centre of their texts with rich emotional, intellectual, and moral interior lives, with which their narrative techniques—first-person narrative in *Theories of Relativity* and character-bound focalization in *Tom Finder*—encourage readers to identify.

But, as this formulation suggests, the narrative strategies of the two novels assume that the readers of the texts are not themselves street kids, that readers must be asked to identify across a gap of privilege. Indeed, these novels are situated firmly within dominant literary modes of production, published by mainstream presses (HarperCollins, Key Porter, Groundwood, and Red Deer), and marketed as children's books generally are, to such adult institutional gatekeepers as the teachers and librarians who are the principal buyers of children's books in Canada.[12] The address of the narratives to young readers housed inside rather than outside the formations of social power is made explicit in an author's note appended to Dylan's narrative:

> It is important that you, the young adult reading this book today, be aware of that kid on the corner of a city street, the one with an outstretched hand. You will grow up to help run this country and will inherit the problem. We must all work toward a solution. (Haworth-Attard 200)

How does one young person become "the problem" that another young person "will inherit" in a projected future? The linkage of the reader with the one who will be authorized to "run this country" is not incidental: as Cynthia Ward has observed, in North America, literacy, "[m]ore than any other factor ... is the means by which class is distinguished" (77). In this explicit confirmation of the ideological designs of the enunciative situation, the young reader's response to the book obviously becomes a marker of his or her cultural place. Like the award-winning novels of Truss, Bedard, Johnston, Aker, and Wynne-Jones, too, all of these novels about homeless young people thematize reading, writing, or other artistic production. In Leavitt's *Tom Finder* and Haworth-Attard's *Theories of Relativity*, in particular, this thematization works to reveal the conditions under which language is authorized and constituted as powerful.

At the beginning of *Tom Finder*, Tom has no memory of how he came to be on the streets or even what his family name is. His only clue to his identity is a notebook he finds in his backpack with some notes about Wolfgang Amadeus Mozart and a pen in his pocket advertising an upcoming performance of *The Magic Flute*. Tom uses his notebook to record what he observes to be true about himself and the world around him: the only name he knows, Tom (21), that he is a "nice guy" (21), that he is "a Finder" (24), that he "can fight" (57), that he "keeps a promise" (57), that "[t]he streets love Tom" (70). He sees himself as "making himself up, inventing the story of himself" (57), but once written, his words have the power to hold his identity in place for him: when he calls himself a "loser," for example, he rereads his self-description and remembers that he is "Not a loser. A Finder" (27). Tom, in fact, speculates that "words are in charge of the world": "What if it's words that makes things real to us, or at least—maybe they're what make us imagine what is real. If that's true, then the most powerful thing in the world you could be is a poet …" (100). Jeans, the friend to whom Tom confides his view of the real, is dubious, cynically observing that "[m]oney is what's in charge of the world" (100). But even Jeans becomes a believer when Tom produces the money to send him home after pointing to the passage in his notebook in which he's written a poem about Jeans returning to Jamaica. The novel ends with Tom beginning to write the stories of the street kids who die in a squat fire, making them real by making them up.

But the narrative is less easily persuaded by its own rhetoric than Jeans is and it reveals its bad conscience in another set of scenes that explore the power of "language" in the larger sense of symbolic system. When Tom first realizes that "[h]e could write anything he wanted in that notebook" (21), he articulates his realization in a mathematical sentence: "He could write $2 + 2 = 5$ if he wanted" (21). But he decides not to do so, because "if he did, nothing would ever make any sense… . [Y]ou had to figure things out" (39). Figures and the language of money punctuate the paradigmatic set of scenes linked through their explorations of city billboards. When Tom scans the city from the top of the Calgary Tower to see if he can recognize his neighbourhood, the only sight that strikes him as familiar is a billboard announcing the performance dates of Mozart's opera. He's convinced that the opera "had something to do with home, with who he was" (32), reasoning that leads him to the conclusion that he should rent a billboard advertising his location to the parents he is sure are trying to find him. Designing and renting the space for two weeks will cost him $5,388, he learns, and he sets out to save what everyone except him recognizes as an impossible amount. Like a conscientious banker, the text dutifully accounts for Tom's money: he has saved $24 (33), when a sympathetic priest gives him "two new twenty-dollar bills" (39), some of which he spends for food, leaving him $62 in savings (51), after which he finds $8.51 in a lost purse, of which he deposits $8 in his bus depot locker (64), adding to that another "twenty-dollar bill" he finds on the streets (70), after which he finds "mostly loonies and toonies and quarters" (71), giving him a grand total of savings of $123.51 (72).

At this point, halfway through the novel and after more than two months of narrative time have elapsed—the passage of time is also recorded in the narrative by the attention Tom pays to an electronic calendar on another billboard—Tom decides to risk all of his savings on a business investment, buying the rights to a corner from a squeegee kid. He never earns a cent from the job, however, and finds himself "back to needing $5,388" (74). While the text continues to document Tom's attempts to earn money—he is paid for two days of window washing and sells one story to a newspaper man he meets in the park—it never again enumerates those earnings clearly, providing a plethora of numbers, but always omitting some of the figures needed to complete a computation. So, for example, the text tells readers that washing high-rise windows pays 50 cents a window and that Tom and Jeans do two "drops" on their first day, but doesn't report the number of windows in each "drop"; at the same time, readers are told that Tom carefully counts the windows "all the way down" (85), that it should, theoretically, be possible to make such a calculation. The text, in other words, attempts to evade the systematic calculus it has earlier insisted on, but it marks those evasions in its gaps. It seems that the magic of the Mozart intertext, referenced in the epigraph to each chapter, has invaded the main narrative, substituting its logic for the need to figure things out: within two weeks of losing the savings he has scraped together over two months, Tom is able not only to buy Jeans an airline ticket to the Caribbean, but also to offer Pam money to escape from her pimp. Jeans's exclamation—"Don't you worry, Tom. The way you save, you have it all back by the time I marry Gina" (129)—marks the incredible turn in the narrative.

The text clearly suspects that the conditions in which "making yourself up" is most likely to be successful include access to sufficient capital, access that it cannot make real but can only imagine to be real for street kid Tom. Words are only "in charge of the world" if they have solicited the attention and recognition of powerful people, such as Tom fantasizes that his parents are. The epigraph from Mozart at the head of the penultimate chapter alludes to this condition of possibility: "What joy it will be, if the gods remember us ..." (136). It is an epigraph that might serve as a gloss on Pierre Bourdieu's description of the magic of recognition that institutes "all forms of symbolic capital" (Language 128). Tom's story about his home and his parents unravels by the end of Leavitt's narrative about him, but the final paragraph in which Tom decides to write the stories of the other street kids demonstrates that he has understood the lesson of marketing himself: "He would write their stories. Everyone of them had a story. The newspaper man would buy it, Tom was sure.

And maybe take him home to meet his wife. He wrote their names. Not their real names, but their street names, the ones they had died in.... He had no trouble finding the words" (141).

Like Leavitt, Haworth-Attard uses a complex of imagery in which skill with a linguistic code—in Dylan's case, computers—is set against a question of capital—here debts rather than savings. Dylan like Tom remains on the streets at the end of the novel. In its conclusion, *Theories of Relativity* also plays with the language of solicitation, with Dylan eventually having to choose whether he will repay his debts by attracting the attention of an empathetic dot-com millionaire or by prostituting himself.

As I have already said, the reader addressed by these texts is not the child who is the subject of the narrative. But children's texts, and the identificatory reading practices often taught to children and assumed by children's writers, typically work to suture the child reader to the child character. As Jacqueline Rose puts it, children's fiction first "sets up the child as an outsider to its own process, and then aims, unashamedly, to take the child *in*" (2). In *Tom Finder*, the close alignment of the narrator with the focalizing character and the frequent use of free indirect discourse give the reader unironic access to Tom's harrowing experiences as he runs away from home, puts himself together as a coherent character, and then watches his story of himself unravel. In other words, the reading position from which the text is "most 'obviously' intelligible" (Belsey 57) is one that recapitulates Tom's emotional journey of unhoming. Like Tom, it seems, readers are asked to know that they have no claim to home, that they too must solicit the recognition that would allow them to move inside. If so, then these texts do appear to be significant departures from the privileged texts of English-Canadian children's literature, which make the child's choice of home the act that constitutes home.

Like most texts of children's literature, however, these texts are preoccupied with the question of what home is, and who belongs there. In other words, they apparently continue to perform the same cultural function as the earlier books, that is, to produce the subject needed by the dominant ideology to reproduce itself. But, if this is so, in what sense might contemporary Canadian culture be said to require a homeless subject? Michael Hardt and Antonio Negri have argued that "the irresistible and irreversible globalization of economic and culture exchanges" that characterize the new form of Empire that now "governs the world" (xi) takes as "its very conditions of possibility" "[c]irculation, mobility, diversity, and mixture" (150). Attempts to block this new form of Empire are futile; any "struggles to contest and subvert" it must "take place on the imperial terrain itself" (xv). In this view, the multiplication of theoretical, metaphorical vocabularies of homelessness can be read as assuming and therefore extending, rather than breaking with, the ideological project of economic and cultural globalization. In the global marketplace, all viable subjects must be mobile and in circulation.

Mobile subjects have been privileged in Canadian children's literature for at least the past three decades. While the meanings of such mobility have shifted, the negotiation between homing and unhoming consistently is used to define the subject of privilege: in the foundational homemaking story of immigration, the mobile subject's refusal to understand herself as homeless underwrites her claim to a settled home; in the allegorical story of choosing home, the upwardly mobile subject can leave behind the traces of filiality and affiliate with the dominant cultured classes; in the story of homelessness, it is the mobile subject who is able to see the ways in which power works and who is able, possibly, to capitalize on that knowledge. In this third story, the right to a settled home belongs to rural folk and to Aboriginal people, both groups tied to landscape in these texts.

Robert Eric Livingston, among many other commentators, has observed that "globalization entails sharpened social cleavages, between those whose translocal mobility has been enhanced and those who are increasingly restricted to assigned locations, socioeconomic as well as cultural and geographic," in addition to its more celebrated functions of unsettling narratives of nation and encouraging the discovery of "more inclusive modes of cultural address" (154). These observations lead Livingston to conclude that the ethical response of literary critics to studying the discourses of globalization is to "do justice to the complexity and possible incoherence of the text under scrutiny" (155). The recent texts of Canadian children's literature that feature homeless central characters invite such a complex response. The mobility of the child subjects is an ambivalent condition. On the one hand, there is a mourning at the heart of these texts, which figure mobility as an expulsion from home and link it to the perils of life on the streets. On the other hand, these novels also propose that the metaphorical untying of home can offer (some of) the unhoused a way in to the intellectual traditions that underwrite privilege.

In *Tom Finder*, for example, the Mozart intertext exists as an event staged within the discourse of the novel as well as an extra-discursive reference that indexes the implied reader's stable position in Leavitt's narrative. Tom not only talks his way into the opera house to see a performance of *The Magic Flute*, but is (mis)taken for a critic by the audience members next to him because of his notebook and pen. In fact, in each of the six recent texts, the central child characters demonstrate an adeptness at the tactical use of public spaces that cultural geographer Sue Ruddick has identified as a skill many homeless people demonstrate as they navigate what she calls the "moral geography of the city" (57). In three of the novels, public libraries provide the best openings for the exercise of such tactics. Dylan in *Theories of Relativity*, for example, first arbitrarily grabs a biography of Einstein from a library shelf as camouflage to allow him to rest in the reading room and to use a warm washroom. But he soon recognizes that Einstein's life and theories have explanatory powers for him and give him the vocabulary through which he articulates his choices. Like Dylan, Tom thinks that a library carrel next to a heating vent will give him a chance to sleep in a warm place; to avoid being evicted by the librarian on duty, he starts to read an anthology of poetry and discovers that, while the poems "didn't let him in easily," if "you didn't give up," they "let you in to play" (107). His pursuit of the meanings of Mozart's opera moves him to remember and then to reject the violent constraints of his family home.

In this representation of public spaces and shared texts, these narratives begin to map a new location of childhood. Sarah Moone in Johnston's novel and Burl Crow in Wynne-Jones's novel choose one family home rather than another, homes with private rooms in which they can learn to read and write themselves. At the end of their narratives, Dylan reaches for a pay phone and Tom sits on the curb of a public street, looking for words that might work to tell the stories that others want to hear.

☐ ☐ ☐

Notes

1 My claims for the pre-eminent place of this narrative in English-language Canadian children's literature are argued in detail in an article written jointly with Anne Rusnak in 2000–2001. As I demonstrate there, fully 40% of the novels that won awards in Canada between 1975 and 1995 follow the pattern I outline here. A second pattern that accounts for a further 28% of award winners also uses several of these elements, notably the new home built on affiliative bonds.

2 *Shadow in Hawthorn Bay* won the Canada Council Children's Literary Prize in 1986; the Canadian Library Association Book of the Year Award, the Canadian Library Association Young Adult Canadian Book Award, and the National Chapter of Canada IODE Violet Downey Book Award in 1987; and a place on the IBBY Honour List in 1988.

3 See Bradford, *Reading Race* (88–101), and Hulme (156–68) for two discussions of colonial representations of the relation between indigenous people and land.

4 See Masschelein (63–65) for a discussion of the ways in which Freud's notion of the *Unheimlich* has been read as "transcendental homelessness" in poststructural theory.

5 See Louise Saldanha's chapter in this volume for a reading of the racialized limits of such heterogeneity in Canadian children's literature generally and Clare Bradford's chapter for a reading of the ethnicized limits encoded in Bedard's novel specifically.

6 While I chose to work with these novels because of their metafictional themes, I've also become aware that all of these novels feature protagonists with unspecified

racial and ethnic identities, but with family names that sound generically Anglophone (with the possible exception of Burl Crow). There are other award-winning novels from the same period (1975–1995) that also use the "away becomes home" pattern and that focus on central characters from ethnicized communities, including Myra Paperny's *The Wooden People* (1976), Barbara Smucker's *Days of Terror* (1979), Julie Lawson's *White Jade Tiger* (1993), Sean Stewart's *Nobody's Son* (1993), Lillian Boraks-Nemetz's *The Old Brown Suitcase* (1994), and Walter Buchigani's *Tell No One Who You Are* (1994). The ways in which the representations of the immigrant child subject as ethnic subject might complicate the narrative patterns and ideologies I outline here needs further consideration.

7   The continuity between the discourses of class and colonialism has been noted by Peter Hulme: speaking of the cultural implications of Defoe's *Robinson Crusoe*, Hulme observes that "the discourse of colonialism provid[ed] the terms with which class conflict can be articulated" (266).

8   This valuing and ordering of possessions is key to the domestic ideology Andrew O'Malley, in his chapter in this volume, sees at the centre of the robinsonade tradition.

9   The farmhouse with the addition Mr. Huddleston has built to accommodate his growing foster family is described by Sara as a "little square house with its ship-like projection, sitting like a promise on the brow of the hill" (Johnston 179); Lazarus House, built by a retired sea captain, makes Ben feel that "he was inside the hull of a ship, massive beams supporting the ceiling overhead while solid oak panels graced the walls" (Aker 188); the window of the Maestro's cottage reminds Burl "of a sail and, like a sail, it seemed alive in the breeze, filled one moment with a reflection of water and sky and the next emptied and replaced with geometric blocks of shade" (Wynne-Jones 35).

10   *Looking for X* won the Governor General's Literary Award for Children's Literature in 2000; *Tom Finder* won the Mr. Christie Award and the Benjamin Franklin Award for Young Adult Literature in 2004 and was shortlisted for the Ontario Library Association's White Pine Award, the R. Ross Annett Award, and the ForeWord Magazine award; *Theories of Relativity* won the Saskatchewan Young Readers' Choice Snow Willow Award in 2005, was shortlisted for the Canadian Library Association's Young Adult Book of the Year Award and the OLA's White Pine Award in 2004, and was shortlisted for the Governor General's Literary Award for Children's Literature in 2003; *Last Sam's Cage* was nominated for both the Manitoba Young Readers' Choice Award and the Snow Willow Award in Saskatchewan in 2006; and *Heck Superhero* won a place on the American Library Association's Notable Children's Book and Best Book for Young Adults lists in 2005, was shortlisted for a Governor General's Literary Award for Children's Literature in 2004, and was named an Editor's Choice book in the *Kirkus Review* in 2004. Jean Little's *Willow and Twig* (2000)—winner of the Mr. Christie's Book Award in 2000 and shortlisted for both the Canadian Library Association's Book of the Year Award and the Violet Downey Book Award—features two young children who briefly live on the streets of Vancouver before being taken to her home by their grandmother. Because it fits easily into the pattern of the conventional home-away-home narrative, it is not discussed here.

11 But see Taylor et al. for an account of the difficulties of using standard "testing instruments" with street kids (3–4).

12 But note Margaret Mackey's observation that this gatekeeping function is changing as publishers respond to the diminished funding of these public institutions and work to sell directly to "the child and its parent" ("Canadian Young People and Their Reading Worlds" 87).

CHAPTER 2

➡ **Les représentations du « home[1] »
dans les romans historiques
québécois destinés aux adolescents**

Danielle Thaler et
Alain Jean-Bart

Récemment, la grande romancière américaine
Alison Lurie rappelait que « dans les classiques de la littérature pour la jeunesse, le héros est généralement un enfant qui quitte son foyer et sa famille
et connaît diverses aventures avant de regagner son foyer » (132). On com-
prend alors pourquoi la critique anglo-saxonne a fait du concept du « home »
un axe essentiel dans sa recherche d'une spécificité de la littérature enfantine : « My impression is not only that home is the dominant place in
children's literature, but also that the house is the chief form it takes[2] »
(Wolf 54).

Mais, le « home » qui mobilise l'attention des sciences humaines comme
la géographie, la sociologie, la psychologie, la psychanalyse, l'ethnogra-
phie et l'architecture reste cependant un concept aux frontières difficiles
à délimiter tant il couvre un champ sémantique étendu et nourrit un large
et riche réseau de connotations[3] (Sopher; George; Hayward). Ces connotations varient non seulement d'une culture à l'autre mais également au
sein d'une même culture, car le « home » est au centre d'enjeux fondamen-
taux dans les représentations de l'environnement géographique, physique,
mais aussi psychique et idéologique. C'est à partir de lui que se conçoit
une vision du monde qui dit le dedans et le dehors, l'ici et l'ailleurs, le même
et l'autre, le moi et le non-moi. Aussi est-il difficile d'envisager un moi dis-
socié de l'environnement dans lequel il a baigné et de répondre à la question « qui suis-je? » sans passer par cette autre question : « d'où suis-je? ».
Nous venons tous de quelque part et nous sommes marqués par les lieux,

les milieux, les paysages que nous avons traversés. Ils ont contribué à la formation de notre personnalité. Ainsi, le « home » est-il fondamentalement un espace « habité », profondément ancré dans la psyché, reflet de l'être et lieu d'une identité qui se forge[4].

Le concept a engendré une abondante littérature critique, à l'initiative, semble-t-il, des géographes comme Yi-Fu Tuan[5], dans les années 1970. Si l'on cherche à saisir dans quelles grandes directions s'est orientée la critique en littérature de jeunesse quand elle reprend la problématique à son compte, on peut avancer qu'elle a surtout tenté de dégager un réseau d'antithèses où le « home » occupe un de deux pôles pour résumer les deux aspirations contradictoires qu'on prête à l'enfant, qui hésite entre la sécurité offerte par le foyer familial et l'excitation de l'aventure promise par le monde extérieur. Nous nous contenterons ici de rappeler hâtivement quelques-unes de ces orientations qui nous aideront à souligner certains aspects des romans du genre historique pour la jeunesse. Lorsque Clausen Christopher s'interroge sur ce qui constitue la spécificité d'un livre destiné aux enfants, il distingue deux visions antagonistes du foyer familial résumées dans l'antithèse « home » / « away »[6]. David Sopher avait déjà, quelques années auparavant, suggéré une opposition entre une conception « domicentrique » où le « home » reste fondamentalement le lieu où l'on se réfugie et une conception « domifuge » où le « home » est un lieu qu'il faut absolument fuir. Pour Jon C. Stott et Christine Doyle Francis, si le « home » favorise généralement l'épanouissement physique et émotionnel de l'enfant, de nombreux récits destinés aux enfants mettent en scène des personnages qui se sentent aliénés dans le milieu où ils vivent et tentent de lui échapper (« not-home »). D'autres oppositions ont été avancées : « home » / « adventure » (Watkins), « home » / « travel » (George 1-2), « home » / « journey »[7]. Il est certes des voyages sans retour, mais le nouvel espace géographique (et psychique?) colonisé et habité n'est-il pas inventé à l'image du « home » perdu? Il est fréquent que l'exilé ou l'immigrant reconstruise son nouvel environnement à l'image de son pays d'origine. Pour Porteous, l'espace géographique s'organise, en effet, à partir de l'opposition « home » / « non-home », car si l'individualisme est marqué par l'anthropocentrisme, l'ethnocentrisme et l'égocentrisme, il est aussi influencé par une vision « domocentrique » de l'espace, c'est-à-dire une conscience de l'espace articulée autour d'un lieu familier dont les représentations sont associées aux idées d'identité, de sécurité (physique et psychique) et d'épanouissement.

Que l'on reste, que l'on revienne ou que l'on s'en aille, ceci est porté, motivé par une vision du « home » et du monde, ce qu'on nomme une utopie. Nombreuses sont les histoires où le désir de partir est stimulé par une insatisfaction. Pourquoi irait-on chercher ailleurs ce que l'on trouve ici ? Si tant de jeunes héros se sont enfuis de chez eux, c'est bien que le moi n'y trouvait pas son compte. Et, si le célèbre adage « les voyages forment la jeunesse » dit vrai, il faut alors accepter l'idée que le « home » ne désigne jamais un univers aux frontières fixées une fois pour toutes, mais que ces frontières sont sans cesse en mouvement et que le « home » s'élargit au rythme des découvertes et des évolutions du moi. Et c'est certainement là que tout se joue, à la limite du connu et de l'inconnu. Jean Starobinski expliquait que le dedans et le dehors sont inconcevables l'un sans l'autre – on peut en dire sans doute autant de « home » et de « away », de l'ici et de l'ailleurs, du moi et de l'autre – et que l'essentiel se passait à la frontière entre les deux univers, à la surface de contact, « lieu des échanges, des ajustements, des signaux sensibles, mais aussi celui des conflits et des blessures » (15).

La fiction historique québécoise pour la jeunesse s'inscrit idéalement dans cette problématique. Elle demeure, en effet, fondamentalement un récit de l'immigration et de la colonisation, un récit d'un aller sans retour. L'acte qui, le plus souvent, inaugure et fonde l'aventure est un départ, car les héros de ces fictions sont des personnages qui s'en vont, et sont bientôt voués à la transformation d'un *ailleurs* en un « home ». Mais, en même temps, à travers l'histoire de la colonisation de ce qui s'appelait jadis la Nouvelle-France, elle n'a cessé de dire aux jeunes lecteurs quels regards ils devaient jeter sur un passé où se forgeait une identité nationale, et donc de leur dire qui ils étaient et d'où ils venaient. Il n'y a pas de vision du « home » innocente puisque celle-ci dit nécessairement comment elle voit le monde. Rien n'est moins surprenant que de trouver le roman historique aux origines d'une littérature qui fait une apparition tardive, dans un pays neuf, après une colonisation délicate et conflictuelle. C'est en effet avec le roman historique que naît une véritable littérature de jeunesse au Québec. Sans doute a-t-il été précédé par la diffusion de quelques contes et œuvres à caractère religieux et moral, mais les premiers auteurs reconnus (Marie-Claire Daveluy, Eugène Achard, Maxine, Marie-Antoinette Grégoire-Coupal) se sont illustrés dans le genre historique.

Et, qu'est-ce que le roman historique ? Une petite fabrique de légendes et de mythes qui remontent aux origines de la création d'un pays, qui déroulent la trame des événements qui justifient son existence et sa raison d'être. Ce n'est pas que la vérité historique soit négligée ou malmenée. Elle est même souvent fidèlement respectée, mais le genre tend à sacraliser des faits qui deviennent les mythes fondateurs d'un état, à sacraliser des personnages qui prennent une dimension légendaire dans leur contribution à la naissance, à la défense ou au développement d'une nation.

Le genre historique, d'ailleurs souvent relayé par des hagiographies qui se préoccupent de la vie des saints et des grandes figures historiques, a ainsi une vocation foncièrement éducative et idéologique qui en fait un genre idéalement destiné à la jeunesse. Ni Marie-Claire Daveluy, ni Maxine, ni Eugène Achard ne s'en cachent. Ils ont le souci de valoriser un patrimoine historique, de participer à l'édification et la propagation d'une épopée nationale, de façon à nourrir chez les jeunes générations un sentiment d'appartenance tout en leur inculquant des valeurs morales, religieuses et nationalistes. Si l'Histoire n'est jamais qu'une relecture et une réécriture du passé, le roman historique est, par excellence, un des genres où s'opère cette métamorphose. Il élabore une vision du monde et affirme ou suggère comment trouver sa place dans ce monde. Il pose ainsi clairement la question de l'intégration de l'individu dans la société, des relations entre l'individu et la Cité.

Toutefois, le genre historique a construit, en grande partie, sa réputation sur un personnage emblématique aux aspirations individualistes fortes : le coureur des bois. Celui-ci est incontestablement devenu la figure privilégiée du roman historique qui traite de la colonisation de la Nouvelle-France. On peut comprendre cette fascination pour cette incarnation de l'aventurier, mais on peut en même temps considérer avec étonnement cette promotion, au détriment de la figure tout aussi légendaire du colon, dans un genre dont les enjeux idéologiques ont été maintes fois soulignés. Le coureur des bois ne symbolise-t-il pas d'abord la liberté, une liberté qui s'accommode mal d'un projet collectif, soit celui de bâtir un pays? David Sopher n'a pas manqué de le signaler : « Set against the myths of home and homeland, we find the myths that challenge them, the myth of the voyager, the adventurer, the mythic quest that takes one forth into and through the world, not reluctantly but eagerly. Let us call these 'domifuge questing myths' […] » (134-135). Ainsi, le coureur des bois, incarnant des valeurs individuelles, se dresserait contre les valeurs de l'autorité instituée et institutionnelle. Cela ferait de lui une figure héroïque antisociale de la contestation du « home ». La réalisation de soi l'emporterait-elle sur la défense et le salut de la Cité, la satisfaction des aspirations personnelles passerait-elle avant tout projet collectif ou communautaire?

À ce personnage emblématique haut en couleurs, il convient d'associer une autre figure tout aussi légendaire et qui trouve naturellement sa place dans une problématique du « home » : celui de l'Amérindien, et surtout de l'Iroquois, incarnation de l'autre. L'autre, c'est-à-dire l'étranger, celui qui est dehors, de l'autre côté de la frontière du « home », figure de l'exclu ou du désir d'intégration, engagé dans un processus d'acculturation ou de contre-acculturation, de contestation ou de légitimation du « home ». Selon Rosemary Marangoly George, la notion de « home » est construite sur un réseau d'inclusions et d'exclusions qui sous-entend la reconnaissance d'une différence, d'une altérité. Le « home » est ainsi défini comme un espace (pas seulement géographique) qui fonctionne sur l'opposition du même et de l'autre, de l'appartenance et du rejet[8]. Le concept ne peut donc être ni politiquement ni idéologiquement neutre.

Nous verrons comment les fictions historiques, d'hier et d'aujourd'hui, destinées à la jeunesse québécoise, exploitent le réseau d'antithèses « home » / « away », et les formules narratives qui lui sont attachées, pour lire et relire le passé, pour fabriquer ses mythes identitaires et ses légendes nationales. L'évolution du roman historique tient certes compte de l'évolution qui a marqué, au cours du siècle dernier, la manière dont nous comprenons le passé et dont nous envisageons l'Histoire : nous sommes, en effet, passés d'une fascination pour les grands hommes et les grands événements à une attention méticuleuse pour le quotidien des petites gens. Cependant, l'évolution touche, aussi et surtout, les représentations de la triade coloniale fondamentale : le colon, le coureur des bois et le Sauvage.

L'utopie de la Nouvelle-France

L'épopée historique de la Nouvelle-France est peuplée d'orphelins. Ceux-ci ont longtemps fait figure, dans la littérature de jeunesse, de personnages à la mode. Le plus curieux est qu'ils le sont demeurés dans les fictions contemporaines consacrées à la colonisation du Québec. Simple respect d'une réalité historique connue? Fidélité à une tradition qui remonte à l'œuvre fondatrice du genre, celle de Marie-Claire Daveluy qui fut la première à jeter deux jeunes orphelins dans l'aventure de la colonisation? Il y a sans doute de cela, mais pas seulement. L'orphelin a quelque chose à voir avec la marginalité. D'abord, il est sans doute, de tous les personnages, l'un des plus disponibles parce qu'il est sans attaches. Il appartient idéalement à la race des héros bâtis pour l'aventure de tous les nouveaux mondes parce qu'il n'a plus rien à perdre et que la rupture lui coûte peu. Ajoutons ensuite que dans les fictions historiques contemporaines, il se rapproche souvent du laissé-pour-compte ou du banni. C'est donc déjà un personnage en exil qui n'a pas, ou plus, sa place là où il est. Privé de famille et de foyer, il lui faut aller chercher *ailleurs* ce qu'il ne trouve plus *ici*. Et cet *ailleurs* du renouveau, où tout est possible, se présente sous les traits attirants de la Nouvelle-France. Mais le voyage est aussi l'occasion d'une renaissance, d'un retour aux origines, car le désir du jeune héros se nourrit souvent de nostalgie, la nostalgie d'un avant heureux (avant la mort du père ou de la mère). Ainsi, l'immersion dans un espace autre, nouveau, est symboliquement associée à un retour vers le passé, à un retour à l'enfance. Le mythe de la Nouvelle-France se rattache au mythe arcadien du paradis retrouvé et la dialectique de l'*ici* et de l'*ailleurs*, en se fondant dans l'opposition du « not-home » et du « home ». Il va mettre l'accent sur tout ce qui sépare la France de la Nouvelle-France. Ce stéréotype, on le retrouvera dans la plupart des romans qui traitent de la découverte et de la colonisation du Canada français. Et l'on peut aisément comprendre pourquoi : la démarche s'inscrit dans un processus idéologique de légitimation de la colonisation.

Tous les récits de l'installation en Nouvelle-France s'accompagnent, ces quarante dernières années, d'un tableau dévalorisant de la France, qui devient le lieu de tous les étouffements et de tous les dangers. C'est la première étape dans le processus de justification. Orphelins, les jeunes héros de ces fictions sont des personnages à qui l'intégration semble refusée ou impossible, quand ils ne sont pas tout simplement menacés dans leur épanouissement et dans leur existence. Étienne (Julien, *Tête*), Matthieu Rousseau (Corriveau), Gabriel (Ouimet, *Mirages*) et Marie-Victoire (Ouimet, *Secret*) sont, en effet, des personnages en danger. Le premier, accusé de vol, et le deuxième, maltraité par son patron, s'embarquent clandestinement à bord d'un vaisseau en partance pour le Nouveau Monde. Humiliée et harcelée par son frère aîné, la troisième doit dissimuler sa véritable identité et s'enfuir : « L'exil … Quelle merveilleuse échappatoire! Finie la peur d'être reconnue. Finie l'angoisse de voir apparaître, un jour ou l'autre, son frère et sa mère tant détestés. Être libre [...] Cette aventure vers le nouveau monde était son unique planche de salut » (Ouimet, *Secret* 41). C'est si vrai que lorsque le personnage reviendra en France, pour une question d'héritage, ce sera pour y disparaître à tout jamais et sans laisser de trace. Quant au jeune Gabriel, victime d'un régime égoïste, il mène une existence misérable dans un monde hostile : « L'espace d'un éclair, Gabriel voit défiler les dernières années de sa jeunesse perdue dans les méandres de la ruse et de l'hypocrisie. Il en a marre de mendier. Comme il espère, encore, pouvoir rêver de vivre une existence calme et sereine! Comme aux beaux jours de son enfance, avant la mort de ses parents. Avant la déroute. Avant l'enfer [...] » (Ouimet, *Mirages* 17); et il est aussi dit :

> À lui seul, ce gamin représente tous les laissés-pour-compte de cette société monarchique qui rejette les enfants, les pauvres et les vieillards sur les routes du royaume de France. Tout occupé qu'il est à faire la guerre à Charles Quint, le roi François ne se soucie guère de ses humbles servi-

teurs. Ce souverain au pouvoir absolu délègue sa puissance à des favoris, à des aristocrates et à des commerçants qui cherchent tous à s'enrichir. Il dirige le pays mollement, ordonnant à ses fonctionnaires, quand il a besoin d'argent, de surtaxer ses sujets. Et que dire des excès de la religion qui envoient bien des gens sur le bûcher! (Ouimet, *Mirages* 18)

Aussi, tout le premier chapitre des *Mirages de l'aube* s'organise-t-il autour d'un axe mort / vie (renaissance), accompagné d'une dévalorisation de l'*ici* (la France) et d'une valorisation de l'*ailleurs* (la Nouvelle-France). Le cas de Jeanne Chatel, l'héroïne de Suzanne Martel (*Jeanne*), est un peu différent. On ne peut pas dire que l'héroïne est en danger même si sa famille a été victime d'une injustice : « La famille Chatel, de petite noblesse, avait été déshonorée et ruinée par un ancêtre tombé en disgrâce auprès d'un roi rancunier. Les calomnies d'un voisin jaloux et puissant, un comte de Villebrand, avaient été à l'origine de ce désastre » (18). Dépouillée de ses biens et orpheline, elle est placée dans un couvent où elle étouffe, car son seul avenir y est de devenir nonne. C'est contre ce destin qu'elle se rebelle : « la porte de sa prison s'ouvre, la grande ouverture commence » (16); « L'orpheline quitte sans regret cette patrie qui pour elle se résume aux murs gris d'un couvent » (35), c'est-à-dire à un enfermement qui contraste avec la liberté dont elle jouissait avant et qui est notamment incarnée par un arbre au milieu d'un parc qui a jadis appartenu à sa famille. Le thème du jardin perdu alimente sa nostalgie du passé et c'est un autre jardin, celui de la Nouvelle-France, qui apaisera son sentiment de frustration et de dépouillement. Dans tous les récits dont il vient d'être rapidement question, le salut est donc dans la fuite.

Il ne faudrait cependant pas croire que cette vision négative a toujours prévalu. Les représentations de la France ont, en effet, évolué dans les fictions historiques destinées à la jeunesse québécoise. Ainsi, les romans de Marie-Claire Daveluy ne brossent pas du pays qu'il faut quitter un tableau sombre. Et, les nouveaux colons gardent des liens privilégiés avec un pays dont ils tentent de répandre les valeurs, surtout les valeurs religieuses : « Comme dans l'épopée traditionnelle, les personnages, assez nombreux, sont engagés dans une action à la fois patriotique et religieuse : accroître le prestige et la prospérité de la France et répandre la religion catholique » (Lepage, *Histoire* 120). Pourtant, Perrine et Charlot sont des personnages qui prennent la fuite, mais c'est pour éviter de vivre auprès d'une tante dont la réputation est épouvantable : « Or, Perrine se rappelle fort bien cette vieille tante, veuve depuis plusieurs années. Elle est d'un caractère acariâtre, dur, impitoyable aux petites faiblesses, très avare. Elle hait les enfants » (Daveluy, *Perrine et Charlot* 12). En fait, se met en place dans cette œuvre une autre thématique : celle de la mère. Premiers orphelins de la littérature de jeunesse québécoise, Perrine et Charlot sont à la recherche d'un nouveau foyer et d'une mère qui puisse remplacer celle qu'ils viennent de perdre. Or, la tante, telle qu'elle est décrite, n'est pas habilitée à assumer ce rôle. La mère disparue apparaît alors à Perrine, dans un rêve, pour lui indiquer le chemin à suivre. À bord du navire où ils ont embarqué, les deux orphelins vont trouver la famille qui les adoptera, et reconnaître en madame de Repentigny une femme ressemblant étrangement à leur mère. Ce retour symbolique à la mère suffit pour légitimer la fuite et l'installation en Nouvelle-France. Ainsi, les personnages d'hier et d'aujourd'hui ont toujours de bonnes raisons pour quitter un pays qui ne peut plus répondre à l'image idéalisée du « home ».

À l'opposé, la Nouvelle-France fait naturellement figure d'Eldorado. C'est la seconde étape de la justification. Les romans historiques des pionniers de la littérature de jeunesse québécoise développent une image très valorisante de la colonie. Marie-Claire Daveluy s'est ainsi lancée, dans les années 1920–1930, dans une légitimation idéologique, morale et religieuse de la colonisation qui la pousse vers une idéalisation des comportements coloniaux et des rapports entre colons : image idéale de la colonie fondée sur la solidarité, la sollicitude, la gentillesse, image d'un bonheur qui n'est brisé que par les incursions iroquoises; sympathie de tous les protagonistes, qu'ils soient historiques ou fictifs, à l'égard de Charlot, sans cesse protégé, même si cette protection n'est pas toujours efficace. Charlot n'est d'ailleurs pas en reste, animé qu'il est par des impulsions généreuses qui lui jouent parfois des tours (il est blessé en voulant séparer deux soldats qui se battent en duel [*Martyrs*]). Bien entendu, l'évangélisation des Indiens contribue à cette idéalisation coloniale du « home ». Porté par une vision manichéenne, le récit divise l'univers de la Nouvelle-France en deux espaces antagonistes, selon un axe « home » / « not-home » : celui de la colonie et celui des Iroquois, ce dernier demeurant cependant, dans une conception purement colonialiste, un inconnu à domestiquer, un « not-home » à transformer en « home ». Cette perception de l'univers témoigne évidemment de l'idéologie dominante d'une époque. Mais, si les représentations ont évolué, les récits les plus récents continuent de s'organiser, du moins dans un premier temps, autour d'une image idéale de la Nouvelle-France. Dans *L'Appel des rivières* d'André Vacher, Pierre Leblanc est un « garçon de dix-huit ans à qui cette appellation de « Nouvelle-France » donnait les plus folles espérances. L'« ancienne », la France des campagnes, l'avait si peu gâté jusque-là qu'il venait véritablement chercher une nouvelle vie ici. Sans rien savoir de ce pays d'Amérique, il en attendait tout » (*Iroquois* 15). Ce roman récent (2000) reprend à son compte une formule déjà abondamment illustrée où la valorisation du « home » identitaire passe par la dévalorisation du lieu originel et la valorisation de la colonisation. On devine les mêmes attentes chez les autres personnages : chez Marie-Victoire, « un pays où la liberté nourrit chaque être humain » (Ouimet, *Secret* 54); chez Matthieu Rousseau, « [l]'océan, tendu comme une route, s'étend jusqu'à l'horizon : loin, très loin, on devine l'Amérique, les pays neufs, l'aventure et la liberté » (Corriveau 12); chez Étienne qui « a souvent entendu parler du Nouveau Monde situé de l'autre côté de la mer. Les marins qui y sont allés relatent toutes sortes d'histoires extraordinaires à son sujet. Et voilà qu'à lui, pauvre petit orphelin, on offre la chance de faire un si merveilleux voyage jusque-là! » (Julien, *Tête* 23-24) et de gagner un pays où « [t]out est à bâtir[9] » (23). Les descriptions prennent alors une connotation légèrement fantastique :

> Les forêts sont tellement denses que l'on peut y perdre la tête en cherchant à s'y retrouver! Et, l'hiver, la neige enterre le toit des cabanes! Mais le plus terrifiant, ce sont les monstres et autres bêtes incroyables qui habitent ce pays sauvage [...] J'en ai visité, des collines et des plaines! J'en ai remonté, des rivières et des lacs! Et j'en ai vu, des bêtes étranges qui n'ont pas leurs pareils en France! (25)

Gabriel succombe lui aussi à cet appel du large et à la fascination pour les terres lointaines de la Nouvelle-France[10] : « Ces gueux avaient su peupler son imagination de paysages de mer, de vagues et de tempêtes. D'animaux plus immenses que les navires. D'îles fleuries où poussent, en toutes saisons, des fruits en abondance. Des contrées légendaires et lointaines où les hommes et les femmes vivent nus sous le soleil » (Ouimet, *Mirages* 10). Tous ces personnages sont les victimes consentantes d'un même mirage aux confins de la légende et de la liberté, esquissant ainsi une image paradisiaque du nouveau monde que confirme la vision idéale et idéaliste de la colonisation de Jacques Cartier dans *Le Vol des chimères* : « De concert avec les indigènes, ces colons feront vibrer de leurs rires et de leurs chants les rives de ce pays. Ils danseront ensemble au son des vielles et au rythme des tambours sacrés [...] » (Ouimet 176-177). Du moins ce rêve est-il fondé sur un métissage des cultures qui témoigne d'une évolution du genre depuis les œuvres de Marie-Claire Daveluy.

Pourtant, sans renoncer à la valorisation de la Nouvelle-France, plusieurs romans contestent cette utopie. Sans doute est-ce dû à l'évolution d'une conscience historique qui remet en question les idéaux du passé. La Nouvelle-France ne jouit plus de la même faveur, ou plutôt, l'axe de valorisation s'est déplacé, provoquant en même temps une remise en question de l'opposition « home » / « not-home ». Cette contestation s'accompagne, bien entendu, d'une révision idéologique qui transforme tout à la fois les images de la colonie et des Amérindiens.

Les romans ont cessé de donner de la Nouvelle-France une image monolithique. Dans le même roman peuvent, en effet, coexister, et entrer en conflit, deux visions du monde : celle où « not-home » / « home » s'incarne dans l'opposition France / Nouvelle-France (c'est-à-dire la colonie), parallèlement à une autre opposition entre la colonie et un *ailleurs* que résume à lui seul le titre du roman d'André Vacher : *L'Appel des rivières*. Déjà en 1964, dans *Le Wapiti* de Monique Corriveau, le héros était condamné à fuir, après avoir été accusé d'un meurtre qu'il n'avait pas commis et alors que nul ne croyait en son innocence au sein d'une colonie où il semblait pourtant avoir trouvé sa place. Après avoir échappé au triste sort qui risquait d'être le sien en France, Matthieu Rousseau était ainsi contraint, une nouvelle fois, d'aller assumer son destin ailleurs, dissipant ainsi le mirage auquel il voulait se laisser prendre. L'image de la colonie semblait alors devoir se ternir pour se rapprocher de celle que le roman donnait de la France. Mais, l'histoire s'achevait fort heureusement sur une réconciliation. Paru en 1980, *Menfou Carcajou*, le premier volume des *Coureurs des bois* de Suzanne Martel, débute par une scène de punition publique, son héros ayant été condamné au pilori. Ce rejet qui signale immédiatement la marginalité du personnage, à travers la méfiance de la société coloniale à son égard, coupe court, dès le départ, à toute valorisation excessive de la Nouvelle-France puisque c'est aussi un lieu qui maltraite et qui exclut, et qui, en procédant de la sorte, semble rejeter de son univers l'espace héroïque sans lequel il n'est pas d'aventure possible. La marginalisation du héros est d'autant plus grande que celui-ci « ne semble pas avoir bien compris le sens de son humiliation » (Martel, *Menfou* 25), et n'adhère donc ni à la morale ni à la vision coloniales. Les deux premiers volumes de cette saga, qui ne formaient qu'un seul volume dans l'édition de 1980, s'achèvent sur un départ, une fuite, le héros rejoignant sa famille iroquoise à la suite d'une déception (la jeune Perrine, qu'il aimait, a épousé le notaire) et d'une injustice (son père adoptif iroquois est emmené sur les galères du roi). En 1999, *L'Orpheline de la maison Chevalier* de Josée Ouimet montre qu'à la solidarité, tant vantée par Marie-Claire Daveluy, des temps héroïques s'est substitué un renouvellement des clivages sociaux et de l'exploitation des plus faibles. Marie Houymel est placée comme domestique dans la maison d'un grand commerçant de Québec pour effacer les dettes de son père, qui vient de mourir, et ainsi aider sa mère et ses nombreux frères et sœurs. Jamais la maison Chevalier ne deviendra un « home » pour la jeune Marie, dont la condition se dégrade, dans un univers clos et étouffant. Elle meurt d'une embolie cérébrale à la suite d'un accident, en 1754. L'opposition dialectique de l'*ici* et de l'*ailleurs*, du dedans et du dehors, du « home » et du « not-home » semble abolie, dans ce récit, pour faire place à une forme de pessimisme : version désespérée qui ne laisse au personnage aucune solution de rechange et l'enferme dans un destin nécessairement noir. Il semble cette fois qu'il n'y ait plus d'*ailleurs* possible. Sans doute faut-il tenir compte, dans cette interprétation, de la dimension symbolique d'un roman dont l'action se situe en 1753, à un moment où les Anglais envisagent la conquête du Québec. Le destin de Marie Houymel préfigurerait ainsi celui de la ville de Québec et de toute la Nouvelle-France[11]. Le roman de Josée Ouimet proclamerait-il, à sa façon, la fin des utopies, la fin du mythe et le retour de l'Histoire? De Monique Corriveau à Josée Ouimet, l'image de la Nouvelle-France se fissure. Celle-ci cesse d'incarner le refuge idéal, témoignant ainsi d'une incontestable révision des valeurs que véhiculaient les romans antérieurs. Il se trouve que cette révision accompagne une revalorisation de la figure de l'Amérindien.

Les représentations des Sauvages dans la littérature de jeunesse québécoise ont beaucoup évolué depuis le début du XXe siècle, et ont ainsi contribué à une réévaluation idéologique du « home ». Dans les récits de Marie-Claire Daveluy, les Iroquois sont accablés de toutes les tares : perfidie, traîtrise, cruauté, lâcheté. Ce sont des barbares qui pratiquent la torture même à l'égard des leurs, peu fidèles, perfides[12], accusés de cannibalisme (Daveluy, *Perrine et Charlot* 139, 142) et dont les gestes sont « dictés par la fourberie, la méchanceté et une jalousie intense » (117-118). Curieusement, un roman contemporain, *Le Vol des chimères*, renoue avec des représentations qui rappellent Marie-Claire Daveluy. Le roman suit deux intrigues parallèles. Le procédé permet de juxtaposer deux points de vue, celui de Cartier (personnage historique) et des Blancs, celui de Shanaweh (personnage imaginaire) et des Indiens. Mais, peut-on vraiment parler d'une véritable alternance des points de vue? En effet, le point de vue indigène se résume essentiellement à celui d'une Amérindienne qui représente le parti de l'acculturation. Shanaweh est, sans doute, l'incarnation de la voix idéologique du roman. À l'opposé, le personnage de Cohenaya devient de plus en plus antipathique alors qu'il incarne les valeurs de la résistance. Et le portrait des autres Indiens n'est guère enthousiaste. S'il est question de ruse (avec une connotation positive) lorsque Cartier tend un piège aux Indigènes, c'est le mot « fourberie » (avec une connotation négative) qui décrit le comportement des chefs de la tribu qui agissent de la même manière. Seuls trouvent vraiment grâce aux yeux du narrateur les Indiens qui acceptent de se soumettre et sont favorables à l'acculturation et au métissage[13]. Sans doute s'agit-il pour l'auteur de défendre un modèle multiculturel, synthèse à partir de laquelle on pourrait construire une identité nationale. Aujourd'hui, à l'exception de ce roman, les Indiens jouissent d'une image beaucoup plus favorable. Mais il semble que c'est en grande partie parce que l'image de l'Iroquois est désormais indissociable de celle du coureur des bois. Ils sont tous deux les représentants d'un territoire qui esquisse les frontières d'un autre « home ». Les deux romans de Vacher leur donnent beaucoup de place et l'auteur s'attarde, après l'enlèvement de Pierre Leblanc par les Onondagas, sur leurs coutumes. Leur image est ambivalente. Ils sont à la fois cruels et généreux, et ils constituent incontestablement une menace pour la colonie, pour le « home ». Mais, en même temps, ils sont aussi les représentants d'un espace naturel habité mais respecté. Ils représentent alors une autre vision du monde. Le point de vue des Amérindiens retrouve donc un certain crédit et leurs doléances sont à prendre en compte dans les représentations du « home » que donnent les romans historiques de la fondation de la Nouvelle-France. Dans le second volume de *L'Appel des rivières* d'André Vacher, sont rappelés les griefs des Indiens à l'égard des Blancs (*Calliou* 98–99). C'est tout un équilibre naturel qui est menacé, rompu, tout un pays qui est saccagé, toute une nation qui est menacée. Un « home » est en train d'être détruit. Le coureur de bois, avant-garde de la colonisation, devient ainsi, à sa façon, un corrupteur d'Indiens, un danger pour les nations indiennes. Si les Iroquois sont une menace pour les colons, les Blancs sont un danger pour les Indiens.

Les représentations de la France et de la Nouvelle-France dans les romans québécois contribuent à justifier la colonisation. Il s'agit quand même de romans historiques, destinés à la jeunesse, qui parlent de la fondation d'un pays, et dont la vocation est d'aider les jeunes lecteurs à une prise de conscience historique et d'esquisser pour eux les contours d'un pays, d'une nation dont ils sont les héritiers. Ces représentations évoluent cependant au cours du siècle, procédant à des révisions idéologiques qui redéfinissent le « home » dans le cadre d'une nouvelle dialectique du « home » et du « not-home ». Quelques romans taillent des brèches dans la vision idéale de la Nouvelle-France pour remettre en question, sinon la colonisation, du moins l'idéologie coloniale. La réhabilitation de la figure du Sauvage est contemporaine de la promotion du coureur des bois. Tous deux semblent indissociables et tous deux incarnent un *ailleurs* que d'aucuns vont trouver plus excitant que l'*ici* de la colonie. Mais, comment cette réévaluation va-t-elle contribuer à redéfinir une identité nationale québécoise?

Le coureur des bois : vers une nouvelle définition de l'identité québécoise.

Le personnage du coureur des bois n'est pas une figure littéraire neuve. La vogue suscitée par Fenimore Cooper a même atteint très tôt des pays comme la France et l'Allemagne. En France, les Indiens sont rapidement adoptés par la littérature enfantine, et des auteurs comme Gustave Aimard (1818–1883) et Gabriel Ferry (1809–1852) peuplent leur univers de trappeurs et de coureurs des bois. L'écrivain allemand Karl May (1842–1912) a obtenu un succès phénoménal avec son Winnetou. Curieusement, le coureur des bois ne semble avoir pris de l'ampleur dans les fictions historiques québécoises pour la jeunesse qu'assez récemment. Cela ne veut pas dire qu'on l'ignorait, mais il n'avait ni la même envergure ni le même statut. Ainsi, le jeune Charlot, le personnage le plus emblématique de la littérature de jeunesse québécoise à ses débuts, n'est pas coureur des bois. S'il a du mal à résister à l'appel de la forêt canadienne, c'est d'abord un soldat, engagé au service de la défense de la colonie. Quelques personnages de coureurs des bois font bien leur apparition dans l'œuvre de Marie-Claire Daveluy, mais ils sont confinés dans des rôles secondaires, comme Olivier Le Tardif et Jean Nicolet, deux grandes figures historiques de la colonisation. Ils prêtent bien leurs silhouettes et leurs noms à l'auteur, mais ils ne font que passer et veiller sur le jeune Charlot. Ils sont toutefois présentés comme des ardents défenseurs de la colonie, ce qui n'est pas le cas du personnage imaginé par Marie-Antoinette Grégoire-Coupal. Celle-ci a choisi un coureur des bois pour en faire le héros de son roman, *La Sorcière de l'îlot noir*, mais le jeune aventurier tombe éperdument amoureux d'une sorcière iroquoise et trahit les siens. Même le Matthieu Rousseau du *Wapiti* de Monique Corriveau refuse de se reconnaître comme coureur des bois. Il est vrai que le portrait que le roman dresse de ce type de personnage est loin d'être flatteur. Il faut attendre les années 1980 et le *Menfou Carcajou* de Suzanne Martel pour que le personnage trouve vraiment grâce aux yeux des romanciers pour la jeunesse et devienne une figure incontournable de la mythologie québécoise.

La fascination pour ces pionniers du nouveau monde s'explique aisément. Ils incarnent la liberté, l'évasion, le voyage, l'aventure, la découverte de mondes inconnus. Ils représentent ainsi une des aspirations de l'être humain que la formule « home-away-home » intègre d'ailleurs dans sa compréhension de la littérature enfantine (Nodelman et Reimer 197–198)[14]. C'est pourquoi le coureur des bois est souvent assimilé à une menace pour la colonie. Nous avons rappelé, dès l'introduction, qu'il échappe à la mythification du « home » dont il conteste les valeurs. Paul Zweig l'écarte d'ailleurs de l'univers authentiquement héroïque lorsqu'il distingue deux types de héros : l'aventurier et le vrai héros. Anita Moss présente cette opposition de la façon suivante :

> Like Virgil's Aeneas, the hero's efforts are devoted to founding and to protecting home and civilization, in contrast to the subversive, antisocial adventurer whose identity is defined wholly in terms of action and whose efforts are in the service of self and in escape from the categories of duty and obligation. (125)

Dans le roman de la colonisation de la Nouvelle-France, les deux rôles sont tenus par le colon et par le coureur des bois. Au colon incombe le devoir, la discipline, l'organisation de la cité et la défense de la colonie. Au coureur des bois revient la satisfaction des pulsions individuelles et la liberté de courir le monde. D'un côté, il y a le « home », le don de soi, des valeurs morales souvent jugées aujourd'hui vieillottes ou dépassées; de l'autre, il y a l'ailleurs, la réalisation de soi, des valeurs individualistes plus à la mode dans notre siècle. Néanmoins, pour séduisante que puisse paraître cette formule, elle demeure assez superficielle, car le coureur des bois reste une figure ambiguë. N'est-il pas tout à la fois le représentant de l'ordre colonial et le représentant d'une rude et naturelle liberté? Comme une hésitation entre nature et civilisation? N'essaie-t-il pas de réconcilier, dans sa personne, des tentations antagonistes? Dans la plupart des romans de la colonisation de la Nouvelle-France, le monde est fondamentalement coupé en deux : un espace plus ou moins civilisé, domestiqué, qui est le domaine du colon, et un espace sauvage, dangereux, qui est le domaine des Indiens. Au milieu, le coureur des bois qui passe de l'un à l'autre, qui a un pied dans chaque camp et sert souvent d'intermédiaire entre les deux mondes. Ni tout à fait ici, ni tout à fait là, il louvoie d'un univers à l'autre au risque de n'appartenir à aucun.

Aussi reste-t-il un personnage très controversé car il entre souvent en conflit avec l'autorité coloniale. Dans *L'Appel des rivières, 1. Le pays de l'Iroquois*[15], Pierre Leblanc, attiré par l'aventure, est un de ces êtres qui se sentent à l'étroit dans l'espace confiné de la colonie, d'une ferme : « Leblanc ne voyait pas d'avenir pour lui à Québec » (30). On peut aussi arguer que son éducation iroquoise en fait un individu particulièrement à l'aise dans la forêt et sur la rivière, et que cet espace naturel est pour lui, comme pour les Iroquois, un lieu qui lui permet de s'épanouir et où il se sent à l'aise. La réalisation des aspirations individuelles entre alors en conflit avec les valeurs collectives et les intérêts de colonie. Le coureur des bois est ainsi souvent critiqué par les colons et les autorités coloniales : « Les *habitants* qui défrichaient, qui labouraient, qui cultivaient, eux surtout ne portaient pas les coureurs de bois dans leur cœur. Ils n'entretenaient aucune illusion sur leur civisme [...] » (57); « Ah! Les coureurs de bois! Ils nuisent plus à la colonie qu'ils ne la servent, ceux-là! Ils sont tout juste bons à nous faire des histoires avec les Sauvages. Ils retardent l'évangélisation, ils nous font une mauvaise réputation » (50). Dans la litanie des reproches formulés par les colons, deux méritent une attention particulière : le coureur des bois nuit aux relations entre colons et sauvages et retarde l'expansion du catholicisme. Il devient donc un obstacle à la réalisation d'un idéal colonial fondé sur des valeurs religieuses et des relations harmonieuses avec les Amérindiens. L'opposition traduit une divergence fondamentale entre des aspirations pratiquement irréconciliables, entre deux visions du monde, et sans doute, en fin de compte entre deux conceptions du « home », deux idéologies : moi par opposition au « home » = liberté par opposition à sacrifice de soi, individu par opposition à collectivité, chasse et commerce par opposition à agriculture, nature par opposition à culture, expansion par opposition à clôture, nomade par opposition à sédentaire.

Pourtant, André Vacher vole au secours de ces aventuriers (8). Quels arguments avance-t-il pour leur défense? Ceux-ci pourraient se résumer à une formule qu'on trouve dans le premier volume de *L'Appel des rivières* : « à la recherche d'un pays qui reculait toujours » (17). Le coureur des bois est celui qui fait reculer les frontières de l'espace familier, rognant sans cesse sur l'ailleurs et l'étranger. Dans le second volume, *Le caillou d'or*, le héros renonce à la traite des fourrures pour s'enfoncer plus avant dans le pays, dans des territoires de plus en plus étrangers et sauvages, jusqu'au pays des Assiniboins, Indiens de la Plaine qui vivent du bison. Cette exploration est une plongée dans une acculturation de plus en plus prononcée. Il faut renoncer à ses racines pour s'immerger dans un monde étranger, pour l'apprivoiser. Et cette immersion n'est possible que si l'on s'adapte au terrain en adoptant les manières de vivre locales. La forêt et la rivière sont aussi un espace culturel et le lieu d'une acculturation puisque Leblanc s'y forge, au contact des Iroquois, une nouvelle identité. Il devient ainsi le type même de l'explorateur. De la même manière, jamais le jeune héros de Monique Corriveau (*Le Wapiti*) ne deviendra un coureur des bois. Il n'a d'ailleurs pas choisi de fuir la colonie et ce sont les circonstances qui l'ont contraint à trouver refuge dans la forêt. Au cours de sa fuite, Matthieu Rousseau est enlevé par les Iroquois. Promis au poteau de torture, il est sauvé *in extremis*, racheté aux Iroquois par un chef SesKanou (tribu inventée par l'auteur), adopté et éduqué. S'il est attiré par les espaces sauvages, ce n'est pas pour devenir coureur des bois, mais découvreur, explorateur, de l'espèce de ceux qui font reculer les limites d'un territoire, les limites du monde connu, et donc colonisable. Tour à tour rejetés et estimés, les deux personnages de Monique Corriveau et d'André Vacher se découvrent finalement la même vocation, mais leur cheminement est différent. L'un doit son statut à une erreur judiciaire avant de retrouver une place au sein de la colonie. L'autre est poussé par une obsession moderne : la réalisation de soi. Ce qui les distingue, c'est finalement tout ce qui sépare un idéal collectif d'un idéal individuel.

Le divorce entre le colon et le coureur des bois est une préoccupation récente dans les fictions historiques destinées à la jeunesse. Dans les premiers romans, cet antagonisme ne semble pas exister, ou du moins n'en fait-on pas mention. Dans les récits de Marie-Claire Daveluy, les deux personnages œuvrent, en effet, de concert, portés par le même idéal. Olivier Le Tardif et Jean Nicolet, incarnations exemplaires du voyageur, sont fort bien considérés par les premiers colons. C'est plus tard que l'image des coureurs des bois se dévalue. Dans les années 1960, ils ont mauvaise presse et le jeune héros du *Wapiti* de Monique Corriveau refuse de leur ressembler. Au cours des années 1990, Olivier Le Tardif reprend du service dans un récit de Suzanne Julien, *Esclave à vendre*, où il jouit toujours d'une image favorable. Mais son compagnon, Marsolet, n'est pas épargné par les reproches et il est même accusé de trahison par Champlain, à qui l'on semble cependant donner tort, le véritable traître de l'histoire étant un colon. Si l'on tient à saisir l'évolution dans les représentations du coureur des bois, il suffit de voir de quelle manière est considéré le personnage de Pierre-Esprit Radisson au fil des œuvres. Dans *Perrine et Charlot à Ville-Marie* (1940) de Marie-Claire Daveluy, il est l'objet d'un véritable culte et sa rencontre avec Charlot est l'occasion, pour les deux personnages, de se faire part de leur admiration réciproque. Marie-Antoinette Grégoire-Coupal fait de lui un zélé patriote qui échoue cependant à convaincre le jeune héros de *La sorcière de l'îlot noir* (1933) de ne pas trahir sa patrie. Mais l'image de Pierre-Esprit Radisson se fissure dans *Menfou Carcajou* (1980) de Suzanne Martel puisqu'il se voit accusé de trahison pour avoir cédé « aux Anglais les forts qu'il avait lui-même construits pour la France à la baie d'Hudson » (153). Menfou prend cependant son parti, estimant que la colonie a fort mal récompensé ses efforts. Mais il est vrai que Suzanne Martel procède à un véritable bouleversement en changeant de point de vue, car c'est vraiment avec elle que le coureur des bois prend toute son envergure et occupe le devant de la scène romanesque. Quant à l'œuvre d'André Vacher (2000), elle est une tentative appuyée de réhabilitation qui laisse penser que le personnage est devenu indispensable dans la mythologie québécoise.

Le cycle romanesque de Suzanne Martel, Les coureurs des bois, est sans doute l'œuvre qui renouvelle le mieux le statut du coureur des bois.

C'est un ensemble de quatre volumes organisé autour d'un couple de personnages, une jeune adolescente, Sophie, et Menfou Carcajou. Ce dernier hésite entre trois identités et partage son temps entre trois lieux. D'abord, il est issu d'une famille de commerçants (les Cormier) dont les ancêtres étaient aristocrates (son véritable nom est Xavier Cormier de Villefoy), famille fort bien installée dans la colonie et qui contracte des alliances familiales avec les Quesnel et les Rouville (Jeanne de Rouville est l'héroïne de *Jeanne, Fille du Roy*), famille particulièrement bien en vue dans la colonie. Menfou fréquente donc Ville-Marie et La Chine où vivent les siens et où il devrait se sentir chez lui. Ensuite, comme il a été enlevé par les Indiens, envoyé au poteau de tortures et adopté par une Indienne, il est devenu Iroquois. Or, le Blanc adopté par les Iroquois est mal vu par les colons. En tant que Sauvage, Menfou représente ce qu'il ne faut pas être et il est un danger pour la colonie. Il rejoint donc régulièrement ceux qui l'ont accueilli au sein de leur tribu. Enfin, il est l'exemple même du coureur des bois qui se livre au commerce des fourrures. Son domaine de prédilection est alors la forêt et les rivières. Ainsi, Menfou existe au croisement de plusieurs clans, de plusieurs milieux et de plusieurs visions du monde, sinon antagonistes, du moins difficilement conciliables. Faut-il lire, dans ce morcellement, l'éclatement d'un être et d'une identité? Ou bien faut-il considérer l'un de ces trois milieux comme un « home » privilégié dont les deux autres ne pourraient raconter que le manque? Dira-t-on de lui qu'il est de nulle part ou bien qu'il est partout chez lui? Est-il condamné à une errance perpétuelle, à la recherche d'un endroit où demeurer et s'épanouir, en quête d'une identité réconciliant les différents morceaux de lui-même?

Le coureur des bois reste donc un personnage complexe, dont les contours sont difficiles à cerner, et qui refuse de se laisser enfermer dans une identité. Il est à la fois d'*ici* et d'*ailleurs*. On peut dire de lui ce que François Paré dit de Matthieu Rousseau, le héros du *Wapiti* de Monique Corriveau : il est « divisé en lui-même et dans sa propre culture » (41). Aucune étiquette ne semble devoir lui convenir comme le prouvent les diverses désignations derrière lesquelles on tente de le dissimuler. On se heurte alors à une série de paradoxes qui disent l'impossibilité de réduire la nature protéiforme du personnage.

Menfou Carcajou se sent profondément Iroquois. Mais ses séjours dans sa tribu sont souvent passés sous silence et correspondent à des ellipses du récit, parfois comblées par des bribes de récits rétrospectifs. Pourquoi ces séjours sont-ils ainsi rarement narrés? Il ne s'agit pas d'une impossibilité à raconter l'altérité, comme on le voit dans le troisième volume, lorsque Sophie est prisonnière des Iroquois. Curieusement, les termes d'« exil » et d'« exilé » reviennent sous la plume de Suzanne Martel pour qualifier les disparitions de Menfou chez les Iroquois. C'est pourtant chez eux que Menfou trouve vraiment sa place. Il est à l'aise dans un univers de forêts et de rivières auquel les colons demeurent fondamentalement étrangers. S'il y est en exil, c'est donc que Ville-Marie et La Chine restent ses ports d'attache. Or, n'est-ce pas là où il est le moins bien traité, vilipendé, cloué au pilori, jeté en prison? D'ailleurs, Hugo de Rupalest et Menfou « considèrent tous deux Ville-Marie comme un lieu d'exil temporaire » (Martel 63). « Que lui importent Ville-Marie, ses contraintes et ses sanctions? Il n'y sera jamais qu'un passant, car Menfou Carcajou est un animal de la forêt, grisé de liberté plus encore que de bon vin » (66). Ni pour l'un, ni pour l'autre, la colonie, Ville-Marie, ne saurait donc être vraiment un « home ». Pourquoi alors Menfou est-il le plus souvent raconté quand il vient perturber la colonie ou qu'il met ses talents au service de la colonie ou des siens? Est-ce à dire que le seul point de vue qui compterait réellement serait celui de la colonie? De la même manière, Matthieu Rousseau (Corriveau, *Le Wapiti*) est désigné par le terme « d'exilé », parfois celui de « proscrit », alors même qu'il est parfaitement à l'aise et heureux dans le milieu qui est devenu le sien. Ses relations avec la tribu évolueront cependant : après avoir été exclu par la colonie, il est exclu par les Indiens. À la fin, il retrouve à la fois sa place parmi les Indiens et sa place parmi les colons. Figure complexe, le coureur des bois serait donc d'abord un exilé mais en exil là où il se sent le plus à l'aise.

En même temps, le personnage de Menfou est régulièrement désigné par le terme de « Canadien ». Les désignations ne sont jamais innocentes. Elles ne changent pas l'espace physique dans lequel se meut le personnage mais l'espace idéologique et mental, sans aucun doute. Dans cet univers, trois désignations fonctionnent sur le principe de l'inclusion et de l'exclusion : Indien (ou Iroquois, Huron …), Français et Canadien. Le terme de « Canadien » permet de distinguer les vrais habitants de la Nouvelle-France, d'une part, des Sauvages, mais aussi, d'autre part, des Français, notamment les militaires, qui ne sont que de passage. Et la méfiance des colons est forte vis-à-vis de ces Français. Ainsi, Rupalest, qui accompagne Menfou dans ses expéditions, reste le « Français ». Seuls les colons et les « colons ensauvagés » comme les coureurs des bois ont droit à cette désignation de « Canadien ». S'opère ainsi une réconciliation idéologique qui n'était pas évidente puisque les romans rappellent régulièrement les griefs des colons à l'égard du coureur des bois. On le craint autant que les Iroquois parce qu'il représente une menace, celle de l'indianisation, du métissage culturel. On l'exclut, parce qu'il est engagé dans un processus d'acculturation.

L'œuvre de Suzanne Martel est sans doute celle qui dépeint le mieux le drame d'un personnage qui hésite entre plusieurs identités culturelles, mais aussi celle qui résume le mieux cette révision idéologique qui fait du coureur des bois une incarnation idéale de l'identité québécoise. Le coureur de bois est sans doute une image de l'acculturation, une sorte de métis culturel, transition entre le sauvage dont il épouse plus ou moins les mœurs, et le colon avec lequel il fait le commerce des pelleteries. On assiste ainsi à une mutation au cours de laquelle le coureur des bois finit par incarner l'essence même d'un pays en train de naître.

Conclusion

La littérature pour la jeunesse contribue à façonner une vision du monde chez l'enfant et l'adolescent à travers les valeurs et les représentations qu'elle véhicule plus ou moins consciemment. Les récits que nous offrons à nos enfants disent comment nous comprenons le monde et son histoire – le passé, le présent, le futur – et comment nous nous comprenons nous-mêmes; ils nourrissent l'imaginaire de l'enfant et de l'adolescent, contribuant ainsi à forger une identité et un sentiment d'appartenance à un groupe. Au Québec, l'ambition a toujours été de produire une littérature de jeunesse canadienne française indépendante. Nombreuses ont été les revendications en faveur de la création d'une littérature de jeunesse qui se libère du marché français du livre et de son influence, et qui contribue à la formation d'un sentiment national. On ne compte plus les appels en faveur de récits qui mettent en scène de jeunes Canadiens français, dans un contexte canadien français et des paysages autochtones[16]. Il était « essentiel que les jeunes aient accès à une grande variété de livres qui célèbrent leur culture, qui racontent leur style de vie, qui décrivent leur milieu, qui rappellent leurs traditions, qui redisent leur histoire, qui reflètent leur société réelle et contemporaine [...] » (Potvin, « Acadienne » 19). Si la littérature de jeunesse québécoise a connu quelques traversées du désert, la volonté de développer une littérature de « chez nous[17] » lui a toujours permis de renaître de ses cendres pour connaître un nouvel âge d'or. Le développement des fictions destinées à la jeunesse témoigne donc de cette ambition sans négliger de refléter l'évolution d'une société, de ses valeurs, de sa vision du monde, des préoccupations de ses lecteurs[18].

Aussi, le roman historique ne se contente jamais de dire comment il faut regarder et comprendre le passé. Il montre également comment le présent relit l'Histoire, réinterprète le passé à sa guise pour se donner du sens. C'est là une évidence qu'il faut rappeler : le roman historique nous parle autant, et parfois davantage, du présent que du passé. La promotion de tel personnage ou de tel événement, les révisions, parfois douloureuses, auxquelles s'abandonne volontiers le genre, participent au renouvellement d'une mythologie qui fonctionne alors comme un miroir. Voilà ce que nous sommes ou voilà comment nous aimerions nous voir. Voilà ce à quoi nous croyons ou aimerions croire aujourd'hui. S'il est facile de souligner les valeurs morales, religieuses, nationales et patriotiques dont se réclamaient les premières fictions historiques pour la jeunesse, c'est que celles-ci étaient clairement revendiquées et prônées, comme le voulait d'ailleurs l'époque. On ne peut sans doute plus en dire autant des œuvres contemporaines. Mais, la rupture qui se produit dès les années 1960 est loin de manquer de signification. La promotion du coureur des bois au rang de personnage principal constitue une rupture idéologique incontestable et essentielle. On ne peut plus lire le monde et le passé de la même manière. Cette invitation à une relecture de l'histoire de la colonisation de la Nouvelle-France brise les anciennes représentations pour lui en substituer de nouvelles, organisées autour d'un personnage qui propose un nouveau modèle identitaire.

Le « home » pose la question des relations entre l'individu et la collectivité. Quelle que soit la manière dont est représentée cette collectivité : la famille, le quartier, la colonie, le pays. De quoi s'agit-il? De s'insérer dans un milieu, de s'insérer dans une culture, de trouver sa place dans *la* société, de trouver sa place dans *une* société. Mais à quelles conditions cette insertion est-elle possible? Toutes les définitions qui tentent d'inscrire les romans pour la jeunesse dans une formule organisée autour des deux pôles « home » et « away » insistent sur une condition déterminante : il faut que l'*ici* favorise l'épanouissement de l'enfant ou de l'adolescent, sinon celui-ci s'empressera d'aller voir *ailleurs*. Le roman de la colonisation s'ouvre toujours sur une rupture avec la France. Il n'y a pas de retour au « home » originel. Les personnages ne reviennent pas sur les lieux de leurs déboires. Ils répondent à l'appel d'un *ailleurs* puisqu'ils ne peuvent se réaliser là où ils sont nés. L'antithèse « home » / « not-home » semble ainsi idéalement représenter l'axe sur lequel se construisent la plupart des romans historiques québécois destinés aux adolescents. C'est qu'elle s'inscrit dans une justification idéologique de la colonisation de la Nouvelle-France.

Mais la prédilection accordée au personnage légendaire du coureur des bois vient subvertir cette opposition initiale pour repenser les relations à l'intérieur du « home » et redéfinir ses frontières. Car certains immigrants et certains colons ne trouvent pas davantage leur place dans cet *ailleurs*, au sein de la colonie, sans doute parce que celle-ci répète un modèle ancien qui générait déjà l'insatisfaction. Ne trouvant pas leur place au sein du

« home », ces personnages choisissent de le fuir pour aller explorer de nouveaux territoires. En fait, il faut distinguer deux tendances parmi les fictions historiques destinées à la jeunesse : une tendance ancienne où la colonie est le refuge idéal, même s'il n'offre pas toutes les garanties de sécurité; et une tendance plus récente qui coïncide avec l'émergence du personnage du coureur des bois et qui témoigne d'une insatisfaction nouvelle. À côté du clivage Nouvelle-France / France, s'impose une autre division de l'espace sur le modèle « home » / « away », mais qui oppose cette fois le territoire de la colonie aux vastes territoires d'un *ailleurs* sauvage non colonisé. Notons cependant que le roman des années 1980 s'achève sur une réinsertion du fuyard puisque le coureur des bois finit par revenir dans la colonie. Il va désormais la servir comme intermédiaire, en s'employant à rapprocher des cultures antagonistes. En retrouvant sa place au sein de la colonie, le coureur des bois apporte avec lui sa part d'Iroquois, donnant ainsi naissance à un nouvel individu. Après le temps des conflits vient celui de la conciliation et du multiculturalisme. Le coureur des bois représente l'éclatement des frontières de l'*ici* et de l'*ailleurs*, car il est tout à la fois d'*ici* et d'*ailleurs*. Il est celui qui fait éclater les frontières du « home ». A mi-chemin entre deux mondes, il en vient alors à incarner une synthèse entre un *ici* et un *ailleurs*, entre un « home » et un « not-home », entre deux cultures; et devient une figure de la réconciliation dans la vision idéalisée d'un métissage qui annoncerait une société multiculturelle. Après s'être enfermé dans une idéologie coloniale, le roman historique renouvelle ainsi ses mythes fondateurs.

◻ ◻ ◻

Notes

1   On gardera le mot anglais, car il nous semble qu'aucun terme français ne convient réellement. Ni le mot « maison » ni l'expression « chez soi » ne parcourent à eux seuls l'étendue du champ sémantique du mot anglais « home ». Dans *The Interpretation of Ordinary Landscapes: Geographical Essays*, David Sopher a souligné la richesse sémantique et symbolique du concept de « home » à peu près intraduisible dans d'autres langues. Il a également rappelé qu'en anglais, à la différence de ce qui se passe dans les autres langues, les mots « home » et « house » ne se confondent pas, le second désignant un espace clos et précisément délimité, ce que le premier n'est pas. Ainsi, selon lui, le mot « maison » que Bachelard utilise dans *La Poétique de l'espace* se charge de connotations que le mot anglais « house » ne peut pas rendre.

2   Pour des points de vue divers sur ce sujet, voir « The World and the Home » de Homi Bhabha, le première édition de *Pleasures of Children's Literature* de Perry

Nodelman, « La littérature pour la jeunesse au Québec » d'Édith Madore et *L'Image de l'autre* de Suzanne Pouliot.

3 De son côté, Witold Rybczynski a montré combien avait évolué au cours des siècles l'idée de « home ».

4 Pour des points de vue divers sur ce sujet, voir Bachelard (*La Poétique de l'espace*); George 21; Porteous 386; Cooper 130-146; Jung.

5 Pour des points de vue divers sur ce sujet, voir Tuan « Geography », « Place: An Experiential Perspective », « Space and Place » et *Space and Place*.

6 « When home is a privileged place, exempt from the most serious problems of life and civilization – when home is where we ought, on the whole, to stay – we are probably dealing with a story for children. When home is the chief place from which we must escape, either to grow up or [...] to remain innocent, then we are involved in a story for adolescents or adults » (Clausen 143). Voir Nodelman et Reimer 197-202.

7 Pour des points de vue divers sur ce sujet, voir Porteous; Tuan « Geography »; Sopher : « "Journey" [...] is an inescapable absence from home, "non-home" if you will [...] "Home" has no meaning apart from the journey which takes one outside home » (133), « People want to make homes and people want to leave home » (134).

8 « Homes and home-countries are exclusive. Home, I will argue, along with gender/sexuality, race, and class, acts as an ideological determinant of the subject. The term "home-country" in itself expresses a complex yoking of ideological apparatuses considered necessary for the existence of subjects: the notion of belonging, of having a home, and a place of one's own. [...] Homes and nations are defined in the instances of confrontation with what is considered "not-home," with the foreign, with distance » (George 2, 4).

9 C'est Champlain qui parle.

10 Cette fascination est déjà celle de Perrine, fascination provoquée par une conversation qu'elle surprend entre le curé d'Offranville et un père récollet qui arrive de la Nouvelle-France. C'est à ce moment-là que Perrine apprend qu'un navire va quitter Dieppe pour le Canada et que prend forme dans son esprit son projet. Notons le cadre où se tient cette conversation entre deux « excellents » religieux : un délicieux jardin envahi de pommiers (Daveluy, *Les Aventures*).

11 Marie et Québec sont d'ailleurs associées dans une même phrase, pratiquement celle qui clôt le roman : « Marie Houymel meurt des suites d'une embolie cérébrale au printemps de l'an de grâce 1754, alors qu'une flotte de navires anglais mouillent au large de Québec » (Ouimet, *L'Orpheline* 102).

12 « il n'est donc pas perfide comme les autres ton étrange compagnon? [...] » (Daveluy 86).

13 La résistance des Amérindiens est dévalorisée; elle serait motivée par la peur. « Peur du changement. De l'ignorance. De la défaite. Peur de se voir imposer des lois qui iraient à l'encontre de leurs traditions. Peur d'être envahis, assimilés, et finalement anéantis ... Cette peur qu'ils s'échangeaient déjà entre tribus et qui les conduisait droit à la défaite. Aujourd'hui, la peur parlait la langue des Européens. Elle avait aussi la couleur d'une peau. Blanche [...] » (Ouimet, *Le Vol* 167).

14 Voir Reimer et Rusnak.

15 Voir notamment l'avant-propos.

16 Pour des points de vue divers sur ce sujet, voir Boulizon et Corriveau.

17 On empruntera l'expression à Joseph d'Anjou.

18 Pour une discussion de cette question, voir l'article « La littérature» de Beckett.

CHAPTER 3

➡ **Le *home* :**
un espace privilégié
en littérature de
jeunesse québécoise

Anne Rusnak

Introduction et références théoriques

Le mot *home* évoque en nous tous des résonances profondes. Ce seul
signifiant, comme l'explique Danielle Thaler dans l'article précédent, a une
richesse de signifiés d'ordre géographique, historique, social, politique et
psychologique. C'est notre « coin du monde », notre « premier univers »
(24) d'après le philosophe Gaston Bachelard. Dans son étude classique, *La
Poétique de l'espace,* Bachelard suggère que l'image de la maison devient
« la topographie de notre être intime » (18) et que c'est en nous souvenant
de la maison que « nous apprenons à 'demeurer' en nous-mêmes » (19).
En d'autres mots, le *home* est un espace intime dont la profondeur psychologique et la dimension symbolique sont liées à notre bien-être.

Toutefois, les résonances du mot *home* ne se limitent pas à l'individu
et à sa demeure. Dans son œuvre de l'historiographie anglo-saxonne inti-
tulée *L'Imaginaire national*, Benedict Anderson propose que, pour comprendre le nationalisme, il faut l'aligner « non sur des idéologies poli-
tiques que l'on embrasse en connaissance de cause » mais plutôt sur « les
systèmes culturels qui l'ont précédé, au sein desquels – ou entre lesquels – il est apparu » (26) au XVIIIᵉ et au XIXᵉ siècles. Poursuivant le travail d'Anderson, Timothy Brennan observe que la montée du nationalisme européen coïncide surtout avec un genre de littérature, à savoir le
roman. D'après Brennan, il s'ensuit que, pour comprendre ce qu'il appelle
« les constructions mentales fictives » que sont les nations, il faut étudier

le « apparatus of cultural fictions in which imaginative literature plays a decisive role » (49). Étroitement aligné sur le projet fictif d'imaginer la nation est le projet d'imaginer le *home*, selon Rosemary Marangoly George. En fait, soutient George dans son livre *The Politics of Home*, la préoccupation de la recherche de « viable homes for viable selves » dans la fiction du XXe siècle serait continue avec la préoccupation de faire des allégories de la nation dans la fiction du XIXe siècle. Ainsi, étudier la représentation du *home* dans la fiction proposée aux jeunes, c'est étudier un aspect de la narration par lequel une nation se produit et se reproduit. Pour emprunter les mots de George, « [i]magining a home is as political an act as is imagining a nation » (6). En parlant de la littérature de jeunesse, Christian Poslaniec spécifie que « la littérature de jeunesse n'est pas aussi indépendante que la littérature générale, elle est même sous la haute surveillance, non seulement des adultes, mais également de l'État » (401).

Après tout, la littérature de jeunesse est une littérature qui est, depuis ses origines, en quelque mesure, éducative. Depuis la publication des *Histoires ou Contes du temps passé avec des Moralités* de Charles Perrault en 1697, deux termes définissent les axes constitutifs de la littérature de jeunesse, à savoir didactisme et divertissement. Perrault souligne dans la préface que les contes s'adressent aussi aux enfants « pour les instruire et les divertir tout ensemble ». Ainsi, depuis le XVIIe siècle, les œuvres destinées aux jeunes expriment ce double souci de la part des adultes. Rappelons-nous que ce qui distingue la littérature de jeunesse de la littérature générale, c'est que l'auteur adulte essaie de rejoindre un lecteur d'un âge autre. Ainsi, la littérature de jeunesse a non seulement un rôle ludique mais aussi un rôle fondamental dans la formation intellectuelle, culturelle, morale et esthétique de l'enfant, d'autant plus que la jeunesse est plus que tout autre moment de l'existence une période de formation intense, d'initiation à la vie sous toutes ses formes. Comme le souligne Françoise Lepage, parmi les facteurs importants qui ont favorisé l'éclosion de la littérature de jeunesse au XXe siècle se trouve « la convergence d'idées nouvelles relatives à la jeunesse en général, à la psychologie de l'apprentissage chez l'enfant, à la montée du nationalisme ... » (*Histoire* 59).

Par conséquent, la production de textes et d'ouvrages destinés aux enfants a toujours subi les pressions et les critiques des adultes. Comme le soulignent Denise Escarpit et Mireille Vagné-Lebas, c'est l'adulte qui, en tant qu'« [a]gent d'éducation par excellence », en élabore les critères et en prescrit les usages (9). Au parent, à l'enseignant, au bibliothécaire, au libraire, à l'éditeur et à « tous ceux qui s'occupent de 'formation' revient cette charge, mais aussi ce privilège » (9). Elles se demandent si, en fait, transmettre les modèles de comportement, « les faire assimiler pour atteindre une reproduction sociale, n'est-ce pas l'objectif, depuis toujours, de toute éducation? » (10).

Puisque ce sont les adultes, à de rares exceptions près, qui communiquent à la nouvelle génération leurs croyances, leurs idées, leurs valeurs concernant leur époque et leur société, cette littérature, selon François Paré, forme donc, dans l'institution littéraire, « une enclave ouvertement idéologique » (*Les littératures de l'exiguïté* 117). De plus, il soutient que c'est la raison pour laquelle cette littérature est marquée par la « défaveur des institutions littéraires dominantes, qui tendent à se distancer de son utilitarisme » (117).

Certes, l'utilité de cette littérature est ce qui explique son abondance. Comme le fait remarquer Dominique Demers et Paul Bleton, plus d'un livre sur trois publié au Québec s'adresse aux enfants ou aux adolescents (24). En outre, ajoutent-ils, non seulement le tirage moyen des livres pour la jeunesse est-il plus élevé mais aussi les réimpressions sont plus nombreuses et les best-sellers plus fréquents (24).

Or, si imaginer un *home* est un acte aussi politique que d'imaginer une nation, il n'est pas surprenant que la notion du *home* soit si importante dans la littérature de jeunesse. Effectivement, le théoricien Perry Nodelman suggère que cette notion du *home* joue un rôle clé dans la structure narrative d'un roman de jeunesse. Le *home*, propose-t-il, est non seulement un lieu, mais aussi un thème dominant en littérature de jeunesse. Plus précisément, il construit la spécificité de cette littérature sur la structure *home-away-home*. C'est-à-dire que le jeune quitte la maison et sa famille à la recherche de l'aventure, qui se passe ailleurs, puis il revient chez lui, transformé et plus mûr, et c'est là où le récit se termine. C'est un voyage circulaire où *home* et *away* se structurent en axe d'oppositions. Selon Nodelman, le *home*, c'est l'adulte, la civilisation, l'emprisonnement, la sécurité, l'ennui, alors que les oppositions binaires de ces thèmes s'alignent sur *away* : l'enfant, la nature, la liberté, le danger, l'aventure. Nous comprenons « aventure » au sens étymologique du terme, comme le définit Ganna Ottevaere-van Praag : « 'adventura' : choses qui doivent arriver. [...] L'aventure est la concrétisation sur le plan narratologique de ce désir de s'immerger dans l'inconnu » (12). L'événement imprévu, surprenant, selon Nodelman, se fait découvrir dans des milieux étrangers, sous des horizons inconnus. Après avoir étudié un vaste corpus de romans de jeunesse, publiés surtout en Angleterre et aux États-Unis, il pose comme principe que cette structure narrative est en fait la caractéristique la plus importante pour définir la littérature de jeunesse comme genre.

Étude préalable

Dans une étude préalable que nous avons entreprise avec Mavis Reimer, nous nous sommes posé la question, est-ce que la structure *home-away-home* est la structure dominante, telle que définit par Nodelman, des littératures canadienne et québécoise proposées aux jeunes? Est-ce que les écrivains voient ce thème de façon identique dans tous les pays? Notre étude diachronique couvrait la période de 1975 à 1995 et portait sur les romans de jeunesse et les mini-romans primés. Nous avons postulé que, puisque ces œuvres ont été couronnées par des lecteurs « cultivés », elles révéleraient les valeurs de la communauté, ce qui serait bon, ce qui serait souhaitable à ses yeux. Nous avons choisi cette période parce que, pendant les années 1970, la production d'ouvrages pour jeunes est devenue une entreprise vigoureuse et créatrice alimentée par l'avènement du nationalisme canadien et du nationalisme québécois.

Nos résultats montrent qu'il faut remettre en question la proposition de Nodelman. Non seulement la structure narrative dominante n'est pas celle de *home-away-home*, mais aussi la structure narrative la plus commune proposée aux jeunes anglophones n'est pas celle proposée aux jeunes francophones. Dans la plupart des textes primés publiés en anglais, l'enfant quitte son *home* présenté en début de fiction et, après maintes aventures, se façonne un autre *home*, ailleurs, ce qui n'est pas du tout le cas dans le corpus francophone de romans primés. Au contraire, il est peu question de quitter son chez-soi qui, en outre, est rarement un lieu de refuge rassurant qui protège l'enfant ou l'adolescent; ce lieu l'ennuie même à tel point que le jeune héros se voit obligé de quitter le foyer pour vivre l'aventure ailleurs. Dans le corpus de romans de jeunesse et de mini-romans publiés en français, c'est plutôt le *away* qui envahit l'espace du *home*.

Présente étude

Pour voir si la structure qui domine dans les œuvres primées est caractéristique de la fiction proposée aux jeunes lecteurs québécois âgés de sept à seize ans, nous avons entrepris la présente étude. Cette fois-ci, il s'agit d'une étude synchronique des romans de jeunesse et des mini-romans non primés publiés au Québec en 1992[1]. Nous avons choisi cette année pour deux raisons : premièrement, elle fait partie de la période étudiée dans l'étude préalable et, deuxièmement, c'est à partir des années 1980, comme le soulignent Françoise Lepage et Edith Madore, qu'il y a eu une expansion phénoménale du roman de jeunesse et du mini-roman. Les romans qui font partie de notre corpus ont un minimum de soixante pages. Nous avons écarté les rééditions, les romans qui se font suite et les romans historiques basés sur des personnages réels. Sur les 102 romans susceptibles de faire partie de notre étude, nous en avons analysé 97 qui nous étaient disponibles. Comme dans la première étude, en partant du postulat du théoricien Perry Nodelman, nous avons classé les romans d'après les quatre structures narratives suivantes : *home-away-home*, *away enters home*, *away becomes home*, et *variations*[2] (voir l'annexe 1.) Ce qui nous intéressait surtout, c'était de voir si, premièrement, dans le corpus de romans publiés en français, la structure narrative *away enters home* continuerait à dominer, et, deuxièmement, si la structure *away becomes home*, celle qui dominait dans le corpus anglophone de livres primés, resterait toujours la structure la moins populaire du corpus francophone.

Résultats

Dans tout le corpus analysé, il est rarement question de quitter définitivement son *home*; cette structure narrative ne se trouve que dans 6 % des romans. La structure narrative que les auteurs québécois proposent aux jeunes dans la majorité des cas (54 %) est celle où *away enters home*. En d'autres mots, un déplacement dans un milieu étranger n'est pas une condition préalable à la rencontre avec l'*aventure*. Ni la structure narrative proposée par Nodelman comme la structure générique de la littérature de jeunesse[3], ni la structure narrative dominante du corpus anglophone ne s'appliquent particulièrement à la littérature québécoise. C'est une littérature qui, semblerait-il, porte la marque du pays qui l'a produite. Il est clair que le *home* présenté en début de fiction, c'est-à-dire l'espace que le jeune habite avec sa famille, est un lieu important dans les œuvres québécoises. Examinons ces résultats de plus près.

La première constatation qui s'impose en analysant le corpus de romans de jeunesse québécois, c'est que dans la majorité des cas, l'*aventure* rentre à la maison du protagoniste central. Les portes ne sont jamais encombrées de serrures ni de clés, de sorte que les frontières entre ce que Nodelman appelle *home* et *away* se brouillent facilement. Il ne s'agit pas de deux mondes clos qui ne se croisent jamais; effectivement, la porte de la maison s'ouvre à l'*aventure*. L'*aventure* se présente sous de multiples formes, telles que l'arrivée d'un étranger (humain ou animal), une maladie, un accident, une malédiction, une tempête ou un concours. Dans *Antoine et Alfred* d'Yves Beauchemin, par exemple, un rat d'égout qui sait parler s'installe dans la maison d'Antoine et perturbe la vie de toute la famille. Bien que le père déclare au début que les rats sont des « animaux nuisibles » et que, par conséquent, il n'y a « pas de place pour eux dans nos maisons » (46), le rat finit par faire partie de la famille et le père lui avoue à la fin : « tu es devenu comme un de mes enfants » (148). On n'a pas besoin de quitter les limites de ses quatre murs pour pénétrer dans un monde merveilleux, comme l'annonce la mère dans *Bouh, le fantôme* de Vincent Lauzon : « Eh bien, je vous jure, il s'en passe, des aventures dans cette maison » (7). Il en est de même pour le public ciblé de douze à seize ans. Dans *Louprecka* de Robert Martel, Alain Brindamour, un adolescent un peu complexé par son acné, devient amoureux, comme son nom nous l'indique, d'une jeune femme belle et mystérieuse qui, apprendra-t-il, a des pouvoirs surhumains. Il entend d'abord sa voix à l'école mais en se retournant, il n'aperçoit que le vieux concierge chauve. Puis, il la rencontre dans la rue; c'est « [l]a plus belle fille imaginable sur ce globe » (45) qui conduit la moto de ses rêves, une Ninja 1000 blanche. À son insu, elle le suit chez lui en se transformant en chat et c'est ainsi qu'elle s'introduit dans sa maison. Elle bouleverse sa vie à tel point qu'il sent qu'il n'est plus le même Alain Brindamour : il lui révèle: « tu as envahi mon esprit, […] tu me domines » (128). C'est son premier amour; grâce à elle, il n'aura plus à « faire le clown » (157) pour qu'on lui prête attention. Quand elle part, l'embarras de l'adolescence a laissé place à la confiance de l'adulte.

Puisque le *home* est valorisé, la demeure et les membres de la famille sont souvent décrits dans les moindres détails. Par exemple, quand Alain invite Louprecka chez lui pour la présenter à ses parents, elle lui annonce « je sais tout d'eux » (131) et se met à décrire d'abord le père d'Alain :

> Ton père s'appelle Simon Brindamour, troisième d'une famille de huit enfants. Il a quarante-quatre ans. Il a fait son cours classique chez les Rédemptoristes, et ses matières préférées étaient le latin et le grec. Il travaille au ministère de l'Éducation depuis vingt-deux ans. Il a fréquenté ta mère deux ans avant leur mariage et ils se sont mariés un premier juillet à 16 h 30. Il adore la photo et la pêche. Son plat préféré est le poulet au citron. Il n'aime pas tellement le hockey, mais quand on lui donne des billets, il se fait un plaisir d'aller voir les Nordiques. (132)

Dans *Le Cœur à l'envers* de Susanne Julien, Sonia décrit minutieusement la chambre de son frère, y compris la corbeille à papier aussi bien que le premier tiroir de sa commode, avant de se cacher au fond de son armoire pendant que son frère et sa copine font l'amour : « La tanière lui semble moche : pas de bibelots, pas de décorations sur les murs, mis à part quelques médailles sportives épinglées derrière la porte. Finalement, elle ne manque rien à ne pas venir ici plus souvent » (10).

Ainsi, dans ces romans, le *home* n'est pas un lieu où règnent la sécurité, la tranquillité et l'ennui, pour n'emprunter que trois des thèmes de la liste de Nodelman. Au contraire, nos jeunes protagonistes y rencontrent souvent le danger, l'inquiétude, l'aventure. Cependant, au terme de l'aventure, c'est-à-dire au dénouement, le *home* se profile plus rassurant qu'il ne l'était au début de la fiction. Le désir d'y appartenir est très fort, comme l'est l'envie d'y trouver réconfort et sécurité. Le héros s'identifie avec son chez-soi où il est bien installé, bien enraciné, comme l'est Ella, l'héroïne du roman, *L'ombre et le cheval*, d'Esther Rochon : « Quand j'étais petite, mon grand-père Anksad me faisait sentir l'eau sous la terre, près du puits. Il me montrait comment s'incurve le sol rouge, si doucement. Nos ancêtres avaient creusé là, et avant eux les anciens oubliés » (6). Cette jeune femme voit menacées les traditions artistiques de son village. Leur manifestation la plus visible consiste à dessiner dans le ciel, au moyen des jets de gaz très précis, de chevaux animés. Héritière de son grand-père, elle doit trouver la vérité pour éviter l'extinction d'une société du désert. À la fin, elle se retrouve encore une fois près du puits où elle se jure de ne pas bouger « plus que le puits, perpétuant une tradition plus ancienne que la mémoire » (121). Le *home* est un lieu privilégié, l'enracinement de l'individu dans le sol natal est souligné. Pour les jeunes protagonistes québécois, il ne s'agit pas de s'enfuir pour trouver la liberté et l'autonomie de s'installer ailleurs. On n'abandonne pas son *home*. Au contraire, on essaye de le rendre plus accommodant, plus rassurant, moins vulnérable. Au terme de l'*aventure*, les liens de famille sont resserrés.

Pour cette raison, il est rare dans notre corpus que le jeune protagoniste choisisse de son plein gré de quitter définitivement son *home* présenté en début de fiction. Si cela arrive, ce qu'on ne voit d'ailleurs que dans six romans, c'est soit parce qu'il n'a pas le choix, soit parce qu'il est à la recherche de ses parents. Prenons comme exemple *Le Septième Écran* de Francine Pelletier, un roman de science-fiction, où la jeune protagoniste, Arialde Henke, une jeune femme de dix-neuf ans, quitte sa planète natale, Arkadie, pour la première fois, afin d'assister à un congrès dans la station spatiale Agora. Elle y aperçoit des gens qui portent des plumes d'oiseaux dans leurs cheveux. Le fait paraît banal, sauf que les plumes proviennent d'oiseaux arkadiens, dont la chasse est interdite. En rentrant chez elle, elle réussit à démasquer les braconniers, avec l'aide de son frère et de ses camarades. Cependant, elle se voit expulsée de sa planète car, en dévoilant les braconniers, elle a transgressé la loi. Ce qui est intéressant à noter, c'est qu'elle monte à bord d'un vaisseau à destination de la Terre, le *home* de ses ancêtres.

Dans le roman, *Otish*, de Gérald Gagnon, on apprend que le personnage principal, Jean, âgé de dix-sept ans, habite chez son oncle et sa tante depuis la disparition de ses parents. Ce qui déclenche sa quête, c'est une lettre qui arrive à la maison quelques semaines après la mort de son grand-père. Ce dernier lui laisse un héritage, mais, pour s'assurer du principal, Jean devra suivre ses instructions à la lettre. Il entreprend un voyage au terme duquel il finira par retrouver ses parents. Dans ce cas, on quitte le *home* présenté en début de fiction, mais c'est pour retrouver ses parents : « Nous nous embrassâmes, mais il n'y eut pas de grandes effusions car tout intérieure était notre joie. Quand, après douze ans, une famille est à nouveau réunie, cela se savoure dans le silence et la paix » (86). Le retour aux parents suffit pour légitimer le départ.

Importance du *home* natal dans la fiction proposée aux jeunes Québécois

Nous avons établi que le *home* en tant qu'espace habité par le protagoniste et sa famille est un cadre très important dans la littérature de jeunesse québécoise. Pour quelles raisons accordons-nous une importance toute particulière au *home* natal dans les romans de jeunesse québécois, ce qui va à l'encontre de ce qu'on trouve dans la structure générique telle que définit par Nodelman et dans la structure dominante en littérature de jeunesse publiée en anglais au Canada? C'est la question sur laquelle nous nous penchons et sur laquelle nous offrons quelques réflexions.

Dans un numéro spécial de la revue *Liberté* (1981) consacrée à l'institution littéraire, plusieurs collaborateurs soulignent le rôle puissant joué par l'État québécois à partir des années 1960 dans la production des œuvres littéraires écrites au Québec. Selon Gilles Marcotte, l'originalité la plus certaine de la littérature québécoise, dans le monde actuel, lui vient « moins de ses œuvres, quel que soit le jugement porté sur elles, que de son caractère institutionnel fortement marqué » (6). Il avance que l'institution littéraire au Québec « précède les œuvres, elle se crée dans une indépendance relative par rapport aux œuvres, elle a préséance sur les œuvres » (6).

Certes, la création de l'organisme Communication-Jeunesse est d'une importance capitale dans l'évolution de la littérature de jeunesse au Québec. Fondé en 1971 par Paule Daveluy et sa sœur Suzannne Rocher, l'or-

ganisme avait pour but de promouvoir la littérature canadienne-française
pour la jeunesse afin que cette littérature « ne disparaisse pas complète-
ment » selon Paule Daveluy (14). Face à la crise de l'édition au Québec en
littérature de jeunesse – l'ensemble des éditeurs québécois n'avaient publié
en 1970 que deux livres pour les jeunes – une vingtaine de spécialistes se
sont réunis, explique-t-elle, pour « stimuler la production et la distribution d'œuvres originales destinées à des enfants en grand danger de perdre, à cause de lectures uniquement étrangères, leur identité et leur sen-
sibilité aux choses d'ici, à leur petite et à leur grande patrie » (Daveluy
13–14). Il fallait une nouvelle politique du livre et des subventions impor-
tantes. En fait, un travail conscient du gouvernement a eu lieu sur la
mise en place d'une littérature et d'une institution littéraire nationale au
Québec depuis 1968, l'année où, comme le fait remarquer François Paré
(*Les littératures de l'exiguïté*), elle se détache « de son cadre pancanadien
et redéfinit ses rapports d'égalité avec la France » (18). Ainsi, une institution « minoritaire », explique-t-il, se hissa au rang des institutions
nationales. Pour le faire, soutient-il, l'institution littéraire québécoise
dispose de « vastes moyens financiers » (18). La littérature pour la jeunesse,
continue-t-il, « autant dans son contenu que dans son interprétation critique et l'usage qu'il en est fait dans l'enseignement, constitue un puissant facteur de cohésion nationale » (116). Ainsi, l'abondance de cette
littérature au Québec, à partir des années 1970, fait partie d'une littérature nationale et de l'institution littéraire au Québec.

Or, si le *home* représente la nation, il n'est pas du tout surprenant que
la littérature de la jeunesse québécoise, à la fin du XXe siècle, soit fasci-
née par le *home*, comme cadre, comme thème et comme destination narrative. En parlant de la littérature générale, Rosemary Chapman remarque
dans son livre, *Siting the Quebec Novel*, que *l'ailleurs* est soit la France,
notamment en tant que pouvoir colonisateur original, soit l'Angleterre
en tant que pouvoir colonisateur conquérant, soit les États-Unis en tant
que pouvoir économique et culturel (273). Chose intéressante, le Canada
anglophone ne fait pas partie de sa liste; aux dires de Chapman, c'est
parce que l'écriture québécoise garde le silence sur le reste du Canada.

Ceci suggère que, dans la littérature de jeunesse proposée aux jeunes
Québécois, un déplacement dans une contrée lointaine ne serait pas une
affirmation mais plutôt une perte de l'identité. L'identité est liée à l'espace
que l'on occupe; le fait de ressentir un attachement profond pour son
home, pour sa famille, pour son pays est de prime importance dans la littérature québécoise proposée aux jeunes à la fin du XXe siècle. Par conséquent, il est rare que le jeune protagoniste choisisse de son plein gré de
quitter son chez-soi pour s'établir ailleurs. On ne substitue pas à son

home un espace nouveau. De plus, il n'a même pas besoin de le quitter pour rencontrer l'*aventure*. Parfois, le cadre est presque exclusivement la maison du personnage principal, comme c'est le cas dans *Les Barricades d'Arthur* de Ginette Anfousse. L'aventure s'ancre dans le quotidien, et le *home* se profile à la fin de l'aventure plus solide qu'il ne l'était au début. Si, au Québec, comme l'a souligné Patricia Smart dans son essai capital, *Écrire dans la maison du père*, l'idéologie de la survivance nationale a présidé la littérature depuis ses débuts (30), il n'est pas du tout surprenant que la maison, le foyer, le chez-soi, soit un lieu valorisé en littérature de jeunesse québécoise. La formation d'un sentiment national est étroitement liée à la valorisation de son *home*.

En outre, ce qui définit le *home*, ce sont les rapports de filiation. C'est la famille qui assure cette survivance de génération en génération. Dans *The World, the Text and the Critic*, Edward Said fait la distinction entre ce qu'il appelle d'une part, *filiation*, c'est-à-dire les rapports fondés sur les liens natals et « the natural continuity between one generation and the next » (16), et, d'autre part, *affiliation*, à savoir les rapports basés sur des liens culturels et sociétaux. Dans notre corpus, il en ressort que mère, père, sœur, frère, grand-mère, grand-père, tante, oncle jouent tous un rôle important. Même une orpheline dès le berceau, comme l'est Rosalie Dansereau, héroïne du *Grand Rêve de Rosalie* de Ginette Anfousse, est entourée de sept tantes protectrices pour souligner de façon hyperbolique l'importance de la mère. Certes, il y a des parents qui sont absents, incompétents ou bien dépassés par les événements. Mais, dans notre corpus, c'est surtout la figure maternelle qui est associée à la maison. C'est elle, que ce soit la mère, la grand-mère ou la tante, qui veille sur l'enfant, qui se soucie au sujet de l'adolescent. « Si j'ai bien compris, annonce Julie Hébert dans *Une peur bleue* de Marie-Andrée Boucher-Mativat, les mères ne dorment que d'un œil, toujours en alerte, prêtes à accourir au moindre cri de leur progéniture » (16). Dans *La Vengeance* d'André Tousignant, Normand Boursier, pensionnaire dans un collège, a hâte de retrouver sa chambre et de se « jeter au cou de maman » (19). Et le narrateur insiste sur le fait que le jeune Rafaël tricote comme son arrière-grand-mère et sa grand-mère (7) dans *Tricot, piano et jeu vidéo* de Sonia Sarfati. Enfin, un titre comme *En exil...chez mon père* de Johanne Robert en dit long sur la séparation d'avec la mère. C'est une expulsion hors de sa patrie que d'aller vivre chez son père qui habite, néanmoins, la même ville. En fait, rares sont les romans où on ne trouve que la figure paternelle[4].

Souvenons-nous du fait que nous avons souvent appelé la société traditionnelle canadienne-française un « matriarcat ». Selon Patricia Smart, le rôle traditionnel de la mère était le fondement même de la société canadienne-française. Cette idéologie de la survivance nationale, qui a présidé à la littérature depuis ses débuts, dépendait entièrement, soutient-elle, de l'adhérence des femmes à leur rôle traditionnel de reproductrices, « car c'était seulement par la 'revanche des berceaux', disaient les dirigeants cléricaux et laïques, que le Canada français pouvait espérer retrouver son ancienne puissance en Amérique du Nord » (30). Dans leurs chapitres dans ce livre, Clare Bradford et Andrew O'Malley parlent d'une configuration coloniale où le *home* est homologue de la nation et où la femme a sa place dans la sphère domestique.

Conclusion

Malgré le fait que la littérature de jeunesse soit devenue pléthorique dès les années 1980, le *home* garde une place solide dans la littérature de jeunesse québécoise. Si le fait d'imaginer le *home* est un acte aussi politique que d'imaginer la nation, il s'ensuit que le *home* natal figure dans cette littérature comme thème, comme cadre et comme destination narrative. La Révolution tranquille a marqué l'imaginaire québécois d'une trace profonde. Ce qui en ressort, au début des années 1990, c'est le manque de fascination avec l'*ailleurs*. Si le voyage favorise la découverte de l'*autre*, force est de constater que le désir est plutôt celui de retrouver sa propre culture. Les « agents d'éducation » qui en ont élaboré les critères à la fin du XXᵉ siècle ont proposé des romans qui mettaient en valeur la société québécoise, d'autant plus que cette littérature était, et l'est toujours, très intégrée aux programmes scolaires au Québec. Ainsi, loin de vouloir s'enfuir de chez soi, le jeune protagoniste prend grand plaisir à y confronter l'aventure, qui sait traverser le seuil du foyer. L'identité nationale et culturelle du jeune et de l'adolescent est liée à l'enracinement, d'où l'importance du *home* dans cette littérature. Dans notre corpus, le voyage que les jeunes protagonistes québécois entreprennent est d'habitude celui qui les mène à l'intérieur de leur être intime et de leur propre culture. Tout cela nous mène à conclure que, si le *home* est un espace privilégié en littérature de jeunesse québécoise, c'est parce qu'il représente non seulement l'individu mais aussi la nation.

Annex 1

Classement de la structure narrative des romans de jeunesse et des mini-romans publiés au Québec en 1992

La Structure Narrative n° 1 Home-Away-Home

Arnau, Yves E. *L'Anaconda qui dort : une aventure d'Edgar Allan, détective.* Illus. de Caroline Merola. Montréal, Éditions P. Tisseyre.

Brochu, Yvon. *On n'est pas des monstres.* Montréal, Québec/Amérique.

Charbonneau, Marie-Josée. *Le labyrinthe écarlate.* Iberville (Québec), Coïncidence/Jeunesse.

Daignault, Claire. *La vie en roux de Rémi Rioux.* Montréal, Éditions P. Tisseyre.

Desaulniers, Diane. *Un cheval en cavale.* Illus. de Michel LeBlanc. Iberville (Québec), Coïncidence/Jeunesse.

———. *La Fuite de Katcadou.* Illus. de Pierre Dagesse. Iberville (Québec), Coïncidence/Jeunesse.

Desjardins, Jacques A. *Tirelire, combines & cie.* Montréal, Québec/ Amérique.

Desrosiers, Sylvie. *Mais qui va trouver le trésor?* Illus. de Daniel Sylvestre. Montréal, La courte échelle.

Émond, Louis. *Taxi en cavale.* Montréal, Éditions P. Tisseyre.

Gauthier, Bertrand. *Panique au cimetière.* Illus. de Stéphane Jorisch. Montréal, La courte échelle.

Gélinas, Isabelle. *Le Mystère du Marloland.* Saint-Laurent (Québec), Fides.

Gravel, François. *Granulite.* Montréal, Québec/Amérique.

Guillet, Jean-Pierre. *Mystère aux Iles-de-la-Madeleine.* Illus. de Huguette Marquis. Waterloo (Québec), M. Quintin.

Huberdeau, Madeleine. *Mission à l'eau!* Illus. de Dominique Jolin. Montréal, Boréal.

Lauzon, Vincent. *Do, ré, mi, échec et mat.* Illus. de Linda Lemelin. Montréal, Éditions P. Tisseyre.

Lebugle, André. *En détresse à New York.* Montréal, Éditions P. Tisseyre.

Lemay, Francine. *Destination : nuit blanche.* Laval (Québec), HRW.

———. *La porte secrète.* Laval (Québec), HRW.

Marillac, Alain. *Le trésor de la citadelle.* Illus. de Johanne Wolfrod. LaSalle (Québec), Hurtubise, HMH.

Michaud, Nando. *Drames de cœur pour un 2 de pique.* Montréal, Éditions P. Tisseyre.

Papineau, Lucie. *Des bleuets dans mes lunettes.* Illus. de Daniel Dumont. Montréal, Boréal.

Rivet, Brigitte. *Le Mystère de la tuque.* Illus. de Pierre Dagesse. Iberville (Québec), Coïncidence/Jeunesse.

Sarfati, Sonia. *La Ville engloutie*. Illus. de Caroline Merola. Montréal, La courte échelle.

Sauriol, Louise-Michelle. *La Sirène des mers de glace*. Illus. de Georgetta Pusztaï. Saint-Lambert (Québec), Héritage.

Tremblay, Carole. *La Nuit de l'Halloween*. Illus. de Dominique Jolin. Montréal, Boréal.

Vandal, André. *Les Voiles de l'aventure*. Montréal, Éditions P. Tisseyre.

Total : 26 romans = 27 % du corpus

La Structure Narrative n° 2 Away Enters Home

Alarie, Donald. *Comme un lièvre pris au piège*. Montréal, Éditions P. Tisseyre.

Anfousse, Ginette. *Les Barricades d'Arthur*. Illus. de Anne Villeneuve. Montréal, La courte échelle.

Anfousse, Ginette. *Le Grand Rêve de Rosalie*. Illus. de Marisol Sarrazin. Montréal, La courte échelle.

Beauchemin, Yves. *Antoine et Alfred*. Montréal, Québec/Amérique.

Bélanger, Jean-Pierre. *Félix et le singe-à-barbe*. Montréal, Québec/Amérique.

Benoit, François. *Carcasses*. Montréal, Boréal.

Bergeron, Alain. *Le Chant des Hayats*. Montréal, Éditions Paulines.

Bergeron, Lucie. *La Grande Catastrophe*. Illus. de Hélène Desputeaux. Saint-Lambert (Québec), Héritage.

Boucher-Mativat, Marie-Andrée. *Une peur bleue*. Illus. d'Anne Michaud. Saint-Lambert (Québec), Héritage.

Brochu, Yvon. *Alexis dans de beaux draps*. Illus. de Daniel Sylvestre. Montréal, Éditions P. Tissyere.

Brouillet, Chrystine. *Une nuit très longue*. Montréal, La courte échelle.

Charbonneau, Marie-Josée. *La Plume de klaxon*. Illus. de Hélène Béland Robert. Iberville (Québec), Coïncidence/Jeunesse.

Clermont, Marie-Andrée. *Poursuite ...* Illus. de Stéphane Jorisch. LaSalle (Québec), Hurtubise HMH.

Clermont, Marie-Andrée. *Roche de St-Coeur*. Montréal, Éditions P. Tisseyre.

Davidts, Robert. *Les Parfums fond du pétard*. Illus. de Philippe Brochard. Montréal, Boréal.

Demers, Dominique. *Toto la brute*. Illus. de Philippe Béha. Montréal, La courte échelle.

Desaulniers, Diane. *Le Chat de Benjamin*. Illus. de Pierre Dagesse. Iberville (Québec), Coïncidence/Jeunesse.

Duchesne, Christiane. *L'Été des tordus*. Illus. de Marc Mongeau. Montréal, La courte échelle.

Dussault, Guylaine. *La Sorcière aux bigoudis*. Illus. de Lucy Saint-Gelais. Shawinnigan-Sud (Québec), CERRDOC.

Fontaine, Clément. *Merveilles au pays d'Alice*. Montréal, Éditions P. Tisseyre.

Gaudet, Johanne. *Comment se débarrasser de Puce*. Illus. de Bruno St-Aubin. Montréal, Boréal.

Giroux, Dominique. *Sacrée Minnie Bellavance!*. Illus. de Hélène Desputeaux. Montréal, Éditions P. Tisseyre.

Goupil, Mylène. *Le Détonateur*. Saint-Laurent (Québec), Fides.

Guillet, Jean-Pierre. *Enquête sur la falaise*. Illus. de Huguette Marquis. Waterloo (Québec), M. Quintin.

Hébert, Marie-Francine. *Sauve qui peut l'amour*. Montréal, La courte échelle.

Julien, Susanne. *Le Cœur à l'envers*. Montréal, Éditions P. Tisseyre.

Labelle-Ruel, Nicole. *Un jardinier pour les hommes*. Montréal, Québec/Amérique.

Landry, Chantale. *Sa majesté des gouttières*. Illus. de Luc Melanson. Montréal, Boréal.

Lauzon, Vincent. *Bouh, le fantôme*. Illus. de Philippe Germain. Saint-Lambert (Québec), Héritage.

Leblanc, Louise. *Ça va mal pour Sophie*. Illus. de Marie-Louise Gay. Montréal, La courte échelle.

Major, Henriette. *Sophie et le supergarçon*. Illus. de Monique Garneau. Saint-Lambert (Québec), Héritage.

Marcotte, Danielle. *Camy risque tout*. Illus. de Doris Barrette. Montréal, Boréal.

Marois, Carmen. *Le Dossier vert*. Illus. de Bruno St-Aubin. LaSalle (Québec), Hurtubise HMH.

Martel, Robert. *Louprecka*. Montréal, Québec/Amérique.

Mativat, Marie-Andrée et Daniel Mativat. *Le Fantôme du rocker*. Illus. de Bruno St-Aubin. LaSalle (Québec), Hurtubise HMH.

Ménard, Josianne. *Mon frère est un zouinf*. Illus. de Marc Auger. Iberville (Québec), Coïncidence/Jeunesse.

Pigeon, Pierre. *Cambriolage au lac Blanc*. Illus. de Mario Giguère. Iberville (Québec), Coïncidence/Jeunesse.

——. *Le Colosse au lac Blanc*. Illus. de Mario Giguère. Iberville (Québec), Coïncidence/Jeunesse.

——. *J'aurai votre peau, sales briseurs de rêves!* Illus. de Micheline Dionne. Iberville (Québec), Coïncidence/Jeunesse.

——. *La Soucoupe affolante*. Illus. de Pierre Dagesse. Iberville (Québec), Coïncidence/Jeunesse.

Plante, Raymond. *Les Dents de la poule*. Illus. de Pierre Pratt. Montréal, Boréal.

Plourde, Josée. *Les Amours d'Hubert*. Illus. de Doris Barrette. Waterloo (Québec), M. Quintin.

Poupart, Roger. *Pelouses bleus*. Montréal, Éditions P. Tisseyre.

Rivet, Brigitte. *Ne m'appelez pas Math*. Illus. de Diane L'Écuyer. Iberville (Québec), Coïncidence/Jeunesse.

———. *Le Virus de la bulle*. Illus. de Marc Auger. Iberville (Québec), Coïncidence/Jeunesse.

———. *Le Voeu d'Élodie*. Illus. de Marc Auger. Iberville (Québec), Coïncidence/Jeunesse.

Rochette, Danielle. *Le Code perdu*. Illus. de Patricia Lapointe. Shawinigan-Sud (Québec), CERRDOC.

Rochon, Esther. *L'Ombre et le cheval*. Montréal, Éditions Paulines.

Sarfati, Sonia. *Tricot, piano et jeu vidéo*. Illus. de Pierre Durand. Montréal, La courte échelle.

Somain, Jean-François. *Le Baiser des étoiles*. Illus. de Stéphane Jorisch. LaSalle (Québec), Hurtubise, HMH.

Tousignant, André. *Josée l'imprévisible*. Laval (Québec), HRW.

___. *La Vengeance*. Laval (Québec), HRW.

Total : 52 romans = 54 % du corpus

La Structure Narrative n° 3 Away Becomes Home

Boucher, Lionel. *Perdus dans une forêt*. Limoilou (Québec), Éditions Permanents.

Foucher, Jacques. *Les Secrets de l'ultra-sonde*. Montréal, Boréal.

Gagnon, Gérald. *Otish*. Montréal, Boréal.

Paré, Louise. *L'Étrange odyssée*. Illus. de Andrée Marcoux. Sainte-Foy (Québec), Éditions La Liberté.

Pelletier, Francine. *Le Septième Écran*. Montréal, Éditions Paulines.

Pouliot, Luc. *Le Voyage des chats*. Montréal, Éditions Paulines.

Total : 6 romans = 6% du corpus

La Structure Narrative n° 4 Variations

Breton, Céline. *Une idée fixe*. Illus. d'Élisabeth Eudes-Pascal. Montréal, Éditions P. Tisseyre.

Briac. *Fichez-moi la paix!* Laval (Québec), HRW.

Cadieux, Chantal. *Samedi trouble*. Montréal, Boréal.

Cusson, Céline. *Échec et Mathieu*. Illus. de Micheline Dionne. Iberville (Québec), Coïncidence/Jeunesse.

Décary, Marie. *Au pays des toucans marrants*. Illus. de Claude Cloutier. Montréal, La courte échelle.

Gagnier, Hélène. *L'Étrange étui de Léo*. Illus. de Danielle Simard. Montréal, Éditions P. Tisseyre.

Héroux, Josiane. *Eve Dupuis, 16 ans ½*. Montréal, Éditions P. Tisseyre.

Lauzon, Vincent. *Concerto en noir et blanc*. Montréal,. Éditions P. Tisseyre.

Laverdure, Daniel. *La Bouteille vide*. Illus. de Daniel Laverdure. Montréal, Éditions P. Tisseyre.

Pelletier, Francine. *La Saison de l'exil*. Montréal, Éditions Paulines.

Pigeon, Pierre. *Pouvoir surnaturel*. Illus. de Pierre Dagesse. Iberville (Québec), Coïncidence/Jeunesse.

Robert, Johanne. *En exil ... chez mon père*. Laval (Québec), HRW.

Somain, Jean-François. *Parlez-moi d'un chat*. Illus. de Stéphane Turgeon. Montréal, Éditions P. Tisseyre.

Total : 13 romans = 13 % du corpus

□ □ □

Notes

1 Dans le corpus de romans de jeunesse publiés en français au Canada en 1992, il n'y avait qu'un seul roman qui aurait pu faire partie de notre étude qui a été publié hors du Québec, à savoir *Exercice Papillon* de Bertrand Simard.

2 On a classé comme *variations* les romans qui ne suivaient pas les trois structures narratives. On y trouve, par exemple, des romans de fantaisie, comme *Au pays de toucans marrants* de Marie Décary où la protagoniste, qui est en train de faire le tour du monde, raconte son séjour sur l'île de Paradis. Ou bien, on y trouve des romans dont le cadre est l'école, comme *Une idée fixe* de Céline Breton, *Échec et Mathieu* de Céline Cusson, *L'Étrange étui de Léo* d'Hélène Gagnier et *La Bouteille vide* de Daniel Laverdure.

3 Bon nombre des romans qui font partie de ce groupe sont des romans policiers qui, comme genre, privilégient l'exploration du monde à l'extérieur du noyau familial et qui introduisent les jeunes aux divers aspects de la société contemporaine.

4 Dans notre corpus, il y a seulement 7 romans sur 97 dans lesquels on ne trouve que la figure paternelle, à savoir : *Les Barricades d'Arthur* de Ginette Anfousse, *Le Chant des Hayats* d'Alain Bergeron, *Au pays des toucans marrants* de Marie Décary, *Tirelire, combines & cie* de Jacques Desjardins, *Sauve qui peut l'amour* de Marie-Francine Hébert, *Le Trésor de la citadelle* d'Alain Marillac et *Le Mystère de la tuque* de Brigitte Rivet.

CHAPTER 4

➡ **Island Homemaking:**
Catharine Parr Traill's
***Canadian Crusoes* and the**
Robinsonade Tradition

Andrew O'Malley

It is perhaps not surprising that one of the earliest Canadian books for young readers tells the story of a group of children of European settlers who survive the elements and the hostilities of the Native people and build a home for themselves in the wilderness. While Catharine Parr Traill's *Canadian Crusoes* (1852) is an early entry in the tradition of Canadian wilderness survival narratives, it is also, as its title suggests, part of a three-centuries-old international and persistent literary tradition of the "robinsonade."[1] This narrative form, as well as the Daniel Defoe novel from which it derives, is generally associated with tales of adventure and exploration. As such, they have participated in what has conventionally been understood as the masculine-coded ideology of colonial adventure and conquest. They are, however, not just stories about discovering strange and exotic places, but about making these places "home" for their adventuring protagonists. In other words, they are stories that also include a strong focus on the usually feminine-coded practices and ideology of domesticity. In this chapter, I am interested in examining how these seemingly contradictory ideological formations have intersected and even sustained each other in both Traill's robinsonade and in examples from the tradition that preceded it. A brief look at this literary/cultural tradition and its ideological implications seems like the natural place to start such a discussion.

The robinsonade became an enormously popular type of narrative in the eighteenth century in England, France, and most pronouncedly in

Germany, where, according to Jeannine Blackwell, over 130 of these stories were published between 1720 (the year *Robinson Crusoe* was translated into German) and 1800 (7, fn 12). The form has lent itself to countless variations, including stories in which children, individual women, individual men, groups of adults, groups containing adults and children, and even stranded animals have survival adventures in remote places—remote from Europe, that is. At the peak of British imperial power in the nineteenth century, the robinsonade was perhaps the dominant mode for boys' adventure stories: examples include Robert Louis Stevenson's *Treasure Island* and almost any of the boys' stories written by R.M. Ballantyne,[2] Captain Frederick Marryat, and others. Such television shows as *Gilligan's Island* in the 1960s and *Survivor* and *Lost* more recently, as well as films ranging from *Robinson Crusoe on Mars* (1964), to *The Blue Lagoon* (1980), to *Castaway* (2000), attest, I believe, to the continued cultural resonance of this basic narrative structure.

Theories abound as to why Defoe's model has maintained such tremendous and widespread appeal. For the purposes of this paper, among the most intriguing of these are Susan Naramore Maher's view that "[t]he island setting ... from Defoe on, serves as an archetypal laboratory for a society's ideology" ("Recasting" 169), Diana Loxley's related but more specifically postcolonial suggestion that narrating an individual (or small group) isolated on an island acts as "the ultimate gesture of simplification ... draw[ing] a line around a set of relationships which do not possess the normal political, social and cultural interference" (3), and Joseph Bristow's view that the isolated settings of robinsonades, especially those for children, provide "the European imagination with an ideal scene of instruction" (94).

Artur Blaim, author of "The English Robinsonade of the Eighteenth Century," one of the few substantial, English-language studies of the genre, suggests that to qualify, a robinsonade must have a number of features and elements beyond the obvious narrative of shipwreck and survival. For example, Blaim observes that robinsonades often also contain sub-narratives of spiritual redemption after the protagonist's descent into despair. This personal spiritual growth is often followed by the conversion to Christianity of some sort of savage indigenous population. Blaim also remarks that robinsonades tend to focus closely on the minutiae of setting up and maintaining a safe *domestic* space in a foreign, alien environment (84). This domestic concern is quite consistent in the form's history but has generally been overshadowed in criticism of both *Robinson Crusoe* and its progeny by the attention paid their more "masculine" attributes of imperialism and adventure (in its various meanings).

Over the last few decades, *Robinson Crusoe* has been studied predominantly in one of two related registers: first, as a narrative charting the emergence of a middle-class, mercantile individualism in the eighteenth century. This reading was popularized by such scholars as Ian Watt in *The Rise of the Novel* (1957), Maximillian Novak in *Economics and the Fiction of Daniel Defoe* (1962), and Stephen Hymer in his article "Robinson Crusoe and the Secret of Primitive Accumulation" (1972). Second, it has been read as a narrative that helped both shape and disseminate the ideology of colonialism in the eighteenth century. While for many critics these two readings are necessarily linked, the latter has maintained the most prominent position in *Robinson Crusoe* scholarship and has had the most influence on recent critical interpretations of robinsonades.

Martin Green was one of the first critics to explore extensively the colonial and imperial (and usually, implicitly or not, masculine) dimensions of Defoe's novel and its imitators in his *Dreams of Adventure, Deeds of Empire*, in which he describes *Robinson Crusoe* as "a central mythic expression of the modern system, of its call to young men to go out to expand [the] empire" (83). In *Colonial Encounters*, Peter Hulme observes how *Robinson Crusoe* works out a myth of origins, typical of colonialist discourse, that has to do "with the primary stuff of colonialist ideology— the European hero's lonely first steps into the void of savagery" (186). Edward Said has famously observed in *Culture and Imperialism* that colonialism and the rise of the realistic novel are inextricably linked, and that *Robinson Crusoe* is at the heart of this shared cultural history: "The prototypical modern realistic novel is *Robinson Crusoe*, and certainly not accidentally it is about a European who creates a fiefdom for himself on a distant, non-European island" (xii). Firdous Azim, in *The Colonial Rise of the Novel*, expands on Said's observation, asserting that the realistic novel is predicated on a kind of European and imperialist subjectivity that depends on the domination of a colonial Other: "It is not surprising that many histories of the novel have alighted on *Robinson Crusoe* as the starting-point for the genre.... It is because the discourse of the novel is based on the notion of a sovereign subject, and the position of that subject is determined within a confrontation with its Other, that the novel of adventure occupies such a significant place in the annals of the English novel" (37).

The large body of postcolonial scholarship that reads Crusoe as a quintessential figure of European imperialism—exploring, cataloguing, naming, mastering, claiming the "New World" and subjugating, assimilating, or eradicating its indigenous population—can be applied, by and large, to many protagonists of eighteenth- and nineteenth-century robinsonades, including those of Traill's *Canadian Crusoes*. Traill's Crusoes, like their namesake and the protagonists in most robinsonades, engage in many of these typical colonizing activities. For example, they name or rename islands and other geographical features like lakes, stake their claim to the land by farming it, and rescue, then undertake the civilizing and Christianizing of an Aboriginal character. As well, the text uses the familiar colonial tropes of the Canadian wilderness, describing, for example, its "trackless forests" (89) and empty fields awaiting the hand of European cultivation and settlement. Indeed, unpacking the deployment of colonial discourse has been a particularly productive avenue of investigation in studies of children's robinsonades from the nineteenth century. For the most part, such studies have tended to assume that the principal function of these "boys' adventure books" was to form masculine, heroic, imperial subjects, and they have considered most robinsonades as narratives of male "penetration" into "virgin" territories, and of "mastery" over feminized lands and peoples.[3]

Perhaps because of the weight of the critical emphasis given to the masculine attributes in *Robinson Crusoe* and its imitators, Nancy Armstrong's remarks on the book's reception in certain eighteenth-century pedagogical circles is all the more surprising. She comments on how Maria Edgeworth and her father, Richard, in their treatise on education, *Practical Education* (1798), thought that *Robinson Crusoe* was more valuable to girls than to boys: "'To girls this species of reading cannot be as dangerous.... [G]irls must soon perceive the impossibility of their rambling about the world in quest of adventures'" (*Desire and Domestic Fiction* 16). This is not an altogether surprising view, given the gendered division of public and private or domestic spheres, especially among the middle classes, that was being promoted in the late eighteenth century. Armstrong, however, goes on to propose that the fact that "educators found his story more suitable reading for girls than for boys of an impressionable age" might have another motivation: "There is also a strong possibility that early educational theorists recommended *Crusoe* ... because they thought women were likely to learn to desire what Crusoe accomplished, a totally self-enclosed and functional domain where money did not really matter" (16). In other words, except for the absence of children, Crusoe has constructed for himself an ideal domestic space: a retreat in which contact with the potential vicissitudes of the public domain of politics, trade, and commerce is neither wanted nor needed.

Such eighteenth- and early nineteenth-century views of *Robinson Crusoe*'s pedagogical utility open up another way of looking at this text and many of its imitators. While robinsonades like *Canadian Crusoes* undeniably participate in the masculinized world of the adventure story, they also very often operate in the feminized register of the domestic story. In fact, the almost ubiquitous concern in robinsonades, from Defoe's original on, over the establishment of home as a safe, and indeed moral, centre suggests that the form lent itself very easily to the promotion of the domestic ideology that was ascendant in the eighteenth century and that became dominant by the nineteenth.

In a 1974 article entitled "Crusoe's Home," Pat Rogers disputes the then newly emerging trend toward reading *Robinson Crusoe* as a narrative of colonial rapine or of early capitalist adventure. Much of the middle section of the novel is, as Rogers points out, taken up with Crusoe's careful cataloguing of his various household goods, his attempts to make such domestic necessities as a table or clay pots, and his methods of growing and preparing food. All of this suggests to Rogers a much humbler, domestic focus to the novel: "It is surely clear that all this is not the language of a marketing man or a capitalist speculator. For much of the time Crusoe is making a nest. His stay on the island represents the *domestic* rather than the mercantile aspect of bourgeois life" (380). By way of refuting the Crusoe-as-colonizer reading, Rogers observes that "Crusoe ... becomes, he tells us, 'a meer Pastry-Cook into the Bargain.' This hardly seems the stuff of which colonial predators are made" (384). Rogers's assertions concerning the domestic bent of the novel, though often sardonic in tone, should not be taken lightly. They require that we consider Crusoe's story more carefully in the light of the domesticity, as a form of social practice and a way of being that had its roots in eighteenth-century middle-class culture and that came to define family life in Victorian Europe and North America.

In *The Middling Sort*, Margaret Hunt traces the roots of domestic ideology to the emerging middle classes of late seventeenth-century Britain. She argues that this group promoted the separation of public and private domestic spheres as a way of gaining access to the political and economic power monopolized by and bound up in traditional aristocratic, inherited privilege.[4] This concept (if not the actual practice) of separate spheres became elaborated, entrenched, and naturalized by the end of the eighteenth and the beginning of the nineteenth centuries, when the middle classes were beginning to assume the central and dominant position in British society.[5] At the heart of domestic ideology is the configuration of home (and of the mother and children who came to embody it) as beyond the reach of the political and the economic. Of course, the construction of the home as a self-contained, self-sufficient, nurturing space, detached from the vices and dangers of the outside (male) world had, since its inception, everything to do with the political and the economic. Domesticity's ability to erase its necessary material conditions and history and to render itself the "natural" mode of family life is what makes it ideological, and its disavowal of the very violence, greed, and exploitation that characterize the expansion of empire make it a perfect counterpart to colonialism.

To view domesticity, however, as merely a justification for or distraction from colonial violence and exploitation would be to oversimplify the relationship between the colonial and the domestic. In *Empire Boys*, Bristow suggests that the framing of the colonizing narrative in familial terms is a kind of reduction or "false consciousness" masking the "real" colonial ends of robinsonades (97–99). Similarly, in her discussion of *The Swiss Family Robinson*, Loxley reads the family's drama of survival on their island as a way of distancing and abstracting the middle-class nuclear family from the capitalist and imperialist economies from which it emerged (90). While I see the merit in such positions, my difficulty with them lies in their subordination of the domestic to the colonial; the prominence of the domestic in robinsonade adventures suggests to me the instrumentality of domestic ideology to the imperial project.

If colonization involves the attempt to reproduce one culture and superimpose it on another, then domesticity in Europe can be seen to have performed an internal colonizing function before it was ever exported to the colonies. Following the pioneering social historians of family life, Leonore Davidoff and Catherine Hall, Mary Jo Maynes describes how, in the late eighteenth and the nineteenth centuries, "domestic arrangements served to constitute the European middle classes, not only demographically but also socially, culturally, and economically" (195). Indeed, she suggests that domesticity was essential to the rise of bourgeois cultural hegemony. The various movements in Europe to reform the domestic economies of both the aristocracy and, more importantly, the lower classes, helped make the middle-class model of home and family life the norm. As Maynes argues, the claimed superiority of middle-class morality was predicated on the domestic sphere, which acted as the foil to the amoral, rational calculations of the market (201). This logic applies equally well to the colony, where middle-class domesticity provided a foil for the amoral calculation, exploitation, and violence of colonial expansion; as Sharon Harrow observes: "[D]omesticity was deployed as a strategy to resolve anxieties about colonial trade" (7). In other words, the domestic creates the framework in which the moral superiority of the colonizer can remain intact.

In the colonies, domesticity and its configuration of "home" also provided, as Inderpal Grewal has demonstrated in the case of India, a space for female participation in the building of empire during the nineteenth century. Travelling abroad as carriers and disseminators of domesticity (and of the national character), "Englishwomen could show their equality with Englishmen by participating in the colonial project that was defined in purely heterosexual, masculinist terms" (65). Indeed, Grewal goes so far as to demonstrate how the colonial and the domestic are ultimately inseparable: "[A]ll constructions of 'home' during this period are implicated within colonial discourses" (8). The feminized, moral quality of domesticity was also understood as a bulwark against the dangers attendant on contact with "other" races and cultures in the colonies. As Sharon Harrow has shown, the threats posed by contact with the colonies were often configured in terms of "sexual, physical, and social infection," dangers against which the home was meant to offer the best protection (9). This observation highlights a perhaps often overlooked, yet crucial association with the idea of "home": as a space not just of welcoming and comfort, but necessarily of exclusion, constructed to keep out unwanted and dangerous elements.

The view that the home should protect against sexual licence led to what Felicity Nussbaum calls "the impossibility of linking domesticity and sexuality" (40). As the domestic sphere was invested with ideas of purity and morality, its security required, paradoxically, a disavowal of the very sexuality necessary for generating nuclear families. In the robinsonade, the anxieties over obscuring the connection between homemaking and sexuality lead to some quite complex narrative contortions. In *Robinson Crusoe*, the tension between female domesticity and sexuality is (perhaps not altogether successfully, given recent queer readings of the novel) defused by keeping women off the island and by configuring the relationship between Crusoe and Friday as one between parent and child. In several later robinsonades involving children, the mother is made absent and her domestic functions are carried on without her. While the feminized practice of domesticity—making and maintaining a safe and nurturing space in which the moral upbringing of children can occur—is crucial to these narratives, the biology of maternity has to be removed from the equation.

Pat Rogers's dismissal of a colonial reading of *Robinson Crusoe* is built on the assumption that colonial adventure/ism and domesticity are distinct to the point of being mutually exclusive. At one level, this seems intuitive: narratives of colonial expansion and exploration are about the "away," while domestic stories are about the "home." Robinsonades of the eighteenth century, however, seem to have little trouble combining these ideological categories. In fact, as such precursors to Traill's *Canadian Crusoes* as *The Female American* (Unca Eliza Winkfield, 1767), *Ambrose and Eleanor* (a 1796 English adaptation of the French children's book *Lolotte et Fanfan* by François Ducray-Dumenil), and *Leila; or, The*

Island (Ann Fraser Tytler, 1839) demonstrate, these narratives bridge the colonial and the domestic by reconstituting, in whatever shape possible, not just the European home but its nuclear-style family as well on the island or other remote setting.

Many eighteenth- and nineteenth-century robinsonades (including *Robinson Crusoe* itself, which opens with Crusoe's critical moment of disobedience to his father) begin with a disruption of the nuclear family unit. Indeed, this seems like an almost necessary element to these narratives—the protagonist must leave or be rent from his or her first home in order to rebuild a new home abroad. This is clearly the case in *The Female American*. The narrator and supposed author of this "true" account, Unca Eliza Winkfield, is the daughter of an English colonist and a Native princess. A domestic rivalry tears the young family apart. A jealous aunt has Unca's mother murdered in the hopes of assuming her place in Mr. Winkfield's affections. Eliza is sent to relatives in England where she receives a thorough formal education and rigorous religious instruction.

While en route from Virginia to England, Unca is deposited by a wicked ship's captain on an uninhabited island, where she makes shift with the help of a survival guide penned and thoughtfully left behind for future castaways by an old hermit. She discovers that her island is visited annually by the sun-worshipping Natives of a neighbouring island[6] and, through what amounts to a ventriloquist's ruse (she hides inside a hollow statue of the sun-god and speaks to the Natives), she manages to convert the heathens to Christianity. Finally, after becoming the spiritual instructor of the local Natives, Unca is found by her cousin, who has spent the years since her disappearance scouring the islands for her. He is a parson's son and is himself intent on missionary work. When he finds Unca, he prevails on her—after repeated refusals—to marry him, and the two remain among the newly converted "savagery" to minister to their spiritual needs. The family she had lost before is thus reconstituted, with her father's relation becoming her husband, and with the Natives filling the role of children, dependent on her for their spiritual upbringing.

Unca's relationship to the Natives she converts is clearly marked in the novel as a parental one. When she first dupes them into believing their sun-god idol is speaking to them, she tells them to follow every instruction of the woman whom the idol will send to them as an emissary. The emissary who will bring them the Christian faith is, of course, Unca herself. Unca as Sun-God gives the Natives these instructions: "You must be sure to show the greatest respect to her, do everything that she commands you.... You must all believe and do as she shall instruct you" (111). A gentle sort of obedience is expected of the natives, and the passage echoes with the fairly common refrains of eighteenth-century pedagogical literature: children should obey their parents—particularly their mothers—or governesses, as they possess both the rationality and the spiritual maturity children lack, and have their best interests in mind. Unca regularly refers to her manner of dealing with the Natives she is instructing in the following terms: "I thus addressed them, with as much affability as I could: yet with an air of authority" (114). Again, the combination of a gentle affability with a definite authority became the model of middle-class maternity in the late eighteenth century.[7] The mother, as centre of the domestic sphere, was meant to be, according to the ascendant domestic ideology of the late eighteenth century, a firm but kindly figure who provided her young with the fundamentals of faith and reason.[8] By ending its narrative of adventure with a reconstitution of the family unit and a confirmation of the maternal ideal, *The Female American* symbolically yokes the colonial objectives of subduing and converting New World savages with a domestic ideology that privileges the function of the mother within the nuclear family model. The colonizers become parents to an Indigenous population, who are slotted as children into a preordained familial role. The colony is made into a suitable home and its inhabitants into a family without the need for the sexual, reproductive act. Indeed, Unca's rejection of her cousin's romantic overtures until the very end of the novel, once the colonial home with Natives as children is already in place, serves to underscore this.

Ambrose and Eleanor is a robinsonade directed, like many others from the last quarter of the eighteenth century on, at a child audience.[9] It performs, however, some similar ideological functions to *The Female American*, which was written with an adult audience in mind. In fact, I would argue that the extraordinary popularity of the robinsonade as a form for children itself highlights its potential for disseminating domestic ideology. This story opens with a colonel in the British colonial army in North America being shipwrecked on an island. He is amazed to discover two English children living there in a state of semi-, albeit basically noble (or at least harmless), savagery. The children, Ambrose and Eleanor, had been left on the island, again by a wicked sea-captain (a popular plot device), when they were only four years old.

The book is clearly inspired by Rousseau's ideas of a "natural education," which he expounded in *Émile*. Nature provides for the child castaways, and their inclinations are, therefore, naturally sweet, honest, and uncorrupted. As the reader finds out only at the end of the story, their presence on the island is also the result of a disruption of the family unit. The union of their parents did not meet with the approval of one of the grandparents, and mother and children were shipped off to the colonies until father could resolve the disagreement. Having lost both of their biological parents, the children are eager to take on the colonel as their surrogate father. The colonel, having left his own family behind in England, immediately acknowledges, and seamlessly assumes, his necessary and ideologically prescribed role on the island: "[H]e resolved henceforth to be to them a father, guide and friend" (20).

Once a version of the nuclear family unit is reconstituted, the colonel sets about creating a proper domestic setting for his new foster children. He removes them from the dank and miserable cave in which they had been living and extracts from it and buries the putrefying remains of the children's deceased guardian, which they had rather grimly been reverencing for several years as the vestige of a lost parental influence. Constructing a true home, in the sense of a protective, nurturing domestic sphere for the children, is the colonel's next obvious step: "a cabin that will shelter us from the injuries of the air, and serve as *an asylum against all alarms*" (22, my emphasis). Even without a mother, whose absence is always felt in the text yet seems necessary to the narrative, the new family thrives and is sustained by the sphere of safety the home represents.

One of the most intriguing parallels between this story and *The Female American* is the reference to sun worship as a kind of Aboriginal given— the assumed state of "primitive" or "natural" religion. Unca Eliza Winkfield manages to correct this inclination in the Natives toward a false, heliological religion. Similarly, the colonel weans his charges from the sun worship to which they have instinctively subscribed. His first lecture on religion to the children begins thus: "[A]t present it will be sufficient to acquaint you that this great Being, who is called God, created all things: the Sun, which has hitherto been the object of your adoration, and which communicates light and heat to all nature, was formed by his word" (40). The assumed "naturalness" of sun worship for both American Aboriginals and untutored European children indicates a shared primitiveness that can be redressed through the domestic and feminine-coded discourse of early education. The primitive and/or infantile tendency toward misguided (and ultimately dangerous) beliefs is best corrected within a domestic framework. This idea, that the home was necessarily the site in which the earliest or foundational religious instruction must take place, was a key element of eighteenth- and nineteenth-century domestic ideology. The domestic and the missionary are connected here in the colonial enterprise at the level of inscribing the nuclear-styled family as the necessary vehicle for transmitting Christian morality and faith.

The colonial and the domestic merge even more explicitly by the end of the novel. After a series of strange and improbable coincidences, the children find their mother while the colonel finds his wife in England. It turns out that the two women had earlier formed a friendship based on their mutual grief over their familial losses. Because of the unjust machinations of his political rivals, the colonel is then exiled from England. This prompts him to "found ... a colony in the island which had so long served him and his pupils as a retreat" (200). The domestic ideology that renders the home a peaceful retreat from an often vicious and corrupt public sphere—here manifested in the campaign of slander and political machination unjustly directed against the colonel—thus dovetails neatly with the objectives of colonial expansion. The "unpopulated" island (as usual, the local Natives "visit" only from time to time) on which the colonel lived with and happily raised his young charges becomes a perfect and natural site for the expression of this ideal of domestic retirement.

Ann Fraser Tytler's *Leila; or, The Island*, a close contemporary of *Canadian Crusoes*, is worth considering briefly here as well, as it represents one of the more exaggerated expressions of the form's domestic ideological possibilities. In this text, the child Leila Howard, her elderly nurse, and her father are all shipwrecked on a spectacularly bountiful yet uninhabited island. Once again, the mother is physically absent even if the social and familial practices she is meant to embody are clearly articulated in the text; as well, the advanced age and clearly marked lower-class status of the nurse defuse anxieties over the possibility of the sexual encroaching on the domestic. In their edenic locale, the makeshift family reproduces with remarkable ease a comfortable (even stylish), upper middle-class British existence, and the island serves primarily as a remote yet ideal setting for the moral education of Leila.

Susan Naramore Maher has rightly remarked on how this particular narrative, like many other robinsonades, acts to reaffirm a patriarchal family order. On the island, "God centers creation, one's father centers family life, and gender determines one's fixed role in this naturalized paradigm" ("The Uses" 155). While the authority of Leila's father is—as is the case with Ambrose and Eleanor's surrogate father—never questioned, the juvenile island narrative still foregrounds most of the activities coded as feminine in domestic ideology: moral economy in the form of early religious training and the nurturing and care of the child, and domestic economy in the form of establishing and maintaining a comfortable, safe home.

Indeed, the transformation of the uncivilized island into an ideal, British, middle-class space of comfort and Christian morality is taken to quite absurd extremes in this text. Leila's father, Mr. Howard, for example, builds a family chapel as well as a bower with the word "Welcome" written in flowers above its entrance. The interior of the bower, which they call their "green parlour" (114), essentially reproduces a bourgeois sitting room: "[I]n a sweet corner close to the window which looked upon the rivulet, there was a little table and a little chair.... [A] pretty cage of white wicker work, with a pair of turtle-doves hung upon a branch by the window" (105).

Catharine Parr Traill, given her own experiences of European settler life in Canada, avoids Tytler's quite silly excesses.[10] Yet, like Tytler's and other robinsonades, Traill's text carries dual ideological charges of colonial conquest-adventure and domesticity. While *Canadian Crusoes'* colonialist qualities are clearly evident, especially in its constructions of the land as abundant and "trackless" and in its representations of the Aboriginal population, a number of critics of Traill's work have remarked on her ambivalent use of this discourse. Robert Fleming has argued that there are many slippages and contradictions in Traill's representations of Aboriginals, which problematize a simple negative reading of her work as imperialist narrative.[11] Suzanne James, I think fairly, suggests that Traill is "almost progressive" in her portrayal of indigenous people, at least in comparison to both her contemporaries, and the architects of "a deliberate policy of cultural genocide" of the generation immediately after Traill's (121). As well, Carole Gerson has pointed out how the figure of "the Native" in Traill's work and Traill's own lived relationships with Aboriginal women in particular are inflected and complicated by gender: "Powerful as white but disempowered as female ... Traill share[s] with Native women some marginal space on the outskirts of frontier culture" (10). Indeed, part of the power of an ideology like colonialism is its ability to contain and elide these kinds of contradictions. What has received less attention in criticism of *Canadian Crusoes*, however, is that the book also presents us with a detailed model of home life, reproducing the domestic ideology that emerged out of eighteenth-century British middle-class culture and became dominant by the nineteenth century.

In an earlier book for juvenile readers, *The Young Emigrants; or, Pictures of Canada* (1826), Traill recounts the transition of the Clarence family from a comfortable home life in England to a difficult settler existence in Canada (a move Traill herself experienced six years later). While this text hardly qualifies as a robinsonade, it provides insights into the reproduction of a distinctly British mode of domestic life in the "wilderness" of Canada that forms such an important part of *Canadian Crusoes*. Among the items the Clarences bring with them from their old estate (called

"Roselands") to their new home are rose bushes. Roses are, of course, the national flower of Britain and one of its national emblems, and in the soil of the colonies they take on the symbolic weight of the British home itself: "These ... we will plant by the porch of our Canadian cottage; and who knows ... but we may, in course of time, possess another Roselands, in the wilderness'" (27). Once the Clarences have established themselves in the colonies, they send for their daughter Ellen, whose poor health required her to remain behind in England. The reunion (an integral part of many robinsonades, *Canadian Crusoes* included) at "the home of that beloved family" takes place, naturally enough, in an iconographic setting of "home": around the "blazing fire" in the cottage hearth (161).

Canadian Crusoes, like so many other robinsonades, begins with some sort of disruption of the domestic sphere and the nuclear family. Hector, his sister Catharine, and their cousin Louis—the titular Canadian Crusoes—leave the safety of their family home and become lost in the wilderness. Their departure from their home comes, like Robinson Crusoe's, partly as an act of disobedience; Louis lies to Catharine, saying her mother has given her permission to join the boys as they look for cattle that have strayed. The anguish Louis feels at his act of disobedience and the anguish the children feel over the suffering their parents must be enduring are recurrent features of the text, just as Crusoe's torment over his own disobedience to his father pervades the original.

As is the case with *The Female American* and *Ambrose and Eleanor*, Traill's robinsonade also includes some sort of reconstitution or reproduction of the disrupted nuclear family in the "away" space. In *Canadian Crusoes* the children re-form a makeshift family with the addition of a young Aboriginal woman whom Hector rescues and whom they name, rather unsurprisingly, "Indiana." Repeatedly, the text refers to Indiana as a child, despite her being the same age as Catharine, thus repeating the pattern of *The Female American*, in which colony becomes "home," colonizers become "parents," and Aboriginals become "children." At one point, Indiana's face is described as being "almost as blank as that of an infant of a few weeks old"; at another it is as "joyous and innocent as a little child's" (113, 114). This blankness and innocence suggest a *tabula rasa* on which the colonizing culture can write itself, demonstrating further how effectively the domestic ideology that recasts the Aboriginal as child works with that of colonialism.

While Catharine calls Indiana her "sister," she acts like her mother. As such, she gladly takes on one of the standard maternal duties, the early and decidedly domestic education of the childlike Indiana: "How did the lively intelligent Canadian girl ... long to instruct her Indian friend, to enlarge her mind by pointing out such things to her attention as she herself took interest in! She would then repeat the name of the object that she showed her several times over, and by degrees the young squaw learned the names of all the *familiar household articles*" (113, my emphasis). Catharine is not just teaching Indiana the basics of the English language, but of English, female domesticity as well, as the attention paid "familiar household articles" suggests.

Finally, as other examples of the form attest, many robinsonades end with the reunion of the disrupted nuclear family and often with marriages, reinscribing and guaranteeing the perpetuation of the domestic sphere into the future. Hector marries Indiana at the end of the story (after she has been baptized and domesticated, as it were), and Catharine and Louis also wed. In fairness to Traill, her model of assimilation is far removed from the genocidal fantasies Defoe's Crusoe entertains and eventually acts out, and it employs a model that can be described as "accommodation" in the making of a new home in the colony.[12]

One of the most telling features of many robinsonades is the detailed attention they pay to the building and furnishing of such new homes. Crusoe is positively obsessive about equipping, maintaining, outfitting, and defending his home. The Canadian Crusoes make a series of homes over the three years they spend on the Rice Lake Plains, starting with a rough lean-to and eventually erecting a comfortable log cabin with a hearth and with cultivated fields around it. In their progression to more and more elaborate and permanent homes, the children re-enact a narrative of cultural evolution from primitive and nomadic to settler-agricultural societies. That the young Crusoes progress through the history of homemaking so rapidly serves to distinguish them from the Aboriginals, who never advance beyond primitive domestic arrangements; the advanced state of the Crusoes' domesticity also underscores the implied claims to the land on which they make their homes.[13]

They spend their first night under a tree, providence protecting and providing for them as it does the birds and the beasts. Their second home is a rudimentary, temporary affair described as "[a] few boughs cut down and interlaced with the shrubs round a small space cleared with Hector's axe" (29). When Traill describes how this dwelling is outfitted, she does so using terms of reference from other primitive, nomadic peoples: the "cedar-boughs that the Indians spread within their summer wigwams for carpets or couches, or the fresh heather that the Highlanders gather on the wild Scottish hills" (30). Their first meal in this dwelling is a partridge prepared "gipsy-fashion" suspended from a stick over coals (30).

Their third home is an improvement: a "summer hut," erected in the style of an "Indian wigwam" (62, 63). Evoking England's own ancient past, Traill remarks that the cedar-bough carpeting "reminds one of the times when the palaces of our English kings were strewn with rushes" (63). The children have evolved by now in their homemaking to a recognizably (albeit archaically) English level. By the time this home is built, they are joined by the family dog, Wolfe, who for weeks had been searching the forest for them. As Kathleen Kete observes in *The Beast in the Boudoir*, by the nineteenth century "the family dog became a cliché of modern [bourgeois family] life" (1). Laura Brown, in *Fables of Modernity*, traces "the socially widespread assumption of household intimacy with a companion animal" to the eighteenth century and points out that the dog was the "[m]ost evident, even ubiquitous" household pet (232, 233). The companion dog is an important feature of many robinsonades (Crusoe himself has one, as does the Swiss Family Robinson, and Leila of *Leila; or, the Island*, for example) because of its powerful association with domesticity. Kete suggests a couple of reasons for this association. First, since domestic ideology has children as its focus, pet dogs became for the middle-class, nuclear family "eternal children, whose care absorbed the family" (77). Second, and more germane, perhaps, to the case of *Canadian Crusoes*, is that domesticity is concerned with overcoming the baser human instincts through the civilizing influence of the home and the mother. The tame, obedient, pet dog, then, acts as a perfect example of the successful domesticating of the wild. In establishing their home-life on the plains, the children are also conquering and subduing the wilds around them, and the addition of their dog Wolfe to the family group reinforces this idea.

The second-to-last home the Canadian Crusoes build is still rudimentary, even by the standards of "the poorest English peasant" (89), yet it manages to provide a humble setting for that idealized vignette of domestic life, the family sitting around the fire at the end of the day: "How cheerful was the first fire blazing up on their own hearth! It was so pleasant to sit by its gladdening light, and chat away of all they had done and all that they meant to do" (89). Although simple and sparse, this house resembles closely enough what the children of European settlers understand as home that they "even entertained decided *home feelings* for their little log cabin" (94, my emphasis). These home feelings bring with them the harmony and close, nuclear, familial bonds emphasized by domestic ideology: "They were now all the world to one another" (94). This is in many ways the essence of the middle-class nuclear family. Being "all the world to one another" stresses the insular and controlled environment the home needs to be in order to provide nurturing and cultivation free from potentially dangerous outside influence. Once Indiana completes the family circle, the Crusoes build one last home that is similar to their previous one, only bigger, better appointed, and more comfortable.

With the Crusoes having by now achieved domestic stability and comfort, Traill's narrative tracks the salutary effects of domesticity as it is exported beyond the walls of their little home and into a nearby Native community. Near the end of the novel, Catharine, who has been a veritable avatar of domesticity throughout the Canadian Crusoes' adventures, is captured by the tribe who had earlier orphaned Indiana and left her to die.

Catharine's status as domestic subject *par excellence* warrants further comment here. Perhaps the most telling outward sign of her commitment to the feminine ideal of domesticity is her extraordinary attachment to her apron over the course of the Crusoes' three years in the wilderness. When Louis suggests they tear her apron into strips for kindling, Catharine's "ideas of economy and neatness [are] greatly outraged" (26). Louis later proposes to use her apron as a fishing net; again Catharine refuses, as this is not the garment's proper domestic use: "It is to keep our gowns clean, Louis, when we are milking and scrubbing, and doing all sorts of household duties" (33). The fact that, at this point, as Louis observes, "you have neither cows to milk, nor house to clean" (33) is irrelevant, as the apron signifies what was lost and what the children must attempt to recuperate in the wilderness. Months and years in the woods take their eventual toll on the apron, but, tellingly, the last use she finds for it is in providing succour to the wounded Indiana: "She bathed the inflamed arm with water, and bound the cool healing leaves of the *tacamahac* about it with the last fragment of her apron" (110).

While in captivity, Catharine busies herself by trying to reform the woeful domestic economy of her keepers. Compared to the continuous improvements she, Hector, and Louis make to their various homes, the state of Native dwellings is shocking to Catharine. She wonders at how her captors erect their wigwams at low elevations where water collects, instead of moving them up a few feet to drier soil: "This either arises from stupidity or indolence, perhaps from both, but it is no doubt the cause of much of the sickness that prevails among them" (194). With this remark, Traill suggests that a lack of attention to domestic matters is the cause of many of this culture's woes. Such a claim elides the impact on Native populations of, for instance, infections and diseases brought by European settlers. The primitive state of Native housekeeping practices and technologies also receives unfavourable mention:

Of the ordinary household work, such as is familiar to European females, they of course knew nothing; they had no linen to wash or iron, no floors to clean, no milking of cows, nor churning of butter.

Their carpets were fresh cedar boughs spread upon the ground, and only renewed when they became offensively dirty from the accumulation of fish bones and other offal, which are carelessly flung down during meals. Of furniture they had none, their seat the ground, their table the same, their beds mats or skins of animals,—such were the domestic arrangements of the Indian camp. (195)

To remedy these deficiencies, Catharine tries to teach the Native women of the camp by example how to tend properly to their homes, sweeping the front of her own tent and replacing the cedar flooring regularly. A footnote Traill provides suggests that efforts at domestic reform such as Catharine's have had their desired effect: "Much improvement has taken place of late years in the domestic economy of the Indians, and some of their dwellings are clean and neat even for Europeans" (fn 195).

She ultimately wins the hearts of the Native women, however, with the attention and affection she shows their children; she cares for them tenderly and washes them regularly. Catharine takes pity on the "dark-skinned babes" whose mothers neglect them, at least by middle-class, European standards of child care; she is shocked to see the babies in the Native camp swaddled and hung from branches, left "helpless and uncomplaining spectators" (193). By the eighteenth century, the practice of swaddling infants was widely condemned in British and continental medical and educational writing as injurious to the health of children. In large part, this was because swaddling was then out of step with the ideals of maternal affection and attention promoted in the emerging domestic ideology. As well, the health and vigour of the child were increasingly linked to the health of the state in pediatric and pedagogical discourses. Catharine's care for the Native babies can thus be read in a few registers: as an indication of her superior maternal sense; as a marker of the unenlightened state of Native women; and in the context of early child care's role in the forming of future subjects in the colony.

This part of the text, dedicated to Catharine as agent of domestic reform, clearly demonstrates the colonizing power of domesticity. The somewhat modified European model of domesticity that Traill's book disseminates is a powerful colonizing agent precisely because of its deployment as a mode of social reform—in other words, precisely because of its ability to effect change outside of the closed, disconnected domestic sphere with which it purports to concern itself exclusively.

The ways in which domesticity and colonialism intersect and inform each other is attested to by the various uses of the term "domestic," along with its verb form, "domesticate," which, although not as complexly nuanced as the term "home," still describe a remarkable range of ideas. My main use here of the term "domestic" has been as an adjective describing objects, feelings, and behaviours relating to the home and to home life, and in particular to the ideological character of a specifically eighteenth- and nineteenth-century, British model of "home" (ideological in its ability to render itself natural and normative and to reproduce and disseminate itself).[14]

The multiple meanings of the verb form are also relevant here. The young Crusoes domesticate in a number of ways: they "familiarize" themselves with their new surroundings and come to "feel at home" there; they "live familiarly" with one another and eventually with Indiana as well. In domesticating Indiana, they "make [her] to be or to feel 'at home,'" but also "tame" her and "civilize" her (usages of the term more commonly applied to animals) and "attach [her] to home and its duties" ("domesticate"). Misao Dean points out in *Practising Femininity* that to domesticate is also to render the alien ordinary and familiar (5–6). Domesticity's power as ideology, in effect, lies in its ability to make its practices ordinary and "homely," to give them the appearance of both the mundane and normal way of being. The domestic ideology I am trying to identify in the robinsonade performs all these functions, and all these functions mesh with colonial ends of establishing a settler society. I think it is also worth noting that the act of domesticating can be applied to what parents do to children, which sheds some more light on the representations of Aboriginals as childlike in these texts. When Catharine domesticates Indiana, she acts as her mother. Discursively, the child and the Native have often been closely linked (it is no coincidence that children are sometimes referred to as "little savages"). Both are imagined to be in a pre-civilized state, which renders them potentially unruly and difficult to manage. One of the functions a mother conventionally has had in domestic ideology, as centre of the nuclear family, is to form her pre-civilized, effectively savage, charges into civil subjects. This model of the maternal/domestic translates with great success into the colonial context in the robinsonade. Further, the domestic activity and objectives of making and managing a comfortable home expand outward to the making, or remaking, of a European middle-class culture.

□ □ □

Notes

1 The term "robinsonade" refers, naturally enough, to texts in the style of, or with many of the same plot elements as, Defoe's 1719 novel, *The Life and Strange Surprizing Adventures of Robinson Crusoe, of York, Mariner.*

2 Ballantyne in particular set the pattern for the Canadian robinsonade with his many tales of adventure set in the Canadian wilderness. His first book, *Hudson's Bay, or, The Life in the Wilds of North America* (1848), is an autobiographical account of his own time spent in the Canadian wilderness. *Snowflakes and Sunbeams, or, The Young Fur Traders* (1856) also contains autobiographical elements relating to his time as a young man working for the Hudson's Bay Company.

3 In "The Robinson Crusoe Story," for example, Martin Green refers to the robinsonade tradition as "profoundly masculinist, both in its characters' indifference to women, and in the stimulus it gave men to find fulfilment exclusively in bonds to other men" (36).

4 See esp. chapter 8, "Private Order and Political Virtue: Domesticity and the Ruling Class."

5 The "reality" of separate spheres has been vigorously questioned recently by a number of scholars who rightly point out the impossibility of clearly and absolutely differentiated spaces and practices along gender lines. See, for example, Lawrence Klein's "Gender and the Public Private Distinction in the Eighteenth Century: Some Questions about Evidence and Analytical Procedure," Michael McKeon's "The Secret History of Domesticity: Private, Public, and the Division of Knowledge," and, for the American context, Cathy N. Davidson's "No More Separate Spheres!"

6 That the Natives inhabit only the neighbouring isle is a fairly common feature of the robinsonade, as it facilitates the necessary myth of origins: the protagonist's island (or other isolated space) itself must not have *permanent* residents. Peter Hulme points out the fallacy of this colonial fantasy, when he refers to the demographic impossibility of such a fertile island as Crusoe's remaining uninhabited, and being used only by cannibals for "periodic picnics" (186).

7 On this model of maternal instruction, see, for example, Mitizi Myers's "Impeccable Governesses, Rational Dames, and Moral Mothers: Mary Wollstonecraft and the Female Tradition in Georgian Children's Books."

8 For a valuable discussion of the moral training the middle-class mother was expected to provide for her children in the late eighteenth and early nineteenth centuries, see chapter 3, "'The Nursery of Virtue': Domestic Ideology and the Middle Class," in Davidoff and Hall's *Family Fortunes*.

9 The value of *Robinson Crusoe* (and later of robinsonades) as a children's text was famously established by Rousseau in *Émile* (147–48). Perhaps the first robinsonade written explicitly for children is Joachim Campe's *Robinson Der Jungere* (1779, translated as *The New Robinson Crusoe* in 1788). For a sense of the tremendous quantity and variety of the form as children's narrative, see Kevin Carpenter's bibliography, *Desert Islands and Pirate Islands: The Island Theme in Nineteenth-Century English Juvenile Fiction.*

10 At the risk of belabouring the point, I will mention perhaps the most extravagant of Tytler's fantasies of castaway comfort. For her birthday, Leila's father

presents her with an ornate, functioning, wicker coach, drawn by a wild goat he has painstakingly tamed and trained for this purpose (194).

11 Fleming makes this point in a variety of ways in his article "Supplementing Self." See, for example, 209, 216, 217.

12 I am indebted to D.M.R. Bentley for his suggestion to me in conversation that Traill makes "accommodations" when making "home." This spirit of accommodation does not, however, imply parity between the two cultures that come into contact, as the settler culture here is depicted as the superior one accommodating elements of the other.

13 The building of more "permanent" houses can be understood, along with tilling the soil, as the kind of investment of labour into the land that constitutes rightful ownership according to Locke's theories in *Two Treatises of Government*: "As much Land as a Man Tills, Plants, Improves, Cultivates, and can use the Product of, so much is his *Property*. He by his Labour does, as it were, inclose it from the Common" (290–91).

14 This is not to collapse differences in domesticity between the eighteenth and nineteenth centuries, but as Misao Dean remarks, the model of proper, middle-class femininity (and domesticity) Traill brought with her to Canada in the 1830s was shaped by late-eighteenth-century ideas and culture: "[Her] ideas on the nature of woman and the expression of that nature by conduct were formed by late eighteenth- and early nineteenth-century British culture" (18).

CHAPTER 5 ➡ **Home and Native Land:**
A Study of Canadian
Aboriginal Picture Books
by Aboriginal Authors

Doris Wolf and
Paul DePasquale

For the past four years, we have been engaged in
the rewarding, though often challenging, task of compiling a comprehensive bibliography of Aboriginal children's literature by Aboriginal authors.[1]
Our work on this bibliography has given us a unique opportunity to survey the wide range of books aimed at or read by audiences up to and
including young adults, written by authors who identify as Aboriginal,
and published from 1967, the year of George Clutesi's *Son of Raven, Son
of Deer*, to the present day. Perhaps the most immediate surprise has been
the sheer number of these books. Although Alexandra West notes in her
historical overview of English-Canadian children's literature in the *International Companion Encyclopedia of Children's Literature* (1996) that,
while "Native writers of adult text are growing in numbers, in children's
literature this is happening more slowly" (866), the number of books and
authors on our list immediately belies this view. Certainly adult fiction has
received more scholarly and popular attention than children's books, but
approximately 300 books for children by approximately 125 Aboriginal
authors are on our list. West further claims that of the two categories that
dominate the field of Aboriginal children's literature—retellings of traditional tales and legends and fictional stories about Aboriginal youths in
historical and contemporary settings—the fictional books have lagged significantly behind the tales (867). Again, our bibliography contradicts this
view. Roughly 70% of the books are fictional stories.

Both categories have, of course, been crucial for Aboriginal children and Aboriginal communities who, given the devastating impact of colonization on the Native peoples of North America, need the positive affirmation of their cultures and identities that these books without exception offer. As Clare Bradford notes in "'To Hold Up Prisms': Australian and Canadian Indigenous Publishing for Children," while non-Aboriginal children might valuably enlarge their horizons of understanding and empathy through these books and are included as part of their target audience, Aboriginal children are typically the primary audience of Aboriginal production. Indeed, Tse-Shaht author and illustrator George Clutesi suggested nearly four decades ago in his introduction to *Son of Raven, Son of Deer* (1967) that Aboriginal peoples' estrangement from their own cultural and artistic traditions "could be part of the reason so many of the Indian population of Canada are in a state of bewilderment today" (12). Motivated in part to counteract this "state of bewilderment," Clutesi, as James Gellert observes, saw his art as contributing not only to a better understanding on the part of non-Indians of Aboriginal cultural and artistic traditions, but also to Native peoples' own understanding of these traditions, in order that they might counteract the "civilizing" influences of alien cultures (79). By helping to recuperate traditions often damaged or lost through colonization, tales and legends have contributed to the resurgence of Aboriginal identities and pride in the past four decades. Many of these books— such as Clutesi's collection of Tse-Shaht legends, *Son of Raven, Son of Deer* (1967); *Tales from the Longhouse* (1973), traditional stories written by Aboriginal children from Vancouver Island and the village of Kingcome Inlet; *Why the Beaver Has a Broad Tail* (1974), an Ojibwa legend told by Susan Enosse of the Wikwemikong Reserve on Manitoulin Island; and Mohawk clan mother Alma Greene's *Tales of the Mohawks* (1975)—draw from a wide range of traditional knowledges that originate in specific First Nations communities. These authors, the forerunners of today's well-known writers of legends such as Bill Ballantyne, Joe McLellan, and C.J. Taylor, sought to record and transmit traditional knowledges to future generations of Aboriginal peoples long before the historical and cultural value of preserving the voices of the elders was recognized, and made, as it is today, even somewhat fashionable.[2] Children are not necessarily the sole intended audience for traditional stories: for example, in its catalogue Theytus Books, an Aboriginal-owned and -run publishing company located in Penticton, British Columbia, which publishes Aboriginal authors only, lists its legends under two categories, children's stories and oral traditions, indicating that adults, too, might well and do indeed read these books for their own pleasure and knowledge.[3]

In the second category, fictional stories, we also encounter a wide diversity of representations encompassing boy and girl protagonists of various ages and Aboriginal affiliations, who are engaged in learning a wide variety of lessons and/or having adventures in various time periods and a number of different locales, including urban, rural, reserve, and non-reserve settings. From Jordan Wheeler's *Chuck in the City*, which recounts Chuck's adventures on his first visit to the city when he gets lost trying to find his Kookum's condo, to Jan Bourdeau Waboose's *SkySisters*, which tells of two Ojibwa sisters' wintertime adventure to see the Northern Lights in their remote northern Manitoba location, these books portray Aboriginal youth in various settings and have helped, along with other multicultural literature emerging in this period, to challenge the dominance of white, middle-class characters and settings in Canadian children's books that continued well into the 1980s (Bainbridge and Fayjean). Crucially, they have offered Aboriginal children an opportunity to see their own history, lives, and experience on the written page.

For our paper here, we focus on the fictional books, specifically picture books, that portray the lives of Aboriginal children in contemporary and recent historical settings. As in the broader field of children's literature, the picture book is the most common form of children's books by Aboriginal authors.[4] In fact, about 75% of all books on our comprehensive list are picture books, suggesting that the form is especially appealing to a wide range of Aboriginal authors writing for children. Yet the picture book also poses a myriad of challenges for these authors. The development of the picture book form throughout the nineteenth century was contemporaneous with Britain's renewed efforts at empire-building. In North America, the rapid influx of settlers led to dramatically deteriorating conditions for Aboriginal peoples, and children's books, including picture books, helped normalize this consequence of imperialism. As recent works such as Jeffrey Richard's collection of essays *Imperialism and Juvenile Literature* and Daphne Kutzer's *Empire's Children: Empire and Imperialism in Classic British Books* have amply shown, imperialism was a complex ideology that was both reflected in and (re)produced by the children's literature coming out of Britain and its empire.

The publishing history of children's literature in Canada, in which the picture book appears as a relative newcomer, has its own particular neo-colonial history. As Joyce Bainbridge and Janet Fayjean remark in "Seeing Oneself in a Book: The Changing Face of Canadian Children's Literature," until the mid-1970s when children's literature began to grow dramatically in Canada, it was typified by outdoor adventure and survival stories, animal stories, historical fiction, and retellings of Aboriginal myths

and legends. Retellings of Aboriginal myths and legends became especially popular in the late 1950s and the 1960s when a number of white
authors, including James Houston, Christie Harris, Robert Ayre, Cyrus
Macmillan, Kay Hill, and Dorothy Reid appropriated the material for a
predominantly white reading public (West 866; Bainbridge and Fayjean).
The first picture book to draw on Aboriginal content was *The Mountain
Goats of Temlaham* (1969) by William Toye, with collage illustrations by
Elizabeth Cleaver. Retelling the famous legend of the Tsimpshian Indians
of British Columbia, where the mountain goats took their revenge on the
men of Temlaham for breaking the law of the hunt, this book was crucial in establishing the illustrated legend as a popular format in Canadian
children's literature. Both author and illustrator were non-Aboriginal.
While contemporary debates around appropriation of voice have helped
to reduce the numbers of non-Aboriginal writers writing about Aboriginal materials, nonetheless the retelling of legends and telling of fictional
stories centred on Aboriginal content by non-Aboriginal authors still
occurs frequently.[5]

Against this heavy colonial and neo-colonial history, Aboriginal authors
writing picture books for children have had to adapt and redefine this
Western literary form to tell their own stories, as well as to negotiate a place
in a publishing industry that has engendered Aboriginal people's inequitable
participation (see Young-Ing). All these things have left an indelible stamp
on picture books in Canada and on Aboriginal writers' negotiations of
this form. And yet Aboriginal authors since the late 1960s and early 1970s
have turned to it as a way to alter the ethnocentrism of Canada and to bring
hope and healing to their communities.

Picture books authored by Aboriginal writers have also been influenced
by another field, that of adult fiction by Aboriginal writers, to which they
are closely connected, sometimes by authorship. For example, Thomas
King, Beatrice Culleton Mosionier, Jeannette Armstrong, Lee Maracle,
Jordan Wheeler, Richard Van Camp, and Tomson Highway have all written both adult and children's books, including picture books. Foregrounding the difficulties in defining Native literature in his introduction to *An
Anthology of Canadian Native Fiction*, Thomas King nonetheless sets out
a number of its most prominent characteristics: an assiduous avoidance
of the historical past, especially the nineteenth century, as setting; the
attempt to bridge oral tribal literature and contemporary written literature
by depicting an egalitarian relationship between humans and other living
things, including the land; and the creation of resourceful, vibrant, and tenacious characters who act as counterpoints to the stereotypes of Native
peoples as an unsophisticated and dying race. These characteristics typ-

ify children's literature by Aboriginal authors as well. Although books such as James Whetung's *The Vision Seeker* and Jeannette Armstrong's *Neekna and Chemai* are set in a distant, pre-colonial past, and others such as Deborah Delaronde's Flour Sack Flora series and Allan Crow's *The Crying Christmas Tree* take place in the mid-twentieth century, most are set in the contemporary moment and avoid the nineteenth century.[6] The non-competitive relationship between humans and the land, animals, and plants is one of the most striking characteristics of the children's fiction we examine here, where the youthful protagonists, who are often resourceful and vibrant, and sometimes tenacious, and who have sometimes adopted Western attitudes toward the land and nature, typically need to learn this Aboriginal worldview and typically do so through an elder, parent, or grandparent, so that the importance of intergenerational influence becomes another main theme in these books.

Perhaps the one striking difference between adult and children's fiction by Aboriginal authors lies in tone. As King notes, early Native writers often wrote about the clash between Indians and non-Indians so that confrontation, conflict, and alienation were major themes in their writing.[7] Agnes Grant in "Contemporary Native Women's Voices in Literature" and Armand Garnet Ruffo in "Why Native Literature?" have made similar observations: "Native literature often confronts readers with a history that is stark and unredeemable," writes Grant, "because the historic treatment of Natives was callous" (125); Ruffo emphasizes that, because many Native Canadian writers see themselves as still always colonized, their writing faces "with an unblinking eye the realities of what it means to be a people under siege. For Native people, this is the history of the Americas and the legacy of colonialism."[8] Native literature for adults then, as Ruffo and Grant emphasize, is fundamentally protest literature, which includes both darkness and anger but also crucially a sense of cultural affirmation, renewal, and hope.

Picture books for children, in contrast, notably lack the anger and siege mentality found in adult fiction. In fact, unlike adult fiction, which tends to foreground such issues as poverty, poor health, substance abuse, lack of educational or employment opportunities, and other inequities still all too prevalent in many Aboriginal communities in contemporary Canada, children's fiction notably avoids the portrayal of these realities. Although some Young Adult novels by Aboriginal authors—for instance, Lee Maracle's *Will's Garden* and Ruby Slipperjack's *Little Voice*—do engage with political issues, past and present, and sometimes even with anger, fictional picture books almost without exception do not. In picture books, no matter the age, location, or specific circumstances of the Aboriginal child protagonist, the child's interactions with both family and setting generally are offered as idyllic. An extreme example is Elaine McLeod's *Lessons from Mother Earth*, where five-year-old Tess visits her grandmother in the country and learns through her help that all of nature is a garden that can be harvested, but only if it is respected. The soft watercolours by Colleen Wood, which emphasize beauty and harmony between the earth and humans, younger and older generations, help to romanticize a scene fundamentally rendered ahistorical through the grandmother's isolated location, clothing, and actions. Similarly, in *Morning on the Lake* by Jan Bourdeau Waboose, the interconnectedness of nature and people and young and old are the main themes of the story in which a young boy goes on a day-long journey with his grandfather into a landscape depicted as untouched by civilization. Again the illustrations emphasize isolation and a world devoid of contemporary concerns or colonial history. Not only do the fictional picture books typically foreground the idyllic, though usually not to the degree of the two examples just given, but readers approaching this body of work typically do so as well.[9]

The pressures to produce, through writing and reading, positive images of Nativeness come from the history of colonization and a desire to counter the contemporary stereotypes of the drunken, lazy, or promiscuous Indian, or the historical ones of the bloodthirsty warrior, Noble Savage, or seductive Indian maiden. Such pressures also emerge from general expectations of age appropriateness surrounding children's literature, especially the picture book form, which is typically aimed at the youngest readers, and particularly from the assumption that children's innocence should be protected. Yet, for reasons we discuss in our conclusion, in the readings that follow, rather than focus on the idyllic nature of these books as is the tendency to do, we would like to read them as a form of protest literature that underscores if not anger and siege mentality, then the sources of anger and siege mentality dramatically foregrounded in most adult Aboriginal fiction. As Emma LaRocque notes, "[M]uch of Native writing, whether blunt or subtle, is protest literature in that it speaks to the processes of our colonization: dispossession, objectification, marginalization, and that constant struggle for cultural survival expressed in the movement for structural and psychological self-determination" (xviii).

In short, we want to borrow from Armand Garnet Ruffo's conception of adult Aboriginal writing as typified by the inclusion of two influences or branches, the spiritual/mythic/sacred and the political/historical/secular:

> It is these inherent traditions and values, then, emphasizing what we may call a holistic, connected, or integrated approach to life, that one finds

throughout the work. However, for those who may think that Native literature is solely about spiritual matters (which much literature about Native people tries to be), I must reiterate that the contemporary Native world-view is postcontact, and therefore also inherently secular/political.

In adult fiction with its darker themes, this secular/political branch is more visible than in children's literature, where the general trajectory of the Aboriginal child needing to learn traditional knowledges through the help of an elder, parent, or grandparent emphasizes the spiritual branch. We argue that, as in adult fiction, both branches exist in many of the fictional picture books, so that locating the secular/historical side becomes a problem of reading and not content. In what follows we foreground a way of reading that teases out the secular/political allusions in the text or pictures or in the relationship between text and picture, and thus emphasizes this body of work as a form of protest literature.[10]

Because the concept of home has been such a politically charged one in Canadian Aboriginal communities and literature, it offers a particularly fruitful site for our readings. What home means and the forces that threaten it have been of concern to Aboriginal authors at least since the publication of Maria Campbell's *Half-Breed* (1973). In Campbell's account of a Métis community in Saskatchewan, "the road allowance people" as she calls them, home is difficult to return to because the independence and pride of the Métis have been eroded by forces that have alienated them from their lands and culture. The challenge depicted in Campbell's text of "returning home," of revitalizing past traditions and reconnecting with the land and peoples, parallels a challenge felt by many Aboriginal peoples across Canada today. For this reason, Anishinabe author Louise Erdrich writes: "We are *nomadic*, both by choice ... and more often by necessity" (qtd. in Eigenbrod 70). For many Aboriginal peoples, this homelessness, which Erdrich terms "nomadic," is not a desired state; it is not the nomadism celebrated by today's poststructuralists who, according to John Durham Peters in *Exile, Nomadism, and Diaspora*, "find illusory the quest for any fixed identity or homesite" (32); it is not the nomadism of Deleuze and Guattari, who use the term to emphasize a commitment to deterritorialization; it is not the "unhoused, decentered and exilic energies" which Edward Said describes in *Culture and Imperialism*.[11] Rather, as Cree scholar Neal McLeod notes, "'[b]eing home' means to be a nation, to have access to land, to be able to raise your own children, and to have political control. It involves having a collective sense of dignity" (17). As McLeod's comment makes clear, the two traditional or spiritual worldviews we want to take up in our discussion below—the importance of family and a non-competitive view of nature—have real-world implications tied to self-determination of the Aboriginal home, both at the level of family and nation. We focus on the portrayal of these two worldviews, which Aboriginal authors have repeatedly returned to in their picture books to create a nurturing sense of home for Aboriginal children, to tease out how they also evoke real-world and historical implications.

□ □ □

A sense of community and family, notes Armand Garnet Ruffo, is considered among the most predominant themes in Native literature. This emphasis holds true for fictional picture books by Aboriginal authors where elders, parents, and especially grandparents figure repeatedly. So common is this intergenerational theme that books such as Jan Bourdeau Waboose's *SkySisters* and Jordan Wheeler's *Just a Walk* stand as notable exceptions. In Waboose's book, two Ojibwa sisters set off on a cold winter's night to see the Northern Lights, emphasizing their close bond, and in Wheeler's book, an Aboriginal boy goes on a solitary walk in the country, stressing his personal relationship with land and animals. Most often, however, older generations are depicted prominently in the books, primarily in teaching roles. From Dave Bouchard's *The Meaning of Respect*, which depicts a wayward twelve-year-old Cree boy being sent home to the reserve to receive counselling from his Moshum (grandfather), to Michael Arvaarluck Kusugak's *Northern Lights: The Soccer Trails*, which shows how Kataujaq's grandmother helps her granddaughter come to terms with the loss of her mother by teaching her an Inuit legend, to Bonnie Murray's *Li Minoush*, which portrays Thomas learning the importance of preserving his Métis language from his mother, fictional picture books by Aboriginal authors typically depict older generations playing crucial roles in helping Aboriginal children establish or strengthen their place in Aboriginal communities through the passing on of traditional knowledges.

The prominence of a sense of community and family for Aboriginal authors comes as little surprise if we recall the role of the bourgeois patriarchal family in colonial societies such as Canada.[12] As Julia V. Emberley notes in "The Bourgeois Family, Aboriginal Women, and Colonial Governance in Canada: A Study in Feminist Historical and Cultural Materialism," this kind of family "would become the most important social apparatus through which to import various technologies of surveillance to further colonial governance during the late nineteenth and twentieth centuries" (61). Not only was the European bourgeois patriarchal family trans-

planted to the colonial environment and mapped onto indigenous kinship relations, but that family structure came to depend on the colonies
to test and secure a representation of itself as "natural." The results were
catastrophic. Modelled on the hierarchical bourgeois patriarchal family, residential school, foster care, and reservation systems destroyed the traditional functioning of communities and roles of elders, parents, and grandparents. Alcoholism, solvent abuse, sexual abuse, poverty, and youth crime
became and continue to be rampant in communities disoriented by foreign kinship relations.

With recent picture books by Aboriginal authors, we come full circle.
These books seek to intervene in and disrupt the very social apparatus that
helped destroy Aboriginal communities—the bourgeois patriarchal family. Given the magnitude of the problems within Aboriginal communities, witnessed voyeuristically by Canadians practically daily through the
media, the mere depiction of warm, caring Aboriginal extended families
and communities that nurture the development of the Aboriginal child protagonist functions as a form of protest to colonial history. Books such as
Deborah L. Delaronde's *Little Metis and the Metis Sash* and *A Name for
a Metis* and Penny Condon's *My Family* re-establish Aboriginal children
in larger kinship networks to learn values such as love, commitment,
interdependence, and humour. Even books focusing on the nuclear family unit challenge the imposition of the bourgeois patriarchal family structure on Aboriginal communities through positive imagery. Leah Dorian's
Snow Tunnel Sisters, for example, depicts an almost clichéd family of two
sisters and a mother waiting for the father to come home from work so
that they can eat supper together; but, through the illustrations, which
reveal the brown skin and dark hair of the girls and their father, and a
poem written by one of the girls at school in which she calls her father "big,
brown, and warm," the book underscores its role in transforming the
image of the (happy) bourgeois family with father as head of the household as normatively white. Similarly, Darrell W. Pelletier's *The Big Storm*
portrays a boy frightened by a thunderstorm being comforted by his father
who burns sweetgrass against the cityscape we see out of the boy's bedroom window. Not only is tradition brought into a modern urban environment, but the father, with his long braid but dressed in shirt and tie, also
disrupts the conventional image of bourgeois father.

If books such as *Snow Tunnel Sisters* and *The Big Storm* depict the
important roles of fathers, and others such as *The Slapshot Star* by Gloria Miller and *Little White Cabin* by Ferguson Plain, the important roles
of grandfathers and male elders, many others focus on the re-establishment
of matrilineal genealogy and maternal order. This common subtheme

within the intergenerational focus of most picture books by Aboriginal authors arises from the particular harshness of colonial rule toward Aboriginal women. Not only did Aboriginal women lose the exercise of political powers that traditional community structures typically offered them, but they were placed in a hierarchal relationship with their men for the first time. Certainly, Aboriginal men were also disentitled to political power, but in accordance with the bourgeois patriarchal model of family, fraternal links were established between Aboriginal and colonial men, which relied on the subordination of Aboriginal women to both groups (Emberley). This double dispossession results in the strong tendency of Aboriginal women authors to document, as Beverley Rasporich notes, a "discourse of protest, grievance and grief ... that is expressly female and maternal: that of lost, stolen, abandoned, or dead children and ... the motif of the struggles of maternity or of its very loss and absence." The celebratory image of Aboriginal women as mothers and grandmothers in picture books by both male and female Aboriginal authors are numerous. From Don Freed's *Sasquatch Exterminator* with its portrayal of a grandmother whose subversive sense of humour helps her grandson cope with a prank by his friends to Jan Bourdeau Waboose's *Firedancer*s with its more serious depiction of a grandmother who teaches her grandchild how to connect with their ancestors' spirits, these positive depictions of a matrilineal heritage become their own version of protest to colonial history.

Some books, however, go beyond offering positive depictions of the family as their sole decolonizing strategy. For example, in underscoring the processes and effects of colonization, a picture book such as *Jack Pine Fish Camp* by Tina Umpherville, we would argue, goes even further as a form of protest literature. This book describes the protagonist's, Iskotew's, life at the fish camp to which her family moves for eight weeks every summer. Iskotew's fun-filled, daily adventures with her friends are set against two backgrounds that problematize the celebratory portrayal of this way of life: one is the serious business of fishing for families who form the small but viable community at the camp. The importance of fishing for the family's economic survival is emphasized not only by the danger the fishermen face on the open water but by an incident in which Iskotew gets drinks for herself and all her friends at the only store on the island. Used to getting groceries for her mother, who always tells her to put them on their bill, she has no concept of credit. Very upset by her generous gesture to her friends, revealing how even a few soft drinks can disrupt the annual economic well-being of the family, her father teaches his daughter a crucial lesson about the capitalist system of enterprise—so unlike Aboriginal systems that emphasized reciprocity and sharing—where credit eventually needs to be repaid. As the book shows, Iskotew never again mistakes store items as "free," though it does lose her a certain popularity among her peers.

The other background is also important for the hardworking community: weekly entertainment for the families living at Jack Pine, who travel to Brochet for Saturday night movies at the old church. While most of the families attend, Iskotew and her dad especially love to watch them, never missing a movie. On the particular Saturday night depicted in the illustrations, a Western is showing and the reader sees an image of cowboys shooting guns on the big screen (see Figure 1). Not only does this image, shown to an Aboriginal community in a church of all places, underscore how the internalization of colonization allows the audience essentially to enjoy watching the history of its own disenfranchisement, but also how a specific Aboriginal father models for his daughter an unproblematic acceptance of Euro-American ways. Other details, such as the incoming planes that pick up fish and drop off Western comic books and treats for the children as well as Iskotew's older brother who has been away attending high school, also emphasize the impact colonialism has had on even remote Aboriginal communities and specifically evokes the circumstances of Aboriginal children, who were taken from these communities by plane only a few decades earlier.

Like *Jack Pine Fish Camp*, Deborah L. Delaronde's *Flour Sack Flora* will not let the reader forget how the mainstream world affects even isolated Aboriginal communities and families. This book tells the story of a young Métis girl named Flora who desperately wants to go to town with her parents on one of their monthly shopping expeditions. Her parents, however, sadly tell her she cannot go with them because she does not have a pretty dress to wear and they cannot afford to buy her one. The book follows Flora on her quest for a dress—a quest that takes her to her grandmother, who eventually makes her one out of a flour sack. As the historical note at the end of the book explains, many remote communities did not have access to fabric, so flour sacks, which were made of unbleached cotton, were dyed to suit many purposes. To decorate her dress, Flora and her grandmother enlist the help of several older women in the community, trading some of Flora's special treasures as well as her services for ribbon, lace, and embroidery thread.

While the book essentially celebrates the resourcefulness of the women in Flora's community and their commitment to the younger generation represented by Flora, the grandmother's role in this picture book is nonetheless far more complicated than those of the purely positive portrayals of matrilineal heritage. Certainly, her actions, that is, the making of a dress for Flora, reveal her love for her granddaughter, but they also reveal how the Métis community depicted here, in spite of its implied isolation, is always affected by the white colonizer's world. The object of desire in this story is a dress, as the illustrations reveal, which conforms to the style set by mainstream society. The grandmother and her friends unquestioningly accept this style as their touchstone of beauty and, more importantly, respectability. One of Grandma's friends, Gladys, fondly recalls her own first trip to town years before and the dress that she wore. In a sense, then, acquiring a mainstream-styled dress becomes a rite of passage to womanhood for these Métis women, a rite in which they themselves actively participate. All the women of her grandmother's generation rally around Flora, letting her trade goods and services for ribbons and lace to make the plain flour sack more beautiful.

Images of the mainstream world are everywhere in the illustrations to *Flour Sack Flora*, from the clothing to the furniture, but they particularly emerge in the bags of Five Roses or Robin Hood flour. These bags become the primary symbol of colonization in the story; because of the frequency of their appearance, they are a constant reminder of the arrival of Europeans in North America and the detrimental impact of this arrival on Aboriginal life. The whole ritual of dressing in mainstream clothes underscores this too. If we think of a novel such as Maria Campbell's *Half-Breed*, in which the negative reactions of the white townsfolk to the materially poor Métis who visited their towns fostered shame and helped erode the spirits of a once proud people, then we can see the shame that is implicit here in Flora's parents' refusal to take her to town in her regular clothes. The degree of shame is highlighted when Flora goes back to her parents with her dress but they still refuse to take her to town because she only has moccasins to wear with it. In the story's conclusion, Flora's parents help to find her a pair of white shoes and we last see her in the car on the way to town. Overall, this book, which celebrates a distinctly women's community and passing on of a specifically female tradition of dressing for town, also importantly underscores the problematic impact of mainstream values on the remote community.

□ □ □

Family becomes a popular site for foregrounding both tradition and colonial history; so too does the relationship between people and land as portrayed in picture books by Aboriginal authors. While images of home in mainstream texts often centre on the physical structure in which a child lives and learns lessons about the self, Aboriginal texts de-emphasize the importance of the physical structure to show that the home necessarily includes both land and natural environment. Indeed, the home evoked in Aboriginal children's literature is rarely limited to the physical structure in which the characters live. Instead, Aboriginal children's books posit that the well-being, happiness, and even the very survival of Aboriginal children, their families, and communities are inextricably tied to an access to both land and resources. For example, the first paragraph of Tomson Highway's *Dragonfly Kites* introduces us to what the author calls the "summer home" of the two boys Joe and Cody and their parents—"a tent near a lake," near where the parents catch their food. But clearly this home is just one of many special places the family has lived, for we are next told that "[t]here are hundreds of lakes in northern Manitoba, so they never stayed on the same one twice. The lakes had beautiful islands and forests and beaches and clear water." The image of home, then, is that of a vast and rich land that this family relies upon for its living. Similarly, in Elaine McLeod's *Lessons from Mother Earth*, Grandma's physical home, a log structure located in a remote, idyllic setting, figures prominently in Colleen Wood's watercolours as an extension of the natural world itself. Not only is her home nestled in a luscious valley teeming with all kinds of flora and fauna, but with no door in the doorway of Grandma's cabin there is little divide between interior and exterior worlds. One of the things both Highway's and McLeod's books do, then, is to make explicit the traditional reliance of many Aboriginal peoples on a large homeland for their sustenance.

Although the two examples just given highlight the interconnectedness of land and people common to Aboriginal worldviews, at work in most picture books, as in real life, are two very different sets of operating principles regarding land ownership. While traditional Aboriginal relationships with the land were communal and conservationist, Euro-Canadians were motivated primarily by private commercial interests (see Peter J. Usher). If, as Marie Battiste states, colonial structures and tendencies "can only be resisted and healed by reliance on Indigenous knowledge and its imaginative processes" (xix), then one of the important contributions of Aboriginal authors is the possibility their books offer readers to explore issues currently in the political arena, such as Aboriginal rights, land claims, and self-determination.

In Deborah Delaronde's *Flour Sack Flora*, which we discussed above, Gary Chartrand's illustrations of the landscape function to at once emphasize and mitigate the impact of colonialism on the Métis community. Like the image of flour sacks, landscapes, usually seen through windows, recur frequently.[13] These images call dramatic attention to the physical and natural beauty of the home that Flora is so eager to leave. Since pictures in picture books not only exercise the visual and aesthetic sensibilities of viewers but also aid in the telling of stories, as Perry Nodelman has observed (*Words about Pictures* vii), the dialectic in Delaronde's book between the "here" of Flora's community and the "there" of the white town warrants close study. The grandmother and Flora often are seen hard at work making the dress against this background. In fact, the term "background," evoking a kind of secondary, less important quality, does not adequately convey the importance of these pictures. Because of their frequency, and because of the ease with which the women work within this environment, the landscape becomes, to echo our earlier quotation, "a landscape of the familiar, a landscape of collective memories." It shapes the very nature and functioning of the community, the necessity for barter, the general resourcefulness, and the working together of the people who live there. Often landscape appears in pictures along with flour sacks (see Figure 2). The balance in this illustration is achieved by putting the women around the window, as far away from the flour sack as possible, with the quilts also between the window and the flour sacks. This progression imitates one of the main points of the story—the mitigating of colonization by insisting on one's own history. Thus we see here the progression from left to right, of flour sacks, the transformation of those flour sacks into the Métis women's own art, to what was always there, even before colonization: the landscape.

The natural environment takes on an even more significant role in Grant Anderson's *Willy the Curious Frog from Pruden's Bog*. The threatened destruction of a marsh home to numerous species of wildlife and waterfowl is the subject of this book, which centres on two characters, Willy, a frog whose home is the marsh and who is described in the first sentence as "an out to lunch but home for dinner sort of a frog," and Benny, a boy who likes to play in the marsh (2). The story goes back and forth between the characters as they each, on their own, set out to stop the development of the marsh into condominiums and a golf course. The parallels in this story between the plight of animals about to lose their homes and the historical reality of homelessness endured by many Aboriginal peoples since the first settlement of Europeans in North America is evident in this book partly because it plays strongly on the oral tradition, in Cree and other Aboriginal cultures, in which animals have characteristics that make them appear more like humans than animals. The young boy Benny functions as a potential colonizer; during their one and only meeting, Benny catches Willy and wants to take him home. Benny's intentions are naïve but nonetheless threatening: he holds Willy up in a vulnerable position and looks at him as though he is a curiosity (see Figure 3). Willy's face expresses fear and shock, emphasizing that Benny needs to learn about the fragility of the natural environment and the detrimental impact even this one small action can have. The lesson begins when his father refuses his son's request that he be allowed to take Willy home, saying the frog belongs in his own home, the marsh, and not in an eight-year-old's bedroom. In addition, Willy and his marsh friends have to learn to work together to stand up for their rights in the face of daunting opposition. When the animals group together to resist the takeover of their land, it is the developers' turn to be shocked and dismayed (see Figure 4). By referencing the earlier illustration of Benny holding Willy, this picture emphasizes the successful reversal of power relations between human and animal/white colonizer and Native.

The word "home" is used many times throughout the book to refer to the marsh where Willy and his friends live but, significantly, is never used to refer to human dwellings. Clearly, the threat to turn Pruden's Bog into homes for people in the form of condominiums draws attention to the fact that the physical spaces that humans occupy are often situated on land that was taken from others, that our homes are built on the homelands of others. This story suggests that stopping or reversing this process is a two-way street. The colonizer has to learn, like Benny, the value of a different way of life, and Aboriginal peoples have to take an active role in reclaiming land, as they are in many real-life land-claim scenarios. If in *Flour Sack Flora*, the landscape mediates the effects of colonialism, so it does here as well. In *Willy the Curious Frog*, however, the landscape, because it is under threat, is more at centre stage than it is in *Flour Sack Flora*. Both books place the fundamental responsibility on the human community. Without people actively working together, the result is a loss of history, culture, and land, as we see in *Willy*.

Conclusion

Not all fictional picture books by Aboriginal authors evoke the historical/secular influences we see in the group of books we look at closely for this paper; for example, we would be hard-pressed to see the spectre of colonialism in the two books we mention in our introduction, *Lessons from Mother Earth* and *Morning on the Lake*. Others we did not discuss evoke a colonial history much more explicitly, for instance, Beatrice Culleton Mosionier's *Christopher's Folly*, where the legacy of Christopher Columbus is alluded to directly. In this book, an Aboriginal boy named Christopher has a dream in which he travels by ship to a land unpopulated by people and through his greed causes the disappearance of the buffalo and wolf. Most, however, follow the pattern of the books we address above, and thus require a reading strategy that teases out the protest from the overlying idyllic images drawn largely from tradition. Marilyn Dumont and Paula Gunn Allen highlight the value of this kind of reading strategy. Thinking about her own position as an urban Métis dislocated from her extended family and Alberta Métis Settlements, Dumont questions the expectations surrounding the role of tradition in Native writing. She argues, "[T]here is a continuum of exposure to traditional experience in native culture, [and] some of us have been more exposed to it than others" (47). In spite of this continuum, the popular image of Native peoples includes notions of rural and traditional; further, Aboriginal writers are supposed to infuse their writing with "symbols of the native world view, that is: the circle, mother earth, the number four or the trickster figure" (47). Paula Gunn Allen, commenting on what she calls the second wave of Native literature (1974 to 1994), similarly notes,

> For the most part, the second wave of Native fiction depicted Native life as exotic and alien. It was portrayed as marginal, and the catchall term "Indian" unfailingly evoked images of Native people as a variety of fauna, as profoundly spiritual, and as dreadfully victimized—sometimes all at the same time. "Real Indians" were identified by feathers, buckskins, tipis, sweat lodges, pipes, vision quests, psychedelic-induced shamanic experiences, or "medicine power," as well as by a belief system that included the idea that buffalo, coyote, bear, and eagle were possessed of supernatural powers to which the good guys of all races could gain access. (9)

In essence, Allen points out, this literature's major popular draw was its "near-caricaturing of Native life and thought" (9). And this is precisely the danger of reading these books without an emphasis on protest. Because of their focus on tradition and the surface romanticizing of Aboriginal ways, as a group these books can too easily be read as caricatures of Aboriginal life and peoples. As Dumont suggests, this romanticizing merely supports, rather than intervenes in, the nineteenth-century idea of Native culture as static, which arose from the notion of the vanishing Indian and was compounded by Canada's Indian Acts and assimilationist policies (47). Thus we want to avoid reading strategies that merely replicate old ways of seeing Aboriginal peoples negatively as a dying race, or conversely, as is more common recently with the advent of new-age spiritualism, as offering Western culture an antidote to its materialistic culture. As Ruffo notes, this "is essentially a reworking of the noble savage motif tempered by the contemporary agenda of self-fulfillment and preservation."

This strategy also allows us to get beyond the idea that the main function of these books, and other multicultural books, lies in having Aboriginal children see themselves in literature, sometimes for the first time. Certainly this power cannot be underestimated. It helped drive the initial boom in Canadian children's books in the mid-1970s when some of the first children's publishers in Canada, such as Annick Press and Kids Can Press, began to produce books so that young Canadians could read books that reflected their own culture, and it has helped to drive the boom in multicultural children's books in more recent years. And, as studies have pointed out, children who see themselves and other ethnic groups in books tend to develop more positive attitudes to differences, their own and others (Wham, Barnhart, and Cook). Yet in what ways does this group of books, which sanitizes the living conditions of Aboriginal youths, accurately represent the daily realities of many Aboriginal peoples and communities today? We barely see any "typical" family strife in these books, much less portrayals of the extraordinary hardships and challenges many Aboriginal peoples encounter. As we have tried to show, however, there are traces of the legacy of colonialism in these works that can problematize a simple portrayal of Aboriginal tradition and offer Aboriginal and non-Aboriginal children a glimpse of the violent and complicated history of North America within a framework that emphasizes hope and renewal. For instance, at the same time that Tomson Highway's *Dragonfly Kites* celebrates the natural world surrounding Joe and Cody's summer home and the boys' exuberance at play, it is also a disturbing story for adult readers of Highway's fictional autobiographical novel *Kiss of the Fur Queen*. The innocence of Joe and Cody in *Dragonfly Kites* recalls the novel's brothers, Champion and Ooneemeetoo Okimasis, fictional counterparts of Highway and his brother René, before they experience the horrors of a Catholic residential school. The connection between these two texts is explicit and deliberate; prior to the scene in *Kiss of the Fur Queen* in which Champion is whisked away from his family in an airplane, Highway tells us that the boys had observed planes before, "drifting in the wind like dragonflies." While younger audiences need not understand the metaphoric significance of Joe and Cody in the children's book catching and transforming dragonflies into kites in order to appreciate the story, the reference to dragonflies forms one of the book's colonial subtexts that could help introduce younger audiences to some of the author's political concerns. Similarly, in *Willy the Curious Frog from Pruden's Bog*, the proposed development of the animals' land into a golf course echoes several recent Native land claims in Canada, such as the Oka conflict of 1990 or the more recent dispute at Caledonia, in which Aboriginal peoples have attempted to block the development of their traditional territories and sacred grounds.

While not all the children's books evoke the spectre of history to the degree that those we explored here do, we believe, with Ruffo, that, because of the magnitude of the upheaval caused by colonialism, "Native writers while writing from their individual perspectives are in a sense adjuncts of the collective experience, of what we may call 'community.'" As a whole, the body of work for children by Aboriginal authors intervenes to offer understanding of and hope for Native communities to Aboriginal and non-Aboriginal children. Challenges to the idea of the bourgeois family, and the connection in children's picture books between a people's survival and their access to land, illustrate the limitations of celebratory readings of these literatures that focus on more "child-friendly" topics. Clearly, a focus on themes such as the spiritual/mythic/sacred undervalues or elides the political contexts and concerns of many Aboriginal authors.

□ □ □

Notes

1 For a more complete description of the aims and challenges of this project, see the introduction to Paul DePasquale and Doris Wolf's "A Select Bibliography of Canadian Picture Books for Children by Aboriginal Authors."

2 The first formal expression in Canada that the traditional stories and histories of the elders "should be collected, preserved, and made accessible ... before it is too late" (Canada 88) was made in the Royal Commission Report on Aboriginal Peoples in 1996.

3 For a discussion of Theytus Books and two other Aboriginal-run presses in Canada, the Gabriel Dumont Institute and Pemmican Publications, see DePasquale and Wolf, "A Select Bibliography" (144–45).

4 Writing in 1987, Judith Saltman observed that the picture-book genre was the fastest-growing, most aggressively marketed, and vital sector of the book publishing industry in Canada (19). More recently, Perry Nodelman and Mavis Reimer write in *The Pleasures of Children's Literature*, "[W]hen most people think of books for children, they think first of picture books: short books that tell stories or convey information with relatively few words but with pictures on every page. They are right to do so. Not only is the picture book the most common form of children's literature, it is also a form almost exclusively reserved for children" (274).

5 See our introduction to "A Select Bibliography of Canadian Picture Books for Children by Aboriginal Writers" for a few notable examples and a discussion of some of the problems with voice appropriation. Laura Smyth Groening in *Listening to Old Woman Speak: Natives and AlterNatives in Canadian Literature* provides a useful background to the issue of the appropriation of Aboriginal voices in Canada (4–5).

6 An exception is Jeannette Armstrong's *Enwhisteetkwa: Walk in Water*, which is set in 1860 in the Okanagan Valley and depicts what life might have been like.

7 Although King indicates this theme has all but disappeared in recent Aboriginal writing, when we think about books such as *Kiss of the Fur Queen* by Tomson Highway, *Monkey Beach* by Eden Robinson, *In the Shadows of Evil* by Beatrice Culleton Mosionier, it seems that confrontation, alienation, and anger continue to appear in adult Native literature.

8 Paula Gunn Allen makes a similar point about the second wave of Native American fiction (mid-1970s to the mid-1990s), stating it reveals a "reasserted often deeply angry, Native identity" (8).

9 In the introduction to our select bibliography we discuss the trend, which we trace to Beverly Slapin and Doris Seale's influential American publication, *Through Indian Eyes: The Native Experience in Books for Children* (1987; repr. 1992), to identify culturally sensitive books by and about Aboriginal peoples. This book's recommendations to help readers identify works that offer non-stereotypical portrayals of Aboriginal peoples promote, we feel, non-critical, highly subjective criteria that tend to romanticize Aboriginal peoples and their traditional ways of life. See 149–50 and 151, fn 5.

10 See Louise Saldanha's essay in this volume for her work on children's books by women of colour in which she addresses modes of reading representations of multiculturalism.

11 For a discussion of Aboriginal responses to post-colonialism and neo-colonialism in Canada today, see DePasquale, "Natives and Settlers Now and Then: Refractions of the Colonial Past in the Present."

12 See Andrew O'Malley's essay in this volume for his discussion of the portrayal of domesticity in the nineteenth-century children's book by Catherine Parr Traill, *Canadian Crusoes*, and its relationship to imperialism.

13 See Deborah Schnitzer's essay in this volume for a very different discussion of windows in *Flour Sack Flora*.

CHAPTER 6

⮕ **At Home on Native Land: A Non-Aboriginal Canadian Scholar Discusses Aboriginality and Property in Canadian Double-Focalized Novels for Young Adults**

Perry Nodelman

This essay will eventually do what its title suggests. But after much anxiety and many false starts, I've concluded I can't discuss Aboriginality in novels for young adults without first discussing my non-Aboriginal, non-young self—specifically, the history of my involvement with one of the texts I plan to consider: *False Face*, a novel about young people and Aboriginality by the also non-Aboriginal, non-young Welwyn Katz. That history has made me uncertain that I should be writing this essay at all, for reasons highly relevant to the issues the essay needs to engage with.

I first read *False Face* in 1987 as one of the three judges of the Groundwood International Fiction contest. The contest was part of a scheme by publishers in various countries to provide young readers around the globe with fictional representations of one another. I assume Groundwood invited me to be one of the judges for the Canadian competition because of the reputation I had developed as a scholar of children's literature. I had what Pierre Bourdieu calls "a capital of consecration": "a known, recognized name, a capital of consecration implying a power to consecrate objects (with a trademark or signature) or persons (through publication, exhibition, etc.) and therefore to give value, and to appropriate the profits from this operation" (*Field* 75). As a judge in 1987, I used my capital to support *False Face* as the book that clearly deserved to win the competition. I did so in spite of my own uncertainty about whether it was realistic enough even to qualify for the competition. *False Face* describes how the discovery of an Iroquois false face mask in a bog in London, Ontario, allows the unsettling release of the spirits the mask contains. As a committed rationalist blind to forces beyond those perceived by my five senses, I have trouble accepting the existence of supernatural creatures generally, including these Aboriginal ones. In 1987, I was arrogant enough to think that the presence of these forces of meaningful significance to members of a culture other than my own marked the novel as a fantasy. Nevertheless, I believed then—I still believe now—in the power of the novel, and I happily used my position as a judge and the power of my reputation as a critic of children's literature to downplay what I saw as its fantasy elements and argue for the realism of its descriptions of contemporary youth and culture. I used my capital of consecration to consecrate it by working to ensure it won the competition.

Now I wonder if I used my capital wisely. In 1987, I was more or less ignorant about Iroquois culture, about Aboriginal cultures generally. To show how very ignorant: a few years earlier, I had felt quite comfortable about publicly stating that we Canadians had a heritage of fairy tales from "our European ancestors" ("Riding Hood" 17), adding that the versions of narratives from Canadian Aboriginal cultures so often published by many Canadian children's publishers "have less to do with us than we assume they should" (17). As Agnes Grant pointed out in a subsequent response, my self-serving universalizing "we" and "us" had erased the existence of Aboriginal Canadians altogether. Knowing better now, I wish I had not spoken so confidently then.

So what now do I know (or at least think I know) better? Most obviously, I've learned to be concerned about issues of appropriation—about the questions that arise when writers, artists, anthropologists, museum curators, and others engage with cultures not their own. Five years after I served on the Groundwood jury, the Anishinabe writer Lenore Keeshig-Tobias wrote, "The issue is not just a white perspective of history, an oversimplification of Native spirituality and lifeways, or mean-spirited and racist rendering of our stories.... The issue is cultural theft, the theft of voice. It's about power" (64). A year later, the Okanagan writer Jeanette Armstrong echoed these views and suggested the practical implications of the misuses of power: "What's at issue there is the ability of ... non-native writers—without malice in most cases—to draw a picture of Native contemporary lifestyle and thinking and so on which creates a false image in the mind of the reading public, and which creates problems for contemporary Native people" ("Body" 11). Thinking about these issues made me conscious of the inadequacy of my earlier views.

In terms specifically of *False Face*, I've realized the negative implications of my reading of its supernatural elements as fantasy. I've also become aware of what I didn't think of at all in 1987: the ways in which, in a novel that is centrally about questions of appropriation—to whom the Aboriginal artifacts it revolves around belong—the non-Aboriginal Katz speaks for and in the voice of a protagonist whose father was Iroquois and who thinks of himself as Aboriginal. In so doing, she may well have created, in Armstrong's words, "a false image in the mind of the reading public." In an article published in an issue of *CCL/LCJ*, the Canadian children's literature journal that I guest-edited, Cornelia Hoogland suggests that she had:

> In creating a distinctly pure (albeit negative) environment [in her description of the Iroquois reserve as a purely non-White space], Katz disallows tensions which need to be voiced and thus the challenges to which native Canadians as well as non-native Canadians need to respond. Otherwise we just replace the injurious *colonist* with the good-intentioned *White lady* writer, replace one ideology with another, one power broker with another. (33)

In a subsequent *CCL/LCJ* interview, Katz complained that Hoogland's views were "unfair, both to me and *False Face*" (Micros 53), and addressed the issue of appropriation: "Some native people have responded ... with such outrage (that I, a white person, should dare to tell 'their' stories; that I, a white person, should use the sacred symbol of the false face in stories at all)" (58). In her defence, Katz argued that "all stories worth thinking about are at bottom about important things like faith, love/hate, prejudice, etc., and there is no way to let such issues into a book if you leave out everything that is sacred to somebody!" (58). Those comments led me to my next public statement about these matters, a response to Katz in *CCL/LCJ* that defended the kinds of readings that so upset her and revealed the extent to which they had changed my own understanding of *False Face*:

> At the end, Tom thinks of his own tears as "not red and not black, not White and not Indian. Just tears from someone who was a person, nothing else" (145). This clearly implies that Tom is most significantly a unique individual—a being essentially separate from his racial background. And in terms of how I read the novel as a whole up to this point, this rings false to me.... I resist the conclusion that what we humans essentially are is something inside us, an invisible entity separate from our bodies and our physical being. To have a body, to be a being with and not just in a body, is to have a skin—a skin whose colour does indeed signal our connections

with various other people past and present in a variety of ways. It matters. To dismiss it is to dismiss a significant aspect of what it means to be human and to live with other people. ("My Own" 91)

My knowledge of the question of appropriation had led me to an awareness of the negative implications of the ways in which the novel made Aboriginality a matter of no significance. If each of us is just "a person, nothing else," then so much for First Nations land claims and efforts to redress past mistreatments people have suffered as members of specific cultural groups.

I still admire *False Face* for many of the reasons I admired it in 1987. It has literary qualities—style, pacing, characterization—I think of as the ones that make a text worthy of consecration. But now I find myself wondering whether what works in it for me might also be what works to support the ideologies I was once unaware of and now find troublesome— whether what I understand to be its excellence might be inextricable from the system of power relations that supports appropriation.

That possibility is supported by the fact that not only *False Face* but also many of the other novels for young adults about Aboriginality that I've been thinking about for this essay have received significant awards or been otherwise identified as possessing quality. Furthermore, all of these novels are by non-Aboriginal writers. Novels for young people by Aboriginal writers tend to be published by more marginal presses—especially ones that focus specifically on Aboriginal texts—and rarely receive as much attention or acclaim from the institutions that have power in the field of Canadian children's literature.[1]

The non-Aboriginal backgrounds of their writers is not the only thing that the acclaimed novels have in common. My interest in thinking further about them stemmed from my growing awareness of their remarkable similarities—similarities that texts by Aboriginals don't seem to share.[2] The ability of the novels by non-Aboriginals to accrue a capital of consecration unavailable to novels by Aboriginals might well have as much to do with their similar views of Aboriginality as with any estimation of their literary excellence that might be assumed to be non-ideological—as I assumed in 1987. Has the field co-opted and promulgated a distorted vision of Aborginality for its own non-Aboriginal purposes? If it has, what am I to make of my own accrual of capital in it?

Despite—in fact, because of—my awareness of the need to ask that question, I see my change of views since 1987 as a move forward. I see more now. The more I see matters to me, as a scholar and as a citizen of my country—especially since part of what I see is an awareness of my own possible complicity that might lead me to find ways of making myself and, I hope, others less complicit. Nevertheless, the change in my views is also what gives me pause here. The more I become aware of the implications of Katz's willingness to write about such matters, to speak of Aboriginality and to do it often in the voice of an Aboriginal character, the more I become aware of the similar implications of my own speaking here. If I believe that Katz might well have thought further before speaking of these things, then what about Nodelman?

Let me consider, first, Nodelman's choice of focusing on texts about Aboriginality by non-Aboriginals like himself and leaving texts by Aboriginal writers unexamined. While I understand that my doing so might replicate the marginalizing of Aboriginal texts in the field of Canadian children's literature, the main focus of my interest in these books—how the culture of consecration operates—requires me to take that chance. As Terry Goldie says of his own study of texts about Aboriginality, "[M]y interest is not in the indigenes but in the image of the indigenes, a white image" (11).

But even that interest is problematic. Speaking of the controversy that developed some years ago over the non-Aboriginal W.P. Kinsella's depiction of Aboriginals in his novels set on the Hobbema reserve, Joseph Pivato says, "The very fact that the cause against appropriation in this case was taken up by other white writers and academics in Canada rather than by the Natives of the community ... reveals the paternalistic position in which this particular group of Native peoples still finds itself. Even their white advocates are guilty of speaking for them." As the comments by Keeshig-Tobias and Armstrong I've quoted show, Pivato is wrong about "Natives of the community" not taking up the cause, but his belief that they haven't is itself revealing. The presence of non-Native voices with more capital of consecration speaking for the Native cause appears to have prevented his consciousness of the Native ones—to, in effect, silence them. As Linda Alcoff suggests in "The Problem of Speaking for Others," "[T]he practice of privileged persons speaking for or on behalf of less privileged persons has actually resulted (in many cases) in increasing or reinforcing the oppression of the group spoken for" (7).

For Alcoff, speech of all sorts is inevitably and already political: "Rituals of speaking are politically constituted by power relations of domination, exploitation, and subordination. Who is speaking, who is spoken of, and who listens is a result, as well as an act, of political struggle" (15). If that's true, then speaking for others or choosing not to are equally political acts, equally prone therefore to re-inscribe the power relations of the context from which they emerge. Choosing not to speak—not to write this essay, for instance, as I have been tempted to do—might represent a self-protective avoidance, "a retreat," as Alcoff suggests, "into a narcissistic yuppie lifestyle in which a privileged person takes no responsibility for her society whatsoever" (17). I must choose, then, to be responsible enough to speak of what I see—but to speak with a consciousness of the implications of my doing so, and therefore with an effort never to forget my own possible complicity or re-inscription of the very same counter-productive ideological practices I am working to reveal in the texts I want to discuss.

I must try, furthermore, to avoid being one of the writers Alcoff describes who "offer up in the spirit of 'honesty' autobiographical information about themselves usually at the beginning of their discourse as a kind of disclaimer ... without critical interrogation of the bearing of such an autobiography on what is about to be said" (25). I will, therefore, consider the degree to which my analysis is complicit in what it critiques once I have done the critiquing.

□ □ □

In the years since appropriation first became a matter of widespread public discussion, I've been aware of the development of an extensive academic discourse on questions of Aboriginality and indigenousness—aware, but only minimally knowledgeable about matters thus far peripheral to my own research concerns. In the light of my awareness of the dangers of writing as a non-Aboriginal about Aboriginal matters and the vast gaps in my knowledge of relevant contexts, it's worth asking how I came to do so in the first place. The answer is simply that the logic of the larger project I was working on led me there. That it did so once more suggests the degree to which these issues of Aboriginality and appropriation are central to the ideology of children's publishing in Canada.

The work began as a project in a course in Canadian children's literature at the University of Winnipeg. Mavis Reimer and I were both teaching sections of this course in the same term, and as we later described in "Teaching Canadian Children's Literature: Learning to Know More," we decided to organize them around the possibility that the specificities of the cultural and economic climate might result in the books for young people published in Canada sharing characteristics that distinguished them from those produced elsewhere. The course resulted in a list of qualities shared by the texts we both taught, including one that particularly intrigued me:

> Most (but not all) of the novels switch repeatedly between two contexts, or
> have two stories going at the same time. For example, the novel might be
> structured around two different points in a series of events (flashbacks), two

different focalizing characters, or two different historical settings.... The two contexts usually oppose the past and the present in some way, with resolutions often valuing letting the past go or moving beyond it. (34–35)

Intrigued by this pattern, I decided to think further specifically about what I came to call double-focalized texts—ones that present the alternating viewpoints of two (and occasionally three) focalizing characters on the events of the story they share. As I reported in two subsequent articles, "Of Solitudes and Borders" and "A Monochromatic Mosaic," I learned that the more than thirty double-focused novels published in Canada in the last few decades tended to express similar concerns.

Of different races, sexes, or social classes, the central characters in these novels offer a version of what W.H. New calls the "boundary rhetoric" (5) prevalent in Canadian writing, an interest in the borders between people and the ways they might be crossed. While the novels don't always insist on the overt cultural or political significance of their characters' differences, they do tend to have a metonymic resonance in relation to Canada's public mythology of multiculturalism and reveal some of the same problematic aspects of that policy discussed by Louise Saldanha elsewhere in this book. As is literally true for members of different cultures in the context of Canadian society as a whole, the focalized characters turn out to be connected despite their own perceptions of isolation, and they alternately express differing views of sometimes different but always connected events until they come to share the same story in the same space—as do Canadians in the public mythology of multiculturalism. The shared space—a home or a cottage or a piece of property—represents a desirable community, one that purports to allow difference but actually tends to erase it. Those entitled to share in that space—claim it as their property—can do so because they've each given up their right to own all of it individually by themselves, and the community forms by expelling those self-seeking isolates who represent a danger to it—as, Saldanha suggests, does the community of Canadian multiculturalism, which "has functioned to neutralize ... the cultural and racial diversity it permits to take shape in Canada" (130). Furthermore, these novels reveal the truth in Robyn McCallum's perception that "interlaced dual narration ... can be a particularly problematic form"—problematic because "[t]he tendency to structure narrative points of view oppositionally often entails that one dominant narratorial position is privileged and dialogue is thus subsumed by monologue" (56). Readers of these novels have insight into the alternating points of view of two characters in order to arrive at agreement with just one viewpoint, an agreement that erases differences. Finally, the past is also erased or reconstituted, by becoming meaningful less in terms of what it meant for those who originally experienced it than as a defining other—what people in the present of the novels need to remember, but remember as over and move beyond, in order to form connections to each other.

Some of the double-focalized novels I read involve encounters between young people of Aboriginal and non-Aboriginal backgrounds: Katz's *False Face* and *Out of the Dark*, Joan Clark's *The Hand of Robin Squires* and *The Dream Carvers*, Monica Hughes's *Log Jam*, Kevin Major's *Red Blood Ochre*, and Martha Brooks's *Bone Dance*. While these novels replicate most of the patterns I found in the other double-focalized novels, they are unlike the others in one important way. They tend not to turn their backs on history as the others do.[3]

There is an obvious reason why that might be so. By and large, my work on these novels has suggested ways in which their recurring patterns might represent a dynamic of multiculturalism—a way of allowing people of differing backgrounds their differences while nevertheless sharing the same space, our home here in Canada. Their shared gesture of making the past significant as taking place elsewhere, in places we must remember primarily as the undesirable opposite of the desirable place we share together now, will simply not work for Aboriginal Canadians. Their history did not take place elsewhere. It occurred nowhere else but on the land we all now occupy together.

It seems, then, that the mere existence of Aboriginal peoples is a threat to what appear to be some key aspects of the multicultural ideologies that are supposed to work to bind Canadians together. If those ideologies are to maintain their power generally—and if they are to include Aboriginal nations among the diverse cultures that define the country as a whole—then ways must be found to circumvent or confront the question of history.

While they do it in interestingly different ways that I'll describe in more detail later, these novels offer surprisingly similar solutions to the problem. They tend to focus on questions of ownership and property, on questions of whom a piece of land or a cultural artifact belongs to. For that reason (and while not always consciously or obviously intending to do so), they resonate in terms of attitudes toward the significant questions about land claims and treaties so central to political and literary discourse about Aboriginals in Canada. The novelists have no choice but to accept that the land on which Canada sits originally belonged to its indigenous peoples, and that, since it was taken from them by force and through the disregarding of treaty rights, they still have a legitimate claim to it. This history still matters and is not yet over.

Nevertheless, these novels make the usual move of double-focalized texts beyond difference and toward community. But in order to move past prejudice and intolerance and/or to find redemption for the guilt of the theft of land and the mistreatment of indigenous peoples by their ancestors and/or contemporaries, the people of non-Aboriginal backgrounds in these novels can and must learn to think and act like Aboriginals—like those shaped by the land they live on. In some of the novels and increasingly in novels published more recently, once non-Aboriginals have learned Aboriginality, they are understood to have become legitimate members of the group of Aboriginals with a claim to the land. While the land of Canada rightly belongs exclusively to Aboriginals, in other words, Aboriginals consist of everyone in Canada who has learned to think and act in an appropriately Aboriginal manner.

Alternatively, Aboriginality is dismissed as counter-productive, along with all other adherence to the cultural forces that divide us from each other. We Canadians are, as at the end of *False Face*, just individuals after all—individuals, therefore, with an equal right to be here together in this place we all own. We are all non-Aboriginal together—and paradoxically, therefore, the rightful inheritors of the land. The opposite viewpoint supports the same conclusion.

Furthermore, these novels tend to represent Aboriginal attitudes to land as significantly opposite to non-Aboriginal ideas of ownership. Like the Australian texts discussed by Clare Bradford in *Reading Race*, they affirm that the land belongs to nobody in particular and everybody as a group, a trust rather than a possession: "Aboriginal spirituality is identified with a pre-industrial golden age, when humans lived in harmony with the natural world. The effect of this shift from the local to the universal is to reconstruct the indigenous sacred as constituting a generalised custodianship over 'the land', instead of connection with a particular tract of land" (58). Those who learn to think in this theoretically Aboriginal way both deny the rights of non-Aboriginal-thinking non-Aboriginals to any specific property and, also, affirm their own rights along with all other "Aboriginals" to the land as a whole. Alternatively, as I've suggested, there is a celebration of individual humanity beyond both Aboriginality and non-Aboriginality that nevertheless equally denies conventional property rights and equally, therefore, denies Aboriginal land claims.

As I've suggested, these novels arrive at these similar conclusions in ways different enough to mask their similarity. Before considering their implications further, I need to show how they do so. I'll explore three novels that have garnered a lot of attention and consecration: Joan Clark's *The Dream Carvers*, Kevin Major's *Blood Red Ochre*, and of course Katz's *False Face*.

For readers who might be interested, my detailed notes on these and the many other similar novels about encounters between Aboriginal and non-Aboriginal young people that I've been investigating are available on the Internet.

□ □ □

As I suggested earlier, *False Face* represents Aboriginality as less meaningful than individuality. Tom, who thinks of himself as Aboriginal, has moved with his non-Aboriginal mother from the Grand River reserve to London after the death of his Aboriginal father, and he feels he does not belong there. The novel works to show that he is right, that he cannot belong in London as long as he insists on being Aboriginal. Not just Tom, but most of the central characters in the novel claim or take on Aboriginality—and it causes them nothing but trouble. A happy ending can emerge only when everyone renounces Aboriginality—becomes equally non-Aboriginal.

As may be expected in a double-focalized novel, *False Face* focuses on questions of isolation and connection. In London, Tom thinks, "[t]hey lived so close to one another they could hear each other's nightmares, but no one seemed to know anyone else. It was a community of strangers" (14). But, by the end of the novel, he can tell Laney, the white girl who is the other focalized character, "We're in this together" (118). The novel mirrors the bilaterally isolated and yet connected nature of its focalization in just about all its elements. Not only is Laney a white middle-class girl and Tom a somewhat Aboriginal and somewhat poorer boy, but both are torn between the opposing qualities represented by their father and mother that they find at war within themselves.

Tom wants to see himself as Aboriginal, like his father: "It was a culture, and it was beautiful. It was his own" (49). But he has to admit a division within himself. "He was Indian! Half an Indian, he corrected himself. Neither one thing nor the other" (18). Laney is similarly divided, albeit in non-racial terms, between her divorced impractical scholarly father and aggressive businesswoman mother. She tries to please her mother by being less like her father, but must deal with their opposite and isolated influences at war within her. The plot of the novel not only connects Tom to Laney, but also allows each of them to connect the separated parts of themselves.

The false face masks of the title are the novel's central symbol of isolation and connection: on both the miniature mask Laney finds and the larger one her mother claims, "[t]he face was divided vertically in half:

the left side, black; the other, red" (19). Laney thinks of that division in terms that match both the novel's alternation between her narration and Tom's and its positioning of her mother's values against her father's and Aboriginal values against non-Aboriginal ones: "Black and red opposing one another, evil and good together. A power to be used. A choice" (78). The implication is that the characters face exactly that kind of choice, and that what they choose will represent how isolated opposites might best be dealt with and, perhaps, connected in their relationship to each other.

The masks represent division in two central ways. First, the novel tells how their separation causes disruption, as their separate ownership by Laney and her mother leads to the expression of harmful urges they would otherwise not act on. When the masks are together (and literally connected), however, the small mask protects the owner of the large mask from its powerful negative effects.

But the connection they represent requires the continuing existence of its separate parts, something that becomes clear in a consideration of the other way in which the masks represent division. They have been removed from a wild bog in the centre of built-up London, where they have been preserved intact for centuries and thus represent the past intruding into the present. Knowledge of the masks' existence interrupts Laney's comforting thoughts of London as home: "the black and the red, the hating and the loving, the two savage, eternal halves struggling beneath civilized appearances" (149). Early on, Tom claims he "ignored history. It was a White subject, anyway" (15). Later, however, he admits something different, a liking for a museum and "the feeling of history it gave him, the awareness that everything was connected. Everything had a place. Everything belonged somewhere" (48–49). The masks removed from the past and intruding into the present then seem to represent a disruption of the orderly, connected way things ought to be—which is an evolution beyond the "savage." As a result, Tom thinks that "he and Laney could rebury the two masks in the bog where they belonged" (94), and Laney, separately, agrees: "Had the bog been protected until now because the masks had been there, the Indian magic keeping it safe?… Everything had been fine with the bog until she had taken the little mask from it" (133). Since the masks so clearly represent Aboriginal spirituality, and by extension, Aboriginality generally, an ending that puts them back in the bog "where they belong," out of the present and safely consigned to the past, resonates in terms of the place of Aboriginality in contemporary life and has a revealing connection to Doris Wolf and Paul de Pasquale's perception, expressed elsewhere in this book, that Deborah L. Delaronde's *Flour Sack Flora*, a children's book produced by a Métis press and by a Métis writer, acts in "the mitigating of colonization by insisting on one's own history" (100). As understood in *False Face*, on the other hand, history might be a white subject after all, a way of connecting past and present that sees the place of Aboriginality as not here and not now.

That view of things is confirmed by the emphasis throughout *False Face* on questions of ownership—ownership not only of the masks but also of land, specifically the bog the masks are found in. Consideration of the masks as property, then, becomes a discourse on land claims. Katz insists that the ownership of the masks is a key to how their power operates. As Laney discovers, "[e]ven the books said that a mask belonged to only one person" (78). So to whom, then, do or should the masks belong? To whom does the Aboriginal past belong? Who has a right to claim the Aboriginal, and the land that once belonged to Aboriginals? The novel offers a variety of answers to these questions.

Laney's mother claims them in terms of the mainstream capitalist views she represents. The large mask is hers to own because she wants to own it, and she wants to own it because she can make money selling it. Not surprisingly, then, her claiming of it is what leads her to her spiteful acts of acquisitive evil—something she allows by refusing the small mask that might balance the power of the larger one. The mask clearly does not and should not belong to her. In a parallel fashion, the novel denies Laney's mother's original position that the bog the masks emerged from belongs to the developer, because, as she says, "[i]t is his land, after all" (10). At the end, the developer responds to the possibility of the bad publicity that might result from Laney's father's attempt to connect it to the Aboriginal past by renouncing his claim and handing the land over to the city for "*permanent parkland*" (152). As that which will keep the Aboriginal past safely buried and unknown and thus protect everyone from its dangerous powers, the land belongs to everybody who rejects any claim to it and to the buried and ideally forgotten Aboriginality it represents.

Laney's anthropologist father and the museum that Tom considers as a home for the masks represent another non-Aboriginal attitude toward Aboriginal property as valuable, not in a monetary way, but as a subject of detached scientific inquiry. This, too, is a claim to property; Tom bristles when a white woman identifies the place where she works as "our museum" (50), and he envisages the museum as a container of the masks' power, for good or ill: "Maybe all that classifying and preserving and studying and analyzing would take enough of the magic out of the mask that it would be safe. Another Indian power destroyed by the White Man" (96).

On the other hand, however, Tom has to learn that the Iroquois do not want ownership of the masks. When he returns to the reserve to inquire

about them, the old man he meets at the longhouse tells him, "It is nothing to do with us" (104); when Tom says, "Those masks will destroy
them" (104), he responds, "Whites have never understood what they have.
They had forests, and they made cities. They had clear streams, and they
made cesspools. The Whites take, and so shall they receive" (105). In
effect, people like Laney's mother deserve the effects of their acquisitive-
ness that the mask will allow.

Many of the other novels under discussion here would agree with that
conclusion. As I suggested earlier, it is a version of what Bradford identifies as a reconstruction of "the indigenous sacred as constituting a generalised custodianship over the 'land' instead of connection to a particular
tract of land," a way of condemning current mainstream culture, which,
when adopted by non-Aboriginals as a presumed form of Aboriginality,
allows them to claim the land. But in *False Face*, Tom rejects the old
man's version of things: after he hears it, "[t]he Reserve was a foreign
place, and he was a foreigner in it. He walked and walked, and felt no
belonging. Go home, he thought. But there was no home. There was only
London, and here" (105).

In the end, then, the novel supports Laney's view that "power like that
was more than any human should handle" (32). The masks are too dangerous for anyone to own and must be returned to the past, where they
really belong. The novel expresses a perverse conviction in the real and
really dangerous power of "savage" magic that requires it to be kept safely
hidden.

As I suggested earlier, then, every central character in the novel who
claims and/or takes on Aboriginality is harmed by it and must finally
renounce it in order to achieve peace. Tom is the most obvious example,
beginning with an assumption of his own Aboriginality and finally coming to understand the value in the fact that Laney "thought of him as a
boy, not an Indian" (96). He begins to think of his Aboriginal father as someone who has already renounced Aboriginality: "The Indian who had loved
a White woman had not belonged on this Reserve. He had seen people as
people, regardless of the colour of their skin. He belonged to a world that
didn't yet exist" (105). Tom finally sees himself as belonging to that world
also, as he weeps "[t]ears, not red and not black, not White and not Indian.
Just tears, from someone who was a person, nothing else" (145). He is Aboriginal no longer, and it is meant to be a good thing.

Both Laney and her mother take on Aboriginality with their possession
of the masks. As the small mask gains power over her, Laney finds herself having nightmare images (139), visions of ceremonies in the longhouse,
and concludes, "God or no god, Indian or White, what was happening

here was wrong" (92)—and so she wisely rejects its power, and in fact, gives it away—to her father, who needs the small mask to protect himself from the forces of the larger one held by her mother. Her mother also renounces the Aboriginal, giving the mask to her husband in response to Tom's plea for her not to hurt Laney because she looks like her father and to pay attention to the "somebody *in* there behind those looks" (145). At this point, Aboriginality is equivalent to deception—the mask that hides the real humanity. It clearly must be renounced.

At this point, Laney's father owns both masks—and being Aboriginal enough to follow the others who took on Aboriginality, he too renounces them, giving them to Tom: "They're your heritage. You'll know the best thing to do with them" (146). But Tom, who has already renounced Aboriginality in favour of basic humanity, firmly renounces it once more:

> The White people didn't want the masks; the Society of Faces didn't want the masks.... He wouldn't keep them. No one could own those two masks, not without risking being owned by them, too. Dr. McIntyre was right. The only safety from the masks lay in giving them up.... White, Indian, half-breed, what did it matter? Nobody was free, and nobody was safe. Everybody had to choose what to let himself be. (147)

This humanely liberal rejection of all the categories that divide people has unfortunate political resonances. For one thing, the novel's conclusion ignores the possibility of any sort of Aboriginal life in the present. While it has earlier taken Tom to the reserve in order for him to be denied his sense of belonging there, the novel's final choice attempts to erase the existence of that reserve—or of any sort of possibility of Aboriginal existence outside a complete absorption of the old traditions in the contemporary world. Furthermore, the surrender of an Aboriginality represented by something one owns in favour of a more basic humanity represents a strong statement against the validity of Aboriginal property claims and land claims generally. As Beverly Haun suggests, the novel's conclusion "echoes past official Canadian policies of assimilation of the Aboriginals of this country into the fabric of the dominant culture—not just with the intent of sharing the dominant culture, but with the sinister agenda of eliminating the Aboriginal ones, reducing them to historical records and artefacts to be studied or examined, displayed or sold" (39).

While Clark's *The Dream Carvers* moves in the opposite direction and celebrates Aboriginality, it ends up in a similar rejection of specific Aboriginal claims to the land. The novel describes the encounter between an eleventh-century Greenlander and a group of Beothuks who call themselves the Osweet. The Osweet capture Thrand, later known by the

Beothuk name Wobee, to replace a man killed by the Greenlanders—to quite literally become an Aboriginal. Three-quarters of the novel offers Thrand's focalization, the other quarter the view of Abidith, an Osweet girl to whom he feels attracted but whose marriage to someone else of another group he must accept as he becomes Beothuk enough to understand their exogamous marriage patterns. Furthermore, Abidith can read Thrand's thoughts, but not vice versa—so even in her narrative the focus remains on him, on his becoming Aboriginal rather than on what it means to be Aboriginal in the first place. *The Dream Carvers* primarily offers readers a non-Aboriginal position to identify with, with Aboriginality as what is in the process of being appropriated and adopted.

At first, *The Dream Carvers* seems to be about the inadequacy of the Greenlanders' and Beothuks' isolation from and ignorance of each other, to be brought together in the usual healthy connection of mutual understanding and allowance as the plot develops. But in fact, it turns out that the Aboriginals have nothing of value to learn from the Europeans. The book insists that the Norse values—figured as representative of contemporary right-wing capitalist North American values—are inferior to those of the Beothuks—figured as representative of contemporary left-wing liberal North American values. The Norse myths are bloodthirsty and require consent, but for the Beothuks, "[w]hat matters is that the story is there for each of us to believe or disbelieve as we choose and in so choosing discover our own truth" (79). Furthermore, "we Greenlanders thought that once we killed a seal, it belonged to us.... The Osweet don't own their goods in the same way Norsemen do. Stealing is unknown to them.... If no one owns anything, it's impossible to steal" (114–15). This applies most exactly to land. The Greenlanders "divide up the land into fields and farms. They believe their reputation depends on how much they own" (177). But "[h]ere the land belongs to the Creator.... It's for his children's use" (169).

As the novel progresses and Thrand becomes one of those children, it is for his use also. Using language that resonates with some very old stereotypes, the novel describes Thrand's transformation into Wobee as, literally, a move from being White to becoming Red. The Beothuk are the red ochre people: "[T]hese skraelings seem to inhabit a world of redness where everything they make or use is red. It's as if they imagine themselves living within a red world of their own that's side by side or within the larger world that I know" (7–8). In fact, the redness moves them out of time and history and into a larger timeless connection with their place: "While she was dancing, my mother, Thoowidith, was transformed into someone else, someone with special powers, someone who saw beyond where we are now. There was a reddish light around her that came from another place. That was when I knew my mother was dancing with our ancestors ... and in so doing, joined them to us" (75–76).

At first, Thrand says, he is "outside their world of redness" (8). The Beothuks hope that he will eventually "become red inside" (178), but first he must become red outside. He does so first as he considers the possibility that he is to blame for the death of the Beothuk he has replaced, and he smears blood over his hands (52)—a taking on of Aboriginality as a symbolic acknowledgement of guilt. Having done that and eventually having learned the superiority of Beothuk values, he finally says, "I have never liked the white parts of my body. To me white is a feeble, weak colour, especially for a man" (181). He becomes red in the way the Beothuks do—with ochre, saying, "The more I think about being red, the more the redness appeals to me" (182). As a result, "[n]ow I look more like the earth.... [T]he ochre is already making me feel I am part of the land, even the forests I feared" (182). Taking on Aboriginality amounts to a land claim.

The novel also suggests that taking on Aboriginality is itself an Aboriginal idea. The Beothuk's plan is to "help him become one of us" (28), and they speak of his doing so as parallel to their exogamous marriage patterns. The grandmother points out that she was once a stranger too: "'[W]e knew in time that we would become the place and the people where we live.... It is difficult,... but eventually we can become part of another place. The trees, rocks and streams of a new place slowly enter us. Our red world is large enough to enclose us all'" (191–92). As the novel makes clear, "all" includes those born white and willing to become red—that is, one of those whom the land has claimed and who can therefore claim the land.

While offering a more even distribution of its two focalizers, once more one Beothuk and one non-Beothuk, Kevin Major's *Red Blood Ochre* offers a similar view of Aboriginality and its relations to land and property. Even though readers learn about as much of the nineteenth-century Beothuk Dauoodaset's thoughts as they do of the contemporary Newfoundlander David's, their alternating narratives and eventual connection with each other tell a similar tale of a non-Aboriginal learning about and taking on Aboriginality.

Blood Red Ochre counterpoints the events of David's life in the present with Dauoodaset's in the past in ways that make David seem shallow and self-indulgent. David is an alienated teenager who isolates himself from his family in self-pity; Dauoodaset is noble, brave, self-sufficient, and concerned centrally with the needs of his people and isolating himself from them only in order to help them. Dauoodaset is strong, but David's "'body has been pampered'" (80). The boys are connected through their relationship with Shanawdithit, the last of the Beothuks, who is to marry Dauoodaset in the past and whom David meets as the newcomer Nancy—"different, foreign almost, a bit mysterious" (5)—in the present and develops a romantic relationship with. As the book reaches its climax, it focuses events for the first time through Shanawdithit, earlier only the object of both boys' focalization, in order to reveal its central point: that she has come into the present to connect David to Dauoodaset, and through him, to his past and to the past of the place where he lives. She has come to make him more aware of the Aboriginal past—and in fact, to make him more Aboriginal.

Dauoodaset's problem is the extinction of his people at the hands of whites. His narrative describes how he sets off to the sea to find food for them. David's problem is also familial. He has just learned that the man he thought was his father is not. In the course of the novel, he must learn to accept that his true family is the one that he lives in—that despite his lack of a blood connection, his stepfather's father, whom he cares for, is in fact his grandfather. David's acceptance of the idea that real families are chosen and that he belongs most significantly in the family and the place that accepts him makes this novel an expression of the pattern Mavis Reimer identifies elsewhere in this book as common in Canadian fiction for children: "[t]he need for the child to choose home" (12). It resonates in its Canadian views of who belongs in Canada—and more specifically, here, in Canadian ideas about Aboriginality as represented in the relationship David develops with Shanawdithit and Dauoodaset. By the end, all the characters isolated by their different blood become connected in the same story in the same time and, above all, the same place—a place that then belongs to them all.

The relationship between David and the two Beothuks is signalled by questions of ownership and property. David's grandfather—significantly not his grandfather by blood—has given him "a Beothuk Indian pendant his own grandfather had given to him as a boy" (3)—a passing on of an object that then signifies family connections, David's right to belong in his grandfather's family. To begin with, David has no idea what the pendant is and understands only that it represents his own sense of isolation—his lack of connection to his heritage: "He knew his wearing the pendant had something to do with his own feeling of having a past that he didn't know much about" (3). The thrust of the novel is to reconnect David to his grandfather's family, but also to the past, and especially the past history of relationships between his non-Aboriginal predecessors and the Beothuk, a history that has left a white family in possession of the pendant.

The pendant was in fact originally a gift from Shanawdithit to Dauoodaset and came into white hands through the murder of Dauoodaset by a white man, so that it represents the history of white violence against the Beothuk. It is this history that David "didn't know much about" and has set out to learn as his assignment for heritage class, and that Shanawdithit has come into the present to draw attention to: "The people from which he has come must feel the hurt they have done to us" (130). When she tells David, "It is your people who are the savages" (131), he is able to tell her that is not in fact true: "The man you were talking about is not my father. I was born before my mother married him" (132). Furthermore, he says, "[y]ou can't blame me for something that happened two hundred years ago" (132).

But if David is to claim a place in his own family, he cannot then deny his responsibility for what happened to the Beothuks; in any case, as Shanawdithit says, "[t]hose who let it happen were as shameful as those who pulled the triggers" (132). At a key moment toward the end of the novel, David acknowledges that returning the pendant to Shanawdithit—a restoration of Aboriginal heritage symbolized by a white gift of originally Aboriginal property back to an Aboriginal—is clearly a better solution to how to deal with that property than the one Shanawdithit spoke of earlier: "Where is there memory of my people? Skeletons in a museum. Bones and clothing and our precious neck pieces to gawk at" (132).

Paradoxically, however, by the time David returns the precious neck piece to its rightful Aboriginal owner, he is in effect an Aboriginal himself. He becomes one by the same means that Thrand does in *The Dream Carvers*—by taking on the redness of the Red Ochre People with his own blood. Dauoodaset wounds David's face, which then takes on redness as Thrand does in *The Dream Carvers*, by means of his own blood: "From one side, with his face smeared red with dried blood, he looks like one of my people" (139). He is, in fact, becoming one with those people; as Shanawdithit says, "I must make him see that I am no longer of his world, that he is now a part of ours" (134).

His being so directly results in his possession of land. The meeting between David and Dauoodaset takes place on Red Ochre Island, "the same island where [David's] grandfather and his family had once lived" (32)—and which has therefore been claimed as white land. Dauoodaset has come there not just to find food for his people, but a new home where "[t]here will be no whiteman there to bother us.... This is new land. It will be our land" (13). It's instructive that Major should set these scenes in a place where the Beothuk claim to the land is as tenuous as that of the whites. When Dauoodaset gets there, a white man is there, with a salmon

FIGURE 1 From *Jack Pine Fish Camp*, text by Tina Umpherville, illus. Christie Rice

FIGURE 2 From *Flour Sack Flora*, text by Deborah Delaronde, illus. Gary Chartrand

FIGURE 3 From *Willy the Curious Frog from Pruden's Bog*, text by Grant Anderson, illus. Sheldon Dawson

FIGURE 4 From *Willy the Curious Frog from Pruden's Bog*, text by Grant Anderson, illus. Sheldon Dawson

As Sue and Jessica were playing, they noticed how sad Molly looked. They didn't like to see Molly looking so miserable. Jessica thought of an idea. She walked over to Molly.

FIGURE 5 From *Molly, Sue … and Someone New!*, text and illus. by Atia Lokhat

FIGURE 6 From *Crabs for Dinner*, text by Adwoa Badoe, illus. Belinda Ageda

FIGURE 7 From *Lights for Gita*, text by Rachna Gilmore,
illus. Alice Priestly

FIGURE 8 From *Anne of Green Gables Souvenir
Magazine*, illus. Erik Dzenis

FIGURE 9 From *A Screaming Kind of Day*, text by Rachna Gilmore, illus. Gordon Sauvé

FIGURE 10 From *Mister Got to Go*, text by Lois Simmie, illus. Cynthia Nugent

FIGURE 11 From *Long Nellie*, text and illus. by Deborah Turney-Zagwÿn

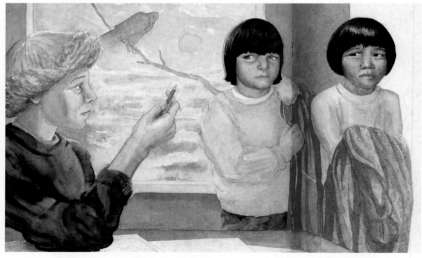

FIGURE 12 From *The Missing Sun*, text by Peter Eyvindson, illus. Rhian Brynjolson

FIGURE 13 From *The Huron Carol*, text by Father Jean de Brébeuf, illus. Frances Tyrrell

FIGURE 14 From *Lights for Gita*, text by Rachna Gilmore, illus. Alice Priestly

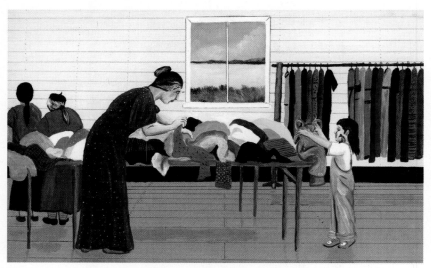

FIGURE 15 From *Flour Sack Flora*, text by Deborah Delaronde, illus. Gary Chartrand

As Grandma sewed, Flora looked through a box of old clothes until she found the prettiest buttons for her dress. She snipped them off and placed them in a bowl. They would be sewn down the back of the dress.

FIGURE 16 From *Flour Sack Flora*, text by Deborah Delaronde, illus. Gary Chartrand

net and a gun, clearly defending what he views as his property. But at the end, David stands alone on this disputed land. He has learned about the Beothuk, even symbolically become one himself. He has taken on Aboriginality and rescued Shanawdithit from the white man who kills Dauoodaset. But he cannot prevent the death of Dauoodaset that happened so many years earlier, and while the novel toys with the idea of Shanawdithit allowing her feelings for David to transform her into Nancy and remain in the present, she finally leaves the novel as the last of her people, paddling out into the ocean and leaving David in sole possession of the land. Earlier, Shanawdithit told David "that he must see us as we are, and he must tell others they have to learn to share this island with us. The food of the waters about this island is not for his people alone" (136). Having learned that, ironically, he is left alone.

One reason for that is simple historical fact. The Beothuk are extinct. But since that's true, why is Shanawdithit so determined to teach David about past history and the need to share the land? It can only be because Major is reaching for larger implications—for a statement about the place of all Aboriginal peoples in Canada generally. Unfortunately, that backfires on him, simply because representing general attitudes towards Aboriginality purely in terms of Beothuk history forces the novel to ignore the continuing existence of Aboriginals in the Canadian present. There are no non-nineteenth-century Aboriginals in *Blood Red Ochre*, an absence that allows the non-Aboriginal David's solitary ownership of the land left to him both by the white grandfather who admitted him into his family and the Beothuks who also made him one of them.

□ □ □

A little further research has shown me that I shouldn't have been surprised by the similarities in these texts. They replicate fairly exactly patterns that Terry Goldie finds generally in non-Aboriginal fiction about Aboriginal peoples: "In their need to become 'native,' to belong here, whites in Canada, New Zealand, and Australia have adopted a process which I have termed 'indigenization.' A peculiar word, it suggests the impossible necessity of becoming indigenous" (13). The cultural forces that drive the urge to indigenization are so powerful that they form what Goldie identifies as "a semiotic field," a field that shapes the responses even of individuals who wish to critique those forces:

> The indigene is a semiotic pawn on a chess board under the control of the white signmaker. And yet the individual sign maker, the individual player, the individual writer, can move these pawns only within certain prescribed

areas. Whether the context is Canada, New Zealand, or Australia becomes a minor issue since the game, the signmaking, is all happening on one form of board, within one field of discourse, that of British imperialism. (10)

Within that field, writers again and again identify Aboriginal culture with what is natural and untainted. Again and again, texts ignore or downplay contemporary Aboriginal culture and position authentic Aboriginality in the past. And above all, again and again whites are indigenized and "indigenizing whites are allowed to acquire nature ..." (Goldie 39), appropriate Aboriginality, and thus claim the land.

While Goldie and I depict this field of semiosis as inherently imperialistic, there are other ways of understanding it. Homi Bhabha, for instance, implies the acceptability of some of the forms and effects of cultural appropriation when he speaks of "a cultural hybridity that entertains difference without an assumed or imposed hierarchy" (*Location* 4). As Bradford says, "[T]here is a powerful utopian attraction about hybridity because of the appeal of a genuinely transcultural and interracial engagement between peoples" ("Transformative Fictions" 195). Indeed, it's the attractiveness of this sort of engagement that has motivated the writers and publishers of the novels I've been considering, which clearly are meant to adhere to ideals of pastoral innocence, self-development, and tolerance that operate in the field of literature for children and young adults generally, and which do so in terms of ideals of intercultural acceptance especially prevalent in Canadian writing for young people. I can view them as thwarting those ideals only by looking beneath the surface and reading against what they consciously declare. I need to do that because, as Bradford goes on to suggest, "dangers lurk behind these apparently benevolent cultural shifts, and they reside especially in the ethnocentrism of western desire. All too often, indigenous traditions become merely sites of abundance and meaningfulness that supply western consumers with what they lack, and in this way hybridity shades into neocolonial appropriation" (195–96). In fact, the Aboriginality being celebrated (or rejected) in the novels I've explored here is hardly hybrid at all, for as I've discovered, it announces itself as a replacement of non-Aboriginality with a pure Aboriginality in those who gain it, and what it represents as purely Aboriginal tends to have little if anything to do with authentic Aboriginal culture at all.

Nor therefore, I have to conclude, does this essay. Goldie asserts that "the white culture has created a semiotic field of such power that no textual representation, very much including the study you are now reading, can escape it" (213–14). As for his study, so for mine. I have inevitably read these texts in terms of my own immersion in the culture of my forebears and my white Canadian contemporaries. It's certainly possible that my awareness of the patterns that strike me as being so clearly present and so worthy of attention in these texts might itself have engendered the patterns—that the texts might well strike other readers less firmly placed in positions of cultural power quite differently. My essay may serve no purpose other than to sustain the very structures of power I hoped to critique and to weaken. Its mere presence in this book confirms the power of the cultural and academic institution that gave me the opportunity to write it and then sanctioned it and agreed to make it available to others, just as similar institutions made the novels I've discussed available to be read and discussed. I'm pessimistic enough to believe that the institutional sanctioning has leached away much of the liberatory force it might have had—even if there were something liberating for others in my original act of appropriating the subject or in my institutionalizing analysis of it.

But I can also see two others aspects of my work here that might be less disheartening. First, speaking of Edward Said's work on orientalism, Goldie says,

> Said seems not to see himself as a position in this equation, as the human being studying the Orientalists. As the white student of the white texts I am constantly aware of this position, as I hope is the text of this study. While I might appear to be claiming that I should be excused from the chain of semiotic manipulation because of my sensitivity to all these problems of distance, this study shows throughout that sensitivity has failed to erase the circumscriptions of the image of the indigene. My claim is not for the perfection of my centre but for the decentring process that I have applied. (8)

I'd like to make the same claim. I hope my awareness and enunciation of the problems inherent in my work will make readers suspicious and encourage thoughtful critical consideration of my conclusions. I hope for responses that explore grounds for disagreement and engage in negotiations with my ideas that might move beyond my own conclusions and might well end up being liberatory.

I hope, in other words, that I am engaged in a dialogue with readers of this essay, just as I have been involved during the project this book represents in a fruitful and ongoing dialogue with the other participants. I agree with Alcoff when she says,

> We should strive to create wherever possible the conditions for dialogue and the practice of speaking with and to rather than speaking for others. If the dangers of speaking for others result from the possibility of misrepresentation, expanding one's own authority and privilege, and a generally

imperialist speaking ritual, then speaking with and to can lessen those dangers. (23)

That doesn't mean this essay isn't dangerous. I merely hope it's less dangerous than it might have been.

Or, perhaps, more dangerous, in a more positive way and for a different reason: because I have been so tentative about saying anything at all. As Judith Roof and Robin Wiegman suggest, "Questioning the relation between identity, experience, and authority and their ties to representation makes visible the ideologies of subjectivity and knowledge that govern contemporary critical speech and the authority for it" (94). I believe that sort of visibility can only be beneficial.

□ □ □

Notes

1 As well as winning the International Children's Fiction Contest, *False Face* was shortlisted for the Governor General's Award. Katz's *Out of the Dark* was shortlisted for the Governor General's Award and the Mr. Christie Award and won the Ruth Schwartz Award. Joan Clark's *Hand of Robin Squires* was a Canadian Centre for Books for Children Our Choice book for three years and won the Alberta Publishing Award. Clark's *Dream Carvers* won the Mr. Christie Award and the Geoffrey Bilson Award. Kevin Major's *Blood Red Ochre* was shortlisted for Canadian Library Association Book of the Year Award and the Geoffrey Bilson Award. Martha Brooks's *Bone Dance* won the Ruth Schwartz Children's Book Award and the Canadian Library Association's Young Adult Book Award.

2 Most significantly, I'm not aware of any that use the double focalizations my readings centre on.

3 These novels form part of larger group of Canadian novels for young people that centrally involve encounters between Aboriginal and non-Aboriginal young people and replicate many of the same themes, but not all of which have alternating double focalizations. Farley Mowat's *Lost in the Barrens* and *Curse of the Viking Grave* most often focalize the story of two boys through the non-specific viewpoint of "the boys" that suggests that both see things in the same way, while a number of novels silence the Aboriginal member of the pair by focalizing the narrative completely through the viewpoint of the white protagonist: John Craig's *No Word for Goodbye*, Ted Stenhouse's *Across the Steel River* and *A Dirty Deed*, and Greg Jackson-Davis's *Digging for Philip*.

CHAPTER 7

➡ **White Picket Fences: At Home with Multicultural Children's Literature in Canada?**

Louise Saldanha

This chapter is a critical effort to think more carefully about the situation of children's texts by writers of colour[1] in Canada. Such books typically attend to the experiences of those traditionally not considered as making up the "mainstream." Such a focus has routinely resulted in their designation as forms of "multicultural children's literature," a category placing such racialized writing in particular relation to the "mainstream." My endeavour, here, is to think through this particular relation of the "multicultural" to the "mainstream" as complicating the commonplaces of "home" and "away" in dominant formulations of both multiculturalism and children's literature. In attempting to place race in Canada, how are standard divisions of here from there, us from them, the familiar from the strange, dis-organized? Simply put: what does it mean for children's texts by writers of colour to make for themselves a "home" in Canada?

Ideas of "home" and "away" centrally occupy children's literature in North America. As a place encoding security and stability, "home" divides itself from "away," producing and securing itself—constantly and variously—against places outside of its familiarity. "Away" marks the space of forests and similar unsettled, unsettling realms, the zone of strangeness and the zone of insecurity. It is hardly surprising that children's literature, generated within imperatives of education and enculturation, teaches its young readers that "home," associated with order, normalcy, and boundedness, is the only place to be. These conventional patterns, however, may not be entirely replicated in Canadian children's literature. As Mavis Reimer and Anne Rusnak discover in their investigation of award-winning texts for children in Canada, "home is not boring or calm; it is not a place safely fenced from danger or hedged against anarchy; it is not a stable location that secures an inside by holding in place an outside" (28). It is Reimer and Rusnak's conclusion regarding the unconventionality of award-winning, decidedly established, Canadian texts that serves, in this chapter, as my point of departure. My critical inquiry here investigates those Canadian children's texts that seem, perpetually, to signify as the less established: the stories of "new" multicultural Canadians of colour. How might Canadian rewritings of "home" display when projected through this multicultural children's literature where being "home" in the private and personal sense becomes enmeshed with being home in the national and public sense?

In Canada, multicultural promises that "we all belong" are preserved within official Canadian policy and, thus, taken as national common sense. Originally developed in response to demands for recognition of all Canada's cultural and ethnic groups, multicultural state policy was initialized as a mechanism to recognize "difference" through policies and practices of "tolerance" and celebration. Yet, despite its widely publicized and self-acclaimed commitment to cultural plurality, Canadian multiculturalism does not live up to what some claim to be its original ideals of recognition and acceptance. Instead, it has functioned to neutralize—rather than seriously engage—the cultural and racial diversity it permits to take shape in Canada.[2] In other words, multiculturalism, perhaps in ways removed from the ideals of its beginnings, has emerged as a strategy managing cultural and racial "difference," shifting its discourse in response to prevailing political and national obligations that have redirected it from its early emphasis on "folklore" to, in the 1980s, "race relations," to its current recasting within "globalization" discourses (Abu-Laban and Gabriel 105–24). In this way, multiculturalism disguises Canadian realities through declamations pronouncing us as all equally ethnic, declamations that make cultural and racial inequities appear not part of Canada:

> Canada is conceptualized as a nation-narrative whose mark of difference consists not in hybridity but in yet another kind of commonality: "all Canadians" are members of the same *ethnos*, Canada. This statement, however, is historically both true and false. It is true in that "all Canadians" are, at least technically, members of equal standing within the state of Canada. But the statement is also false in that it dehistoricizes the social and political conditions that have discriminated against many Canadians, the same

conditions that, through colonial history, contributed to the formation of the Canadian state. (Kamboureli 100–1)

In order to be at "home" in the Eurocentrically bounded Canada, our "away," as people of colour, remains, for all intents and purposes, outside of things, our exoticness perhaps celebrated but not actually included in any material, transformative, manner.[3] To this end, the participation of non-white cultures is encouraged and financially supported mainly within the cultural and symbolic sphere rather than within the social and economic sphere.[4] As a result, our Otherness is fixed in time and place through colourful cultural spectacles advancing the tolerance and acceptance of us as just as beautiful as everybody but in our own way. We are constructed as, essentially, something outside *to* and apart *from* the living of life within the "home" of the Canadian nation. From "out there," as outsiders, we are then accepted *in* by multiculturalism's diversity rhetoric, but our residency is largely inconsequential to the Canadian space. Multicultural inclusion—as South Asian, as Caribbean, as Chinese—becomes little more than a prefix to the "Canadian" as a sign of "enrichment" (Hage, *White* 117)[5] of Canada itself, rather than a meaningful marker of a process of continual negotiation and renegotiation.

Since official, institutional, and popular approaches to multiculturalism fail to facilitate our ability, as people of colour, to influence substantively what gets understood and felt as "Canadian-ness," the very multicultural policies and practices that seek to fit us into national spaces, ironically, also work to aid in people of colour experiencing Canada, itself, in many ways, as *not*-home. Consequently, the terms of multicultural inclusion identifying Canada for "mainstream" Canadians as home, comforting and comfortable in its cultural harmoniousness, work to make Canada feel not-home for people of colour. This, I suggest, seems to be how we are caught up in the convoluted formula of Canadian cultural diversity: as non-whites, we are typically taken, in Canada, to represent "away." And, despite multicultural exertions to the contrary, we are often then left experiencing Canada as "away," a place of non-belonging, a place not-home.

Hence, children's books by writers of colour enter into existing mainstream multicultural paradigms that are powerfully shaped by specific understandings of the place of non-whiteness. Dominant multicultural ideologies attach to racialized children's texts fixing them, racially and culturally, in one dimension so that they all the better can be paved into the tranquil cultural mosaic. But how do renovations to common sense frameworks of "we're-all-the-same-but-not-quite" look? My focus, here, is on the ways in which children's literature by writers of colour in Canada occupies not only the multiple places of "home"—as both the private, familial location and the public, national one—in order to work out the terms of belonging, but, perhaps more complicatedly, the multiple places of "away." For, parallel with how we inhabit and are inhabited by Canadian multiculturalism, many of these books do depict "away" in the context of distant-from-Canada lands, but they also offer varied responses to our experiences of estrangement *inside* Canada—that sense of being racially excluded and "away" in the public, national space where we should, as multiculturals, be feeling "at home." Given this, can standard structures of "here" and "there" easily hold us? In what follows, I take up both the possibilities and limits of some children's texts by writers of colour to negotiate the inadequacies of constructions of "home" and "away" as discrete, stable settings where opportunities for one's personal growth, it is implied, rely on the leaving behind of one for the other. In this context, how do children's texts by writers of colour in Canada take up the space currently made for them? And to what extent do they circulate *both* within and in excess of established multicultural realms in order to tell their stories?

FITTING IN   The picture book *Molly, Sue ... and Someone New,* written and illustrated by Atia Lokhat, recounts the experiences that the non-white "someone new" has in taking her own personal "newness" out into the public Canadian multicultural space (in the form of her neighbourhood). The conflict begins when Molly, who is playing with her best friend Sue, refuses to include "the someone new," Jessica, her neighbour, because she does not like the latter's purple dress. The illustrations accompanying the written text, however, establish that the problem is hardly Jessica's faulty fashion sense. Molly and her best friend Sue are white, and Jessica is of colour; the story is obviously meant to show its readers that racism is hurtful. Certainly, the book's depiction of racism defies the ubiquitous impulse to offer children a world that is always good and safe. Yet its representation of racism (and its ultimate alleviation) is produced within the context of its surrender to the middle-class values conventional in children's literature. In particular, Molly and Sue have lots of books and toys and live, as does Jessica, in bright, spacious houses. Molly and Sue also have wardrobes ample enough to accommodate Jessica's "difference," for the story ends with a reconciliation and the reassuring promise that "'tomorrow we can all wear purple because purple is nice too.'"

Further, *Molly, Sue ... and Someone New* centres on racism through a white reference point privileging, in both its narrative and its illustrations, a white perspective. For instance, Molly enjoys full and unrestricted representation at least twice during the course of the book, occupying the entire page and facing the reader directly, while Jessica, the girl of colour, is introduced to us behind objects. In addition, the narrative offers no other possible friendships for Jessica other than one with Molly and Sue. Most disturbing is the fact that, although Molly is the one who excludes Jessica, the text stresses Molly's ensuing suffering. As a result, Jessica, sorry to see how "miserable" Molly looks, offers the gesture of reconciliation (see Figure 5). Assuming the caretaking role, Jessica generously declares, "Molly, I know you don't like my purple dress, but that doesn't mean we can't still play together. Would you like to play 'catch' with us?"—all so Molly can realize: "Maybe her new neighbour was nice after all." Thus the conflict between the girls is managed within a liberal framework of interpersonal relationships, deferring to the dominant multicultural vocabulary that narrates ethnic identity as a matter of individual choice to be freely donned or discarded, like purple dresses, at one's free will.

All in all, this effectively performs an (officially) multicultural aestheticization, and subsequent neutralization, of "difference." Jessica, as the unnamed "someone new" of the book's title, finds "home" in multicultural Canada, but it is one acquired by posing no real challenge to current racial and cultural arrangements. Still, we cannot discount that, even in its ability to fulfil, "safely," the mandate for ethnically diverse representations, *Molly, Sue . . . and Someone New* makes visible, however apprehensively, the material effects of racism in the lives of people of colour.

Positioned both within and by the Canadian multicultural mosaic, children's books by writers of colour in Canada can also be said to occupy an in-betweenness, an interstitial space between competing cultural discourses, a "third space" from which to affect authoritative ideologies of nation, multiculturalism, childhood, and race. "It is that Third Space, though unrepresentable in itself," Homi Bhabha has said, "which constitutes the discursive conditions of enunciation that ensure that the meaning and symbols of culture have no primordial unity or fixity; that even the same signs can be appropriated, translated, rehistoricized and read anew" (*The Location of Culture* 37).[6] What, then, is the potential of children's books by writers of colour in Canada to articulate "Canada" and "difference"—not in the sense of offering an alternative to the mainstream—

but in the sense of fulfilling the promise of being in-between: the promise of transgression, subversion, resistance? For the position of racialized texts is one that can be also rendered productively ambivalent.

BETWIXT AND BETWEEN   Indeed, it cannot be denied that Canadian multiculturalism makes available vital space for racially and culturally diverse expression historically pushed aside. And many of the children's books by writers of colour in Canada open with acknowledgements of the financial support of government-funded multicultural programs and initiatives. This acknowledgement places these texts in a somewhat complex and ambivalent relationship with official and ideological Canadian multiculturalism and the ways in which it offers entry into Canadian society. In fact, the various and varied methods of children's texts by which writers of colour end up taking possession of the "home" made for them in Canada points to how their narratives may be approached as strategic mediations of the very multicultural ideologies granting them presence.[7]

While some writers have produced texts with glossaries translating non-English (often emphasized by italics) words, others take advantage of the form and reception of children's literature, itself, to "teach" readers about cultures or about the hurtfulness of racism for individual children of colour. Undoubtedly, choosing to write books aligned with dominant multicultural aesthetics may be politically adroit, as such books have, possibly, a wider market appeal, making them more attractive to disseminators of children's literature (publishers, educators, librarians, and the like).[8]

Still other writers choose not to foreground, explicitly, issues of race, endeavouring, instead, to "normalize" the experiences of children of colour as equally three-dimensional as those of white children. While these books' potential to be read as "accessible" and "universal" confers on them similar promises of wider appeal and distribution, such narratives might also demonstrate different strategic choices that refuse essentialist conceptualizations of children and writers of colour whereby their lives are singularly defined by the colour of their skin. For instance, both Hiromi Goto's *The Water of Possibility* (a fantasy novel about Sayuri's adventures in the magical world of Living Earth to which she and her brother are transported) and Cheryl Foggo's *I Have Been in Danger* (which deals with Jackie's adventures on a camping trip through which she confronts questions about identity, relationships, family, and growing up) characterize their protagonists as living lives multiply situated and whose adventures, perhaps, could be those of any child. But, in each text, the use of racialized names, histories, food, and other such markers underline the racial and cultural specificities of the "heroes" and their stories. There is, therefore, a certain usefulness (but one not without encumbrances) in dwelling in-between that makes it possible for us to encounter representations of race and children that we might very well not have encountered at all.

TRANSGRESSIONS In many ways, the focus on food and cultural tradition in *Crabs for Dinner* by Adwoa Badoe and *Lights for Gita* by Rachna Gilmore caters to customary multicultural celebrations of culturally colourful, non-threatening "difference." *Crabs for Dinner* and *Lights for Gita* capitalize on dominant multiculturalism's celebratory focus on customs and food and its emphasis on "teaching about." But the fact that these books take for granted the likes of "fufu" and "Divali" in their protagonists' lives is validating and affirming for children of colour who habitually have learned to read themselves as not-there. Gilmore does provide an explanation of "Divali" in her book while Badoe's use of "fufu" simply occurs without the obligatory multicultural glossary, but, in both texts, the use of "foreign" words enacts a powerful strategy of resistance positioning mainstream readers as outsiders of the text.

Furthermore, although "away" is evoked, in these stories, in keeping with multicultural constructions of faraway countries of origin (represented in both cases as the place inhabited by grandparents), it is neither fixed nor secured in the exterior of the dwelling place of the protagonists living in Canada. Instead, "away" intermingles at "home" as an intrinsic actual or remembered presence, and "Canada" is imagined as an expansive and generative space able to hold "here" and "there" as interactive and dynamic processes of homecoming. In portraying "home" elastically, these texts reveal how, for people of colour in Canada, truly belonging requires the roominess of more porous spaces and a way of living where "home" and "away" are not stabilized within national or cultural borders and categories.

"I do not like crab. I do not like fufu. I do not like palm nut soup.... So when my aunties and uncle come to dinner [my sister and I] eat chicken or french fries or pizza or hamburgers and we never touch the stuff the grownups are eating," declares the multiculturally divided protagonist in the beginning of *Crabs for Dinner* (Badoe). After exchanging many stories with his visiting Ghanaian grandmother, however, the protagonist realizes a way of being that is more relational and fluid than can be enclosed within the narrow, nostalgic conceptions of identity, history, or home characterizing dominant multicultural ideologies. This fluidity is made clear in the text's image of the grandmother telling her grandchildren stories of "away" while in their "home" against an outline of a map of Ghana: a representation of "away" that, here, is quite literally at "home" (see Figure 6). "Away" (the "foreign" land of Ghana, fufu, and palm nut soup) and "home" (the dinner table where the Canadian protagonist refuses any fufu and palm-nut-soup-eating) thereby come, during the course of the story, to reinforce each other, culminating in the protagonist's final decision to taste his grandmother's palm nut soup the week before her return to Ghana. His concluding discovery that the soup he had rejected in the beginning of the story is, in fact, "[e]xquisite!" and wonderfully acceptable after all gestures toward a reconstruction of "away" as intrinsic to home (although the fact that the grandmother's soup is more delicious than the living-in-Canada mother's because it has the "original taste" maintains problematic multicultural orientations toward the "authentic" as a mark of purity, uncontaminated by mixing in with the dominant culture).

Lights for Gita is a picture book that relates Gita's first Divali celebration in Canada. Last year's Divali in New Delhi had been "warm and joyful," but this year, in Canada, freezing rain puts an end to the traditional fireworks Gita had planned to enjoy with her friends. Gita's memories of the past contrast with the bleak prospects of her present life far from her loved ones. She longs for "[a]ll her aunts, uncles, and cousins [who] would be together at her grandparents' house. They'd be laughing, talking, and exchanging sweets with friends and neighbours." Meanwhile, the modified traditional celebrations she and her parents have planned in their Toronto apartment are literally eclipsed by a power failure. "How could such a place ever be home?" Gita laments, but the recurrence of the pictures of Gita looking out the window of her house suggests she is on the threshold of permeable boundaries of "here" and "there." Indeed, the book, in its interweaving of past memories and present circumstances, reveals that, in the end, "home" is a place of becoming.[9] By the story's end, the lights for Gita result not from the traditional display of fireworks as she had expected, but from the ice crystals outside her window where "[t]he whole world glistened! The sidewalks, every branch, every twig, the lamp post, even the blades of grass!" (See Figure 7.) While perhaps *too* cute, this leads to Gita recreating Divali with her "Canadian" friend, Amy.

But since, as I am proposing, at the site of children's literature by writers of colour, the significance of "home" and "away" is multiple, "away" also may be represented as a more near-away, the public and social space of Canada itself. In books such as Hiromi Goto's *The Water of Possibility* or Cheryl Foggo's *I Have Been in Danger*, for example, the Canadian national space, which, according to dominant ideologies of multiculturalism, *should* be "home," is neither felt nor depicted as one and, therefore, is experienced more as an "away" by the protagonists of colour. Indeed, it is occupied, variously, by cruel or ignorant neighbours, employers, classmates, teachers, and the like who exist just beyond the protagonist's four walls and who, often profoundly, impose on the protagonist's sense of self, family, and place. Similar to books such as *Crabs for Dinner* and *Lights for Gita*, these texts also show "away"—although here conveyed as a place much closer to home—as a location intimately connected to the characters' experiences of themselves and of their place both within and beyond their four walls.

INSIDE   At the same time, the re-visioning these texts offer is compromised by the ways in which they also perpetuate received notions of Canadian multiculturalism. While the reformulation of "home" and "away" may not be unique to children's books by writers of colour in Canada, we cannot overlook how, in these books, "home" is usually more affected by "away" than the converse. That is, these books seem to suggest, if Canada, the national space, is to be experienced as the "home" of multicultural promises, we need to surrender to its terms of cultural expression as a personal difference rather than engaging it as a means to affect sustaining and systemic change. In other words, in books such as *Crabs for Dinner* and *Lights for Gita*, personal homes may be reconfigured as structures where "here" and "there" can cohabitate. What, fundamentally, stays undisturbed, however, is the near, more immediate, public home space of Canada.

In these books, as in multicultural conventions, our differences are best left mainly behind closed doors. These narratives make clear that it is the private home space inhabited by people of colour that must find a way to include the outside, which is Canada, in its construction, while the outside Canada appears impervious to any reconstitution in kind. By these stories' conclusions, neighbourhoods, workplaces, and schools remain structurally unaltered. The sharing of food or traditions or the expressions of sorrow and anger and other emotions in response to racial injustices are present in these books in ways that, ultimately, remain irrelevant to Canada.

We see this in the representations of the enlarged senses of self achieved by both protagonists in *Lights for Gita* and *Crabs for Dinner*, which do not reach beyond the happy endings depicting the "brown" family eating "their" food or celebrating "their" cultural traditions from far-off lands in private. All the sharing that occurs, therefore, troubles little the public mainstream of Canada. In fact, Amy, Gita's white friend, in the only words given to her in the book, greets Gita's Divali-in-Canada celebrations with almost complete disregard, saying only, "Gita, tomorrow we can go sliding. It'll be like flying." The multicultural "home" of Canada endures as a domain barely affected by the presence, in its midst, of the Other.

Instead, it is the racialized protagonists, in order to overcome feeling "away" in Canada, who must make it "home" by conforming to, rather than transforming, its structural requirements as a white normative space. In the end, this homemaking only ensures we continue to be kept "away." And, by not really showing their characters imprinting the public space, these books seem to confirm that our state as at-home-but-not-quite in Canada is natural and inevitable (just as the equally inevitable "multicultural" question, "But where are you really from?" always returns our belonging—even as Canadian citizens—to somewhere else).

OUT OF BOUNDS   This expansiveness of "home," in its private and familial sense, but not of "home," in its political and national sense, however, is not generalizable to all children's books by writers of colour in Canada. As such, the novels *Coloured Pictures* (Himani Bannerji) and *A Group of One* (Rachna Gilmore) are among the few texts that do demarcate the public space as re-formed in any abiding way.[10] In *Coloured Pictures*, the protagonist Sujata's campaign against racism results in collective action crossing race, class, and gender lines, which transforms her entire community of family, friends, teachers, and neighbours, rather than any one individual. As the plot unfolds, Bannerji traces the manner in which the familial home (where Sujata's family shares not only food and traditions, but their painful experiences of racism) intersects with places outside the home—the Canada often felt as "away" (here represented by Sujata's neighbourhood and school).[11]

This intersection can also be found in *A Group of One*, a novel about a young woman of colour named Tara Mehta, and a novel in which Gilmore resists the multicultural obligations of promoting the peaceful good vibes holding sway in her *Gita* picture books. The climax of the novel occurs when Tara, who is trying to survive life as a teenager (family, boyfriends, best friends, and obnoxious teachers), courageously delivers an oral report about her visiting grandmother's experience of the Indian Independence Movement to her junior-high history class. The result of this bravery brings "home" (the place Tara lives with her family) into the public space of Canada, which, up until the time of the story's climax, Tara has only been able to move through as an "away," a fact confirmed in the reminder from one of her teachers that she is excluded from the rank of "plain old regular Canadian" (152).

This book, however, points to the potential there is to belong in Canada truly, differently. Throughout Tara's story, Gilmore insists on this connectivity between "home" and "away." Tara's best friend, for example, who is not South Asian, loves eating the samosas at Tara's house, and Tara's mother teases her guests with euro-accents. While, to me, these events feel somewhat contrived, what is particularly well done in Gilmore's story comes later in the novel through the intensity of the responses Tara receives to her oral report about her grandmother's experiences. Rather than offering a pat and happy end to Tara's presentation about colonialism and resistance, Gilmore presents the results (which are quite in distinction to Tara's dream that her report is greeted by everyone with joy and immediate understanding) as realistically ambiguous. At her house, after giving her report, Tara relates how "the back of my neck loosens. It's such a relief to be at home, where they understand" (159). But, at school, reactions to her assertion that she is a "regular" Canadian are mixed:

> Most of the kids are nodding. But Lynne and Mel are still shuttered, and a few others are puzzled. They just don't get why it's a big deal; they probably think I'm a real freak, bringing it up. My heart twists. All these faces, all these stories. There's such a chance to interweave and come together here. It could be so different.
>
> For a split second I have the same feeling I had in the dream that night, all of us *together*. Then it's gone and I'm back in the class with old friends—but there's also Pete, who is troubled; Nadia, who's never thought about *regular Canadians* and who still doesn't get it; and Mel; and Jeff. But mostly friends. (153)

Although we cannot claim Tara's intervention is a radical alteration of the Canada existing beyond the familial domain,[12] we can appreciate Gilmore's emphasis that, at least partly, Tara has made a "difference" to Canada as "away"—a sphere Tara, obviously, has been able to occupy thus far only as an "irregular" Canadian. Still, it is significant that Tara's struggle to voice her grandmother's personal story is depicted as touching, quite deeply, many of her classmates and teacher as it does, throughout the novel, her family and boyfriend (in sharp contrast to the depiction of Gita's friend Amy and her unmindful response to Gita's cultural celebration). In so doing, Gilmore demonstrates Tara's success in affecting not only the shape of the place she shares with her family, but also, crucially, the shape of the housing of her diversity, more broadly, in Canada.

This, then, is how racialized children's texts can dispatch possibilities of reconceptualizing "difference," auguring at least the possibility of interventions—both great and small—that can expose, expand, and potentially exceed the limits of established multicultural "homes" and "aways." In order to expose these possibilities, my approach to these texts has endeavoured to pay them different attention.[13] And, in order to trouble naturalized multicultural readings of these texts, I have pursued them for how and where they might, in fact, miss the mark of both hegemonic literary and cultural diversification pressures as these come to bear on representations of race in children's literature in Canada. As such, my analyses here have intentionally refused customary concerns with supposed literary goodness or badness, for it is always possible that these texts might crumble under the freight of such normative standards.[14] Instead, my focus is on a different mode of reading that heeds different things in order to acknowledge the varied ways children's literature by writers of colour in Canada takes up space within current agendas of racial and cultural diversity. Such engagements read these racialized children's texts as strategies of negotiation that demarcate organizations of racial power and privilege, which reside in prevailing multicultural definitions, expectations, and claims in Canada.[15]

Indeed, reading Others in "other" ways, as I have attempted to perform in this chapter, supports an anti-racist critical pedagogical project that resists any easy and untroubled consumption of racial and cultural difference. While multiculturally designated children's literature can never completely escape from the social and political scripts that configure its presence, a reading practice that points out how such texts outline the contours and parameters of their dictation can reveal the modifications, the foreclosures, and the omissions at work in containing race and culture in Canada. In this sense, racialized children's texts can function as remarks on current paradigms and agendas not simply where and when they challenge and transgress but, equally importantly, where and when they defer in apparent well-adjustedness. Exposing structures and regimes of containment insists we take notice of children's texts positioned amid the mar-

gins in Canada, not simply as transparent portals of connection or identification with people of colour, but as places where hegemonies of race enter
visibility. "Encounters between dominant and subordinate groups cannot
be 'managed' simply as pedagogical moments requiring cultural, racial, or
gender sensitivity. Without an understanding of how responses to subordinate groups are socially organized to sustain existing power arrangements, we cannot hope either to communicate across social hierarchies
or to work to eliminate them" (Razack 8).

As I have attempted to show, some texts internalize—and are internalized by—these agendas, and other texts attempt to weave in and out
of designated programmatic structures, spilling over the edges that enfold
"home" and "away" as simply one thing or the other. While I do not want
to abandon the variety of attitudes and strategies existing in children's
books by writers of colour in Canada in favour of vast and sweeping gen-
eralizations, I hope that what emerges from these readings is the potential of racial representations to move inside, to move through, to move
against stifling Eurocentric designs on the nation space. For in the end,
while we can hardly claim the genre of "multicultural children's literature" as a revolutionary oppositional discourse, the vision of inclusive-
ness it negotiates can usefully be regarded as an opportunity to engage,
counter, resist, transform the terms by which its "diversity" becomes
lodged.

□ □ □

Notes

1 Although I recognize the dangers of reductiveness in doing so, I mobilize the
   categories "writers of colour" and "people of colour" not as homogenizing and
   essentializing classifications but, strategically, as occupations that are no more
   stable or definitive than the category "white." My intention in naming subject
   positions this way, while indeed risking the reproduction of narrow categories of
   sameness and difference, is to evoke the racial systems and structures at work
   in sorting out our place in the nation.

2 For a detailed historical tracing of the various, and sometimes competing, ideals
   and manifestations of official multiculturalism in Canada, Augie Fleras and Jean
   Leonard Elliot's *Engaging Diversity: Multiculturalism in Canada* is an invaluable resource.

3 My argument, here, is contextualized in the critiques of Canadian multicultural
   policies and practices as separating people of colour from the national space
   advanced by Himani Bannerji's *The Dark Side of the Nation: Essays on Multiculturalism, Nationalism, and Gender*, M. Nourbese Philip's *Frontiers: Essays and*

Writings on Racism and Culture, Arun Mukherjee's *Postcolonialism: My Living*, Eva Mackey's *The House of Difference: Cultural Politics and National Identity in Canada*, Rinaldo Walcott's *Black Like Who? Writing Black Canada*, and Sherene H. Razack's collection *Race, Space, and the Law: Unmapping a White Settler Society*.

4 See, for example, Yasmeen Abu-Laban's and Christian Gabriel's chapter "Multiculturalism and Nation-Building" for an analysis of the grant proposals favoured by the current Canadian multiculturalism program and the increasing emphasis on multiculturalism as private, familial, and communal rather than as the public responsibility of the state.

5 Ghassan Hage's critique of the theme of "enrichment" as it appears in Australian multicultural discourses applies equally to its appearance in the Canadian context:

> For the White Australian articulating it, the discourse of enrichment still positions him or her in the centre of the Australian cultural map. Far from putting "migrant cultures," even in their "soft" sense (i.e. through food, dance, etc.), on an equal footing with the dominant culture, the theme conjures the images of a multicultural fair where the various stalls of neatly positioned migrant cultures are exhibited and where the real Australians, bearers of the White nation and positioned in the central role of the touring subjects, walk around and enrich themselves. (*White* 118)

6 I am also aware of the criticism this formulation has received for its abstractness and failure to attend to the difficulty of inhabiting, concretely and bodily, such spaces. The living in between the dominant and non-dominant cultures is often a space of violence and painful struggle. As such, I do not proffer the third space as a romanticized, emancipatory, pure, revolutionary space but as a space of difficult and complex negotiation and strategy:

> It is a constant challenge to develop this notion of interstitial space.... I see the position of women, for example, as being radically difficult.... [I]n terms of subject positioning you can only thrive on fragile ground. You are always working in this precarious space where you constantly run the risk of falling on one side or the other. You are walking right on the edge and challenging both sides so that they cannot simply be collapsed into one. (Trinh, *Framer Framed* 173–74)

7 This is in keeping with Kamboureli's argument concerning ethnic anthologies where editors, likewise,

> acknowledge indebtedness to the official [multicultural] policy because of the financial support they received through multicultural programs, but also, and most important, for the policy's sanctioning of ethnicity. In this sense, one may conclude that the Canadian Multiculturalism Act has succeeded in fulfilling one of its principal mandates, namely the "enhancement" of diasporic experience. Conversely, the self-contradictory images of ethnicity that emerge from these anthologies defy the ideological assumptions of the Canadian Multiculturalism Act. (134–35)

8 These disseminators are, in turn, themselves also often circumscribed by various political demands and policies that require the multicultural children's literature they pick up to perform Canada in particular ways.

9 And, indeed, Gilmore has written more books dealing with Gita's various experiences in Canada establishing her home, including *Roses for Gita* and *A Gift for Gita*.

10 Although imposing "home" on "away" has been, historically, a colonialist gesture, efforts to transform the public, hegemonic "away" when advanced from colonized or non-dominant positions, I believe, signifies differently.

11 I discuss Bannerji's *Coloured Pictures* more fully in the chapter "Bedtime Stories: Canadian Multiculturalism and Children's Literature," in *Voices of the Other: Children's Literature and the Postcolonial Context*.

12 It is certainly a troubling aspect of the plot, for example, that the burden of proof that she is a "regular" Canadian lies with Tara, as a person of colour.

13 The importance of bringing new reading practices to bear on racially marginalized children's literature in Canada is also addressed in DePasquale and Wolf's chapter in this volume.

14 Moreover, this choice of not focusing on the "supposed literary goodness or badness" of racialized children's literature can also be understood as a refusal to take up the role of consecrated (and consecrating) reader Nodelman discusses in his chapter in this volume.

15 Further complicating my readings of the racialized representations advanced by these children's texts is the overt commitment to multiculturalism of many of the presses publishing them. It is worth considering, therefore, how children's texts by writers of colour in Canada published by presses with no clearly stated obligations to multiculturalism might construct home/away differently. An interesting example presents itself with Cheryl Foggo's *I Have Been in Danger*, which I have discussed in this chapter and which is published as part of Coteau's In The Same Boat Series, described by the publisher as "a wonderful new series of novels that celebrate the diverse cultures of our country." As I discuss the novel here, the depiction of home/away within racialized spaces may negotiate more directly the complexities of such spaces than Foggo's earlier novel *One Thing That's True*. This earlier novel was published by Kids Can Press whose goal, as it appears on its website, is less clearly defined: "Our company's goal is to offer books that entertain, inform and delight the most important audience in the world—young readers."

CHAPTER 8

➡ **Windows as Homing Devices in Canadian Picture Books**

Deborah Schnitzer

Lucy Maud Montgomery's 1908 *Anne of Green Gables* introduces Anne's first morning through an opened window that conjures an opportunity seemingly unrealizable:

> But it was morning and, yes, it was a cherry-tree in full bloom outside of her window. With a bound she was out of bed and across the floor. She pushed up the sash—it went up stiffly and creakily, as if it hadn't been opened for a long time, which was the case; and it stuck so tight that nothing was needed to hold it up.
>
> Anne dropped on her knees and gazed out into the June morning, her eyes glistening with delight. Oh, wasn't it beautiful! Wasn't it a lovely place! Suppose she wasn't really going to stay here! She would imagine she was. There was scope for the imagination here.... Anne's beauty-loving eyes lingered on it all, taking everything greedily in; she had looked on so many unlovely places in her life, poor child; but this was as lovely as anything she had ever dreamed. (*Annotated Anne of Green Gables* 75–76)

The "look" out this 1908 window on Anne's first Green Gables morning acquires a host of Canadian associations that derive from homemaking practices generated by this peculiar, orphaned, immigrant, alien, and female child. An intriguing iconographic correlative comes from a *Souvenir Magazine* for the original 1965 musical production of Anne (see Figure 8). Freckled, open-faced, and larger than life, this Anne is an Alice overflowing the frame, her extraordinary view taking in everything as wonderland, including the miniaturist cast of community players who salutes her Tom

Sawyer–ish and Cinderella-esque dream-come-true potential. Given Anne's initial status as "almost" refugee and flawed hired hand, the view expresses an irrepressible desire for the possession of a world reduced to a pathetic fallacy.

The politics and styles of imagined homes, the performative character intrinsic to acts that would take possession, as well as their trickiness and ambiguities, are wonderfully involved in the stigmatized view Anne conjures, expressive of her tendency to meddle in things that don't belong to her.[1] Mary Claire Helldorfer's 2001 adaptation of the Anne story incorporates windows to dramatize things that will belong to her. The claim is incarnated in the dreamed-woman dress held by Anne as she is embraced by Marilla and Matthew in her finally "real" home at Green Gables. Homized by "adoption," re-dedicated and re-bound to the "civilized" world, Anne is doubly settled by a prospect of marriage, the logical extension of a Canadian child's ABC, where D might represent the de-fusion, domestication, and dowry she has acquired through Cuthbert affiliation. At the end of the story, in the final scene visualized by illustrator Ellen Beier, the view out the closed, frosted window defers to the view of an interior, articulating that "centripetal bias" Gaile McGregor suggests as compulsively produced by "new" Canadians. The winter sky revealed in the background window is absorbed by the colouring of the store-bought, gifted dress staged as Anne's growing-up toy. Its sheer presence, furbelowed and flowing, echoing the see-through curtains that dress the window behind, secure containment in terms of family and the "puffed sleeve[d]" dreams of marriage (Helldorfer), deepening the resonance of home-growing processes that turn the gaze inward toward enclosed and enclosing spaces. These properties suit Anne's hyphenations as "new," "restored," perhaps "former" (even recovering), Canadian insofar as she passes through orphaned, immigrant, alien, and redeemable: fiery and yet compliant, adventuresome though capable of yielding to the sensible, a "queer" but ultimately "becoming" Canadian. As a lovingly rehabilitated "heathen," she reappears as a windowed subject in various guises in our picture book history, integrally related to the "border epistomologies" of homemaking and homebodies.[2]

Windows pictured in Canadian picture books seem particularly able to define the shifting, dynamic, and often subtle "here" and "there" dialectic intrinsic to working definitions of home as developed in stories choreographed by conceptions of belonging, identity, and sanctuary. Carefully placed, allied with correlative forms that frame openings, views, thresholds, and passages,[3] they help distinguish the routes of resistance, initiation, and transformation that reveal how children are to understand their places. The lines windows draw to mark inside and outside spaces beguile; the fragility of such interfaces—even when they present as imposing and secure—heighten our awareness of the provisionality of home concepts and emphasize the assailability of homemaking practices that set out to build sheltering realities. In this chapter, I am introducing representative examples of seven windowscape chronotypes that develop specific "here-there" movements and exposures that in themselves both secure and trouble feelings of connection and claim: distress; opportunity; cellophane/envelope; two-stor(e)y/third-space; stained, ROSTA/ROSTA-*gris*; and picture window.[4] While William Moebius distinguishes between iconographic and graphic codes in his discussion of intra- and extra-literary referents,[5] I am going to use the term "iconographic" to suggest the blending of these pointing systems with regard to the iconic and verbal materials being examined. In naming the chronotypes, I am aware that a single window can exhibit and accommodate a variety of codes within an iconotext. However, inflected by the tale's particular theme and related narrative variables, a specific emphasis prevails and so distinguishes the type. I have been fascinated by the way in which these types emerge, the specific nature of the compositional elements that contribute to their expression, and the patterns they establish to determine who and what belongs in any given landscape. Inherent in my own study is its bias toward an inter-arts method and a close reading of those elements, so that I might understand how a particular type of window organizes and focuses our attention on the possibilities of homemaking it makes visible. As well, my study is biased toward windows as conceived primarily through a Eurocentric architecture. Most traditional Aboriginal dwellings in Canada, by way of contrast, do not incorporate openings like this western window, which in its composition privileges the eye as a way of naming and knowing place, and seems concerned with concepts of occupation that involve the politics and possibilities of ownership and permanence in material terms.[6]

distress windows

Often raised as second and/or third, attic stor(e)y windows where damsels are imprisoned by malignant spirits, distress windows can also occur at ground level to exhibit forms of house arrest where rogue characters, locked in and/or out, are denied access to significant aspects of their freedom, identity, and sense of home. They are confined or feel confined in spaces that present as alien, unforgiving, hostile, tricky, and/or dangerous.

Marie-Louise Gay's *Rumpelstiltskin* (1997), a whimsical retelling of the Grimms, deploys the prototypic sealed, attic distress window to exhibit the distraught miller's daughter contemplating her demise. Idiomatic in fairy tale and legend, central to its themes of inaccessibility, longing, and lost intimacy, the trope is absorbed and revised in Robert Munsch's "almost" subversive girl hero Elizabeth who saves and then drops the boy in *The Paper Bag Princess* (1980). More toady than princely, Ronald appears in the barred window in the upper reaches of the dragon's hold, hailing his would-be singed and paper-bagged princess just at the moment of her triumph, having rendered the dragon impotent. A distress window composes the frontispiece of *A Christmas for Carol* (2002), written by Len Gasparini and illustrated by Aino Anto, the story of a neglected, young "Raggedy Anne" child whose sallow, exilic state is co-signed by upperstorey, cloaked, and blind windows in the rooming house where she lives with her "hussy" of a mother, surrounded by seemingly disordered eccentrics, consoled in part by a neighbouring boy whose attentions mitigate Carol's almost cheerless existence.

The properties of the distress window—suspended in time and space in plastic and verbal terms—convey tensions between desire and actuality. It is worked by Rachna Gilmore in *A Screaming Kind of Day* (1999) with illustrations by Gordon Sauvé (see Figure 9). Frustrated by her mother's home work and tormented by her brother's teasing, Scully "escapes" outside, unable to resist the call of rain, "the way the green sings with" it and the way she shouts back (12). Having disobeyed and run the further risk of compromising her hearing aids, Scully is "grounded" by her mother, pulled screaming to her room, and stranded in front of a window. Her connection to the home space is represented as damaged and lost insofar as every aspect of the house disappears except the window itself. The sense of filiation persists, however, in echoes: the intricate moulding of the window frame finds parallels in the colouring and construction of the picture of a woman hung on the back wall, who seems, by the costume and sepia effect, to have come from another time and place. She is a grandmother perhaps—an ancestral figure whose mothering connection to Scully offers a trace of the home feeling that the child cannot access in these moments when the house is experienced as cellar and crypt, equivalents for the attic tomb.[7]

The distress window holds two stories inscribed by means of the simultaneous, diptychous presence of the present-day Scully and the pictured past relation—a rain-stained visual correlative for the mechanism of projection in the written text:

I stare out the window. The rain is falling soft and sad.
All I wanted to do was dance, dance with the rain,
to shout with the green.

Mom doesn't know how it pulls at me.
No one understands.
I'm not crying,
the rain is.
   (*Screaming Kind of Day* 28)

Distress windows, and attendant themes of un-homing and potential re-homing, make their way into Paulette Bourgeois's *Oma's Quilt* (2000), illustrated by Stéphane Jorisch, which begins with two threshold windows marking the transition about to unfold. Elizabeth's Oma is moving from her "house on Maple Street" to the "Forest View Retirement Home." The word "house" is deliberately chosen to facilitate the sense of leave-taking. The text continues to absorb what Gaston Bachelard describes as "the signature of intimacy" engendered by the "real houses of memory," smells that linger as part of the protective force field within the "original shell" (*The Poetics of Space* 4–14) that this Oma unwillingly relinquishes: "The house is empty, but it still smells like cabbage soup, warm yeasty dough, lemon polish and vinegar." Iconographically, the redoubled but shadow window on the floor inscribes the significance of this soon-to-be abandoned interior whose contents in the form of the single chair, as yet untaken, counter the almost content-less and blank view to the outside world. The distress of the moment is imaged in the frame that follows: Emily and her Oma take one last look out the window—a window suspended and shot from below to convey the feelings of entrapment and loss.

And yet the feeling of loss is blended here: there is optimism—seen not only in the colour values and the gentled, playfully rendered figures of grandmother and granddaughter, but also in the way this window is gaily dressed in butter yellow mouldings and drip cap. These dressings[8] suggest modes of reconciliation that are happily embraced by the lighter sides of Bourgeois's tall tale as satisfactory, resolvable endings persist and thrive. In the dressed window that follows during the very first day that Oma enters the Retirement Home, the sense of provisionality is conveyed through the lack of symmetry in the framing of the window whose presence and view Oma are encouraged by her daughter to appreciate. Oma's resistance is structurally present in the awkward vector constructed by the left-hand sash moulding and the brown diagonal that falls off the sill to suggest a second jamb. Yet there's a tentative, hopeful gesture achieved through the greens that connect the ribbons dancing from Oma's hat to the edge of the frame and the tops of weeping willows sketched beyond, which themselves contribute to the interior casings of the window itself. This optimism will further find expression in patterns of continuity and exchange in the quilt given by the granddaughter and daughter to memorialize the past sense of life on Maple Street. Reread, the opening windows simultaneously mark dislocation and potential relocation, yielding in cipher form the anticipatory qualities of homemaking that are explicit from the outset in the window of opportunity.

windows of opportunity

Windows of opportunity are charged with homemaking/keeping roles and responsibilities. Often as formulaic and self-conscious as distress windows, they are easily and insistently quoted in a variety of texts preoccupied with strays—human, animal, sometimes vegetable—and with the ruminating processes that translate "raw" matter into prospect and sanctuary.

A prototype for home defined by the transformation from interloper to pet is *Mister Got to Go* (1995) by Lois Simmie with illustrations by Cynthia Nugent.[9] The picture book depends on windows telling a story that begins as many do: "One dark and rainy night at the edge of a city on the edge of an ocean, a stray cat came walking down the beach." The black cat stops in front of the Sylvia, arrested by one version of the uncanny: "[A] strange, warm feeling [stirs] inside him. I think, thought the cat, I am tired of being a stray." There are multiple iterations of rectangular, windowed forms that highlight the way in which concepts of stray and home are "caught" in this picture book. These range from the opening illumination of Mister's form straddling the light and dark planes created by taxi headlights that simulate cat's ears to focalizations from the interior of Mr. Foster's office with Mister knocking on a rain-spattered window of opportunity looking for room at the inn (see Figure 10).

This window holds a range of lit and unlit exterior windows in an indifferent outside. The rain, glazed as tears and cats' eyes, textures the windowed frontier whose shore geography—ledger, filing cabinet, pencil and ruler—coddled in warm tones and bright light, code refuge, order, and safety. As the hotel, its manager, and staff learn how to contain Mister, sister and surrogate windows of opportunity track that opening and the ironies involved as the stray passes as guest and then fledgling member. This movement up the ladder is colour- and class-coded as well through the cup with the picture of a "bowled" goldfish eyed by a lighter, domestic cat partially seen through the bowl itself on Foster's desk. The image of cat and fish is framed twice: a bold red box bordered by dainty red paw prints. While the goldfish signs trapped, it also signs meal ticket in the chain of being as determined by an insider ideology that translates wild into tamed. The coding reminds us that windows of opportunity and the lightening of loads depend on the interests of the observer, the degree of agency, and the quality of the fit that can be imagined and constructed. Stories within stories reveal the delicate series of checks and balances that define how pets depend on the seeming integrity of their owners. The goldfish "survives" because of the protection its prison affords; the cat is fed but lives tormented by the view of a naturally occurring food source denied. These fragile home arrangements are further dramatized by related storybook characters. The pink pig eraser housed on the manager's pencil (a far cry from the brick home built as defence against the wolf) allows predator/protector, real/fake, transient/permanent values to flourish simultaneously and continuously.

This recurrence of the window as the "home" opportunity is achieved in another kind of stray-as-newcomer story fostered in the immigrant experience and the making of home in a forbidding but potentially rewarding Canadian West.[10] In William Kurelek's *They Sought a New Land: The Story of European Immigration to North America* (1985), an illustrated history with paintings and comments by Kurelek and additional text by Margaret Engelhart, a domestic interior, "The Taste and Smell of Home," is presented with the further title "Food linked the kitchen of the New World with that of the Old." Kurelek observes in the book's epigraph that he chooses "to record the crises, the calamities, the hunger, thirst, sweat, toil of the people settling into an untamed country. This I feel is nothing to be ashamed of. On the contrary, it glorifies the courage, the service, the toughness." The glorification is amplified in the verbal extensions Englehart provides for the painting:

> Holding the family together
> The immigrant was always in "two places"—the Old Country he longed for and the New World where he lived. It was the immigrant woman, the Mother, who held the two places together, just as she held her family together. Her kitchen where she prepared foods such as her mother had done in Europe—a time-consuming task—was the center of family life and the cosiest room in the house. Here everyone sat, talked and ate while children played or studied. (35)

The accompanying window of opportunity is opened in two ways: the sash is lifted and the right-hand jamb is absent. Threads for that further opening are sown by the scissors and spool on the sill, which exhibits agricultural, culinary, digestive, and generational tracts that cut into evolving home grounds outside and inside the window. Especially intriguing with regard to the tropes for growth and transformation is the potato become native as crop and perogie, manna-esque miracles to be polished off by the growing "wilderness" family whose spread is handsomely supported by the omnipresent paternal line framed as a photograph of the patriarch hung in all its glory adjacent to the open window. Metonymic and synecdochical figures seen through and in front of the window amplify and gender the bounty by juxtaposing parallel lines of harvest, sites for male—plough, fencepost, woodpile—and female—rolling pin, table, spool—homemaking activity.

The window of opportunity can come with special features as in Maxine Trottier's *Prairie Willow* (1998), with paintings by Laura Fernandez and Rick Jacobson. After the dedication, "To immigrants, then and now, who came understanding the promise / and carrying the hope / of our parents and grandparents among them," the covered wagon cradling the children opens in the text: "They built a house from the earth. Like moles, Mama and Papa dug the sod and piled it up. Emily fed the chickens and played with Jack. At night they slept in the wagon. It rocked gently in the wind like a ship in the dark. Emily held her doll closely and dreamed of trees." From this exodic ark, we share a view of a cleared and seemingly "uninhabited" landscape, take possession of its expanse, and ally our fortunes with these "first" parents in a synergistically resonant and new world. Of course the implications are alarming: I will speak more directly about this kind of erasure of identity and history in relation to Aboriginal peoples in relation to the stained window. At this point, I can say that few picture books seriously or even tangentially encounter First Nations peoples as distinct from, though perhaps in relation to, the immigrant story. Most envision an empty country, government-sponsored/sanctioned cheap land, and the possibility of prosperity contingent on hard work, fate, and sometimes "good" fortune.

The window of opportunity in the immigrant experience is face-lifted and transported to the present in *From Far and Wide: A Canadian Citizenship Scrapbook* (2000) by Jo Bannatyne-Cugnet with illustrations by Song Nan Zhang. The story begins with a hinge[11] and winter window that marks the moment before Xiao Ling Li, dressed in Canadian colours, leaves with her family for the Canadian citizenship ceremony at Queen Elizabeth School on King Street. This day, which coincides with national flag day, offers a time and experience Xiao Ling Li decides to commemorate in "scrapbook" form for her unborn brother who will be "born Canadian" in what by that afternoon will be a "Canadian family." And, as is perhaps typical of the way in which the refugee homeland is represented in multicultural picture books meant to celebrate Canada's open arms, the paratext observes that *From Far and Wide* is "not only the story of one special little girl, but is also a useful resource" working in harmony with "naturalization" processes developed by Citizenship and Immigration Canada. The church-sponsored Ethiopian refugee family seated in the row in front of Xiao Ling Li comes from a place that is remarkable only insofar as it has been escaped: "We were in the second row, behind Sophia and Maria. They are twins. They are in kindergarten at Queen Elizabeth. Their parents had to escape from Ethiopia at night, or maybe be killed."

The problematic nature of these biased representations of "failed homes"[12] is readily apparent in what I call the "Beirut" window of opportunity in *From Far Away* (1995) by Robert Munsch with illustrations by Michael Martchenko. Conceived through the letters Saoussan Askar writes about the 1991 immigrant experience that brought her from "war-torn" (Jones and Stott 368) Beirut to Scarborough, Ontario, the picture book sees Beirut only as a site of departure on a make-haste road toward Canada. To exhibit the transition, a makeshift, hinge window created by the mortar fire that has destroyed part of the family home is decorated by an improvised sill garden supervised by the girl's mother who proudly holds "the plane tickets to Canada." Saoussan translates a benign Canadian Halloween through the "bad dreams" of a homeland that fades as she learns "enough English" and names Canada a "nice place." Beirut is not missed. Homesickness (significantly Saoussan is motion sick throughout a plane ride, where "[n]obody wanted to sit near me") is represented by traumatized projections that disturb an otherwise secure Canadian peace Saoussan finally comes to welcome as real. In parallel ways, Saoussan is less a "real" little girl in her pre-Canadian phase; the transitory nature of her filiation is revealed through Beirut's damaged and dismissed reality and performed when she announces that she will change her name from Saoussan to Susan. Her mother, hands on hips, bolstered by the reflection of a no-trespass window behind, tells Saoussan to "change it back," but that command has only superficial resonance for a child now happily revealed as Canadian. Her tricky passage is masked and muted in simplistic Canadianizations that overwhelm this seeming collaboration.

cellophane/envelope windows

In the cellophane window, the subject is inextricably involved in, built through, and developed by parts of the window architecture: the mouldings and sashes, the jambs, muntins, sills, stools, and window dressings such as curtains, fringes, and rods. These kinds of windows create a fused content that helps manage the often nei-ther-here-nor-there, the in-between, revealing the libidity that characterizes the transient form. Often magical entities, figures who don't belong, these forms bring strange and sometimes trans-formative opportunities from alternative, unknown, and/or exotic worlds with them.

This kind of liminality is whimsically expressed in the magical plastic and verbal status of the windowed, "unhungry" snow cat who appears as a prayed-for playmate in *Snow Cat* (1992) by Dayal Kaur Khalsa. Elsie lives all "alone at the edge of the woods" where "the only face you ever see is your own, when, at the turn of the stairs each night you hold the can-dle aloft and catch a glimpse of yourself in the sleek black window, waver-ing like the moon fallen into a well." The wavering and unknown nature of the strange and potential pet who gives Elsie's wish flesh is cornered by the dimensions of the bewitching window, which can comprehend only one stage of its enormous visitor at a time. Of such "curious" propor-tions, it looks first "like a whole hill of snow piled against the window" and then "just a tall thin pillar of snow wagging against the sky." The tail and hind section of the cat are carved by the muntins that compose its quadrants, dramatizing both the size of the cat in relation to Elsie's hum-ble cottage and the impossible nature of the relationship that cannot be sustained by owner and pet. The snow cat doesn't survive inside Elsie's home but melts, morphing into a pond that will amuse and console throughout the change of seasons and thus relieve the isolation that Elsie has experienced.

The fascination with outsider and the edge on which the outsider is sit-uated as both migratory and possible extended family is central to the iconographic codes that work with envelope/cellophane windows and themes of perceived homelessness that have to do with status assigned by economic, regional, cultural, and species-driven assumptions and expectations.[13] *Long Nellie* (1993), by Deborah Turney-Zagwÿn, is dedi-cated to the author's "gypsy parents ... who raised me on the outskirts." The "homeless" Long Nellie, "as thin as a curved rake and as tall as a bent stepladder," gets by as a scavenger on the "outskirts" of the "village." The text is rich with references to the "at-the-edge" nature of her world: she is a castoff and homely, a recycler who collects junk from the "neighbor-hood dumpster"; hers is "a pretty lonely occupation" and "[n]o one thanks her for it." Long Nellie lives in a "scarlet trailer," a mobile home marker that Rosemary George notes is perceived often as "violating the 'true' image of the neighborhood," its occupants coded as "transients" and "read as 'unstable'" (24). Given Nellie's nickname and appearance, she is a freak as well. Her trailer appears with a "kinked pipe" that smudges the sky with grey wood smoke and "plastic veiled ... windows," "cloudier than smoke." Inscrutable and "unsung" define the threshold of the caravan itself as constructed by those who *really* do belong: "Neighbours couldn't see in. Long Nellie couldn't see out." Ironically and predictably, Long Nellie is "re-homed" by Jeremy, a young budding metrosexual who "mates" her with a stray cat found in the family's garbage can, an "orphan" like Long Nellie, "skinny, scruffy, alone." An inversion of the Exodus, Jeremy as insider and mini-sahib plants the cat, a basketed Moses, in the dumpster, the "living treasure" that Nelly might discover as playmate and kin.

There's a bit of an accident—Nellie hurts her foot because a poorly hidden Jeremy frightens her—and immediately Jeremy "rescues" that which he now ensures is broken. Nellie is no longer mobile, and so too the caravan loses its autonomy. There is the seeming restoration of Nellie's agency so that her "Gypsy colours!", her "amazing" "patchwork nest adorned with bottles of every hue,... butterfly colours," can "shine" with the light outside through "real" rather than no-trespass windows. Nellie's "gypsy" shawl, clothespinned to a rope inside the caravan, is windowed now in the door (see Figure 11) of a "snug," de-scarleted caravan advancing toward assimilation and permanence, supervised by Jeremy hanging tar paper for a "rainy day." This process requires disabling Nellie to begin with and placing her "outside" visually to code her reclamation. Taking cover and making shelter involve the removal of the occupant. Nellie's fetishized shawl replaces her; her former outdoor attire is revised and normalized. The born-again trailer is heavily pumpkin-esqued, a "not-quite" Cinderella coach that the reader imagines taking up residence as the rehabilitated "neighbour" next door with Nellie, less odd and wonderfully petted, whose new door boasts the shawl as window dressing and a miniature door for her own domestic.

two-stor(e)y/third-space windows

> This chronotype draws attention to the fact that alternative and sometimes competing stories of home are simultaneously present in a single window whose plastic and verbal implications are variously modified by the changing conditions of the unfolding story. Certainly the effects achieved can be intriguingly related to palimpsest and pentimento processes.

Two-stor(e)y/third-space polysemantic/iconic synchronicities are kin to, yet different from, two-stor(e)y effects that are managed sequentially. In *The Moons of Goose Island* (1997) by Don Philpot with illustrations by Margaret Hessian, for example, a grandmother's story, "The Moon of the Returning Geese," told to console a newly orphaned David, is replaced by the story David calls "The Moon of the Weeping Heart." The first bedroom window stages the grandmother's story; it is redressed by David's suffering in a second bedroom window, anticipating pictorially the particular way in which he will recover his balance and sense of home. By way of contrast, in Munsch's *The Boy in the Drawer* (1986), Martchenko's half-blackened window operates as graphic correlative for the provisional status of Shelley and her alter ego, that imaginary culprit who messes things up in Shelley's world, grows to "human size" if rebuked, and disappears if treated lovingly. The range of secular imaginary friends who score two-stor(e)y/third-space window surfaces to test concepts of home and not-home, the lost and the found[14] includes Tim Wynne-Jones's *Zoom Away* (1985) with pictures by Eric Beddows. A high Arctic revealed through the galley's portal window is reworked by the letter from Zoom's elusive Captain Roy. The written convention is disturbed pictorially because of the way in which the scene is shot: the letter, exhibited from the back, arcs into the portal window. While accessible insofar as it is "read" in the written text, it is, at the same time, cryptic for the pictured script is illegible, mimicking iconographically Uncle Roy's ability to evaporate into the unknown. The enigmatic values rendered here animate Zoom's renewable dreamscape at the close as he imagines "travelling with Maria and Uncle Roy to rescue the Catship once the ice melted." In *Waiting for the Sun* (2001) by Alison Lohans with illustrations by Marilyn Mets and Peter Ledwon, Mollie's newborn brother Benjamin, small and "ugly," disappoints Mollie. Her sadness is iconographically conveyed by the blank window countered by the grandmother's consoling presence. The window exists simultaneously as an empty slate and as a tablet inscribed with her more long-range vision of how this alien baby will be naturalized: "One of these days, he'll be running around all over the place. You two will have such fun."

More politically marked two-stor(e)y/third-space values are revealed in *The Missing Sun* (1993), written by Peter Eyvindson and illustrated by Rhian Brynjolson. Emily is confronted with two contrasting versions of Inuvik's missing sun within a single pane (see Figure 12). Emily's mother, a meteorologist, has moved the family from Regina. Her scientific explanation—"Right now, we are in the shadow of the earth. You see, when the sun shines directly on the equator, the whole earth is equidistant from the sun's rays and therefore, everywhere on earth receives the same amount of sunshine. But when the earth spins outward from its axis ...."—is countered by Emily's friend Josie Tucktoo's legend of Raven, the "tricky one" who will steal the "old sun."

These two versions co-exist in a single window. The disjunction registers the faltering of the mother's master narrative, hand-held in human-made pencil and paper and diminished verbally by her own daughter as "meteorological mumbo jumbo." This account occupies the same space as Josie's Story of Raven, which is simultaneously accessible and mysterious. Heard as "squawking," visually held in the tree branches, and perceived through the disappearing sun, Raven maps seasonal change in terms indigenous to the region. The third space, indebted to a vital "jarring of meanings and values" (Bhabha, "DissemiNation" 312), is further reorganized in the narrative, insofar as increasing weight is given to the accounting conceived and received by the Inuit as the story unfolds. This shift is prepared for here and coded iconographically: the foreground "white," interior and academic knowledge system (reinforced by the intensely lit windows of the sprawling Sir Alexander Mackenzie School that follow) has no more authority than the background and exterior, traditional telling. In fact, the latter expands, for the right margin is doubly supported by both Josie and Emily, while the mother's seeming inside/r knowledge is constrained by the skeptical looks on the children's faces, the singleness of her position, and the way in which the Raven extends beyond the border of her own head space. The artist challenges the value we typically assign near and far, such that background subjects assume foreground significance as Emily as newcomer is informed by northern climate, companion, and story. Hierarchies are further confounded at the close of the story as a continuing part of the strategy that would re-set subaltern and master points of view insofar as the "old sun" is not returned. While Emily demands that Raven "bring back" the old sun, an interpretation she receives from her mother who "says the sun is hiding ... behind the earth" and will "be back any day now," Josie corrects her friend: "No, Emily. That old sun isn't coming back! He was too small. And too easy for Raven to steal. We need a new sun. A big sun. So big that Raven will never be able to steal it from the sky again." The trickiness of the tale— the way in which conceptions of the "new" will inevitably be re-absorbed and jostled by and into conceptions of the "old"—is part of the inside joke that Josie laughingly spins at the picture book's close, a teaching brokered by the contrasting worldviews first conceived through the two-stor(e)y / third-space window.

stained windows

> The uncontested adventurer/tourist and open space in fantastic voyages become more problematic when the imperial eye lives in historical time and remains seemingly unaware of its damaging imposition. These degradations often are most tellingly revealed in the stained window. "Tainted"[15] by the stories inscribed in or on them, they are rooted in the historical and political realities of occupation and reveal racist and related death-dealing practices.

In *Peter's Moccasins* (1987), with illustrations by Philip Spink, the staining emerges in what I would call a "golden book" third space, one so mediated by neo-colonial eyes that the author herself, Jan Truss, would not claim sole responsibility for its production. Raymond Jones and Jon Stott explain:

> Given her interest in the treatment of minorities in Canadian history, it is not surprising that Truss agreed to do the text for a picture book that would give contemporary Native children a positive vision of their culture. Truss was so frustrated with producing a book acceptable to educators and bureaucrats, however, that she insisted the editor [Nancy MacKenzie] who changed her text share cover credit. In its published form, *Peter's Moccasins* is insipid. (454)

Though embarrassed by his new homemade moccasins and reluctant to share them during an in-class show-and-tell, Peter is so eager to play at recess he slips into them so that he can join the other boys outside. The stained window exhibiting this moment carries the trappings of a sluggish assimilationist edge that the editors may have felt redeemable as "admirable social values" (Jones and Stott 454). Its seemingly consoling cultural mosaic includes a store-grown touristy toy moose, Peter's abandoned "made-in-Canada" outside shoes, "western" clothing and sports equipment, Peter's moccasins, falling leaves, and cloud-shaped rustic-coloured bushes. The happily-ever-after character of this display McWindow endorses the would-be "true north" coalition that fails precisely because a reductive, anodynous, materialist treatment prevails.

As crude, but perhaps even more alarming, are the stained window actualities realized in *The Huron Carol*, originally told by Father Jean de Brébeuf, a Jesuit missionary who worked with the Huron at Fort Ste. Marie (now Midland, Ontario) from 1627 to 1649. Brébeuf, it seems, was killed during an Iroquois raid. The back-cover note for the picture book explains that the Huron Carol is "Canada's most beautiful Christmas carol"; kept alive after Brébeuf's death for one hundred years, translated into French, and then written in English by J.E. Middleton in 1926, it is republished in this 1990 version with illustrations by Frances Tyrrell.

The unsigned explanatory closing note, "The Story of the Huron Carol," reveals the under-story incentive for the picture book: "Many of the Christian Missionaries who came to the New World did not understand that the native peoples already had religions of their own." To his credit, Father Brébeuf "recognized the strength of the Huron beliefs" even while he "translated many books into the Huron language" and composed the carol, which "was sung in the Huron language for one hundred years." The note further commends Tyrrell's "accurate" illustrations: Tyrrell "tried to make each picture accurate. For instance, the constellations that appear in the borders are those that would have been in a December sky in 1648. The chiefs who come from afar are wearing the clothing of the Kootenay from the Pacific coast, the Sioux from the Plains and the Shawnee from the Woodlands. The palisades and the longhouses look like those that would have surrounded Fort Ste Marie when Father Jean de Brébeuf lived there."

In this Eurocentric fantasy with all its problematic inclusivities intact, the iconographic "drag" of the "saving fiction"[16] is accompanied by "translations" like the following: "The chiefs from far / before Him knelt / With gifts of fox / and beaver pelt." The stained glass effects that are created by the choice of a church window as frame for this invading "nativity" ironically exhibit issues of appropriation and misrepresentation that the note self-consciously pretends are resolved. The apology underlines the neo-colonial ideology: "Lack of respect for other people's beliefs has brought much heartache and suffering. But the Huron carol deserves to be remembered and enjoyed because it touches something in all of us: its message—that even in the darkest winter there is the promise of light and new birth— is one of hope which we all can share." To demonstrate this "truth," and thus avoid its totalizing character, the publisher quotes from the Grand Chief of the Huron-Wendate Nation, Max Gros-Louis: "Today there are over 2,000 people living on our reserve at the heart of Quebec City. This Nation is a dynamic one. We operate schools, a bank, a radio station, and our own justice system. We are pleased that this book tells a part of our common history."

The juxtaposition of these two excerpts intensifies the vexing nature of this rationalization of racist practices many Canadians rarely acknowledge, have been trained not to acknowledge, or too quickly re-frame as "only doing one's job," a following of orders—in this instance, Jesuit ones. The settler standing in place of the Other, re-enacts an old-world/Word origin story through violations that masquerade as "authenticities," promoting those asymptotic negotiations Alan Lawson explores in his study of the settler as "a narrating subject" seeking to "establish a nation" and therefore needing "to become native and to write the epic of the nation's origin" (27). The stained windows so gloss the reality of imposition/purchase that the reader "almost" renders unto the church what was not and is not the church's, reading into its colonization legitimacy rather than disavowal (see Figure 13). The renascent "Imaginary Indians," palliatives for "earnest" colonial desire, are hailed by the divine inspiration recorded in the text that accompanies the viewing of the baby inside the curtained doorway of the dwelling staging the event:

> Come kneel before
> the radiant Boy
> Who brings you beauty,
> peace and joy.

> "Jesus your King is born,
> Jesus is born.
> In excelsis gloria!"
>   (De Brébeuf, *Huron Carol*)

Neo-colonial values proliferate. The "angels" wallpapering the viewing of the Christ child energize the good father's quill as he sits before the fire composing the commemorative carol in the penultimate image of the picture book. Appropriately dressed in Jesuit robes, his performance intact and "Word" uninterrupted, Brébeuf is haloed in sweet, scrolled clouds of smoke. Tyrrell's "innocent" Hallmark iconography enshrines those "little leeway[s]" Roderick McGillis tracks in Welwyn Wilton Katz's appropriations in *False Face* (227–34).

The political implications of the stained window can also demonstrate opportunities for resistance and redress—express, in fact, the loss incurred by First Nations peoples savaged by "noble" colonial ideals. *old enough* (1986), a story by Eyvindson with illustrations by Wendy Wolsak, references the master tools that haunt peoples made homeless in their homeland. The elders are gathered in the kitchen with an etiolated map of the Provinces of Canada that shows through a complicated redoubling of panes in partially opened fore- and background windows, themselves suggesting themes of imprisonment and release. This staining of the land, the often unacknowledged stealing of homelands by the federal government, is windowed here in a story that traces how a father's absorption with the political means that will redress that wrong almost leads to the loss of contact with his own son. The de-fathering of the federal claim coincides with the re-fathering of the elder–son relationship. I find in this window opportunities for an edginess and critique that may well develop related *gris* elements, properties intrinsic to *film gris*, a sub-genre that involves *film noir* characteristics by exposing the shortcomings of prevailing, dominant ideologies, yet preserves the possibility of happier endings. Windows cited in these terms may find more frequent articulation as Canadian picture books challenge more consistently and compellingly the assimilationist, narcotic, and narcissistic reaches of contemporary, official multicultural policy and performance whose limitations Louise Saldanha, for example, explores in this volume.[17]

ROSTA/ROSTA-*gris* windows

I am adapting the ROSTA window integral to 1920s Russian political poster art. Blending educational and political goals, its form became both the first cultural ABC-picture book and the propagandist newspaper.[18] Set by illusions of security and preserve, formulaic and fully expressive of embedded points of view, the home-sweet-home settler story and "O Canada" ROSTA window dominate empire-building initiatives and related nostalgic renderings of a national home. Windows that interrupt the enthusiasm for an uncomplicated ROSTA introduce *gris* elements that discover in seemingly up-beat resolutions troubling compromises and losses.

Belle's Journey (1993) by Marilynn Reynolds, illustrated by Stephen McCallum, for example, exhibits back-cover promotional material that names the tale as "[a] moving and touching story of devotion and a heroic fight for survival," endorsed by praise from *Canadian Geographic*: "Maybe the most touching children's story ever" produced in Canada. The "little farmhouse," garrisoned, "almost hidden in the storm," glows however "dimly," guiding Molly and her trusted Belle through the blizzard back to the "familiar shape" of home and the windowed silhouette of her watching parents. The interior golden light secures Molly in the iconographic means that follow, catching the outline of father and horse outside her bedroom window, haloing those uncanny instincts in Belle that kept home intact throughout the storm. These means animate stabled ROSTA resonances that prevail in the secular glorifications of a prairie "native." Certainly this sense of "just-enough" courage and the miracle of the return are part of the pragmatic heroics in many settler stories that involve Anne's metaphysical sisters—those young girls who combine pluckiness with fortitude and some luck … as they make and re-make home.[19]

The ROSTA window, in its most hyperbolic iterations, is as distressingly one-sided as it is formulaic. One of the most troubling representations comes from Ian Wallace's *Sparrow's Song* (1986). Set in the Niagara

Falls of the turn of the century, this is a "true story" about an orphaned sparrow whose mother is shot by Katie's brother's sling. The sparrow is foster-mothered by Katie, whose ministrations in the attic give view to an idealized farming community, further sedated by the accompanying "pictures" that secure the rituals of a colonial past. The collected artifacts represent the history of occupation, domestication, and commodification: a Union Jack hangs from the rafters; a lifebuoy inscribed with MAID OF THE MIST is coupled with a "primitive" rendering of a naked mist maiden taking the falls in a birch bark canoe. She faces a mannequin, a metaphysical twin, whose face is composed of a blank mirror. Processes of erasure and reification involve the redoubled but falling right breast composed by the hanging, bare light bulb that illuminates a series of memorabilia pieces that share a caged/framed form. These include the playpen that houses the sign for the Ridley Regatta; the antique wooden cart that might have been pulled by the wooden horse; the caged sparrow directing its song toward Katie's breast; the window that secures the picturesque; the painting of Katie's forbears in turn-of-the-century costume propped by an old-world trunk; the noose made from the wire of a hanging bulb that is revealed as an isomorphic cousin to the mirror; and the skeletal frame of the mannequin that appears as almost ambulatory underneath the padded torso.

Katie absolves her brother of the murder and they return again to "nature," re-homing the orphaned sparrow by simulating their own "noble savagery." Like the "helpmates" and "partners" in the imperial enterprise discussed by Rosemary George (144), the children "mother" the bird under the watchful eye of their own human mother (realized in a suitable Canadian gothic). The bird is successfully restored to its "natural" state, returning in the fall while the children are playing checkers to bid farewell, singing, in "english," "I'm fine ... I'm fine," an example of the "thematical wild" Gary Snyder explores in nature writing (299).

The picture book takes its leave with another far too-easily resolved, unnatural and problematic homeland security: an opened, dressed, and attic ROSTA window that is pointed clearly into an uncomplicated "happily ever after" supported by the reliable, permanently homed, mechanical rooster weather vane, gay kites expertly managed from the ground, the perfectly formed V of southbound Canada geese, and the serene, methodized view of a prosperous, settled countryside. This view is enjoyed by the soul-mated, sensitive, tousle-haired, blond Canadian boy and girl, silled, their shadows delicately staining the opened casement window as if to emphasize the "rosier" view they've acquired in "training" the orphan and themselves. Re-homed in their retreat, they are bolstered rather than distressed by the old-world power plays that are coded through the window behind them: the picture of a castle hung on the wall and a friendly game of checkers underway.

Bereft of the edges that might subvert Anne's kindred spirits or challenge the golden flounce and green-gabled values intrinsic to performances of the colonial home and past, this potent image and pattern is fully expressive of conventional ROSTA windows and the plastic and verbal idioms that achieve them. These conventions are absorbed by, yet complicated within, the 1994 *Lights for Gita*, as Gilmore initiates the story of being settled in a new home's unsettling dimension. Insofar as certain ROSTA values are challenged in *Lights*, the story apprehends some of the window *gris* implications I note may increasingly develop in Canadian picture book window architecture and story.

Interestingly, a more one-dimensional sense of a Canadian ROSTA window emerges in Gilmore's later *A Gift for Gita* (1998). The book is dedicated by Gilmore "To all the children who are newcomers to Canada—welcome home!" This paratext appears in tiny font at the very back of the book, a hiding of place-name that suits the internationalist agenda of the book itself. Were it too peculiarly Canadian it might not appeal. The national, cultural, and geographical codes are soft: Canada is not mentioned in the story, though markers like canal, camping, canoeing, the Rockies, and ice skating invite insider identifications. So too, the ROSTA effects persist, for the suffering through and anxieties about re-location and becoming Canadian are equally soft. Momentarily overwhelmed, Gita struggles with her attachment to both place and person. These loyalties figure in seemingly acculturated sill and stool visualized from the outset through the Indian nesting dolls and the "favourite maple tree." This tree is consistently windowed as a kindred spirit, the companion that Gita consults as she wrestles[20] with the fact that her beloved Naniji will return to India while Gita and her parents will "root" themselves permanently in Canada. The "India" that once existed is but "a blur of distant colour and voices, an echo. Here was full and clear, loud and now. Home." The ROSTA concept, repeated in the windows that picture an Ottawa fall, depends on tranquil motherland realities. While a subsequent image may suggest viable hyphenated identities and the consolation of memory, acculturated values dominate.[21]

There are seemingly darker possibilities that undercut the ROSTA optimism in *Gifts* in the terms Gilmore establishes in her earlier *Lights for Gita*. Gita's desire to share a "first" Canadian Divali festival of lights with her friends is thwarted by a winter ice storm. The Canadian climate infuriates Gita—this "November gloom" so different from the New Delhi she remembers "brilliant with fireworks," rich with family gathered at her grandparents' house. Gita's anxiety is pictured in the distress window of their "new home," scored iconographically by Poe-esque branches and bird, barren and sharp, and in the two abridged windows that follow: the branches strike as lightning, "[n]eedles of ice" sting the windows, the unlit *diyas* on the sill impotent against the darkening sky. Gita wonders: "How could such a place ever be home?" Yet, even as the power fails, "one by one" the "golden flames" of the *diyas* quiver and spring to life mingling with the "warm fragrance of mustard oil," "beat[ing] the darkness."

This story of transformation finds a related pulse in the Divali festival itself, which celebrates the homecoming of Prince Ram and his wife Sita after years of exile. The story as told in the Hindu epic *Ramayana* is recalled by Gita's mother even as she reminds her daughter of the poignancy intrinsic to stories of endurance and continuity: "'Gita,' said Mummy softly. 'Divali is really about filling the darkness with light. Fireworks can't do it for us. We must do it for ourselves.' Mummy's smile was bright, but also sad—like grandmother's smile when they'd said goodbye." The third-last picture book window shows Gita's face inscribed as a reflection whose joy and spirit is echoed in the redoubled *diyas*, glowing, "bright, brighter, brightest—filling the living room with light" and annotating the night sky. The use of the mirrored window gives concrete definition to the transference and self-reflexivity the story celebrates. The world outside is adopted by this Indian child and this Indian ceremony: "Gita ran to the window. The *diyas*' reflection made it seem as if there were another shining room outside." Interestingly, the verbal code maintains the military model that pits Canadian and Indian realities against one another: "'We beat the darkness, we beat the darkness!' Gita clapped her hands." Gita's mother further consoles, feeling the performance is a sign of the "wonderful luck" the family will enjoy.

The deceptively "Indianized" outside gives Gita renewed hope, and the partially abridged yet persistent golden glow emanating from her apartment window is retained in the penultimate window (see Figure 14) with Gita outside, about to greet her Canadian friend Amy, finally come to share the evening's celebration. Gita's vigil does in fact seem to claim the kind of "luck" that makes a difficult world home. The story concludes with a celebration of what a Canadian ice storm, hailed by the *diyas* and Gita's longing, can do to duplicate the "brilliant" fireworks of New Delhi: "Gita took a few cautious steps. She stopped, eyes wide. The whole world glistened! The sidewalks, every branch, every twig, the lamp post, even the glades of grass! In the dark city, only their windows blazed with the steady glow of *diyas*. The ice, reflecting their light, sparkled and danced like fireworks." Gita will write to her grandparents "about this Divali in her new home," these *diyas* "singing in the heart of the ice."

This is a complicated ROSTA-*gris* window capable of turning on itself in significant ways. It can be interpellated through the figure of the nation-as-refuge, adept enough to hold a promising dialogue between Canadian and Indian realities. Yet it appears equally as illusory as Anne's "imagined" possession of Green Gables, engagingly congruent with the paradoxical aspects of the classic that had enthralled Gilmore, herself, as a child in Bombay, when her grade four teacher, Mrs. Chaubal, "a red-haired lady, perhaps Canadian or English," read it to the class, "[f]irst thing in the morning," in what Gilmore states was "the best private school in Bombay," "run by the Anglo-Scottish Education Society" (Jenkinson).

Homemaking paradoxes reverberate: this capacity to sing "in the heart of ice," to play hide-and-seek in a magical outside, occurs "while the power's still out." The power will come back: the usual Canadian mosaic conditions that define who is visible and what belongs will be reinstated. The suspension of "real" Canadian conditions is thus as precarious as the Divali light momentarily suspended in the third-stor(e)y apartment window. The returning "power" prevails even as a more consoling, though uncertain, ephemeral shared space is constructed, which would allow Gita to hold to family traditions insofar as she momentarily colonizes the Canadian landscape in Indian terms. The "new home" promise and reconciliation of here–there tensions the story seems to endorse are intriguingly eroded, though that complexity may seem underdeveloped in the "new home" celebrated in the written text. The imbalance, however, is coded pictorially in the final image itself of the two friends arm in arm just before Gita takes "one last look at the light" and the two "race ... upstairs" back into Gita's apartment. While the girls are rendered as equals in terms, their foreground position carefully balanced within the frame, and while red and saffron motherland colours cooperate, the scarf around Amy predominates, visually underlining both girls and signifying the prevailing status of the Canadian winter, the seasoned Canadian native, and the accommodations that must be made as the immigrant is threatened, naturalized, perhaps erased.[22]

picture windows

The making of home is often built by processes of exclusion[23]: lines are drawn, limits are set. Their arbitrariness is most readily experienced, perhaps, in the off-kilter quality of dressed windows that emphasize dislocation and distress among inside and outside forces. Renditions of the elastic and constructed status of home can be

> achieved equally by kiltered views through windows that sponsor
> balanced and regularized treatments—picture windows whose sur-
> face quiet reveals concepts of refuge and risk by playing with mime-
> sis and simulacrum, copy and construction as they relate repre-
> sentations of "actual" and "imagined" space–time realities.

In the work of Aboriginal and Métis writers and illustrators, such picture windows often help achieve the presence of equally significant historical and dream worlds.[24] This is particularly true of the work by Joe
McLellan, who, with his wife Matrine, creates *Nanabosho Grants a Wish*
(2000), illustrated by Lloyd Swampy. The opening picture window establishes the site of Nonie's birthday party where Billy's wish—"I hope it
snows a lot"—leads to a cautionary tale told by the grandfather that shows
the dangers that might attend ill-conceived wish-making. The relationships in the outside view are carefully preserved, not only as a way of
measuring the increasing snowfall, but also as a way of securing the building blocks that showcase the more conventional here-and-now coordinates of the home place. That convention is disturbed in part to reveal what
Maria Nikolajeva and Carole Scott have defined in their picture book
typology as enhancing and counterpointing image–word relationships
(12). The interior picture window, which shows ordinary time passing
through accumulating snow, exhibits a right-hand lower corner rediscov-
ered in the circular willow window. The slight re-drawing anticipates the
presence of different time senses in a single composition, a simultaneity
that increasingly interests the narrative and emphasizes the art of framing itself. The green leaves hatching from the willow encourage the forest green outside the window to communicate within. Progressively human
and natural forms intersect and travel to baffle conventional inside–outside, here–there boundaries, exercising thematic opportunities that dramatize how the series of wishes work. The story concludes with a picture
of the gathered family seen from a distance through the western living-
room window, snowed in by a "fierce" night blizzard. The sky itself exhibits
two oval portraits of the children along with written text framed within
the shape of a turtle. The latter is built in the spirit of the recurring, long-
ago home window that exclusively exhibits the written story initiated
inside the circular willow window at the outset of the story. Its iconographic disposition absorbs specific story details that distinguish the
scenes marking the series of requests that are made of Nanabosho. The
techniques that establish framed views, space-time realities, and life forms
involve enigmatic conversations with picturing and related concepts of
artistry and reference.

Picture-window iconographies revealing the dialectic among space–time realities are emphatically present in the work of Deborah Delaronde and Gary Chartrand in books that make up the Flour Sack Flora stories, tales of survival and inventiveness placed in the 1930s to 1950s rural Métis community of Duck Bay, Manitoba. In their discussion of Virginia Lee Burton's *The Little House,* Nikolajeva and Scott note its "unique" and "fixed point of view, where the reader/viewer is placed in front of the house, as if it were a theatre stage. However, while the perspective does not change, the scenery does: from day to night, spring to summer, fall to winter, and then through a rapid urbanization and technologizing" (15). This sense of staging both change and stasis is integral to the home concept achieved through the recurring series of picture windows in the Flora stories. Interestingly, these windows emphasize the presence of landscape, which, while inflected by signs of human habitation by way of docks, houses, hanging laundry, and distant boats, almost entirely excludes the representation of human forms and often employs a "flat distance" technique to achieve effects of stillness and openness.[25] The absence of human figures and the presence of signs of human habitation in the landscapes drawn outside the window relate intriguingly to a sense of the way in which natural and human-made structures co-exist in communal spaces that bear but transform the impress of colonial forces.

Flour Sack Flora (2001), the first of the Flora books Delaronde has written, tells the story of the homemade "town" dress crafted by Flora's grandmother with the help of a number of other community women whose handicrafts depend as well on the unbleached cotton cloth sacks they recycle as "aprons, towels, and dishclothes," pillow and cushion covers, and "table cloths, doilies, napkins and pillow cases." In her thanks to Robin Hood Multifoods for giving her permission to use their company flour sack and logo and to Five Roses Flour for the use of their 1926 company flour sack and logo, Delaronde reminds us of their pervasive influence: "[T]he first mill was in operation in 1881 in Winnipeg, Manitoba, 1886 in Montreal, Quebec and 1913 in Medicine Hat, Alberta. In 1915, the first Five Roses cook book was published, the cook book was in daily use in nearly 600,000 Canadian homes."

The process of making the dress is drafted in a number of community dwellings with shared renderings of the exterior scene, emphasizing the collective, secure, and sustaining values of the community. In fact, ten of the twenty-four visual texts involve interior views of windows that in some way look out on the outside world. (Eleven, if you count the view outside taken from inside the car that carries Flora, in her spiffy new dress, and pet frog Mucky into town.) The stability of the external environment is supported by the fact that the view is, at some levels at least, an ontic rather than phenomenal presence. None of the inhabitants in the story are ever pictured looking out the window. The reader sees the out-of-door scenes regularly unfold, unmediated in any direct way by the interior points of view, though of course indirectly mediated by Flora and her community, as well as by the developing sense of the Other and the mainstream world far away, which is nonetheless insistently present in the flour sacks, emissaries from "trusted" Robin Hood and Five Roses flour companies elsewhere.

Recurring framing treatments persist to the extent that particular examples might in fact double as both "actual" windows and "actual" paintings. The distinction does not settle. For example, while there are no double mouldings, as there are in what appear to be living room windows, no muntins to block the pane as at Kookoo Marta's Second Hand store (see Figure 15), no knobs and hinges to suggest an opening as in the kitchen window, the views exhibited while Grandma and Flora measure, draw, cut, and sew (see Figure 16) might be windows rather than paintings. They do not differ substantially from any of the other stylistically and conceptually related views of the landscape out the window. By meddling with distinctions between art and nature, repeated in a number of dwellings, Chartrand demonstrates the shared understanding of what "home" looks like among community members.

That conceptual realism—the idea and ways of home—is informed by choices Delaronde considered as she collaborated with Chartrand.[26] The transcending of the binary, the playing with illusionist techniques in "pictures" that pose as landscape paintings, and "windowed subjects" that pose as painted spaces is also evident in related framing practices. The emphasis on making and exhibiting works of art further achieved through translation is also present in the hangings of the raw and finished materials composed of flour sacking: clothespinned flour sacks, laundry lines stretched outdoors, curtains in windows and under sinks, second-hand dresses in Kookoo Marta's store, the measuring and hanging of the emerging dress as well as the variety of quilts, runners, wall hangings, and hand-crafted items displayed by artists. The sack cloth, stripped of its signatory identity and/or "original" and problematic purpose, although reconstituted in any number of creative ways, of course retains the tracings of its colonial form and presence, recalling the concept of the transculturated that is part of studies of "mutual transformation," the "various kinds of serendipitous, mutual, strategic and subversive cross-cultural borrowings and more transgressive masquerades" that translate colonial presences and reconceptualize home.[27]

While this sense of agency and resistance is never explicitly verbalized by characters in *Flour Sack Flora*, every dress-making action distinguishes the transformative processes of a collective strategy, homegrown wisdom, creativity, and steadfastness that show the polyglot character of goods re-thought and repackaged by equally homegrown practices. The specific impact that defines the fortunes of the Robin Hood and Five Roses Flour companies and the struggling, makeshift, and make-do resourcefulness of the community reveal the asymmetrical character of the power relations: the community's idiosyncratic activist accommodation is nonetheless unmistakably tied to town. Flora requires this "pretty girl's" *and* "granny's" dress so that she might go and shop, following in the footsteps of her mother and father, who regularly fill the shopping lists of family and friends. How that tricky space is managed as an act of translation is revealed in part by the windowed landscapes built by the correction lines of a home seemingly secure.

These paradoxes are strikingly presented in the final scene of the book, the home landscape appearing through the car's cellophane window as they gather speed on the "gravelled road" that brings Flora closer to her first close encounter with dolls in store windows. That passage is accompanied by an ongoing dialogue with Mucky in which Flora wonders aloud about asking her grandma and her friends "to sew … a doll just as pretty as any doll sold in the stores!" We recall the imaginative acts of possession that made home for Anne, at the outset of this exploration, the first-hand longing from a second-story window of opportunity constructed by an orphan with nowhere else to go. In *Flora*, we discover picture-window homemaking practices that help ground a process that enables a young Métis girl to fit into a tempting world away from a home that in itself endures, where she does in fact belong, and that ingeniously supports her round trip.

My exploration of window types within this chapter encourages us to see the way in which particular types function to define pivotal home-making practices and activities. Each specific instance of the type is con-structed by a range of verbal and visual values. While the specifics will cer-tainly vary according to the pictorial style and thematic preoccupations of the individual story, the type itself establishes conventions that are reit-erated in clear and compelling ways. As we become more adept at read-ing the types themselves, we discover opportunities we may have over-looked. One-sided or one-dimensional representations of home are complicated, for example, by two-stor(e)y/third-space and ROSTA-*gris* techniques that exhibit the presence of contrary, competing, or opposing claims within a single window. Such devices dramatize the permeability, changeability, and instability of home front assumptions and the illusions of security those assumptions may have initially hoped to maintain. It seems that, as picture books explore more difficult, controversial, and risky subjects in relation to national dreams and nation building, as they reveal the complications of the past and the present, as they insist on sharpening rather than dulling our understanding of the forces that make and un-make home, so too the homing devices windows display become less static and formulaic, more responsive to the political implications of the processes of oppression, transformation, and resistance that reveal our various histories.

☐ ☐ ☐

Notes

1 Anne characterizes her tendency to "meddle" as a series of "mistakes" she learns through experience to amend. The fiction she creates in her view out the window is as responsive to the topophiliac panorama that McGregor suggests as the centrifugal and potentially "claiming gaze" characteristic of the American experience of seemingly "unmapped," "virgin," or "unclaimed" space (16) or what John Berger in *The Shape of a Pocket* calls the "mimetic sweep" of dominant world-pictures that would obliterate alternative and diverse points of view that in themselves ruin or refuse such representations (209–15). As such, the view constructed is also available to discussions of the "desire" and "disavowal" Alan Lawson, Roderick McGillis ("'And the Celt Knew the Indian'"), and Stephen Slemon, for example, identify as crucial to the asymptotic settler practices that stain existing terrain with the colonial gaze. As well, the claims can be associated with what might be called "see-through" or open-window gestures that sustain the *trompe l'oeil* fascination of single-point perspective and infinite regression through seemingly empty and/or unclaimed space. Certainly my understanding of here and there has been informed throughout by the pivotal work with home and away patterns that Perry Nodelman explores and in studies inspired by that analysis as expressed, for example, in Mavis Reimer and Anne Rusnak's "The Representations of Home in Canadian Children's Literature/La représentation du chez-soi dans la littérature de jeunesse canadienne."

2 I note happily the helpfulness of John Kraniauskas's discussion of various frontier knowledge systems in "Hybridity in a Transnational Frame: Latin-Americanist and Post-Colonial Perspectives on Cultural Studies" in *Hybridity and Its Discontents: Politics, Science, Culture*, 239.

3 In "Introduction to Picturebook Codes," William Moebius notes:

> I would point out that the frequent depiction in picture books of gates, doors, windows and stairs, of roads and waterways, and the changing representations of light, artificial and natural, to accord with different degrees of character understanding, are not accidental or fortuitous phenomena, but downright basic to the symbolic force of the story. A char-

acter who looks out the window or stands in the door, as Max does in *Where the Wild Things Are*, is implicated in the unspoken meanings of thresholds. Whether stairs, steps or extended ramp, the incline may provide a measure of the character's stature or of progress towards a depth or height of understanding or confusion. There is nothing doctrinaire about such pronouncements. Nothing should tie interpretation of stairways or doorways and such in picturebooks to a single intention or effect. Such pieces of the symbolic code work differently in different stories, and will lend themselves to different interpretations. But they should not be overlooked. (146–47)

My own sense of window types involves the specificity that Moebius describes, as well as a pattern of emphasis that can reveal commonalities among particular manifestations and thus operate as "spoken" thresholds. Though I've not encountered explorations devoted to the study of picture-book windows alone at this point, many and engaging references to their significance occur in the various analyses of what Moebius describes as thresholds and related "buffer" zones between the known and the unknown.

4 The windowscape taxonomy I am developing involves fifteen types overall, including dressed, hinged, spell, spill, sill, no-trespass/closed, window seat, and seasoned window, in addition to those I discuss here.

5 Detailing this distinction in "Introduction," Moebius observes: "Graphic codes do not depend on the relation of objects to each other in a world outside the text; these we would call 'iconographic'" (148). He further observes in an accompanying note that "[t]o read iconographical codes, we need to know much more, often, than the text can tell us about symbolic usages. We acquire our knowledge of these figures from sources outside the text ..." (148). While I am not convinced the distinction Moebius is making holds, I appreciate the contextual processes he's exploring and the further distinction he makes in this section of the "Introduction":

> To be able to read a graphic code we must consider the disposition of objects on the page, the handling of line and colour, we must examine the "presentational process." It would be misleading and destructive of the possibility of an "open text" to say that within the graphic codes, this particular gesture means one thing or another, regardless of the specific text. We must speak of "dominances" and "probabilities," to borrow from the language of Beaugrande. (148)

6 My developing understanding of these distinctions involves a conversation with Herbert Enns, professor of architecture at the University of Manitoba and the analysis Paul DePasquale and Doris Wolf provide in "Home and Native Land," as they suggest that the sense of home in Aboriginal texts is less reliant on the physical structures of home and more involved with shared space than might be the case in non-Aboriginal texts. The further complications that obtain because of such distinctions, while not part of this study, will deepen my continuing research into viewed space and homing devices.

7 Cf. Gaston Bachelard, *The Poetics of Space*, 17–25.

8   The term "dressed" implicates a range of views, coverings, and colourings that give truncated, abridged, and annotated views of and through the window, that turn us toward impending actions ranging from the disastrous to the fortuitous.

9   The story is based in fact: *Mister Got to Go* has been immortalized in the landmark Sylvia Hotel in Vancouver, B.C., where he found a home given by the hotel manager who reluctantly capitulated to his charms. Mr. Foster is based on the real concierge, Axel DeVerrier, who has been the manager of the Sylvia for twenty-five years. Mr. Got to Go lived in the hotel for twelve years—from about 1981 until 1992. There's a new cat—Ms. Goddess Day—but she lives in the basement and doesn't interact with guests. There is an entire catalogue of stray-pet, in-between figures in Canadian picture books. The convention is represented in *SnowPaws* by Mary Alice Downie, for example, where a "toy" companion fashioned by Sam's older brother and sister to soothe his loneliness, enters Sam's bedroom and together they soar over and into the city throughout the winter.

10 Immigrant kitchen windows of opportunities proliferate in Canadian picture books as illustrated in Sue Ann Alderson's *Ida and the Wool Smuggler* (1987), where a nineteenth-century West Coast Canadian Little Red Riding Hood sets out with a basket of bread for Mrs. Springman, outwits smugglers along the way, and is rewarded by being allowed to hold Mrs. Springman's newborn, having proven herself "clever, brave" and "big enough now." Many of these kinds of windows will combine the window of opportunity promise with ROSTA home-and-native-land visual and verbal anthems.

11 Hinge is a term conceived by Jane Doonan in her analysis of *When Sheep Cannot Sleep* by Satoshi Kitamura. Doonan explores the showing of a particular moment when Wooly the sheep is pictured at work: "Before [this moment], he is something of a sheep, but at work and thereafter he is very much a child in sheep's clothing" (32). A related concept, the notion of a "critical window" in which "specific parts" of the subject's "brain are the most ready to be altered and learn from experience," has been introduced by Max Cynader, director of the Brain Research Centre at UBC (McIlroy). It is no accident that visual and verbal codes for these openings involve windows. Canadian picture books that explore the metamorphic potential of the hinge window include *The Olden Days Coat*, a 1979 Margaret Laurence story illustrated by Muriel Wood in 1999; Ann Blades's *Mary of Mile 18* (1971); Jan Andrews's *Very Last First Time* (1985); Jean Speare's *A Candle for Christmas* (1986); Sheryl McFarlane's *Waiting for the Whales* (1991); Peter Eyvindson's *The Missing Sun* (1993); Julie Lawson's *Midnight in the Mountains* (1998); Maxine Trottier's *Dreamstones* (1999); Marie-Louise Gay's *Stella Queen of the Snow* (2000); Adwoa Badoe's *Nana's Cold Days* (2002); Ian Wallace's *The Man Who Walked the Earth* (2003).

12 Rosemary George speaks of how "native" homes are represented in colonial novels as "ruins," "rubbish," "decay," and "decline"—homes and selves are "deemed inappropriate or inadequate," perceived "as spaces where non-subjects live in 'informal circumstances'" (23–25).

13 Themes of the outside/r, and "pattern[s] of select inclusion and exclusion" (George 2) persist in various envelope windowscapes including David Booth's *The Dust Bowl* (1996) to recount the Big Dry hardships and Dayal Kaur Khalsa's

Tales of a Gambling Grandma (1986), which realize *bubameises*—grandmother stories—and so reveal hideaways for the legendary underworld criminal Dutch Schultz stored in his imposing brick building. They occupy the field of *The Hockey Sweater* (1999), the "Canadian" "classic" by Roch Carrier, translated by Sheila Fischman, illustrated by Sheldon Cohen and adapted from the original collection of short stories published in 1979. *Hockey* uses the envelope to intensify feelings of estrangement and entrapment that will build two-stor(e)y/third-space effects to actualize 1946 tensions between French and English Canada.

14 Related two-stor(e)y/third-space windows are revealed in Susan Bosak's *Something to Remember Me By* to reveal how a young woman's face exhibits the trace of her grandmother's battle with Alzheimer's, using graphic techniques that establish the concept of home in terms of continuity within family resemblances that themselves seed the inevitability of the defective conditions that disorientate and un-home in old age. The difficult process of accommodating two worlds is central to the two-stor(e)y/third-space iconography in Priscilla Galloway's *Jennifer Has Two Daddies* (1985) where pivotal windowscapes represent the tension between conflicting filiations. In *SnowPaws*, the two stories cannot intersect in the story time itself except through the work that the reader/viewer does in imagining their intercourse, an imagining made possible through the two synchronized stories revealed in the closed window: the outside snow cat is decorated for Christmas by the children while the inside, pregnant Emile watches, entwined in the crèche displayed on the sill.

15 The sense of the stained window involves the stained-glass window and the history of religious imperialism it can represent. This characterization finds correlatives in Lawson's exploration of the "'settler's' desire to 'stand in' for the native" that "produces ultimately and perhaps inevitably the unspeakable desire for miscegenation—what in South Africa was once called 'taint.' The insertion of the settler into the (physical and discursive) space of the indigene is simultaneously characterized by desire and disavowal. The movement into indigenous space must be asymptotic: indigeneity must be approached, even appropriated, certainly photographed, but never touched. This produces in the settler subject an anxiety of proximity" (34).

16 "Saving fiction[s]" central to *Heart of Darkness* reveal the damnable consoling racist textualizations related to Benedict Anderson's discussion of the aristocracy's appearance in "national drag" (86–87). These might apply in inverted form to a picture book like *The Huron Carol*, insofar as the imagined Indians are either (a) drawn in religious or (b) drawn in and toward imperialist drag so that they might be "subjects" of a "common history."

17 Louise Saldanha introduced me to Tin-An Chen's *Little Pria's Big Canadian Adventure*, which is full of ROSTA windows informed by the desire articulated in the paratext to "promote ... the cultural diversity that flourishes in our country." Any distress Pria may experience is silenced by the magical, welcome-wagon properties of a Canadian goose, Lucy Esmeraldo Olivia Goosington of the Canadian Goosingtons who provides a coast-to-coast tour that unabashedly endorses the usual range of multicultural caricatures and stereotypes. My sense of how what Saldanha defines as the "tranquil cultural mosaic"

might be disturbed is suggested by the concept of the ROSTA-*gris*, which emerges from exploration of the *gris* adaptation of the *film noir* style and vision. While capable of happier endings, *film gris* is as occupied with the ambiguities and contradictions that expose and critique the underside of National Dreams and their attendant customs, conventions, and treatments.

18   In *Children's Literature Comes of Age*, while tracing the 1920s development of children's literature intended to express emerging social realist cultural agendas that would offer "living images" of proletarian rather than bourgeois culture in Russia, Maria Nikolajeva introduces the so-called ROSTA window. ROSTA was the Russian news agency, later called TASS, and its official style in the political propaganda posters from the period involve "vivid colours and simple, concrete contours, with an accompanying catchily rhymed short verse of usually two lines. The principle for the first picture books for children was exactly the same" (83).

19   The gloss and comfort of the happy ending defined by the recovery of rootedness to family and place is secured in the closing window in *The Olden Days Coat* where all is well: Sal and her grandmother share an "early present" that recovers the magical links with her gran's "heirloom" story. So too, the closing home scene in *Waiting for the Sun* shows more porch-lit windows wombing the growing family welcomed within. Intriguing palimpsest effects are achieved in the ROSTA window in Barbara Smucker's *Selina and the Bear Paw Quilt* (1995) as the quilt squares that exhibit Selina's former life are echoed in the window panes, with tracings that include the iconic reference to the tracks the family has made by train during their "escape" from persecution of Mennonites during the American Civil War. In Marsha Forchuk Skrypuch's *Silver Threads* (1996) nativity, matrimonial, and immigrant stories conjoin forces told through a miraculously webbed ROSTA window whose light guides a just-released Ivan home.

20   The sense of wrestling with the dominant culture pervasive in Canadian literature is noted by Victor Ramraj in "The Merits and Demerits of the Postcolonial Approach to Writings in English," as he recalls earlier work he had done in his 1998 paper "Postcolonial India: Nation Building in Polycultural Societies," which suggests that

> unlike India's postmodern multiplicitous multiculturalism ... Canadian multiculturalism is always an issue of how the minority cultures (and here we can include the Quebecois) relate/negotiate/wrestle with the dominant culture; there is always that dominant culture which defines centrally Canada and Canada's nationhood. (265)

21   This formula is apparent in a subsequent image that composes the female line in front of the living room window at the critical moment when Naniji must tell them she will turn away from Canada. Her shawl, with its own scattered leaf design, disrupts the rich, illustrated frame, but the foliage iconography of a Canadian fall outside colours the doll, the design on Gita's sweater, her own mother's blouse, the window curtains and, of course, the maple tree on guard. Gita renews her vows: "'Naniji, I want to be with you, but ...' she held the doll against her heart. 'Everything's here. Everything, but you.'"

22 In her own discussion of "myths of sameness" and "romanticised and hom-
ogenised views of child experience," Clare Bradford explores how suggestions of
common ground between the white and original girls in Hashmi's *You & Me, Murrawee* are unsettled by "fluctuating and ambiguous markers of modality" that often
privilege the "reality" of the white girl as "the status of a norm against which Murrawee's existence is compared." She advises: "[T]he uncomfortable facts of colonial history, and the equally uncomfortable facts of Aboriginal dispossession in
the 1990s, work against any scheme that represents the white girl and her Aboriginal counterpart as inhabiting the same notional space" (*Reading Race* 116–19).
In many ways, the troubling of a hoped-for equal footing in *Lights* expresses
important and parallel ambiguities that relate equally to the uneasy truce achieved
within the "cult" of mainstream multiculturalism and the "limits of diversity"
Neil Bissoondath examines in *Selling Illusions* and Saldanha discusses in her
chapter in this book, as racialized protagonists are pressed to conform to "white
normative space."

23 Rosemary George observes for example:

> At the risk of implying a universal humanism, I will suggest that if any
> common pattern can be traced in the many versions of home that contem-
> porary cultures provide us with, it is one of exclusions. Homes are not
> about inclusions and wide open arms as much as they are about places
> carved out of closed doors, closed borders and screening apparatuses. When
> different groups or individuals jostle each other to establish space as their
> own, as an exclusive manifestation of their subjecthood, this struggle can
> become as urgent as keeping oneself alive. As a result, "home" becomes
> contested ground in times of political tumult either on the level of power
> struggles at a national communal stage or at the interpersonal familial
> level. (18)

24 In Thelma Poirier's *The Bead Pot*, a bead pot gifted through the matrilineal generations within a family of Wyandote people of the Great Plains magically refills
itself every night so that the protagonist in this episode, Toniya Wakanwin, might
continue to craft her designs on moccasins. The history of that magic and the
passage of time that is part of it is pictured in a series of windowscapes that
show the continuity of the sense of place and tradition that persists even as
Toniya moves from the Plains to an adobe house with her new husband, then
to a trailer home, and finally to a lodge where she welcomes her own passing even
as she bequeaths the bead pot to her granddaughter.

25 John Stephens discusses related interrogations of illusionist traditions in his
analysis of the work of Allen Say and anti-mimetic devices that "would privilege
devices of stasis" in "Picture Books, Mimesis and Competing Aesthetics of Kinesis and Stasis." He references Francois Cheng's definition of the Chinese convention of flat distance (*p'ing-yuan*) landscape—"from a nearby position, the
onlooker's gaze extends to infinity with complete freedom" (95)—as well as
related alternatives to Western single-point perspective such as the laying out of
a scene as "a receding series of flat planes," which is very much a part of the strategy in many of Chartrand's landscapes in *Flour Sack Flora*.

26 Delaronde-Falk writes that Chartrand "was the only artist 'old' enough to remember what life was like 40 years ago" (e-mail, 25 May 2004). This ensured that they could meticulously reproduce the household items, the sense of authenticity and "accuracy" (Gary's word for what he was after during a May 25, 2004, telephone conversation about his collaboration with Deborah, an accuracy that could represent the "happiness" of that time, the serenity and "comfort"). Delaronde-Falk wanted to depict the "dirt poor" realities the community faced, "not to elicit sympathy from the reader. Rather the purpose was to educate children about the living conditions of the Metis people AND the pioneer life experienced by early settlers prior to electricity and all its benefits that we take for granted today." In showing the "ingenuity born out of necessity to make use of everything," Delaronde-Falk is careful to preserve distinctions about "WHO" is using the flour from the two companies represented in both *Flour Sack Flora* and *Flour Sack Friends*:

> This was a consideration as I struggled to find story situations where I could place these bags and maintain the integrity of the story. My reasoning was because not all people could afford to buy "Robin Hood Flour." According to the Robin Hood flour company AND elderly people that I interviewed. Robin Hood produced a quality flour that never failed in baking under the fluctuation of heat from wood stove conditions. Also ... according to my research not all stores would sell Robin Hood flour. This was due to the higher price AND their regular customers/community's financial situations. Another consideration for storekeepers in selling Robin Hood Flour is that the color dye never fully washed out. So people who purchased Robin Hood would STILL use the fabric to sew "bloomers" and use the cloth for household items such as dishcloths, etc. Knowing the popularity and affordability of "Five Roses Flour", the storekeeper would order more of this flour as opposed to the more expensive flour. Robin Hood Flour was simply a preferred choice for higher income earners or for Metis and Native people who would buy one to keep for special occasion cooking. You'll be interested to know that not only did the color dye wash out of the "Five Roses" flour bag, but that the company sold their flour in plaid, checkered and flower patterned sacks! This proved extremely popular as people could then sew dresses, curtains, etc. by matching and purchasing multiple bags of flour with the same pattern.:-) Yes ... a lot of thought and research went into the writing of "Flour Sack Flora". And Yes ... the resourcefulness of the Metis, Native people and early pioneers is exemplified in the use of the flour sacks whether they are hanging on a clothesline or seen through a picture window. (E-mail 29 June 2004)

27 Introduction to *Hybridity and Its Discontents* (Coombes and Brah 10). Related explorations among many involve Paul Gilroy's explorations of a Black Atlantic, reinventions of Englishness in Britain, and Néstor García Canclini's analysis of Latin American modernization.

CHAPTER 9

⇒ **The Homely Imaginary: Fantasies of Nationhood in Australian and Canadian Texts**

Clare Bradford

My involvement in the "Home" project over the last three years has necessitated a continuous process of comparative reading: my encounters with Canadian texts have been shaped by my knowledge of Australian children's literature, and conversely I now read Australian texts in the light of Canadian material. The connections between the two literatures, as between the preoccupations that drive Australian and Canadian scholarship in children's literature, are both obvious and elusive. For one thing, the shared histories of Canada and Australia as British settler colonies are complicated by the fact that Canada had two founding powers, Britain and France. Again, geographical similarities—the vast spaces of the north in Canada, the desert regions of Australia—signify differently and are inflected by Australia's relative isolation as an island continent and Canada's contiguity with the United States. Third, while in both nations the development of settler cultures depended on the dispossession of indigenous peoples, treaty discourses are prominent in Canadian discussions of relations between indigenous and non-indigenous citizens and cultures, whereas the Australian nation was founded on the doctrine of *terra nullius*. Thus, even as I look to the discourses and ideologies that the two discourses and their literatures have in common, I am reminded of the historical and cultural influences that differentiate them.

As many postcolonial theorists have pointed out, one of the principal effects of colonization was the separation of space and place, described by Bill Ashcroft as follows: "The movement of European society through the world, the 'discovery' and occupation of remote regions, was the necessary basis for a separation of space and place and the creation of what could be called 'empty space'" (152). The notion of "empty space" was fundamental to the legal concepts that shaped British colonial practices—in particular, the principles that planting, farming, and fencing land established a claim to ownership and that land that did not show the signs of cultivation (according to the colonizers' definitions of cultivation) was waste land, waiting to be "improved" by being put to profitable use.[1] In Canada and in Australia, colonial processes of mapping and claiming the land transformed places hitherto known, named, and occupied by indigenous peoples into empty space, envisaged as a vast resource to be used and enjoyed by European settlers.

Citing two Canadian writers, Robert Kroestch and Dennis Lee, Ashcroft observes that in settler societies a sense of displacement manifests in "uncertainties about the location of value, ambivalence or argument about certain kinds of cultural or political affiliation, social contestation over the 'proper' use of language, confusion about the use of the word 'home'" (155). Like children's texts more generally, Canadian and Australian texts tend to centre on the identity-formation of young protagonists, played out in represented processes of growth, change, and acculturation. Many of these texts exhibit the sense of displacement described by Ashcroft, often centring on imaginings of "home" and proposing interrogations and contestations of the cultural and political meanings that attach to those imaginings.

Any formulation of home incorporates a sense of who is included and who is excluded or marginal. In *White Nation*, Ghassan Hage outlines what he refers to as "the homely imaginary of nationalist practices" (38), noting that discourses of home are frequently marshalled to justify the strategies of inclusion and exclusion that determine who is "at home" in the nation. According to Hage, dominant groups in nation states maintain their dominance in this way:

> A nationalist practice of exclusion is a practice emanating from agents imagining themselves to occupy *a privileged position within national space* such as they perceive themselves to be the enactors of the national will within the nation. It is a practice orientated by the nationalists' attempt at building what they imagine to be a homely nation. (47, my italics)

My focus here is on the extent to which a "privileged position within national space" is figured through the homes and the homely places that feature in selected Canadian and Australian novels for children. I begin with two texts published around the beginning of the twentieth century,

Lucy Maud Montgomery's *Anne of Green Gables* (1908) and Ethel Turner's *Seven Little Australians* (1894). Later I move to a consideration of two novels that usher in the twenty-first century, Michael Bedard's *Redwork* (1990) and David Metzenthen's *Boys of Blood and Bone* (2003). It is not part of my argument that the authors of these texts "imagine themselves to occupy a privileged position within national space" in any conscious sense, but rather that their writing is shaped by discourses that accept as given the idea that national identity in both Australia and Canada is built on Whiteness and Britishness. My discussion, which considers the assumptions and rhetorics of examples of "mainstream" children's literature, is offset by two chapters, Doris Wolf and Paul DePasquale's "Home and Native Land" and Louise Saldanha's "White Picket Fences," which focus on the politics and cultural discourses that inform children's texts by and about marginalized groups within Canadian national space.

Viewed as products of what Stuart Ward calls "a global imperial history" (44), *Anne of Green Gables* and *Seven Little Australians* illustrate the busy traffic of texts shuttling between colonial and metropolitan readerships around the turn of the twentieth century. *Anne of Green Gables* was first published in the United States and Britain, with an Australian edition appearing in 1924, and is, according to Cecily Devereux, "one of the best-selling English-Canadian novels ever" (12). *Seven Little Australians* exemplifies a similar pattern of production and reception. Published in London, Turner's story of family life in 1890s Sydney was an immediate success, winning plaudits from Mark Twain and George Meredith.[2] According to Brenda Niall, "[I]t would be hard to think of any other Australian book which is so widely known" (2). The two novels thus have much in common: both are canonized texts, regarded as icons of nationhood; both have been continually in print since first publication; both have been adapted for the stage and as television series, films, and telemovies. Like canonical texts generally, they embody cultural capital, serving as touchstones of "quality" and markers of national identity.

In line with what Hage says about the "homely imaginary" of nationalism, *Anne of Green Gables* and *Seven Little Australians* represent nationhood in relation to a normative Whiteness.[3] The Whitest characters in both novels are the middle-class, Anglo-Celtic children central to their narratives. Those excluded from this privileged position are outsiders not merely because of class, race, or ethnicity, but more fundamentally because they are marginal to the fantasies of nation that underpin the representations of settler childhood exemplified by Montgomery's Anne and by Turner's seven little Australians.

As Anne Shirley makes her first journey to Green Gables in Matthew Cuthbert's buggy, her behaviour mimics British colonial practices of viewing, mapping, and naming. Like a young colonist, she closely observes the lineaments of land and vegetation; at the crest of a hill she surveys the land spread out before her; and she renames two features that possess less resounding names than she believes they deserve: what locals call "the Avenue" she claims as "the White Way of Delight" (22), and she renames "Barry's pond" the "Lake of Shining Water" (23). In a quasi-religious reference, a star shines "like a lamp of guidance and promise" (24) directing Anne's gaze toward Green Gables, which she recognizes as "home" without being told. So insistently does the text establish Anne's instinctive and natural sense of being at home, that the delay between her arrival and Marilla Cuthbert's decision that she is to remain at Green Gables reads more as a deferral of citizenship than as a threat of eviction. Indeed, the novel's title functions proleptically as a promise that Anne will be granted citizenship in this house.

The landscape of Avonlea affords a model of the style of British settlement which Patricia Seed describes, in that the land is owned and put to use, its "snug" (24) farmsteads signalling good order and industry; its church spire testifies to the godliness of its inhabitants, a godliness that Anne must learn as one of her first duties when Marilla sets her to memorize the Lord's Prayer. The orderliness of Avonlea suggests a formulation of nationhood in which nature is controlled, subdued, and rendered homely. Only one episode in the novel suggests that features of the landscape might evoke the uncanny or the forbidden. In their desire for gothic imaginings, Anne and her friend Diana Barry give the name "the Haunted Wood" to the spruce grove near their homes, investing it with ghostly presences: apparitions of a white woman, a murdered child, a headless man. Marilla's action of requiring Anne to walk through the spruce grove "for a lesson and a warning" (141) expunges these horrors, persuading Anne to be content with "commonplace places" (142). A critical aspect of this episode is that the ghosts of the Haunted Wood, like its name, are ersatz, invented by Anne and Diana to provide excitement. In *Anne of Green Gables*, unlike Janet Lunn's *Shadow in Hawthorn Bay*, there are no shadowy presences equivalent to the marginalized, homeless, outlawed, and Aboriginal figures who, as Mavis Reimer demonstrates in her chapter, haunt "the unconscious of the text" (7). What does haunt *Anne of Green Gables*, in a muted and allusive way, is the memory of Anne's unhappy life prior to Green Gables, referred to at several points in the narrative and drawing attention to the significance of home as the ground of identity. That poverty, illness, and personal misadventure are capable of excluding citizens from the simple, peaceful lives experienced by the inhabitants of Avonlea is an idea never explicitly addressed but present as a warning of the unhomely.

Anne of Green Gables ends with Matthew's death and Anne's decision to return from her studies at Queen's in Charlottetown so as to remain with Marilla. While the narrative hinges on Anne's transformation from orphanhood to a state of being at home, a parallel process occurs in which Marilla is transformed from spinster to mother, instantiated in her words to Anne: "I love you as dear as if you were my own flesh and blood" (246). These ameliorative trajectories map Anne's progress onto a version of identity in which, to borrow a phrase from Deborah Schnitzer's chapter, Anne becomes a Canadian, at the same time that Green Gables becomes a more homely and nurturing national space.

I noted earlier that immediately she sees Green Gables Anne instinctively knows that this is her home, but the narrative also foregrounds Marilla's sense that Anne is "like us." As Marilla and Anne drive from Avonlea to White Sands, where Marilla seeks an explanation for Anne's arrival in place of the orphan boy she sought, Marilla poses the following questions: "Where were you born and how old are you?"; "Did you ever go to school?"; and "Were those women … good to you?" (38–40). These questions test Anne's origins, her education, and her character, probing not merely what she says but how she says it. On all counts Anne's responses are satisfactory: Marilla judges her to be "ladylike" and her parents to have been "nice folks" (40). Even Anne's lack of systematic education is not a disadvantage, since it renders her more susceptible to training—or, as Marilla says, she is "teachable" (40). While the criteria Marilla uses relate to class and breeding, Anne's Whiteness is a naturalized component of her acceptability, embedded in the distinction between her and the French-Canadian outsiders, Mary Joe and Jerry Buote. By virtue of a bundle of attributes represented as innate and essential, Anne is thus judged worthy of the "privileged position within national space" (Hage, *White Nation* 47) that is symbolized by Green Gables.

To be sure, the novel's narrative drive depends on Anne's failures to align her behaviour with the ideals of godliness and propriety that Marilla places before her, but Montgomery is at pains to emphasize that her escapades result from high spirits, imagination, or honest mistakes rather than from defects of character. Moreover, Anne's progress from her arrival at Green Gables to her final utterance, "God's in His heaven, all's right with the world" (256), tracks her gradual conformity to cultural norms as she becomes godly, domesticated, self-controlled, and—in the final moments of the narrative—romantically attracted to Gilbert Blythe and hence assured of a heterosexual relationship leading to marriage and children. A century and a half on from *Canadian Crusoes, Anne of Green Gables* sustains the narrative of domesticity described by Andrew O'Malley in his chapter. Anne is not, like Catharine in *Canadian Crusoes*, an "avatar of domesticity" (82); nevertheless, the closure of *Anne of Green Gables* accords with the colonial configuration where the home is homologous with the nation, and where women are located within the domestic sphere.

Despite the fact that both Canada and Australia are predominantly nations of city-dwellers, in both countries myths of nationhood revolve around concepts of wilderness. In Canada, wilderness takes the form of what Erin Manning describes as "the myth of the 'great white north,' a myth that imagines Canada as a land with unmediated landscapes peopled by those of strong, pure character" (9). Montgomery's emphasis on the orderliness of Avonlea, its disciplined and known landscape, its models of "strong pure character" exemplified by Marilla and Matthew, invites speculation as to what lies beyond these controlled and godly spaces. In Australia, a mythology of the bush locates Australianness in the outback, where strong, laconic settlers struggle with an inhospitable land. Misrule, the home of the Woolcot family in *Seven Little Australians*, is located in a suburban setting that mimics country life, with its "big wilderness of a garden, two or three paddocks, numberless sheds for hide-and-seek, and, best of all, the water" (13). Captain Woolcot, the children's father, is a career soldier who has remarried following the death of his wife in childbirth, so that his children's young stepmother, Esther, is only four years older than Meg, his eldest daughter.

The novel revolves around thirteen-year-old Judy, who bears a striking resemblance to Montgomery's Anne: "She was very thin, as people generally are who have quicksilver instead of blood in their veins; she had a small, eager, freckled face, with very bright dark eyes, a small, determined mouth, and a mane of untidy, curly dark hair that was the trial of her life" (11). Playing on the nationalism of an Australia seeking to distinguish itself from Britishness, Turner sought to distinguish Australian child characters from those others, "[i]n England, and America, and Africa, and Asia,… [who] may be paragons of virtue…. [I]n Australia a model child is— I say it not without thankfulness—an unknown quantity" (7). The rackety, haphazard household of Misrule resembles an anarchic state more than a settler nation: the children's father absents himself as much as possible from his troublesome offspring, and their young stepmother, Esther, is given to lamenting, "Seven of you, and I'm only twenty!" (34).

At first glance, then, Misrule appears to present a very different analogy of home to nation than is the case in Green Gable's ordered, controlled, godly space. I would argue, however, that the two texts share a common agenda—that of demonstrating how wild colonial girls are tamed and rendered domestic and hence docile. Turner's narrative follows a more melodramatic direction than Montgomery's: Judy, sent to boarding school because her father regards her as uncontrollable, runs away from school and embarks on a week-long walk to Misrule, sleeping outdoors and developing pneumonia during her journey. To recover from her illness she is sent with her stepmother and siblings to Yarrahappini, the cattle station owned by Esther's parents. Here, during a picnic with her siblings, Judy rushes to save the General, her baby stepbrother, and is crushed under a falling gum tree, dying surrounded by her sorrowing brothers and sisters.

Judy's death in *Seven Little Australians* circumvents the narrative difficulties that Turner would have faced if, in subsequent novels, she had been required to imagine such a wild girl growing into adulthood, since, as Richard Rossiter argues, "there is no place for the rebellious, highly individualized character in the Australia of this period" (64). Whereas Anne is "tamed" by Marilla, the spinster who becomes a mother, Judy is subjected to the arbitrary and harsh regime of her father, who is indirectly responsible for her death. In *Anne of Green Gables*, Matthew Cuthbert is a secondary presence, interceding with Marilla on Anne's behalf and seeking to soften her austere regime. In *Seven Little Australians*, Esther performs precisely the same function, while Captain Woolcot harshly disciplines his children (often through corporal punishment) so as to form them as Australian (and British) citizens.

I have already drawn on Ghassan Hage's discussion of the "homely imaginary" of the nation, and in *Against Paranoid Nationalism* Hage's explication of "the imaginary of the fatherland" offers a way of thinking about the contrasting yet complementary significances of Green Gables and Misrule. Hage proposes that, whereas the imaginary of the motherland is embodied in references to home, mother, and nurturing, the imaginary of the fatherland resides in the notion of individual subjects "gaining the capacity to utter the transcendental national 'we' and feeling legitimized to impose order 'from above'" (34–35). At several points during *Seven Little Australians*, the narrative depicts Captain Woolcot's reflections on the threat offered by Judy not only to his discipline but to larger notions of order. At one point he tells himself: "There will be no end to my trouble with her as she grows older" (125). Judy is, then, the unruly subject who refuses assimilation into the "we" of the father's rule and, in a homologous sense, into the "we" of the nation. In describing the relation between motherlands and fatherlands, Hage comments that "[t]he nation as community, home, or motherland without a fatherland to order it and protect it would not be a very satisfying nation to belong to" (36). Judy presents an anomalous figure in that, on one hand, she does not have a "real" mother and refuses to conform to the gendered discourses that shape ideas of home and motherland; and on the other hand there is no place for her in a fatherland where she rejects the order and control that produce the national subject.

In *Anne of Green Gables*, the principal threat to the security of the home is Matthew's unworldliness, exemplified in his loyalty to the Abbey Bank because "old Mr. Abbey" (243) had been a friend of his father's. Marilla, who wants Matthew to draw their savings out of the Abbey Bank, is powerless to influence him, and his sudden death, caused by the shock of discovering that the bank has failed, can be read as a warning about the dangers of trusting in corporate power. Seen in this light, Anne's resolution to give up her scholarship to Redmond and return to Green Gables represents both a retreat from the world outside (and a diminution of opportunities) and also an affirmation of the feminine realm as home. In *Seven Little Australians*, Judy herself represents the principal threat to the law of the father. But her death occurs not at Misrule but at Yarrahappini, a fact that evokes the contrary mythologies of the bush[4] as a place where Australians are simultaneously at home and in danger from both natural and uncanny forces.

Turner treats Yarrahappini as a site where maternal and paternal realms are readily distinguished: inside the house, domesticity, sustenance, and comfort; outside, a world of manly activities and adventures. An analeptic account of the beginnings of the station accords with Seed's description of British land ownership as constituted by labour: Esther's father, Mr. Hassal, "worked harder than any two of his own stockmen," while Mrs. Hassal "scrubbed and cooked and washed as many a settler's wife has done before, until the anxiously watched wool market had brought them better days" (145–46). The presence of Tettawonga, the "station black," mutely signals that before Mr. Hassal fenced and cultivated his property, indigenous people lived on this land but did not own it, in the sense that the British defined ownership. Tettawonga is provided with accommodation and daily rations because, fifteen years prior to the events of the narrative, he saved Mrs. Hassal and Esther from two bushrangers who attempted to rob the young family; but it is because of Mr. Hassal's generosity and loyalty that Tettawonga now lives at Yarrahappini (an "Aboriginal" name), where he "did little else than smoke and give his opinion on the weather every morning" (146), not because he has any claim to the property. Rather, his presence bestows a kind of legitimacy on Yarrahappini, demonstrating the Hassals' benevolence and humaneness. There is, of course, no prospect that Tettawonga will ever be "at home" in the inner circle of the Hassal family, and in this sense Tettawonga's place at Yarra-happini is metonymic of the marginalization of indigenous people in the nation, expressed a few years after the publication of *Seven Little Australians* by the White Australia Policy, which operated from the time of Federation in 1901 and into the 1960s.[5]

The scene in which Judy dies is based in part on the many deathbed scenes with which Turner was familiar, in Victorian texts such as *The Daisy Chain* and *The Wide, Wide World*. Australian inflections are present in the location of events within "the strange silence of the bush" (183), and in Turner's account of the ministrations of Tettawonga, who "soothed the General off to sleep.... And he had made a billy of hot, strong tea, and asked the children, with tears in his eyes, to drink some, but none of them would" (184). As Judy lies dying, surrounded by her siblings, her sister Meg recites the words of the hymn "Abide with Me," a reference that folds notions of a heavenly home into that of the homely space where Judy is buried, in a grave on a hilltop where wattle trees are "gold-crowned and gracious in the spring" (188) and surrounded by a fence of white palings. Uncontainable and disorderly in life, in death she is hemmed in by a signifier of domesticity and control. The pathos of Judy's death and burial is offset by a sense, in the novel's final chapter, that Misrule is a more homely place for her death: the behaviour of her siblings is less wild than before, and her father fonder of his six remaining children, "though he showed his affection very little more" (192). The systems of surveillance and control that ensure the maintenance of the fatherland are secure now that Judy is no longer present to breach them, and the two imaginaries, of the motherland and the fatherland, are restored to their complementary and dialogical roles.

The thematics of home, place, and death that traverse *Anne of Green Gables* and *Seven Little Australians* are evident as well in *Boys of Blood and Bone* and *Redwork*, texts that look back in time to Australian and Canadian involvement in the Great War of 1914–1918. Between the beginning of the twentieth century and the beginning of the twenty-first, momentous cultural shifts occurred in both Canada and Australia, among them the impact of feminism; the transformation of both nations into multicultural societies; the dismantling of Britain's economic, political, and cultural authority over its colonies. The first of these, the impact of feminism, is palpable in representations of female figures in the two contemporary texts, notably Maddy in *Redwork* and Janine in *Boys of Blood and Bone*. These characters, romantically associated with the novels' protagonists, are forceful, independent young women whose horizons are not circumscribed by associations with domesticity and the nurturing of the young—or, as in the case of Judy in *Seven Little Australians*, with the tragic trajectory of the untameable colonial girl.

As to the second and third of the cultural shifts I have identified (the adoption of policies of multiculturalism in Canada and Australia, and the loosening of ties to Britain), the two contemporary texts afford more ambivalent versions of home and nation. Like *Anne of Green Gables* and *Seven Little Australians*, both these texts concern themselves with White characters and sociocultural settings (although, as I will show later, *Redwork* alludes to the presence of non-White others). Neither text evidences anything like the fervour with which *Seven Little Australians* announces its nationalistic project of advancing the story of an Australia where "the land and the people are young-hearted together, and the children's spirits not crushed and saddened by the shadow of long years' sorrowful history" (7). Nonetheless, both *Redwork* and *Boys of Blood and Bone* map "home" onto "nation" by tracing the experiences of young men who fought in World War I and by engaging with questions about the significances of those events for contemporary characters.

In *Boys of Blood and Bone*, a double-stranded narrative tells the story, in alternating sections, of a contemporary young man, Henry Lyon, who is temporarily trapped in the rural town of Strattford when his car breaks down, and of Andy Lansell, a young soldier from the same area, who fights and dies in the trenches in France. In *Redwork*, the contemporary character, Cass Parry, moves with his mother, Alison, into an upper-floor flat in a decrepit house owned by Mr. Magnus, a reclusive old man who relives his experiences as a young soldier in dreams uncannily shared by Cass. Canadian and Australian mythologies of nationhood alike fix upon the Great War as the birth of nationhood. Reimer notes that "[a] popular version of Canadian political and military history is to represent World War I as the event that forged a nation from a colony" (15), and similarly in Australia the events of April 1915, when the Australian and New Zealand Army Corps (ANZAC) undertook its first major military action, are regarded as pivotal to the nation's history.[6]

The contemporary protagonists of both novels initially experience a sense of being at odds with the practices of their cultural and familial settings. Henry, in *Boys of Blood and Bone*, feels obscurely oppressed by the expectations of his girlfriend, Marcelle, and of his parents; Cass, in *Redwork*, is a bookish and sensitive boy who does not readily make friends and who regards himself as an observer of life rather than a participant: "It seemed as if he had spent most of his life living over stores, stationed invisibly at windows, watching" (17). By treating Cass as the main focalizing character, the narrative both shows events and characters through his perspective, and provides an entrée into his interior world of dreams and thoughts. Cass's mother is in the last stages of completing her MA thesis on William Blake's poetry and makes a tenuous living as a house-cleaner. When Cass and Alison are given notice to vacate their apartment, their move takes them to Deer Park, a neighbourhood of old homes recently discovered by renovators, where Mr. Magnus's house stands out because of its rundown state. Both novels mobilize the narrative schema, so common in literature for adolescents, in which young men, initially insecure and uncertain, experience events that endow their lives with meaning and purpose.

Once he moves into the old house, Cass hears the sounds of Mr. Magnus going about his daily activities in the flat below and observes his nightly visits to the garage in the backyard, where the old man builds a fire each night in order to conduct the alchemical experiments with which he is obsessed. In a box of photographs left in the flat, Cass discovers a picture of Mr. Magnus as a young soldier, and following this he begins to experience the old man's dreams of the muddy trenches of France, dreams full of death and horror. Observing both Mr. Magnus and how he is treated by those who live in the neighbourhood, Cass realizes that the old man is a site of meanings projected onto him by the fears and desires of others. Thus, Cass's next-door neighbour Mrs. Wharton, who is concerned above all with property values, regards Mr. Magnus as out of place, a shabby, smelly presence in a rapidly gentrifying suburb. The schoolchildren in the area, who call him "old man Maggots" (168), believe that he is a witch; Sid Spector, the leader of a gang of young men who frequent the park opposite the house, exploits the old man's reputation for profit, extracting protection money from the local children and conducting a campaign of intimidation against the old man.

Cass finds a job as an usher at the Palace, a run-down cinema where he develops a friendship with Maddy, who serves at the candy counter. When Maddy and Cass visit Mr. Magnus, they find that his flat is cluttered with old furniture, newspapers, and boxes. In entering this space, with its smell of "smoke and dirt and things shut in too long" (154), the two young people gain admittance to a world of memories. In comparison, the other old houses in the neighbourhood sport sandblasted walls, looking to Cass like "old people desperate to look young" (7). While they gain cachet from their age, these homes represent the rejection of national memory, just as their inhabitants neither know nor care about Mr. Magnus's wartime experiences. Later, when the old man's garage burns down and his neighbours gather to observe what has happened, Cass regards them as voyeurs who take delight in observing a way of life whose marginality reassures them as to their own normality:

> Here people were not supposed to limp, grow old, talk to themselves, be different. People here were supposed to be happy and whole and have neatly trimmed lawns and sandblasted facades and scrubbed, exceptionally gifted children. Mr. Magnus had been a worrisome reminder of everything they wanted to do away with. (265)

In Ghassan Hage's terms, the world of Deer Park is governed by the imaginary of the fatherland, since it is concerned with an imagined "we" unified by a common desire for uniformity and order. There are here no signs of a motherly, nurturing presence, but only of a national capitalism that engenders its own panoply of goals and desires in a perpetual competition for the latest and best of material possessions.

Magistrale's Fruit and Vegetable Market, operated by a family of Italian migrants, functions as a marker of otherness in Deer Park. Eighteen-year-old Tony Magistrale and his sister Maria are minor players in the narrative, but they are represented in ways that suggest the ambivalence concerning "certain kinds of cultural or political affiliation" (155) identified by Ashcroft as characteristic of settler societies. Cass is "utterly unraveled" (58) by Maria, who is associated with images of voluptuousness and sexual availability, while Tony is cast as a muscle-bound drudge working in his parents' shop. Later in the narrative, when Sid Spector and his offsiders threaten Cass, Tony comes to his rescue, and Cass realizes that Maria has alerted her brother to Cass's plight. While Tony and Maria are shown to redeem themselves by aligning themselves with Cass and against Sid, they are nevertheless located outside the "privileged position within national space" (Hage 47) occupied by Cass and Maddy.

In their descriptions of military action, *Redwork* and *Boys of Blood and Bone* resist the hero narratives that inform hegemonic versions of masculinity, focusing instead on the psychological, emotional, and bodily experiences of young men caught up in processes they do not understand. Mr. Magnus, recalling his experiences as a fifteen-year-old who lied about his age to join the army, reflects that the trenches of World War I were "full of boys—none of them nearly old enough to vote, but all of them more than old enough to die" (219). His account of trench warfare, like Metzenthen's descriptions of Andy's war in *Boys of Blood and Bone*, highlights the fear and confusion of the soldiers, their dogged endurance and the moments of camaraderie that sustained them. In *Redwork*, the pointlessness of war—and in particular Mr. Magnus's war—is offset by his quest for the Philosopher's Stone, which symbolizes his yearning for a personal and psychic transformation. Broader questions about the politics of the Great War and the role of "the British Dominions" are barely addressed except obliquely, in Mr. Magnus's reflections on the foolish patriotism of his young self, who believed that war would be "just a glorious adventure" (219).

The novel concludes at the Palace, where Cass and Maddy serve patrons who attend a screening of Charlie Chaplin's silent films. Alison and her partner Murray arrive, accompanied by Mr. Magnus. This tableau, incorporating Mr. Magnus into a cross-generational "family" where he is the revered senior member, constructs the homely nation in relation to Whiteness, access to European cultural pursuits, and membership in the middle class. The downside of this formulation of national identity is the exclusion of those who do not belong—Sid Spector and his gang, Tony and Maria Magistrale, and those who live behind the sandblasted facades of the old houses of Deer Park.

In *Boys of Blood and Bone*, Henry's enforced stay in Strattford introduces him to a hitherto unfamiliar Australia. When his car breaks down just outside the town, Henry is obliged to wait for a passing motorist to notice his plight. As he waits he notices that small plaques engraved with names, initials, and numbers are placed in front of the avenue of trees leading to the town, and he deduces that these acknowledge the men of the district who died in the First World War, which seems to Henry "like something from the Middle Ages" (2). The novel traces Henry's journey from this moment of idle speculation to a sense of identification with Andrew Lansell, the author of the journal dialogically placed alongside the story of Henry's sojourn in Strattford, and its aftermath.

Henry comes from Malvern, an upper-middle-class suburb of Melbourne; his mother has loaned him her Volvo to drive to the beachfront property where he plans to stay with his friends. Henry's ignorance of mechanics, his reliance on his mother, and the fact that he is driving a Volvo make him feel like an effete and pampered outsider when he is rescued by Graham Trotter (Trot), a local young man. When Henry is obliged to stay in Strattford for two days while his mother's car is repaired, he meets Trot's girlfriend, Janine, who loans him Andy Lansell's diary. Commencing with an entry written by Cecelia Hainsworth, Andy's intended wife, in January 1917, the diary ends with words written by his friend Darcy after his death: "On this day, the 9th of August, 1918, Private Andrew Richard Lansell, volunteer soldier of the AIF, died at Villers-Bretonneux Field Hospital, France, of wounds received in battle. He was one of the best. He always was, and he always will be" (291). Henry's reading of the diary collapses time and place, producing a sense of intersubjective engagement that transcends the distance between him and Andy Lansell. The diary entries, bare and cautious in their descriptions of events, are all that Andy is willing to expose to public scrutiny, while the sections that follow each entry, focalized through Andy's perspective, trace his actions, thoughts, and emotions during the last year of his life. The alternating sections focus on Henry's experience over a similar period, from his arrival in Strattford until the novel's close, when he returns to the town, once more driving his mother's Volvo.

Andy's story incorporates his discovery, relayed in a letter he receives while on leave in England, that Frances-Jane Kelly, a young woman with whom he had sex shortly before his departure, is pregnant with his child. In line with the mores of his time he writes to Frances-Jane to offer marriage, and to Cecelia to confess to his misdeed. During a second furlough in London, he receives the news that Frances-Jane has delivered a daughter, whom she has named Eliza. In the contemporary story, Henry meets Cecelia Hainsworth, by now a centenarian who has never married and who is the town's "living, local, legend" (19), and it gradually emerges that Janine is Andy's great-granddaughter. Over the same period that he is pursuing the story of Andy Lansell, Henry's relationship with Marcelle founders; later, Trot is killed in a car accident; and later still, Janine and Henry travel to France after Cecelia Hainsworth offers Janine what she terms a scholarship—enough money to visit Andy's grave, "see the place, and learn some things" (213).

Through its interweaving of lives and stories in the two time schemes, the narrative situates individuals against a backdrop of national and international events. While Andy is at first overcome by shame at having disgraced his family and effected an estrangement with Cecelia, he comes to regard the baby he has fathered as "beyond light, beyond words—she was like the goodness left in the boys' souls after they had walked from the battlefield" (224–25). Caught between the experience of death in the trenches and his reflections on the new life he has engendered, Andy questions a moral scheme where he is paid as a soldier to kill people, while he expects that his responsibility for Eliza's existence will be regarded in his home town as "a foul and despicable crime" (74).

When Andy thinks of home, his memories linger on the materiality of his life on the land: the smell of hay, the sounds of the farm, the sensations of physical work. The novel's treatment of the contemporary setting of Strattford folds its culture and values into those of the earlier setting—thus, the warmth and directness of Trot and Janine mirror the same qualities in Darcy and Bob, Andy's army companions from Strattford, just as the pleasure Henry takes in the details of country life echoes Andy's recollections of his home. These parallels enforce a sense that the country is the "true" Australia and its inhabitants proper Australians—as Janine says of her impression of Andy from an old photograph, "I thought he looked so *Australian*. With those clear eyes that could look forever" (102). The romanticism and nostalgia of this version of Australia disguise the extent to which it is based on relations of inclusion and exclusion similar to those that inform *Seven Little Australians.* Hage says of the homely nation that "[i]t is a place of nurture, love, serenity and peace *because* it is a place of power and subjugation, a place where the will of the father is trying to ensure that everything is positioned in a way that suits the national subject" (*Against* 37). Thus, Andy's anxiety about the treatment that might be meted out to Frances-Jane speaks to his awareness of the harshness with which the borders of propriety are patrolled.

As I have noted, *Boys of Blood and Bone* constructs a strikingly White version of Australia. Henry's father Walt is Canadian and likes to use the word "mate," "although with his faded Canadian accent Henry was not convinced that he should" (165). To be Canadian, however, is to be almost Australian; on hearing of Henry's parentage Cecelia Hainsworth remarks, "The Canadians were well thought of by the Australians. They were very good fighters" (20). Henry's friend Nick remarks that his own great-grandfather fought in the Great War, "'[e]xcept that he was on the other side. You know, the dirty Germans.... Sorry about that, folks. You know, it's okay, though. We lost'" (141). These Commonwealth and European connections are, however, readily incorporated into the White world of the novel. I am not here arguing that the novel might have been "improved" if non-White characters had been incorporated into its narrative, but rather that its construction of the homely nation draws in such a reflex manner on mythologies of a White Australia that it naturalizes a narrow and exclusive version of the nation.

The phenomenon of the "cultural cringe"[7] manifested by settler societies insecure about their standing inflects how *Boys of Blood and Bone* represents relations between Britain and Australia during the Great War. As in *Redwork,* the narrative does not engage in interrogation of the colonial relations that impelled Australia into the war, or the self-serving mythologies that justified the slaughter of thousands of Australian and Canadian soldiers. When Andy and Bob take leave from the front, spending their time in London and Edinburgh, they engage in conversations in which they are praised specifically for being Australians; for instance, a man on the train travelling to London tells them, "[Y]our boys have been doing well" (230). Through such exchanges readers are positioned to assent to the gratification and pleasure "naturally" experienced by Australians reassured

as to the legitimacy of the nation, exemplified by the exemplary performance of its soldiers.

Both *Redwork* and *Boys of Blood and Bone* lay claim to continuities of
individual and cultural identities across time. In the epilogue to *Boys of
Blood and Bone*, as Henry returns to Strattford, he ponders the potency
of places as signs—specifically, the avenue of memorial trees: "There
weren't too many places, he thought, where you could actually see where
the past, the present, and perhaps your future met, but this was one"
(292). Similarly, Cass in *Redwork* comes to think of himself as closely
connected with old Mr. Magnus: "They were but different moments in the
one cycle" (230). Time and place meet in these textual moments when protagonists experience a sense of themselves as participants in larger structures of thought and feeling that centre on myths of nationhood. As they
are constructed in the four texts I have considered, the homely nations of
Canada and Australia have more in common than their histories as British
colonies. Informed by naturalized understandings of who is included and
who excluded, these texts situate their protagonists in privileged positions within national space, proposing versions of nationhood where citizens are nurtured and loved insofar as they conform to the will of the
national imaginary.

□ □ □

Notes

1 See Patricia Seed, *American Pentimento: The Invention of Indians and the Pursuit of Riches*, for an analysis of the differences between English and Spanish
colonial systems in regard to the ownership and usage of land.
2 See Brenda Niall (7–33), for an account of the novel's reception in Australia and
Britain.
3 I follow Hage in his treatment of Whiteness as "a fantasy position of cultural dominance born out of the history of European expansion" (*White Nation* 20). For discussions of the Whiteness of *Anne of Green Gables*, see Devereux (20–25); of
Seven Little Australians, see Bradford (3–5).
4 The term "bush" in Australian colloquial language refers to regions remote from
cities and towns. It is associated with national mythologies that enshrine the bush-
man as the "true" Australian—stoical, egalitarian, disrespectful of authority.
5 The White Australia Policy privileged British culture over all others, using harsh
immigration policies to discourage non-White migrants and actively seeking to
"breed out" indigeneity by removing indigenous children from their families and
confining indigenous people to missions and reserves.
6 ANZAC Day, celebrated on April 25 in Australia and New Zealand, commem-
orates the landing and subsequent campaign of the ANZACs in Turkey as

they attempted to capture the Gallipoli Peninsula and Constantinople (now Istanbul).

7 This term was first used by the commentator A. A. Phillips in 1958, to refer to Australians' internalized conviction of their inferiority to British culture and institutions, even following political independence.

CHAPTER 10

➡ **Home Page:
Translating Scholarly
Discourses for
Young People**

Margaret Mackey
with James Nahachewsky
and Janice Banser

Margaret Mackey

Introduction

A group of scholars meets, discusses, writes, critiques, meets again. A rich and exciting discussion of ideas of "home" in Canadian children's literature develops. The project leaders wish to make their ideas available to a wider public than the strictly academic circles in which it initially occurs. My role in this project is to find ways of bringing these ideas to a broader readership.

This chapter describes the processes of exploring potential conduits to a wider world, a fascinating and very challenging operation. In taking on this task, I was ably supported by two graduate students at the University of Alberta, James Nahachewsky and Janice Banser. In this chapter, making use of a very different intellectual framework from those developed in other chapters in this book, I will describe our developing understanding of the challenges as we created a website and returned it to the larger group for scrutiny. I will attempt to analyze the divergences that arose between and among the scholars and the website creators. In the end, this chapter tells the story of a pilot project that ended in initial failure, but the processes and pitfalls we negotiated offer interesting and potentially productive implications. The project we undertook was bound by different constraints: academic disciplinary priorities, discourses, and delineations; technological possibilities and constraints; and the strengths and weaknesses of the kinds of virtual collaboration that are made necessary by distance.

The Disciplinary Challenge

Children's literature is a field spread among at least three disciplines: English, education, and library and information studies. In general academic activities, scholars and practitioners in this field usually find that they have more in common than they hold distinct, and that most differences can be turned to productive use. In this project, where academic ideas were to be "translated" into material accessible to a more general public, however, disciplinary issues were highlighted in unexpected and interesting ways.

The Technological Challenge

The book of which this chapter is a part and which represents the major outcome of this project is fixed and linear in the normal book-like ways. We proposed a website that would present the ideas in a very different format, with relatively small units of text that could be linked in a variety of ways. The development of a coherent argument looks very different in this format, and we, as a collective, never did fully resolve the questions that arise from such a shift.

The Geographical Challenges

The project team was located in a variety of sites across western Canada, for a variety of compelling reasons. The "translation" of the scholarly work into something that would be of interest to a more general public on a website was a delicate operation, calling for the kinds of subtle and nuanced communication that are most easily accomplished face to face. E-mail and even telephone proved to be clumsier substitutes for personal meetings than we initially anticipated. The normal complications that confound any long-term project involving numerous participants—illnesses, new jobs, new babies—resulted more than once in lengthy e-mail silences that seriously interfered with the development of momentum and a sense of shared progress.

The Intellectual Challenges

These challenges overlapped in many ways and complicated what was already a formidable intellectual challenge: to comprehend the elegant and substantial arguments of a group of academics whose significant individual achievements were further enhanced by the constructive scaffolding of the group approach and to *re-address* these arguments in such ways that they could be rendered accessible to readers who would otherwise never open this book. The story of our successes and failures in this ambitious project is a complicated one, and I will first lay out the chronology of the website development and the group response before returning to the issues I have outlined above.

The Messiness of the Early Thinking

Hindsight has a way of making sometimes happenstance developments look much more purposive than their origins might justify. Space considerations make it impossible to do justice to the ebb and flow of many different ideas that made up the early days of the project. Our initial discussions about my role in this project could best be described as inchoate. From the very beginning, we were interested in finding ways to introduce other voices into our discourses. We considered vehicles that might enable exchanges of opinions between scholars and young readers, discussing the different potential made possible by working through classroom arrangements or exploring the possibility of setting up some kind of exchange with a public library's teen advisory panel. Our first look at the potential of the Internet was in pursuit of this idea, and our later decision to explore the establishment of a website grew out of this idea of finding venues for readers to exchange their different perspectives.

At the outset of the project, it was not at all clear to me what my own role might involve, and I spent some extended time exploring the complex question of whether reading about "home" is a distinctive kind of reading process. Do we read differently when the cadences of the writing are, so to speak, "mother" cadences, utterly known and familiar to us from our earliest consciousness? Are our patterns of arousal different when we recognize the landscape being described as it has been inscribed in our brain's early schemata, not merely by our eyes but also by our exploring feet? Is there a cognitive and affective vividness that attends reading about "home" in ways that have no equivalent in any other kind of reading?

I still think this question has much provocative potential, but with regard to the project, we ultimately decided that it would be more productive for me to explore ways of presenting the research of the group to the world rather than to pursue my own question. The thinking about variations of reading responses did not disappear entirely, however, as it evolved into questions about ways of reading that rematerialized in the diagram below. Ironically, I find it difficult to make room on my continuum for such a focused "home reading," a fact that reinforces my interest in the original question of how personal and ungeneralizable such forms of reading may be. The untransferrable singularity of such an experience literally took it off my schematized map of reading and it may well be that the intractable uniqueness of this kind of recognition is not very susceptible to outside observation.

The conversations about this intimate and visceral form of reading informed my thinking at the outset. In the end, however, the idea of exploring this notion further was abandoned in order to enable me to work on ways of translating the thinking of the group to a wider public. We began to frame the issues of reading in more public ways, yet the very personal notion of "home reading" survived in a form of half-life at the private end of the reading scale I later developed.

Reading as Play and Work

As the group discussions matured, we began to focus more singularly on the idea of creating a website and looked at ways of making it useful. One obvious route from the academy to a broader readership lies through the school classroom; a set of lesson plans is always a possibility for making new ideas available to a particular public. My own interest in this challenge included the arena of looking at the playful potential of these ideas as well as considering them as objects of work and study. At the very least, a pincer movement that takes account of reading as play as well as reading as work might offer more vehicles for effecting change. I did not want to abandon the classroom approach but neither did I wish simply to turn the group's insights into a set of lesson plans (though lesson plans were certainly one substantial component of the initial overall scheme). My plan, the ambitiousness of which is probably clearer to me now than it was at the beginning, was to attempt to find ways to address the separate strengths of classroom reading and recreational reading.

If we define the word "literate" in broad and multimodal ways, a vivid model for literate play is the DVD with its many extra tracks exploring the art of a film. Viewers opt in out of sheer interest and pleasure. Another model may be discerned in the wide variety of websites built to accompany and expand the experience of different children's television programs, as Julian Sefton-Green describes. In many cases, however, both of these examples are commercially rather than critically motivated. Attention may be drawn to the surface of the text in order to celebrate the cleverness of that surface, or, indeed (and paradoxically), to extend the sense of being immersed—but implicit assumptions are very rarely questioned and issues of framing remain invisible. While we wished to achieve the engaging and playful stance of these models, we were far more intent on introducing a critical component.

A website was an obvious vehicle for such an experiment. Creating a website would involve translation of the insights of the scholars into more widely accessible language—and also transformation of the linear material of their essays into a more mobile and dynamic format. But in constructing such a website, before I began to look at the particular content, I needed to be clear about my model of readers who might explore this site, and also to articulate some ideas about how I wanted to reach and affect these readers.

A Model of Forms of Pleasure Reading

Reading can happen on a number of planes and I was interested in clarifying a model that would not exclude either recreational reading or classroom reading. Before beginning any other work on this project, I set out to clarify my thinking about ways of reading for pleasure and what, for lack of a better shorthand label, I can best describe as reading for growth (these two categories are definitely not mutually exclusive). Robert Protherough, Jack Thomson, and J.A. Appleyard have proposed developmental models that represent how readers mature, but, on this occasion, I was more interested in considering how the same reader may adopt varied reading approaches to take account of text and context. It would be easy to read the model I developed as hierarchical, but that would be too linear a description, despite the linear and horizontal shape of Figure 17. In non-developmental and non-hierarchical ways, readers choose frames of engagement for their encounters with a story according to the occasion, the mood, and the text itself. They may actually shift stances throughout even a single reading event. One form of reading is not invariably and exclusively better or more appropriate than another in all circumstances.

Bearing this fluidity in mind, then, let us consider some ways of reading for pleasure, keeping in mind that space constraints allow for only a very simplified description. One way of reading recreationally is what I have called the *good-enough reading* (Mackey, "Imagining," "Good-Enough"). A good-enough reading experience involves a personal balance between the requirements of momentum, of keeping going through the story, and the requirements of accountability, of having some relatively clear sense of what the words are actually saying. (See Edward A. Chittenden, Terry S.

Salinger, and Anne M. Bussis for a fuller account of momentum and accountability.) Different readers find different balance points on this spectrum. Some readers will read very fast, assuming that difficulties in comprehension can be solved by forging ahead. Some readers are very slow and careful, reluctant to turn the page till they are clear about every detail. There are advantages and drawbacks to each approach, and of course readers can be found at all points in between as well. In order to read at all, everyone must simply *keep going* and this process sometimes involves compromises.

A good-enough reading always runs the risk of being *not* good enough, and readers are variably comfortable with that risk. On the other hand, a good-enough reading is not invariably just an inferior substitute for "better" kinds of reading. Many highly literary readers will find themselves shifting into good-enough mode as a story overtakes them.

A good-enough reading may have a perfunctory quality to it, and this distinguishes it from another form of recreational reading: *immersion*. J. Yellowlees Douglas and Andrew Hargadon describe an immersed reading in the following terms: "When immersed in a text, reader's perceptions, reactions, and interactions all take place within the text's frame, which itself usually suggests a single schema and a few definite scripts for highly directed interaction" (156). An immersed reading involves a reader in the sense that the medium is transparent, that the sole role of the words is to convey readers *into* a fictional world that absorbs all available attention. It is usefully contrasted by Douglas and Hargadon with what they call *engagement*, a form of reading experience they describe as follows: "Conversely, in what we might term the 'engaged affective experience,' contradictory schemas or elements that defy conventional schemas tend to disrupt readers' immersion in the text, obliging them to assume an extra-textual perspective on the text itself, as well as on the schemas that have shaped it and the scripts operating within it" (156). An engaged reading treats the vehicle of the text as opaque; readers not only notice what is happening inside the fictional world, but also pay attention to the elements that combine to create this world. Much classroom work, in both schools and universities, occurs on the level of the engaged reading. It is exactly this territory, only with regard to viewing rather than reading, that the DVD explores so thoroughly. Numerous websites addressing details of television programs, movies, and some books, also invite forms of engaged reading. Many readers move back and forth between immersion and engagement very readily.

The distinction between immersed and engaged reading may call to mind Roland Barthes's opposition of readerly and writerly texts. Barthes defines the writerly text as a text that a reader may write (rewrite) today, "to desire, to put forth as a force in this world of mine" (4). He values this capacity to rework a text highly: "Why is the writerly our value? Because the goal of literary work (of literature as work) is to make the reader no longer a consumer, but a producer of the text" (4). The readerly text is the "countervalue" of the writerly text, measured by "its negative, reactive value" (4).

The potential for active reading that is implied by the concept of engagement, the possibility of moving in and out of the text, does connect in interesting ways with the idea of the writerly encounter. To label an immersed reading as "readerly" and as a form of consumption raises an issue of value judgement that goes to the heart of disciplinary differences between English studies and library and information studies, a topic to which I return later in this chapter.

What we might call *meta-reading* is a more thoughtful and reflexive version of the engaged reading. Thomson's model does not attach labels to the stages of reading he describes, but his account of stage six sums up many of the qualities I am subsuming under this heading: "Consciously considered relationship with the author, recognition of textual ideology, and understanding of self (identity theme) and of one's own reading processes" (360). Meta-readers are more aware of how the text is working *on them as readers*, in verbal, cultural, social, and aesthetic ways, and may be involved in working out their own identity issues in texts and themes. Such a meta-reading, as I conceive it, involves an enjoyment of the processes by which the story is created and perused, and it involves a highly attuned and always increasing personal awareness of the *self as reader*.

Yet another stance involves *critical reading*. Of course, such reading is not simply a negative approach, looking for flaws. It involves readers in considering challenges to the text and its assumptions. It is often what Judith Fetterley calls a resistant form of reading, which may involve deconstructing the assumptions that the text implicitly takes for granted and exploring political, psychological, and social implications of the text. This kind of expansion of the engaged reading is much less well represented on the alternative tracks of the commercially available DVD, which more often produce engaged celebrations of the text rather than critical counterinterpretations.

It is possible to represent this model graphically in terms of increasing self-consciousness (see Figure 17), though I consider it important not to think of these distinctions as value judgments. Each kind of reading has its place in the life of a reader.

FIGURE 17

A Non-heirarchical Model of Forms of Reading for Pleasure

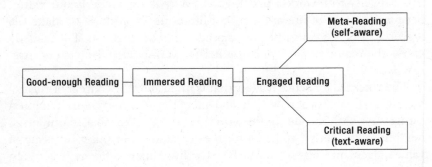

Meta-reading and critical reading often involve work at least as much as play, but it is also possible to account for them by means of a term of Seymour Papert's: "hard fun" (qtd. in Chris Johnston 12). It was my intention that the website should assume that young people can be appealed to by means of the route of "hard fun" (and I would certainly hope that intellectually stimulating "hard fun" would also occur in the nation's classrooms). Such an approach, however, is ambitious and complex.

These five approaches made up my basic model of reading for the purposes of thinking about the "home" website. It is certainly not an exhaustive schema of reading stances, but it proved helpful to my purposes—which were, in a nutshell, to move readers past the immersed reading into the territory of more engaged and critical reading, while still honouring the reader's right to take pleasure in any given text.

Creating this schema of reading approaches also helped me to clarify what I would *not* attempt to achieve in the website. Although I think both good-enough and meta-reading are extremely important processes with significant implications for the development of readers, I think they are less open to being influenced impersonally from a distance. I would not argue that good-enough reading needs no help; many readers fail to build up fluency because they never learn that it is sometimes all right to settle for the good-enough and so they reject the pleasures of recreational reading outright. Nevertheless, what is good-enough for the moment of reading is a highly personal decision and not really amenable to being affected by an impersonal outside agency. Similarly, the reflexive processes of meta-reading are very personal and often better established through local conversation and reflection than through a remote approach in a website. A website is no substitute for informed and personal teaching or for conversations with other readers.

FIGURE 18

A Modified Model of Reading Processes to Be Addressed in the Website

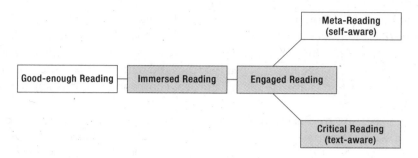

So I decided to focus on three of the five elements in my little schema. See Figure 18.

Not coincidentally, many of the readings offered by the scholars in this project also largely reflect the more social and impersonal qualities of being engaged and critical. For the most part, in their chapters in this book, they do not discuss their own good-enough reading or any immersed early readings. There are a few examples of meta-reading, particularly Perry Nodelman reflecting on his changing perspectives concerning double-voiced fiction. His chapter is as rare as it is valuable in critical writing about literature in that it entails a reflection on a reading that no longer seems good enough. It may be that if we had pursued the web work for long enough we could have used this chapter as a productive model for pursuing a more self-reflective kind of reading. In general, however, the scholarly discourses of this book take account of the more public end of the reading spectrum, and it made sense for the process of dissemination and diffusion to follow the same path, at least to begin with.

So my project description became more specific: design a website with the potential to meet young people as they experience an enjoyable but not necessarily thoughtful process of immersed reading and offer them other ways of thinking about their story. It is worth noting that much scholarly critique actually bypasses the immersed reading also, taking it as a given, or *as read*. The academic discourse often begins at the level of engagement, moving on to more critical reading. I wanted the website to meet readers at the point of immersion rather than starting with the assumption of engagement. A playful approach to reading acknowledges the power of immersion as a significant and often primary engine of reading pleasure. My own ethos as a one-time English teacher incorporates the importance of finding ways to introduce the pleasures of immersion into a classroom, while acknowledging any teacher's need to move on from simple immersion to other ways of looking at a text. But my librarian instincts also champion the importance of respecting the reader *as is*, of meeting the reader at the site of pleasure and acknowledging the significance of that pleasure as part of the intellectual framework of the discipline of understanding reading. I hoped that the fluid nature of a website would make room to encompass the paradoxical components of this apparent contradiction.

Supporting an engaged reading might involve ways of enabling readers to look at the surface of the text as well as through that surface into the imaginary world being created. What decisions has the author or illustrator made? How do they affect my response? What conventions are being assumed? How does what I know about the world and about other books feed into how I think about this book? Louise Saldanha's chapter in this book offers an example of engaged reading as play (despite her very serious purpose) as she experiments with fonts and borders, and there is scope for a website to follow this model in interesting ways.

Providing help in the development of a critical reading is a complex operation involving many factors. One important element entails raising questions about what is not included in the text. Do the missing components seem to have been left out deliberately or by oversight? What assumptions are being made about the world in general and about this story world in particular? How can we usefully question these assumptions? Are there ways of looking at this text that raise new questions? How have the elements of the text been framed and focused?

My ambition for the website was that we would be able to find ways of meeting young readers as they pick up a book for pleasure and to acknowledge and respect that pleasure while also finding ways of making these young readers *think*, of disrupting the kind of complacent reading that never raises a question. Such an aim was always rife with paradox and our first pass at achieving it was not successful.

Models for Communication

In creating a website to support pleasure reading, we began to define our job in two ways:

1. We were to expand the ways of thinking about particular texts (Canadian children's books featuring the idea of "home" in some way) from the immersed to the engaged and the critical.

2. We were to do so in ways that strive to respect the conditions of pleasure reading, to present some ways of questioning the texts under consideration, and to offer materials that teachers might find useful for the classroom—and, at the same time, to respect the critical work of the scholars.

We also hoped to produce a website that was pleasing to view and transparent to use.

Almost our first decision involved the reading audience. We decided that a readership at around the grade six to grade seven level would be interested in many of the books under discussion and able to adjust to more abstract forms of discussion. We decided to speak directly to those eleven- to twelve-year-old readers, as well as incorporating materials that their teachers might find useful.

In setting about this project to build a website, we were dealing with two dynamics: the technological and the intellectual. On one hand, it is possible to speak usefully of how these two dynamics fed into each other and constrained each other in stimulating ways—but simultaneously (and also paradoxically) even to make the distinction is misleading because the technological exercise was undeniably intellectual in nature, and vice versa.

In the end, the website was abandoned because of the impossibility of reaching consensus among the group on its tone and content, within the financial constraints of this particular project. But we started our project full of optimism.

The Technological Parameters

Some of the technological issues were basic, though not necessarily simple. Janice Banser was the site builder and she began with certain specifications in mind, based on criteria for usability:

- The site should be visually appealing but not so overloaded with technological extras that it would require lengthy download times on older computers. (At the end of 2005, according to a large survey by the Media Awareness Network, 94% of Canadian children had domestic access to the Internet but approximately 40% of that access was through dial-up rather than broadband.) Our intent was not to exclude that 40% of Canadian children from accessing our site at home, and to include all those many schools whose classroom computers are old, slow, and frustrating.
- The site organization would be transparent, and navigational tools would be clearly available at all locations on the site.

- The design elements would be distinctive but not overwhelming. Our budget was strictly limited, so this component was based on financial considerations as well as those of taste and utility.
- The web design would serve the intellectual content, but the intellectual content would have to be shaped in such a way as to take best advantage of the affordances of a website.

James Nahachewsky took responsibility for content and his job was twofold. In the beginning he worked on sample screens that could serve as placeholders for the building of the site organization. As the design of the site clarified, he then needed to refine his writing so that it would do a more precise job of conveying levels of thinking about the themes developed by our academic colleagues. This later stage would involve communication back and forth with the originators of the material.

Web Discourses

From the outset, we moved back and forth between considerations of design and considerations of content. The genre of web writing is new but the parameters are clarifying rapidly. A workable unit should not tax the limits of screen reading; links play a vital role in connecting those restricted single units. As an academic writer, I am of course familiar with the standard templates for organizing scholarly discourse: problem, hypothesis, research question, literature survey, et cetera. I also know that an organizational framework for a piece of writing, sometimes just an extended metaphor that exists nowhere but in the mind of the writer, can bring life and suppleness to a thinking exercise in ways that may range from the invisible to the elegant. The larger the work, the greater the utility of some such mental support structure to aid the organization of complex thoughts.

Not all academic writing lends itself to metaphorical shaping, and I have been inclined to think of such patterning as a luxury element in the standard discourse of the kind of scholarly material that is written for publication on paper. But working with the website sharply demonstrated the importance of establishing strong patterns early on in our thinking. A certain elegance of design, rather than featuring as a bonus, soon manifested itself as a *sine qua non* for productive work. If our website were not to be shapeless, it would have to be shapely. There was little in the way of a standard neutral template to fall back on.

Issues of Design

We rapidly fixed on a title ("The Home Pages" was an obvious choice) and Janice began work on creating a visual and organizational identity for the project. The early stages involved many design decisions that are outside the purlieu of the average piece of academic work—line drawings? full pictures? photos? font choice and size? use of colour? In the early stages, James took on the challenge of reading the drafts of the academic papers and providing some placeholder translations to allow Janice to keep building. This early stage of the project involved many small decisions that added up to an overall effect, and it surprises me now, looking at the website as it finally evolved, to remember the detailed labours of the building process. Those who know websites as consumers only are all too ready to regard its design as transparent—just as readers may regard the book as something always already "made."

The danger of this process was the potential for the site simply to expand in uncontrolled and unuseful ways. We had a variety of themes to incorporate from the different studies of the scholars, as a perusal of the other chapters in this book will make plain. To limit sprawl and create a focus that was both constructive and dynamic was our immediate requirement.

Issues of Discourse

Finding a voice for the writing on the website was an enormous challenge for James. For the early stages, he experimented with levels of complexity. The opening screen for the windows section, for example, was aimed at a notional reader at around grade 6 level and read as follows:

Does your home have windows? What type are they—large or small, picture windows or storm windows?

Where do the windows in your home look out onto—a busy street, a park, a friend's house? Have you ever tried to read just by the light that comes through your window?

Windows are interesting. Things always seem to be changing outside our windows—from morning to night, from summer to winter.

Windows are intriguing. They let you look two ways—inside and outside.

Sometimes you may even notice your own reflection in a window. This is what good books do. They let us see out to other worlds, and sometimes they reflect who we are.

Many Canadian authors and illustrators have used windows in their books to let us see people and places, to experience things that we can't see outside our own windows.

Some of the views through these windows are comforting, and others are very strange. We couldn't imagine such experiences or possibilities without being able to see through these other windows. We wouldn't be able to see through these other windows without visiting great Canadian books.

The next time you look through a book that has illustrations, a book you may be reading now or one that you read when you were younger, take some time to visit the windows in these other homes. It is good to be in another light for a while.

But the section marked "a deeper look" borrowed much more extensively from Schnitzer's stance and vocabulary and began in the following, very different terms:

A single window can exhibit or accommodate a variety of codes of meaning. This is particularly evident in Canadian picture books such as: *A Screaming Kind of Day* by Rachna Gilmore with illustrations by Gordon Sauvé; *The Missing Sun* by Peter Eyvindson with illustrations by Rhian Brynjolson; *Oma's Quilt* by Paulette Bourgeois with illustrations by Stéphane Jorish; *Snow Cat* by Dayal Kaur Khalsa; and *Mister Got to Go* by Lois Simmie with illustrations by Cynthia Nugent. The codes which exist in a dominant manner, or co-exist within the illustrated window, co-operate to tell the overall story of the picture book. Such window codes may be better understood when discussed as: distress windows; two-story/third-space windows; hinge windows; envelope/cellophane windows; and windows of opportunity.

This section ran at some length and, correspondingly, the font for this deeper exploration was two sizes smaller than the font in the opening screen. Our intent, of course, was to augment the lists in this passage with links to visual and perhaps verbal examples. We were not committed to either piece of prose but we were committed to the idea of experimenting with levels. Finding fruitful ways to link between different levels of discourse on the site was a design challenge that was not easy to solve. When we inserted the two entries on windows, we experimented with a system of buttons to indicate level of complexity, but this was a solution that felt rather more forced than intrinsic or elegant.

These pieces of writing are drafts rather than finished examples, but it is interesting to explore their location on the diagram of reading approaches (Figure 18). Even in their undeveloped form, we can see progression from immersed reading ("Windows are intriguing. They let you look two ways—

inside and outside") to a more engaged approach ("The next time you look through a book that has illustrations ... take some time to visit the windows in these other homes") to a much more critical discourse ("A single window can exhibit or accommodate a variety of codes of meaning"). The movement from one kind of reading, from one level of discourse, to another is relatively clumsy in this example, but it does give an indication of our intent.

The process raised very interesting questions about the use of the hyper-link as a connector. Linear prose, no doubt in part to compensate for its linearity, offers us a supple and varied range of connectors. "And" and "then" allow us to keep going; "however," "but," and "nevertheless" warn us that the prose is about to make a turnaround. Beyond the set of single words, we have other resources: "looking at this argument from an alternative perspective," "addressing this question at a deeper level," and other such locutions allow us to finesse the development of a line of argument. The hyperlink is more of a blunt instrument. It can act as a boundary marker as well as a connector, and readers may not feel immediately clear about which kind of role a particular link is playing. It offers fewer indications for clarifying the shape of a developing argument.

We need a rhetoric of hyperlinking, a set of conventions that we may learn to read as we read the cuts and connections of shots in a film. At present such a rhetoric is nascent at best, and in developing the Home Page website we often felt as if we were dealing with an unsubtle tool set.

Though we felt this lack of supple links as an impediment, there are interesting arguments on both sides. Shelley Jackson provides an intriguing alternative perspective on the role of connectors. As a hypertext author, Jackson is suspicious of linear prose, which she describes in the following terms, contrasting it with hypertext to the general intellectual advantage of the latter:

> The trick [of continuous print writing] was to allow the reader only one way to read it, and to make the going smooth. To seal the machine, keep out grit. Such a machine can only do two things: convince or break down. Thought is made of leaps, but rhetoric conducts you across the gaps by a cute cobbled path, full of grey phrases like "therefore," "extrapolating from," "as we have seen," giving you something to look at so you don't look at the nothing on the side of the path. Hypertext leaves you naked with yourself in every leap; it shows you the gamble thought is, and it invites criticism, refusal even. (244–45)

Words like "naked" and "gamble" carry powerful connotations of the kinds of risk that are perhaps more easily braved alone than as a collective. It is a tricky operation to find ways of gambling with the nakedness of other people without causing trouble. I am sure that the newness of the form and its lack of established "smoothers" was a factor in the difficulty of our task.

Windows, Voices, and Belonging: Part 1

From the outset, I assessed the chapter on "windows" as the most productive starting point, as it would link readily to many other themes from the project and provide some concrete and accessible visual material for the lead-in. James and I began some preliminary communication with Deborah Schnitzer about possible entry-points to the "windows" pages. However, as the organization of the website progressed, the idea of starting from a single initiating point began to seem a very linear and hierarchical approach for what we had in mind. After some unproductive experimentation, Janice, James, and I held a crucial team meeting in Edmonton and expanded that opening theme to three equal topics: windows, voices, and belonging. Instead of beginning with a single initial focal point, we would start from a dynamic interaction among three themes. Our design would incorporate movement among ideas right from the outset.

From that point onwards, the website took much clearer shape in my mind. The idea of windows would incorporate Schnitzer's work and would link to other topics: for example, the picture books used by Saldanha and by Doris Wolf and Paul DePasquale included windows that could be categorized through Schnitzer's taxonomy. But both the work on the writings of women of colour and the work on Aboriginal writing would also link to the other two themes of voices and of belonging. Danielle Thaler and Anne Rusnak's material on French-Canadian literature and Andrew O'Malley's work on *Canadian Crusoes* would also fit under both the latter headings. Nodelman's work on dual narrators would clearly fit in the category of voice, and Mavis Reimer's project on homelessness had its most natural home under the heading of belonging.

At this stage, I began to envisage quite a large website. Under our main headings, we would include James's translations of the academic work on particular themes and topics. But I wanted to link in other directions as well, to make use of the affordances of the web to incorporate teaching plans that could be linked to one or more themes, and to include particular book titles with a paragraph or so of annotation (one screen per title), that could be linked both to the explications of the themes and to the teaching plans—which would themselves be linked to curriculum guides

FIGURE 19

The Home Page: A Partial Site Map

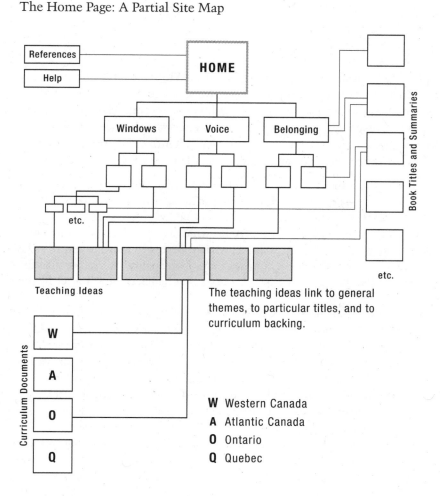

The teaching ideas link to general themes, to particular titles, and to curriculum backing.

W Western Canada
A Atlantic Canada
O Ontario
Q Quebec

from the different parts of the country. I drew up a schema for the overall design (see Figure 19) and we sent samples of our work so far (still with placeholder text) round the group.

This design had the potential to include all three earmarked reading stances. The annotated book titles offer one route into immersed reading; I was interested in allowing readers of the site to develop and explore their own matrix of primary reading. I envisaged the teaching plans as beginning at the level of engaged reading, with the potential to move on to critical reading. The core sets of windows, belonging, and voices, I pictured as providing an introduction that led rather more directly to the critical readings based on the academic work, but with the kind of "immersed to engaged" lead-in that we see in the sample above.

Response to the Prototype

The largest group in the project is based in Winnipeg, and this group got together to view the prototype website we sent them. Unfortunately they were not able to open the scanned diagram of the overall schema of the site. They did respond to those elements of the website that were mounted at that stage—and they were not happy. Mavis Reimer, the principal investigator, summed up their concerns in a detailed e-mail, which read in part:

> 2) We agreed that we understood the objective of this project to be to provide an opportunity to engage young people in critical discourse about literary texts. We were intrigued by the fact that, when the audience was conceptualised as being young people, what we coded as "language arts discourse" took over: for example, what appeared to move to centre stage were the general themes of homelessness, aboriginality, etc., rather than the critical discourses about particular texts that had been put in place by the researcher.
>
> This led us to our second principle: 3) As we talked about this, it became clear that a primary principle of translating scholarly discourses should be close consultation with the scholar whose work is being translated. Most of us do not have expertise in the pedagogy of young people, but we do have expertise in the research we're doing and we have some clear ideas about how that work could best be framed. Finding the right vocabulary might be the work of the "translator," but the "text" of the work already exists in our research and writing.
>
> This is closely related to the next point: 4) The translation must respect the politics and the ideological framing of the scholar, not seek to diffuse or soften those politics. If it is not possible both to respect these politics and to address young people, then this impossibility itself becomes a very interesting question to discuss: what might this tell us about the attitudes to young people in this culture, or the containing and constraining "thought practices" assigned to young people or assumed to be safe for young people?

Windows, Voices, and Belonging: Part 2

This first response to our website was intriguing. At one level it represented a reaction to the placeholder writing, something we had anticipated. There also seemed to be concern about the introductory kinds of writing that I have labelled as "immersed," but that the group described as "language arts discourse." I was a little bit more surprised by the resistance of the group to our request to supply us with three to six book titles from their list, complete with a paragraph or so of annotation. The Winnipeg group, according to a telephone conversation with Reimer, did not want to lay unpoliticized annotations side by side with their critical readings. What I had perceived as an invitation to immersed reading as part of the broader sweep of the website seemed to have been perceived by them as a betrayal of the politics of their work.

Clearly this rejection could be taken simply as a sign that I had failed in making my intentions for the site clear enough in the prototype, and such a failure is undoubtedly a major contributor to this particular breakdown. There are, however, other ways of reading this disagreement. Applying a critical reading to this point of tension in our differing intentions for the way the site would work raises some very interesting questions about disciplinary approaches to the processes of reading. In extremely simplified form (although, since I have a university degree in each of these three disciplines, it is at least a kind of insider simplification), the librarian wishes to organize opportunities for the reader to choose, taking account of intellectual principles of access and a theoretical understanding of reader behaviours; the teacher wishes to meet the reader where he or she is now and cause that reader to change and develop, drawing on developmental and educational theories; and the English studies academic wishes to focus on the texts themselves, raising issues of interpretation and questioning the ways in which the texts are framed and presented and drawing on a critical discourse of interpretive strategies.

I would not defend these distinctions between these three disciplines in any detailed way (and I certainly would not say that any participant in this project was constricted to a single approach), but, for a broad sweep, this account has the merit of explaining some of the uneasiness expressed by the Winnipeg group. Among many other issues, I do think we were seeing a disciplinary faultline at work in this point of disagreement. I am a librarian with a background as a teacher; James is a doctoral student in education; Janice is a library school student who has also worked as a teacher; and the Winnipeg participants are concentrated in the English department. Work in children's literature crosses these disciplinary boundaries as a matter of routine, but in the normal run of academic exchange the demarcations of the disciplines are fairly thoroughly smudged. To use a helpful concept expressed in an ugly word, it was the challenge of "operationalizing" the scholarly insights in forms accessible to a wider public that brought this potential for breakdown at the boundaries to the fore.

The academics' perception that the politics of their readings had been diffused and defused in the translation to a more popular level of discourse was entirely correct. James and I did not agree that such reduction was an essential component in creating what the group chose to describe as "language arts discourse," but we were more than ready to concede that the placeholder writing had raised this threat. The lesson plans were clearly problematic to the academics as well, and the Winnipeg group voted to abandon this element of the website at least in the early stages.

Questions concerning the politics of immersive and/or playful reading and the role of rereading also arise out of this response. Where does the idea of a resistant reading begin? Individual readers may differ in their preferences: some may choose to produce a compliant reading to begin with before turning a deconstructive eye to the text on subsequent rereadings; others may prefer to bring a more combative style to their initial reading and to resist the text from the outset. Whether one approach is preferable to the other is debatable. The first reader runs the risk of succumbing to the seduction of the authorial stance; the second reader is in danger of overlooking or overriding the pleasures that the text has to offer. Personal habits—even whether one is a fast or a slow reader and whether one likes or objects to rereading—may unduly inflect reader preferences for one approach or the other. An entire chapter could be written on the nuances of when the pleasures and challenges of critical interpretation can or should be introduced to readers, especially voluntary readers outside the classroom.

As I mulled over the response from Winnipeg, it occurred to me that we were seeing our categories of windows, voices, and belonging now being played out in the different field of our cooperative project. If for "windows" we substitute the idea of "framing," it seems clear that the academics in Winnipeg were concerned about a kind of appropriation of voice, a co-optation of their work to fit and "belong to" a sanitized classroom discourse, a reframing of their insights to reduce the impact for conflict. At this level, their reaction was reasonable and illuminating, and it offered us a chance to refocus the writing, in ways we had already anticipated doing.

An issue of process also became important at this stage. The e-mail response, unlike its conversational equivalent, arrived already reified in some important ways. Although it was certainly not designed to shut down negotiation, it was hard not to feel its impact as representing views already achieved and articulated, as much less tentative and open than the kind of give and take involved in conversation. In retrospect, I consider that we erred in making too little use of the telephone over the course of this project. A conference call between the Winnipeg group and the website creators in Edmonton would have provided a more flexible venue for preliminary responses to the prototype. Misunderstandings about how we in Edmonton perceived the highly tentative nature of the writing could have been cleared up immediately, for example; when we realized that the Winnipeg scholars could not open our electronic diagram of the web architecture we could have made instant arrangements to send a fax instead. We resorted to some telephone communication in the summer of 2005, particularly between James and Deborah Schnitzer, but, although it proved to be a productive way to work, it was almost certainly too little, too late. E-mail seemed like a logical, electronic way to discuss an electronic operation, but, in my view, by relying too heavily on e-mail we lost opportunities for timely and genuine debate.

Issues of Translation

Some general and some specific barriers to the translation of academic discourse into an address to a broader public became apparent throughout this project. Specifically, and very significantly, we were dealing with drawbacks of geography. A writing collaboration conducted at a distance is a complex operation. (See Muriel Robinson and Margaret Mackey for an account of the complications of a different virtual writing partnership.) In this case, we were adding the extra dimension of not simply co-writing but also changing medium, so that the possibilities and limitations of writing for the website also became a factor in the discussions. Not being able to meet face to face on a regular basis to explain different priorities and deal with potential problems was a problem in itself. It is striking that, when the group met in Winnipeg in June 2005, about three months after the meeting that led to the Reimer e-mail quoted above, the participants readily agreed to add the book annotations back into the website. A decision that had been complicated by distance became relatively simple face to face.

Yet the issue of geography was not simply an artificial constraint that could have been eliminated by better planning and a more locally cohesive group. To write about the idea of "home" in Canada is to face geographical barriers almost by definition. In all our discussions it was apparent that at least some level of geographic and linguistic dispersal was essential to do any kind of justice to the topic. A group of Canadians based in a single city or even province runs a serious danger of being limited by regional perspectives; from the outset we have seen it as a strength of our group that we were more widely dispersed. So it was always necessary to find ways of rising above problems created by distance—but the problems remained real and significant.

The other issues that arose over the course of the project were probably more general in nature, though none the less interesting for that. One intriguing complication lay in the interaction between questions of intellectual property and questions of address. To what extent did the content of the material inhere in its particular expression as seen in the other chapters of this book? What did we do to that material when we changed its form of address and its potential audience? Did changing that address actually change the purpose of the writing?

The question of different disciplinary priorities also raised issues about what room should be created for readers to react to the "home" stories in different ways. Clearly the Winnipeg group felt uncomfortable about the amorphous nature of the teaching component of the website and they were opposed to the simplicities of the annotated lists; at our end, James and I were uneasy about too much foreclosure of divergent reader response if only critical perspectives were presented. This is not a right-or-wrong question; each position begins from a different stance. The question we had to address collectively was a simple one: how much room for compromise can there be when the result is a singular outcome—even one with the protean potential of a website?

This led to a different kind of question: what kind of trust among the different participants was appropriate and what was actually possible—especially at a distance? I am not speaking here of personal trust; I do not think that such a question was an issue in this group at any time. I am more concerned with the issue of what might be labelled as a kind of disciplinary trust: faith that different disciplinary groundings are rigorous even if one does not immediately recognize the basis of that rigour.

The question of trust leads to a related question of time. The need for exchanging numerous iterations of the translations of the chapters, back and forth between participants in this project, made major demands on the time of the busy academics involved. In practical terms, the constant potential for delay was probably the single biggest constraint on the whole project.

Resource implications were also significant. After the collective Winnipeg response came in, James and Deborah Schnitzer began to communicate over the telephone and by e-mail. It became clear that they could readily agree on many aspects of how to present the "windows" section of the website—but this agreement would involve a degree of graphic support that was not immediately forthcoming within the budget of the project, which was now in its late stages.

The final complication was that, while I was present at every group meeting except the first one that set up the project proposal, members of the team did not know James at all. The absence of a personal contact was more of a deterrent than I had anticipated. Whether the virtual generation now growing up with a vast network of "Internet friends" would react in the same way in a similar situation is an interesting question but not one to be addressed here. We decided it was essential to bring James together with at least some of the team members for some intensive face-to-face work at least once before we reached a final decision on the website project.

The combined impact of all these factors was that a job I had always envisaged as large turned out to be enormous. Challenging and fascinating, raising numerous intriguing questions, a good project to be working on—but huge. It was not the nuts and bolts of thinking and writing that magnified the scale of the challenge; these elements were often daunting but they unfolded more or less as I had anticipated. The sticking point lay with the imponderables of the collective diversity. As long as we were all working on separate chapters for this book, the plurality was productive and always interesting. Creating a singular vehicle that honours such plurality and represents the complexity of divergent points of view without simply turning into an abbreviated rewrite of the scholarly book called for a kind of managerial politics that I simply had not anticipated sufficiently.

Most of the participants in this project are represented in the other chapters of this book. James Nahachewsky, the graduate student who undertook the challenge of creating the content for the website, also deserves to have his voice heard. (Janice Banser chose to be represented by a paraphrase of her priorities—see above.)

James Nahachewsky

The Translator Speaks

In the summer of 2004 when Margaret approached me to join in the task of presenting chapters from a book on the notion of "home" in Canadian children's literature I was intrigued by the possibilities of the project. At the time I was in a very liminal space personally and professionally, being in the midst of Ph.D. work in the Faculty of Education at the University of Alberta while raising a young family after completing degrees in English literature and education, a master's degree in education, and several years of middle-years and high school classroom teaching. As an emerging academic whose interest lies in expanded notions of text in relation to multi-literate practices in contemporary classrooms and curricula, as I have discussed before, I was keenly aware of the possibilities of children's literature, particularly picture books, in engaging students in critical discourses in relation to the plurality of identity and experience in Canadian society, as Ingrid Johnston and Jyoti Mangat suggest. I was also intrigued by the multivocal and multimodal possibilities afforded by online technologies in representing print material that Gail E. Hawisher and Cynthia L. Selfe and R.P. Stoicheff discuss.

My work as writer on the project began in earnest in the later part of September 2004, when Margaret loaned me the collected drafts of the Winnipeg group's chapters. Over several weeks, I read to familiarize myself with the authors' diverse voices, perspectives, and considerations of home in Canadian children's literature. In addition, I spent time in the Education library stacks searching for and reading materials that were interpreted throughout the chapter drafts and which I was not already familiar with. During this prewriting phase, I also examined several web pages devoted to children's literature—authors' pages, publishers' pages, student-constructed sites. My main concern as I began to write was with the tone(s) that I would construct for this particular situation to engage the broad range of possible readers of the website—most likely individuals who would gain knowledge of the academic book and selected children's literature through the website itself. In this prewriting phase I was constructing a sense of the chapters' content and sources as well as an implied audience. In these first few weeks I was also familiarizing myself with the evolving genre of online writing and envisioning possibilities for our website. I did this as I was very much considered a co-constructor of the site along with Margaret and Janice—being critical of our process and product while the process and product of writing/construction continued throughout the fall and into the winter.

I worked during this time, meeting with Margaret and Janice every two weeks or so, to provide drafts of web text that would act as placeholders for the various web pages that Janice was designing and placing onto the Internet. These pages' content and tone were intended for diverse implied readers (whom I understood, through the scheduled conversations with Margaret, to be intelligent and multi-literate early adolescents, educators, and librarians). Interestingly, the web pages that I was writing both drove and were directed by the emerging architecture of the site—conceptualized as a multi-dimensional and dynamic text geared to be cross-referential through reflexive readings. Three categories, windows, belonging, and voice, were decided upon as organizers for the broad range of topics addressed in the book's chapters. Margaret suggested that I flesh out several teaching ideas that we had brainstormed to complement the ideas considered in the book's chapters and the content of the picture books— providing further depth for the site and engagement for educators. Margaret hoped to provide a substantive site in the early spring for the Winnipeg group to read and view with an eye for giving advice regarding the content and architecture of the site.

In the text I was writing for the various web pages of the developing site, I was appropriating each chapter author's utterances to form a heteroglossia, as defined by Mikhail Bakhtin, to engage the implied readers. This process, for me, was evident in the product, which did not follow a one-to-one ratio of representation. I did not represent each chapter as a separate entity. Rather, as website author I was intending to allow for inter-textualities to form within and between the website and the various readers' textual and personal experiences. I was working to convey academic authority particular to literary interpretation without being too authoritative— rather I was writing to open spaces of navigation, understanding, and critical discourse inherent in online texts through a variety of levels of voice and tone for a variety of readers. After the Winnipeg chapter authors had the opportunity to view and respond to the drafts on the website (through many pointed and grounded criticisms), I have attempted to bridge the gap between authorial intentions—casting forth with more direct representations of the single chapters and reeling in productive responses as to the meaningfulness of these representations for the various chapter authors.

The act of writing is, at the best of times, very complicated. When the process involves as many divergent relations (ideological, technological, philosophical) as this project has, these complexities multiply. At times I have felt like Pirandello's six characters in search of an author—understanding myself at various times to be explorer, translator, editor, copy writer, web creator, and academic underling. At other times, I have felt like a writer with nine editors. Importantly though, throughout this process, I have come to understand not only the complicated nature of the multiple and contemporaneous processes involved in writing for a website, but also the elegant appropriateness of this particular multidimensional site for the public's exploration, consideration, and questioning of "home" in Canada.

Margaret Mackey

The End of Chapter One

In January 2006, James and I made a brief visit to Winnipeg to meet with the group of scholars located there. James arrived a day ahead of me and spent the first day with various members of the group, assisted by a web

producer whose time was generously supplied by the University of Winnipeg. As we expected, it was much easier to clarify the important questions on a face-to-face basis. The outcome of these sessions, however, was
intriguing, not at all what I had anticipated. This expert did not suggest
a solution to the immediate problems of discourse, register, and purpose
that were dogging our translation exercise. In effect, he proposed the possibility of a detour. Drawing on the graphic potential of the web, he suggested that the framing discourse could be visual rather than verbal. Instead
of our introductory words, we could offer graphic support to scaffold the
entry into the critical readings being offered by the various chapters.
Instead of running what was clearly perceived as the risk of producing
"language arts discourse," the introduction could be pictorial—a drawing
of a conventional house, for example, with a few introductory words of
introduction in the doorway and windows that "exploded" with leads to
particular chapters.

There are numerous multimodal routes to a critical reading, particularly of a picture book. It might be possible to draw on the "pop-up" convention of the CD-ROM image to highlight critical questions by drawing
the mouse across an image from a relevant book. It might be useful to draw
on the conventions of the DVD by including alternative, critical audio
tracks to the reading of a book. "Child windows" on the screen (inserted
smaller screens) could provide a home for disruptive points and queries.
The list is not necessarily endless but it is large and full of potential.

It is possible that the visual scaffolding would supply a sufficiently
inviting structure to entice immersed readers to take a new look at their
stories. It is certainly likely that a well-crafted visual schema would seem
more transparent to the scholars who rejected the "re-voicing" of their
chapters. In short, the visual translation seems like an experiment worth
pursuing, a way, to paraphrase Jackson, of unsealing the machine, insert-
ing grit into the works, raising troubling questions. How such a visual
approach might coexist with the pleasures of absorbed reading is a fascinating question awaiting the first tentative answers. It may well be that
a visual form of critical reading offers more ways to respect and coexist
with the initial pleasures of immersion, that it may be seen less in the
"spoiler" role of analytical overkill that results in the hostility of many
school readers.

To conclude this chapter, I posit the existence of some form of visual
scaffold and revisit the issues that became part of the original challenge
of the first website. To compare the pilot project with the new vision is to
deal with apples and oranges—the concrete limitations of the initial website with some of its options pinned down, however provisionally, must

certainly seem constrained and inadequate in contrast with the boundless potential of its wholly imaginary alternative of graphically enriched content. With regard to "operationalizing" this new variant, it is worth considering what problems may be solved and what problems may remain. To create such a website will involve, at the very least, a new budget and a level of technical support and expertise beyond what was available in our pilot project. The potential is certainly very exciting. Nevertheless, some questions still need answering.

The simplest questions arise out of considerations of geography. Our experience with the first website suggests that the initial foundations of this kind of project can be established more successfully on a local basis— that removing the complication of communication over distance at least for the opening stages is one simplification that is easy to organize. With hindsight, it seems clear to me that it would be easier to establish local decisions and precedents on a face-to-face basis with the largest single group, and then move outward to include the further-flung members of the group. I do not say that it is impossible to establish a virtual framework of communication at a distance; I do say that it is difficult, especially with a group for whom time is always at a premium, and that the factor of distance communication represents one difficulty that can be reduced relatively painlessly.

The most exciting positive question involves how much of the complexity of the chapters can be retained through the use of visual metaphors. One of the major issues of the original website involved the perception by the scholars that our reworking of their material was reductive. Would a pictorial translation be perceived as more neutral and/or more all-encompassing? Even if we assume a positive answer to this question, there remain other significant issues. The potential for sprawl would continue to be a danger, and such a site would need a strong editor or run the risk of becoming too prolix to be engaging. A website can be enormous without being "sticky," that is, without appealing to readers enough that they persevere through its options on any single visit and/or return more than once. The chapters are complex and dense and any kind of translation into a more popular form is going to run the risk of reductiveness. Issues of visual grammar will also need to be confronted; the site will have to be readable.

As for the interdisciplinary questions (to my mind, the most interesting complication of the whole project), they call for much more delicate consideration, and a simple and robust solution is not immediately apparent to me. How can we raise critical questions about a text without simply interrupting absorbed and happy readers with a lecture along the lines of "This is what is wrong with how you are reading right now"? Such a question, needless to say, is a caricature of intrusive and destructive pedagogy, but even in this crude form it outlines a genuine problem. Barthes's dismissal of readerly behaviours by use of the pejorative word "consumption" (4) is a reminder of disciplinary priorities in literary studies. The challenge of how to understand and address the issue of immersed reading is complex and fascinating, and it is heightened when we are speaking to voluntary rather than conscripted (classroom) readers. DVD alternative tracks extend the awareness of viewers with regard to the composition of a movie, but they don't necessarily challenge or disrupt viewing pleasure in critical ways. Discovering a means of inviting voluntary readers to experience the challenge of new forms of critical reading as sufficiently enjoyable and intriguing that they are happy to keep reading remains a pedagogical challenge—and a challenge of voice and address. There is no shortage of young people who are sufficiently disheartened by some version of the caricatured approach I describe above that they simply stop reading.

It may well be that the visual route supplies a form of pleasurable scaffolding that was clearly difficult to achieve through our verbal texts. However, as long as the intent of the website is to speak to voluntary readers, the threat of the off-switch never goes away. As Todd Gitlin reminds us, we are all obliged in this era of information overload to develop "stratagems of inattention" (118), and readers who feel their enjoyment is being "spoiled" by too many disruptive questions have an easy out, by means of a single click. Awareness of that click must always feature in how the design of the new website is shaped.

Or alternatively, and perhaps more simply, the creators of the projected new website may simply decide to pass over the immersed stage of reading, to abandon the librarian framework, and to focus mainly on classroom readers by means of addressing their teachers. Such an address would short-circuit some of the subtleties and problems of dealing with volunteer readers. It may be that we were trying to achieve too many complicated aims at once in our initial project and that including the untroubled immersed reading as a starting point simply makes the scale of the project too vast.

The role of immersed reading, perhaps especially in the field of children's literature, is subject to a great deal of mixed feeling and confused discussion. Stephen D. Krashen provides evidence to suggest that free voluntary reading is necessary to turn people into readers, and that the foundations of pleasure are an essential part of the final edifice. With young, new readers in particular, there are many subtle questions about when to let them read freely and perhaps thoughtlessly, and when to introduce ways of critical, resistant, and more deeply informed reading processes and habits. Such questions are significant for the study of children's literature in all corners of the academy: English departments, education faculties, and library schools.

With the original website, James and Janice and I attempted to work with such questions but our first pass at the challenge did not succeed. The significance of our original purpose and the importance of whether we should even attempt to address the immersed as well as the potentially critical reader in the same package was lost in subsequent discussions of the inadequacies of the provisional voice we had offered. I suspect that, as with many of the issues involved with the creation of the website, conversations about such questions among representatives of the three major disciplines of children's literature might be more productive on an incremental day-by-day basis rather than structured as an occasional large-scale debate—another reason for work of this kind to begin locally.

In the final account, it may be that English scholars, teachers, and librarians cannot find a single voice to speak to child readers. It may be that the field must inevitably remain multifaceted rather than singular. It may be that the complications of distance and time that dogged this project simply camouflaged the fact that we were shooting for an unachievable goal. I do not pretend to know the answer. What I do know is that we attempted something worth trying and that one failure does not prove this aim impossible. The issues that were raised and highlighted by this project are well worth pursuing on another occasion.

➡ **Homeward Bound?**

Neil Besner

I

When Mavis Reimer invited me to join this project in 2002, she asked that I work as a "metacritic," along with Australian metacritic Clare Bradford; we were to provide a kind of oversight of the group's work, commenting on how their inquiries into the meanings and functions of home operating in Canadian children's books might resonate in the wider context of more general discourse and scholarship on Canadian and Australian writing. Of course the prospect of working in this way presented several questions, first among these, what the relationship might be between writing for children—and the scholarship attending this writing—and Canadian and Australian writing and scholarship in general. And what kind of oversight might Clare and I bring to bear? These questions remain very much alive.

"Metacritic": then as now, the term led to another series of questions. It seems to me that scholarship in Canadian children's literature—a good deal of which I have had the privilege of observing at close quarters for nearly twenty years at the University of Winnipeg, which now has, without doubt, the largest and most productive cohort in the country of scholars in the area—has a distinctive ethos that precludes, at least in theory and certainly in practice, the aerial point of view implied in "oversight." What I believed entering the project, I believe more strongly as we finish this stage, four years later: there is no simple position available to this metacritic, or indeed a critic by any other name, as he thinks through the work exemplified in this collection of essays. What might be available, though, is a series of responses to the riches of the various discussions, some of which seem to me to be engaged in a dialogue with each other that is strikingly similar to the kinds of conversations that have been resonating across Canadian criticism over the last twenty years.

Before I address these remarkable echoes, however, a word about the three years and more leading to this collection of essays. Every summer, the working group assembled in or near Winnipeg for a mini-conference of two days at which members presented progress reports, discussed each other's projects, and talked about the shape of the collection of essays. (Of course, there was extensive e-mail conversation at all times between the meetings, and since the majority of the group lives and works in Winnipeg, there were also countless opportunities for ongoing conversations in smaller subgroups.) These intense summer meetings produced, cumulatively, a growing sense of familiar conversation; of the provenance of our agreements and our disagreements; and a growing familiarity, too, with the discourse of the whole group, which shaped a conversation inflected and engaged with difference at every level—a discourse that encouraged difference. I'm struck now by how that tacit agreement, never explicitly articulated, has survived, even thrived, in these essays, which at once bristle with cross-talk and cohere in their difference. How this alchemical and paradoxical state was reached remains mysterious. But it has been and is invigorating.

And last, another word about metacriticism, oversight, and scope. I have not pretended to respond to every essay, or to every argument in every essay in what follows, both because that would be tedious and because such a response implies a position I am quite uncomfortable with, and implies as well a hierarchy that I do not subscribe to, in which scholarship on Canadian children's texts might be understood to circulate in a location accessible to "oversight." What follows, rather, is a sideways series of comments in which I have tried to articulate an outsider's perspective and at the same time—in keeping with the spirit of the collection—to ask, as often as possible, where, when, and whether "outsider" is the most accurate position or perspective from which to write.

II

Even a glancing familiarity with Canadian criticism in general since well before the turn of the last century will reveal a striking focus on the meanings of "home" now available, or lost, or in the process of being redefined. Rewriting and rethinking "Canada" in postcolonial terms; writing on race and interrogations of multiculturalism; redefinitions of region and nation; the reinscription of local senses of space and place in the context of the global; the persistent thematic of the borderland; the at once central and marginal(ized) place of Aboriginal writing—all of these contemporary fibres and filaments of our discourse, not surprisingly, emerge in this collection as well. Nor is it surprising that the critics writing here should so often invoke, alongside the scholars like Sheila Egoff, Perry Nodelman, or Rod McGillis who focus more centrally on children's literature, the Canadian critics working more generally in the field: W.H. New, Cynthia Sugars, Stephen Slemon, Smaro Kamboureli, Terry Goldie, Patricia Smart, Cecily Devereaux, Jonathan Kertzer, and Deborah Keahey, for example. And the necessarily international character of Canadian criticism is of course reflected here as well, through frequent commentary on the work of Bhabha, Bourdieu, Berger, Rosemary George, Bradford, Said, and others. In fact one quite visible (and more vocal) argument implicitly made by this collection is that there is no clear border—in criticism or in the primary texts—between writing for children, and its attendant scholarship, and other Canadian writing. If in our classroom practice, many of us teach *Where the Wild Things Are* alongside "adult" texts, or *Robinson Crusoe* alongside *Canadian Crusoes*, *Anne of Green Gables* alongside *The Colony of Unrequited Dreams*, Thomas King the novelist alongside King the storyteller, and ditto Margaret Laurence and Margaret Atwood and Mordecai Richler, then perhaps the entire precinct of children's writing migrates more often across a more permeable border than the traditional segregations of the discipline might have imagined. In this sense this collection, although this was not its primary intention, performs another valuable service.

I agree with Mavis Reimer's perception, implied in the order of the essays, that a central position in this collection is occupied by Doris Wolf and Paul DePasquale's essay, "Home and Native Land," which aptly underwrites many of the book's premises, complementing Perry Nodelman's related and provocative argument in his "At Home on Native Land" and Louise Saldanha's equally provocative and revealing discussion in "White Picket Fences." Aside from providing the surprising information that Wolf and DePasquale found "approximately 300 books for children by approximately 125 Aboriginal authors" (87), this essay's tracing of the "heavy colonial and neo-colonial history" (90) of the Aboriginal picture book, along with its telling analysis of how (and why) Aboriginal children's fiction "notably avoids the portrayal of these realities" (91) of the colonial condition, underscores a particular instance of the didactic and ideological functions of children's fiction and re-situates representations of Aboriginal experience from the historical margin to the contemporary centre. And of course, as Wolf and DePasquale make perfectly clear, Aboriginal writing for children is not entirely separable from Aboriginal writing for adults, even if the latter is more often and more strongly inflected with more thoroughly realist, and far less idyllic, portraits of Aboriginal experience in Canada.

I remain intrigued by Danielle Thaler's and Anne Rusnak's persuasive demonstrations that there is no satisfactory equivalent for "home" in French. This defies common sense, and yet, as they both show, it is so. How can a word and idea so charged, so freighted with meanings in English that it appears in innumerable book, song, and poem titles (including the titles of three contemporary books by the Canadian critics named above), and indeed provides the major impetus for this project, be untranslatable? My first (misguided) temptation was to seek an answer in proto-Canadian terms—to find, in Quebec's position in the nation, and hence in writing from Quebec, an explanation in our history and geography that would account for this powerful linguistic displacement and erasure. But French and English both precede us, and as Thaler's and Rusnak's pieces show us, there is no easy or monolithic accounting for the place of children's writing from Quebec, just as there is no equivalent or approximation in English for the culturally complex and liminal figure of the coureur de bois. And here as elsewhere in the collection, there is no assurance that the home-away-home pattern discerned in some writing for children is either generalizable or secure.

Nowhere in this collection do I feel more like an admiring outsider looking in, amazed, through an impossibly variegated series of picture windows, than in reading Deborah Schnitzer's formidably detailed and precise taxonomy of the kinds of vistas enacted, enabled, or performed in the representations of windows she analyzes in children's picture books. It is not only that my own reading of picture books is shown to be impossibly naïve, although that is so; more importantly, Schnitzer's discussion opens out, in visual terms (and thus keenly raises the question of the visual effect for and on children of the pictures in picture books), many of the implications of Reimer's reminder early in the collection that children's literature is the only genre in which adults write for a different target audience. Move for one moment beyond the glib supposition that it is only adults who read (see? perceive? interpret? decode?) the significances inherent in the windows, real, imagined, sketched in, painted, that Schnitzer reveals; and move, as well, beyond the equally glib supposition

that the "insides" and "outsides," the restrictions, permissions, and inter-
dictions that Schnitzer shows to be so intricately coded in the windows
of every kind, on any storey in the houses, sometimes the homes, depicted
in these books—and you find yourself in a world in which picture and
word are signs whose powers and relations you are newly uncertain about
and eager to think about. No other essay in the book engages in such a
thorough rereading of pictures of windows; no other essay left me as certain that "metacriticism" and "oversight" were polite fictions, stand-ins
for some other, less attractive designation.

If Schnitzer's essay is invaluable because it so strikingly extends and
directs the discourse of the collection toward the visual, then Andrew
O'Malley's piece on the robinsonade, the place of *Canadian Crusoes* in this
tradition, and the seemingly contradictory place of the domestic in the masculine coding of the form, performs another invaluable operation, by
broadening the reach of the collection—as Danielle Thaler does in her
discussion—to include, explicitly and specifically, a longer historical sweep
and vision. It has long been a (somewhat simplified) commonplace of
Canadian criticism to see the Strickland sisters, Susanna and Catharine,
as having incarnated twinned but opposing views of the new colony:
Moodie's vision, melancholic, gothic, and despairing, best illustrated in
Roughing It in the Bush, while Traill, the straightforward, optimistic, no-
nonsense pioneer, exhorted the new settlers to make do, forge ahead, and
stay busy, as exemplified in works like *The Backwoods of Canada*. But
what is lost in this polarization are many of the nuances of Traill's vision
(and both Moodie and Traill reappear regularly in contemporary Canadian poetry and fiction as iconic characters or voices; see, for example, the
haunting Moodie of Atwood's imagination, or the vigorous Traill, or
"C.P.T." of Laurence's in *The Diviners*); O'Malley's reading of Traill into
other contexts with strong roots in another tradition helps to problematize her status, and that of her best-known work.

Over the last several years, I have listened to several iterations of Louise
Saldanha's argument about the skewed representation of conflicts (and their
shallow resolutions) between visible minorities and the mainstream in
Canadian children's fiction; like Smaro Kamboureli in her work on multiculturalism, Saldanha is one of the most careful and astute readers of
Canadian multicultural policy and its intersections and contradictions
with cultural practice—and of textual representations of this cultural
practice. What intrigues me now, reading the final version of "White
Picket Fences" (and seeing precisely how layout and typography can mirror, reflect, and embody meaning, not only in pictures but in text) is how
persuasive Saldanha's argument has become in the company of Perry

Nodelman's contestations of easy accommodation to Aboriginal ways of living and being, and also in relation to Wolf and DePasquale's discussion. It is not that the writers have set out to complement or contradict each other, and this is true of all the contributors; rather, it now seems to me as if the several years of conversation have animated every writer's (allegedly) solitary essay, so that the cumulative effect before us is a group of essays that at once advance a particular argument *and* speak across that argument *to* each other. It is one thing to convene a conference on a given topic and then to publish the proceedings, and we can certainly think of many fine collections of essays with just that provenance; it is quite another thing to engage in a years-long conversation among fewer than ten people on a topic such as the meanings of "home" in Canadian children's literature, and then to circulate, re-convene, and re-circulate and discuss drafts of each other's essays.

III

I commented earlier that I agreed with Mavis Reimer's suggestion about the centrality of Wolf and DePasquale's essay in this project, and suggested, as well, that I see Nodelman's and Saldanha's essays as complementary arguments, from very different vantage points, to be sure, both to the Wolf/DePasquale discussion and to each other. It's also true, I think, that in Clare Bradford's and Mavis Reimer's (unintentionally) complementary readings of children's texts that are central, respectively, to Australian and Canadian writing for children, there emerges another commonality that extends beyond nation and beyond genre and mode: it is not only that, as Bradford points out, "Canadian and Australian texts tend to centre on the identity-formation of young protagonists, played out in represented processes of growth, change, and acculturation" (178), but that, as well, and extending beyond Canadian children's literature, Bradford's perception resonates with Reimer's comment that "[t]he movement of child subjects from given bonds of filiation to chosen bonds of affiliation appears to align Canadian children's texts with postmodern celebrations of mobile subjectivities" (2). What I read in Bradford's and Reimer's syntheses—and this echoes across the whole collection—is, finally, a rearticulation (I had to suppress "recapitulation," but let that stand, too) of the wider colonial history that informs both Australian and Canadian cultures, and that has recently been shown as so instrumental in postcolonial work across these and many other colonial cultures. That is why the meanings of "home," and of movements away and toward old and new figurations of home and homelessness, of locations, dislocations, and relocations; the strange but distinctive histories and cartographies of the emptying out and then the filling up of national space; and the restlessly "mobile" reconfigurations of identity that seem so typical, and so powerfully constitutive of writing for children in both cultures should also be typically and powerfully recurrent in writing more generally, at least in Canada. Pick a handful of recent Canadian novels and place them alongside Reimer's and Bradford's comments: Johnston's *The Colony of Unrequited Dreams*, Atwood's *Oryx and Crake* or *The Blind Assassin*, Toews's *A Complicated Kindness*, Bergen's *The Time in Between*, or King's *Green Grass, Running Water*, Ondaatje's *Anil's Ghost* or *The English Patient*, or Richler's *Barney's Version*, or Shields's *The Stone Diaries* or *Unless*, or, again, Kogawa's *Obasan*, or Michaels's *Fugitive Pieces*, or Bock's *The Ash Garden* (or virtually all of Munro's or Gallant's short fiction, although that is another long story)—and ask whether these fictions often perform or narrate the identity-formation of young protagonists (they do), and whether there is a corollary movement in many from given bonds of filiation to chosen bonds of affiliation (there is); and whether many, if not all of these fictions present us with mobile subjectivities (they do).

My conclusion, therefore? First, that I continue to understand very little about writing for children, but that what I do understand is not foreign to my understanding of Canadian writing more generally. On the contrary: I have learned much from this project that sharpens my general understanding. Second, that it seems somehow fitting that a collection such as this one should have been produced by a group of critics located, mainly, at once on a cultural margin in Canadian terms—Winnipeg—and also, geographically, in the centre of the country. Third, that a concentration of scholars in the area of children's literature such as the one at the University of Winnipeg has uncannily and to welcome effect replicated and then interrogated many of the ideological tensions and cross-currents afoot in the country at large and brought them together between the covers of one book. There is something keenly fitting in this, and it speaks well, too, of the variously formidable energies that have been gathering in this field at the University of Winnipeg for over twenty-five years. And finally, that the conversations and the voices arrested for a moment in print here, where they only seem to be at a pause, drawing a breath, are, in reality, just for openers.

□ □ □

WORKS CITED

Primary Works—English

Anne of Green Gables Souvenir Magazine. Illus. Erik Dzenis. Confederation Centre of the Arts, 1986.

Aker, Don. *Of Things Not Seen.* Toronto: Stoddart, 1995.

Alderson, Sue Ann. *Ida and the Wool Smugglers.* Illus. Ann Blades. Toronto: Douglas & McIntyre, n.d.

Anderson, Grant S. *Willy the Curious Frog from Pruden's Bog.* Illus. Sheldon Dawson. Winnipeg: Pemmican, 2002.

Andrews, Jan. *Very Last First Time.* Illus. Ian Wallace. New York: Margaret K. McElderry, 1985.

Armstrong, Jeannette. *Enwhisteetka: Walk in Water.* Penticton, BC: Theytus Books, 1982.

———. *Neekna and Chemai.* Penticton, BC: Theytus Books, 1984.

Atwood, Margaret. *Oryx and Crake.* Toronto: McClelland & Stewart, 2000.

———. *The Blind Assassin.* Toronto: McClelland & Stewart, 2003.

Badoe, Adwoa. *Crabs for Dinner.* Toronto: Sister Vision, 1995.

———. *Nana's Cold Days.* Pictures by Bushra Junaid. Toronto: Groundwood, 2002.

Ballantyne, R.M. *The Coral Island.* 1857. London: Collins, 1966.

———. *Hudson's Bay; or, Everyday Life in the Wilds of North America.* W. Blackwood & Sons: Edinburgh and London, 1848.

———. *Snowflakes and Sunbeams; or, The Young Fur Traders.* London: T. Nelson & Sons, 1856.

Bannatyne-Cugnet, Jo. *From Far and Wide: A Canadian Citizenship Scrapbook.* Illus. Song Nan Zhang. Toronto: Tundra, 2000.

Bannerji, Himani. *Coloured Pictures.* Toronto: Sister Vision, 1991.

Bedard, Michael. *Redwork.* Toronto: Stoddart, 1990.

Bergen, David. *The Time in Between.* Toronto: McClelland & Stewart, 2005.

Blades, Ann. *Mary of Mile 18.* Montreal: Tundra, 1971.

The Blue Lagoon. Dir. Randal Kleiser. Perf. Brooke Shields and Christopher Atkins. Columbia Pictures Corporation, 1980.

Bock, Dennis. *The Ash Garden.* New York: Random House, 2001.

Booth, David. *The Dust Bowl.* Illus. Karen Reczuch. Toronto: Kids Can, 1996.

Boraks-Nemetz, Lillian. *The Old, Brown Suitcase: A Teenager's Story of War and Peace.* Brentwood Bay, BC; Port Angeles, WA: Ben-Simon Publications, 1994.

Bosak, Susan. *Something to Remember Me By.* Illus. Laurie McGraw. Whitchurch-Stouffville, ON: The Communication Project, 1997.

Bouchard, Dave. *The Meaning of Respect.* Illus. Les Culleton. Winnipeg: Pemmican, 1994.

Bourgeois, Paulette. *Oma's Quilt.* Illus. Stéphane Jorisch. Toronto: Kids Can, 2001.

Brooks, Martha. *Bone Dance.* Toronto: Groundwood, 1997.

Buchignani, Walter. *Tell No One Who You Are: The Hidden Childhood of Régine Miller.* Montreal: Tundra, 1994.

Campbell, Maria. *Half-Breed.* Toronto: McClelland & Stewart, 1973.

Campe, Joachim Heinrich. *The New Robinson Crusoe.* London: J. Stockdale, 1789.

Carrier, Roch. *The Hockey Sweater.* Illus. Sheldon Cohen. Trans. Sheila Fischman. Toronto: Tundra, 1984.

Castaway. Dir. Robert Zemeckis. Perf. Tom Hanks. 20th Century Fox, 2000.

Chen, Tin-An. *Little Pria's Big Canadian Adventure.* Illus. Angela Hodge. Mississauga, ON: Cornucopia, 2004.

Clark, Joan. *The Dream Carvers.* Toronto: Viking, 1995.

———. *The Hand of Robin Squires.* Toronto: Clarke, Irwin, 1977.

Clutesi, George. *Son of Raven, Son of Deer.* 1967. Disney, BC: Gray's Publishing, 1975.

Condon, Penny. *My Family.* Illus. Penny Condon. Saskatoon: Gabriel Dumont Institute, 2001.

Craig, John. *No Word for Goodbye.* Toronto: Peter Martin, 1969.

Crow, Allan. *The Crying Christmas Tree.* Illus. David Beyers. Winnipeg: Pemmican, 1989.

de Brébeuf, Father Jean. *The Huron Carol.* Illus. Frances Tyrrell. Toronto: Key Porter Kids, 1990.

Defoe, Daniel. *Robinson Crusoe.* 1719. Oxford: Oxford UP, 1998.

Delaronde, Deborah L. *Flour Sack Flora*. Illus. Gary Chartrand. Winnipeg: Pemmican, 2001.

———. *Flour Sack Friends*. Illus. Gary Chartrand. Winnipeg: Pemmican, 2003.

———. *Little Metis and the Metis Sash*. Illus. Keiron Flamand. Winnipeg: Pemmican, MB: 2000.

———. *A Name for a Metis*. Illus. Keiron Flamand. Winnipeg: Pemmican, 1999.

Dorian, Leah. *Snow Tunnel Sisters*. Illus. Roberta Dorion. Winnipeg: Pemmican, 2000.

Downie, Mary Alice. *SnowPaws*. Illus. Kathryn Naylor. Toronto: Stoddart, 1996.

Ducray-Dumenil, François. *Ambrose and Eleanor; or, the Adventures of Two Children on an Uninhabited Island*. Trans. and adapt. Lucy Peacock. London: R. and L. Peacock, 1796.

———. *Lolotte et Fanfan*. Paris: Le Prieur, 1793.

Ellis, Deborah. *Looking for X*. Toronto: Groundwood—Douglas and McIntyre, 1999.

Enosse, Susan. *Why the Beaver Has a Broad Tail*. Written by Mary-Lou Fox. Trans. Melvina Corbiere. Illus. Martin Panamick. Cobalt, ON: Highway Book Shop, 1974.

Eyvindson, Peter. *old enough*. Illus. Wendy Wolsak. Winnipeg: Pemmican, 1986.

———. *The Missing Sun*. Illus. Rhian Brynjolson. Winnipeg: Pemmican, 1993.

Foggo, Cheryl. *I Have Been in Danger*. Regina: Coteau, 2001.

———. *One Thing That's True*. Toronto: Kids Can, 1997.

Freed, Don. *Sasquatch Exterminator*. Illus. Myles Charles. Saskatoon: Gabriel Dumont Institute, 1999.

Galloway, Priscilla. *Jennifer Has Two Daddies*. Illus. Ana Aluml. Toronto: Women's Press, 1985.

Gasparini, Len. *A Christmas for Carol*. Illus. Aino Anto. Toronto: Seraphim Editions, 2002.

Gay, Marie-Louise. *Rumpelstiltskin*. Toronto: Groundwood, 1997.

———. *Stella, Queen of the Snow*. Toronto: Groundwood, 2001.

Gilligan's Island. Dir. Sherwood Schwartz. CBS-TV. 1964–1967.

Gilmore, Rachna. *A Gift for Gita*. Illus. Alice Priestly. Toronto: Second Story, 1998.

———. *A Group of One*. New York: Henry Holt, 2001.

———. *Lights for Gita*. Illus. Alice Priestly. Toronto: Second Story, 1994.

———. *Roses for Gita*. Toronto: Second Story, 1996.

———. *A Screaming Kind of Day*. Illus. Gordon Sauvé. Markham, ON: Fitzhenry & Whiteside, 1999.

Goto, Hiromi. *The Water of Possibility*. Regina: Coteau Books, 2001.

Greene, Alma. *Tales of the Mohawks.* Illus. R.G. Miller. Don Mills, ON: J.M. Dent, 1975.

Hashmi, Kerri. *You & Me, Murrawee.* Victoria, Australia: Penguin, 1998.

Haworth-Attard, Barbara. *Theories of Relativity.* Toronto: HarperCollins, 2003.

Helldorfer, M.C., adapt. *L.M. Montgomery's Anne of Green Gables.* Illus. Ellen Beier. New York: Random House Children's Books, 2001.

Highway, Tomson. *Dragonfly Kites.* Illus. Brian Deines. HarperCollins, 2002.

———. *Kiss of the Fur Queen.* Toronto: Doubleday, 1999.

Hughes, Monica. *Log Jam.* Toronto: Irwin, 1987.

Indian Children of British Columbia. *Tales from the Longhouse.* Sidney, BC: Gray's Publishers, 1973.

Jackson-Davis, Greg. *Digging for Philip.* Winnipeg: Great Plains, 2003.

Johnston, Julie. *Adam and Eve and Pinch-Me.* Toronto: Stoddart, 1994.

Johnston, Wayne. *The Colony of Unrequited Dreams.* Toronto: Knopf Canada, 1998.

Katz, Welwyn Wilton. *False Face.* Vancouver and Toronto: Groundwood— Douglas and McIntyre, 1987.

———. *Out of the Dark.* Toronto: Groundwood, 1995.

Khalsa, Dayal Kaur. *The Snow Cat.* Montreal: Tundra, 1992.

———. *Tales of a Gambling Grandma.* Montreal: Tundra, 1986.

King, Thomas. *Green Grass, Running Water.* Toronto: HarperCollins, 1993.

Kogawa, Joy. *Obasan.* Toronto: Penguin Canada, 1983.

Kurelek, William. *They Sought a New World: The Story of European Immigration to North-America.* Additional text by Margaret S. Engelhart. Toronto: Tundra, 1985.

Kusugak, Michael Arvaarluk. *Northern Lights: The Soccer Trails.* Illus. Vladyana Krykorka. Toronto: Annick, 1993.

Laurence, Margaret. *The Diviners.* Toronto: McClelland & Stewart, 1974.

———. *The Olden Days Coat.* Illus. Muriel Wood. Toronto: Tundra, 1998.

Lawson, Julie. *Midnight in the Mountains.* Illus. Sheena Lott. Victoria: Orca, 1998.

———. *White Jade Tiger.* Victoria: Beach Holme, 1993.

Leavitt, Martine. *Heck Superhero.* Red Deer, AB: Red Deer P, 2004.

———. *Tom Finder.* Red Deer, AB: Red Deer P, 2003.

Little, Jean. *Willow and Twig.* Toronto: Puffin Canada, 2000.

Lohans, Alison. *Waiting for the Sun.* Illus. Marilyn Mets & Peter Ledwon. Red Deer, AB: Red Deer P, 2001.

Lokhat, Atia. *Molly, Sue ... and Someone New.* Toronto: TSAR, 1994.

Lost. Dir. Jack Bender, Stephen Williams, et al. ABC-TV. 2004–present.

Lunn, Janet. *Shadow in Hawthorn Bay.* Toronto: Puffin–Penguin, 1986.

Major, Kevin. *Blood Red Ochre.* New York: Delacorte, and Toronto: Doubleday Canada, 1989.

Maracle, Lee. *Will's Garden*. Penticton, BC: Theytus Books, 2002.

McFarlane, Sheryl. *Waiting for the Whales*. Illus. Ron Lightburn. Victoria: Orca, 1991.

McLellan, Joe. *Nanabosho Grants a Wish*. Illus. Lloyd Swampy. Winnipeg: Pemmican, 2000.

McLeod, Elaine. *Lessons from Mother Earth*. Illus. Colleen Wood. Toronto: Groundwood, 2002.

Metzenthen, David. *Boys of Blood and Bone*. Camberwell, AU: Penguin, 2003.

Michaels, Anne. *Fugitive Pieces*. Toronto: McClelland & Stewart, 1996.

Miller, Gloria. *The Slapshot Star*. Illus. Gloria Miller. Winnipeg: Pemmican, 2001.

Mosionier, Beatrice Culleton. *Christopher's Folly*. Illus. Terry Gallagher. Winnipeg: Pemmican, 1996.

———. *In the Shadow of Evil*. Penticton, BC: Theytus Books, 2000.

Montgomery, L.M. *Anne of Green Gables*. 1908. North Ryde, AU: Angus & Robertson, 1987.

———. *Anne of Green Gables*. London: Sir Isaac Pitman, 1908.

———. *The Annotated Anne of Green Gables*. Ed. Wendy Barry, Margaret Anne Doody, and Mary E. Doody. New York: Oxford, 1991.

Moodie, Susanna. *Roughing It in the Bush*. London: R. Bentley, 1852.

Mowat, Farley. *The Curse of the Viking Grave*. Toronto: McClelland & Stewart, 1973.

———. *Lost in the Barrens*. 1956. Toronto: McClelland & Stewart, 1974.

Munsch, Robert. *The Boy in the Drawer*. Illus. Michael Martchenko. Toronto: Annick, 1986.

———. *The Paper Bag Princess*. Illus. Michael Martchenko. Toronto: Scholastic, 1980.

———, and Saoussan Askar. *From Far Away*. Illus. Michael Martchenko. Toronto: Annick Press, 1995.

Murray, Bonnie. *Li Minoush*. Illus. Sheldon Dawson. Trans. Rita Flamand. Winnipeg: Pemmican, 2001.

Ondaatje, Michael. *Anil's Ghost*. New York: Alfred Knopf, 2000.

———. *The English Patient*. Toronto: McClelland & Stewart, 1992.

Paperny, Myra. *The Wooden People*. Illus. Ken Stampnick. Boston and Toronto: Little, Brown, 1976.

Pelletier, Darrell W. *The Big Storm*. Illus. Darrell W. Pelletier. Regina, SK: Gabriel Dumont Institute, 1992.

Philpot, Don K. *The Moons of Goose Island*. Illus. Margaret Hessian. Sandy Hook, MB: Hinterland, 1997.

Plain, Ferguson. *Little White Cabin*. Illus. Ferguson Plain. Winnipeg: Pemmican, 1992.

Poirier, Thelma. *The Bead Pot*. Illus. Nona Foster. Winnipeg: Pemmican, 1993.

Poulsen, David A. *Last Sam's Cage*. Toronto: Key Porter Books, 2004.

Reynolds, Marilynn. *Belle's Journey*. Illus. Stephen McCallum. Victoria: Orca, 1993.

Richler, Mordecai. *Barney's Version*. Toronto: Vintage Canada, 1998.

Robinson Crusoe on Mars. Dir. Byron Haskin. Perf. Paul Mantee, Victor Lundin, and Adam West. Aubrey Schenck Productions, Inc., 1964.

Robinson, Eden. *Monkey Beach*. Toronto: Vintage, 2001.

Rousseau, Jean-Jacques. *Émile*. 1762. Trans.Barbara Foxley. London: J.M. Dent, 1974.

Sendak, Maurice. *Where the Wild Things Are*. Toronto: HarperCollins Canada, 1988.

Shields, Carol. *The Stone Diaries*. Toronto: Random House, 1993.

———. *Unless*. New York: HarperCollins, 2002.

Simmie, Lois. *Mister Got to Go*. Illus. Cynthia Nugent. Red Deer, AB: Red Deer College P, 1995.

Skrypuch, Marsha Forchuk. *Silver Threads*. Illus. Michael Martchenko. Toronto: Penguin, 1996.

Slipperjack, Ruby. *Little Voice*. Regina: Coteau Books, 2001.

Smucker, Barbara Claassen. *Days of Terror*. Toronto and Vancouver: Clarke, Irwin, 1979.

———. *Selina and the Bear Paw Quilt*. Illus. Janet Wilson. Toronto: Stoddart, 1995.

Speare, Jean. *A Candle for Christmas*. Illus. Ann Blades. Vancouver: Douglas & McIntyre, 1986.

Stenhouse, Ted. *Across the Steel River*. Toronto: Kids Can, 2001.

———. *A Dirty Deed*. Toronto: Kids Can, 2003.

Stevenson, R. L. *Treasure Island*. London: Cassell & Co., 1883.

Stewart, Sean. *Nobody's Son*. Don Mills, ON: Maxwell Macmillan Canada, 1993.

Survivor. Dir. Mark Burnett. CBS-TV. 2000–present.

Toews, Miriam. *A Complicated Kindness*. Toronto: Knopf Canada, 2004.

Toye, William. *The Mountain Goats of Temlaham*. Illus. Elizabeth Cleaver. Toronto: Oxford UP, 1969.

Traill, Catharine Parr. *The Backwoods of Canada*. London: C. Knight, 1836.

———. *Canadian Crusoes: A Tale of the Rice Lake Plains*. 1852. Ottawa: Carleton UP, 1986.

———. *The Young Emigrants; or, Pictures of Canada*. London: Harvey and Darton, 1826.

Trottier, Maxine. *Dreamstones*. Paintings by Stella East. Toronto: Stoddart Kids, 1999.

———. *Prairie Willow*. Paintings by Laura Fernandez and Rick Jacobson. Toronto: Stoddart Kids, 1998.

Truss, Jan. *Jasmin.* Vancouver: Groundwood-Douglas and McIntyre, 1982.

———, and Nancy MacKenzie. *Peter's Moccasins.* Illus. Philip Spink. Toronto: Reidmore Books, 1987.

Turner, Ethel. *Seven Little Australians.* 1894. North Ryde, AU: Angus & Robertson, 1988.

Turney-Zagwÿn, Deborah. *Long Nellie.* Victoria: Orca, 1993.

Tytler, Ann Fraser. *Leila; or, the Island.* 2nd ed. London: J. Hatchard, 1841.

Umpherville, Tina. *Jack Pine Fish Camp.* Illus. Christie Rice. Winnipeg: Pemmican, 1997.

Waboose, Jan Bourdeau. *Firedancers.* Illus. C.J. Taylor. Toronto: Stoddart Kids, 1999.

———. *Morning on the Lake.* Illus. Karen Reczuch. Toronto: Kids Can, 1997.

———. *SkySisters.* Illus. Bryan Deines. Toronto: Kids Can, 2000.

Wallace, Ian. *The Man Who Walked the Earth.* Toronto: Groundwood, 2003.

———. *The Sparrow's Song.* Toronto: Groundwood, 1986.

Warner, Susan. *The Wide, Wide World.* New York: George P. Putnam, 1850.

Wennick, Elizabeth. *Changing Jareth.* Vancouver: Polestar, 1999.

Wheeler, Jordan. *Chuck in the City.* Illus. Bill Cohen. Penticton, BC: Theytus Books, 2000.

———. *Just a Walk.* Illus. Bill Cohen. Penticton, BC: Theytus Books, 2000.

Whetung, James. *The Vision Seeker.* Illus. Paul Morin. Toronto: Stoddart, 1996.

Winkfield, Unca Eliza. *The Female American.* 1767. Peterborough, ON: Broadview Press, 2001.

Wynne-Jones, Tim. *The Maestro.* Vancouver: Groundwood–Douglas and McIntyre, 1995.

———. *Zoom Away.* Illus. Eric Beddows. Toronto: Groundwood, 1985.

Yonge, Charlotte M. *The Daisy Chain, or, Aspirations.* London: Collins, 1856.

Zweig, Paul. *The Adventurer.* London: Basic Books, 1974.

Primary Works—French

Alarie, Donald. *Comme un lièvre pris au piège.* Montréal, Éditions P. Tisseyre, 1992.

Anfousse, Ginette. *Les Barricades d'Arthur.* Illus. d'Anne Villeneuve. Montréal, La courte échelle, 1992.

———. *Le Grand Rêve de Rosalie.* Illus. de Marisol Sarrazin. Montréal, La courte échelle, 1992.

Arnau, Yves E. *L'Anaconda qui dort: une aventure d'Edgar Allan, détective.* Illus. de Caroline Merola. Montréal, Éditions P. Tisseyre, 1992.

Beauchemin, Yves. *Antoine et Alfred.* Montréal, Québec/Amérique, 1992.

Bélanger, Jean-Pierre. *Félix et le singe-à-barbe.* Montréal, Québec/Amérique, 1992.

Benoit, François. *Carcasses*. Montréal, Boréal, 1992.

Bergeron, Alain. *Le Chant des Hayats*. Montréal, Éditions Paulines, 1992.

Bergeron, Lucie. *La Grande Catastrophe*. Illus. d'Hélène Desputeaux. Saint-Lambert (Québec), Héritage, 1992.

Boucher, Lionel. *Perdus dans une forêt*. Limoilou (Québec), Éditions Permanents, 1992.

Boucher-Mativat, Marie-Andrée. *Une peur bleue*. Illus. d'Anne Michaud. Saint-Lambert (Québec), Héritage, 1992.

Breton, Céline. *Une idée fixe*. Illus. d'Élisabeth Eudes-Pascal. Montréal, Éditions P. Tisseyre, 1992.

Briac. *Fichez-moi la paix!*. Laval (Québec), HRW, 1992.

Brochu, Yvon. *Alexis dans de beaux draps*. Illus. de Daniel Sylvestre. Montréal, Éditions P. Tissyere, 1992.

———. *On n'est pas des monstres*. Montréal, Québec/Amérique, 1992.

Brouillet, Chrystine. *Une nuit très longue*. Montréal, La courte échelle, 1992.

Cadieux, Chantal. *Samedi trouble*. Montréal, Boréal, 1992.

Charbonneau, Marie-Josée. *La Plume de klaxon*. Illus. d'Hélène Béland Robert. Iberville (Québec), Coïncidence/Jeunesse, 1992.

Charbonneau, Marie-Josée. *Le Labyrinthe écarlate*. Iberville (Québec), Coïncidence/Jeunesse, 1992.

Clermont, Marie-Andrée. *Poursuite ...* Illus. de Stéphane Jorisch. LaSalle (Québec), Hurtubise HMH, 1992.

———. *Roche de St-Coeur*. Montréal, Éditions P. Tisseyre, 1992.

Corriveau, Monique. *Le Wapiti*. Québec, 1964. Montréal, Fides, 1978.

Cusson, Céline. *Échec et Mathieu*. Illus. de Micheline Dionne. Iberville (Québec), Coïncidence/Jeunesse, 1992.

Daignault, Claire. *La Vie en roux de Rémi Rioux*. Montréal, Éditions P. Tisseyre, 1992.

Daveluy, Marie-Claire. *Les Aventures de Perrine et de Charlot*. Montréal, Bibliothèque de l'Action française, 1923.

———. *Charlot à la Mission des Martyrs*. Montréal, Librairie Granger frères, 1938.

———. *Perrine et Charlot à Ville-Marie*. Montréal, Librairie Granger frères, 1940.

Davidts, Robert. *Les Parfums fond du pétard*. Illus. de Philippe Brochard. Montréal, Boréal, 1992.

Décary, Marie. *Au pays des toucans marrants*. Illus. de Claude Cloutier. Montréal, La courte échelle, 1992.

Demers, Dominique. *Toto la brute*. Illus. de Philippe Béha. Montréal, La courte échelle, 1992.

Desaulniers, Diane. *Le chat de Benjamin*. Illus. de Pierre Dagesse. Iberville (Québec), Coïncidence/Jeunesse, 1992.

——. *Un cheval en cavale.* Illus. de Michel LeBlanc. Iberville (Québec), Coïncidence/Jeunesse, 1992.

——. *La Fuite de Katcadou.* Illus. de Pierre Dagesse. Iberville (Québec), Coïncidence/Jeunesse, 1992.

Desjardins, Jacques A. *Tirelire, combines & cie.* Montréal, Québec/Amérique, 1992.

Desrosiers, Sylvie. *Mais qui va trouver le trésor?* Illus. de Daniel Sylvestre. Montréal, La courte échelle, 1992.

Duchesne, Christiane. *L'été des tordus.* Illus. de Marc Mongeau. Montréal, La courte échelle, 1992.

Dussault, Guylaine. *La sorcière aux bigoudis.* Illus. de Lucy Saint-Gelais. Shawinigan-Sud (Québec), CERRDOC, 1992.

Émond, Louis. *Taxi en cavale.* Montréal, Éditions P. Tisseyre, 1992.

Fontaine, Clément. *Merveilles au pays d'Alice.* Montréal, Éditions P. Tisseyre, 1992.

Foucher, Jacques. *Les secrets de l'ultra-sonde.* Montréal, Boréal, 1992.

Gagnier, Hélène. *L'Étrange étui de Léo.* Illus. de Danielle Simard. Montréal, Éditions P. Tisseyre, 1992.

Gagnon, Gérald. *Otish.* Montréal, Boréal, 1992.

Gaudet, Johanne. *Comment se débarrasser de Puce.* Illus. de Bruno St-Aubin. Montréal, Boréal, 1992.

Gauthier, Bertrand. *Panique au cimetière.* Illus. de Stéphane Jorisch. Montréal, La courte échelle, 1992.

Gélinas, Isabelle. *Le mystère du Marloland.* Saint-Laurent (Québec), Fides, 1992.

Giroux, Dominique. *Sacrée Minnie Bellavance!.* Illus. d'Hélène Desputeaux. Montréal, Éditions P. Tisseyre, 1992.

Goupil, Mylène. *Le détonateur.* Saint-Laurent (Québec), Fides, 1992.

Gravel, François. *Granulite.* Montréal, Québec/Amérique, 1992.

Grégoire-Coupal, Marie-Antoinette. *La Sorcière de l'îlot noir.* Montréal, Bibliothèque de l'A.C.-F., 1933.

Guillet, Jean-Pierre. *Enquête sur la falaise.* Illus. de Huguette Marquis. Waterloo (Québec), M. Quintin, 1992.

——. *Mystère aux Iles-de-la-Madeleine.* Illus. de Huguette Marquis. Waterloo (Québec), M. Quintin, 1992.

Hébert, Marie-Francine. *Sauve qui peut l'amour.* Montréal, La courte échelle, 1992.

Héroux, Josiane. *Eve Dupuis, 16 ans ½.* Montréal, Éditions P. Tisseyre, 1992.

Huberdeau, Madeleine. *Mission à l'eau!* Illus. de Dominique Jolin. Montréal, Boréal, 1992.

Julien, Suzanne. *Le coeur à l'envers.* Montréal, Éditions P. Tisseyre, 1992.

——. *Esclave à vendre.* Iberville (Québec), Coïncidence/Jeunesse, 1993.

————. *Tête brûlée.* Iberville (Québec), Coïncidence/Jeunesse, 1992.

Labelle-Ruel, Nicole. *Un jardinier pour les hommes.* Montréal, Québec/Amérique, 1992.

Landry, Chantale. *Sa majesté des gouttières.* Illus. de Luc Melanson. Montréal, Boréal, 1992.

Lauzon, Vincent. *Bouh, le fantôme.* Illus. de Philippe Germain. Saint-Lambert (Québec), Héritage, 1992.

————. *Concerto en noir et blanc.* Montréal, Éditions P. Tisseyre, 1992.

————. *Do, ré, mi, échec et mat.* Illus. de Linda Lemelin. Montréal, Éditions P. Tisseyre, 1992.

Laverdure, Daniel. *La bouteille vide.* Illus. de Daniel Laverdure. Montréal, Éditions P. Tisseyre, 1992.

Leblanc, Louise. *Ça va mal pour Sophie.* Illus. de Marie-Louise Gay. Montréal, La courte échelle, 1992.

Lebugle, André. *En détresse à New York.* Montréal, Éditions P. Tisseyre, 1992.

Lemay, Francine. *Destination : nuit blanche.* Laval (Québec), HRW, 1992.

————. *La porte secrète.* Laval (Québec), HRW, 1992.

Major, Henriette. *Sophie et le supergarçon.* Illus. de Monique Garneau. Saint-Lambert (Québec), Héritage, 1992.

Marcotte, Danielle. *Camy risque tout.* Illus. de Doris Barrette. Montréal, Boréal, 1992.

Marillac, Alain. *Le trésor de la citadelle.* Illus. de Johanne Wolfrod. LaSalle (Québec), Hurtubise HMH, 1992.

Marois, Carmen. *Le dossier vert.* Illus. de Bruno St-Aubin. LaSalle (Québec), Hurtubise HMH, 1992.

Martel, Robert. *Louprecka.* Montréal, Québec/Amérique, 1992.

Martel, Suzanne. *Jeanne, Fille du Roy.* Montréal: Fides, 1982.

————. *Menfou Carcajou.* Les coureurs des bois. 1980. Montréal, Fides, 2002.

Mativat, Marie-Andrée et Daniel Mativat. *Le fantôme du rocker.* Illus. de Bruno St-Aubin. LaSalle (Québec), Hurtubise HMH, 1992.

Ménard, Josianne. *Mon frère est un zouinf.* Illus. de Marc Auger. Iberville (Québec), Coïncidence/Jeunesse, 1992.

Michaud, Nando. *Drames de coeur pour un 2 de pique.* Montréal, Éditions P. Tisseyre, 1992.

Ouimet, Josée. *Les mirages de l'aube.* Ottawa, Éditions P. Tisseyre, 2001.

————. *L'Orpheline de la maison Chevalier.* Montréal, Hurtubise, 1999.

————. *Le Secret de Marie-Victoire,* Montréal, Hurtubise. "Atout histoire." 2000.

————. *Le vol des chimères.* Montréal, Éditions P. Tisseyre, 2000.

Papineau, Lucie. *Des bleuets dans mes lunettes.* Illus. de Daniel Dumont. Montréal, Boréal, 1992.

Paré, Louise. *L'Étrange odyssée.* Illus. d'Andrée Marcoux. Sainte-Foy (Québec), Éditions La Liberté, 1992.

Pelletier, Francine. *La Saison de l'exil*. Montréal, Éditions Paulines, 1992.

Pelletier, Francine. *Le Septième Écran*. Montréal, Éditions Paulines, 1992.

Pigeon, Pierre. *Cambriolage au lac Blanc*. Illus. de Mario Giguère. Iberville (Québec), Coïncidence/Jeunesse, 1992.

———. *Le colosse au lac Blanc*. Illus. de Mario Giguère. Iberville (Québec), Coïncidence/Jeunesse, 1992.

———. *J'aurai votre peau, sales briseurs de rêves!*. Illus. de Micheline Dionne. Iberville (Québec), Coïncidence/Jeunesse, 1992.

———. *Pouvoir surnaturel*. Illus. de Pierre Dagesse. Iberville (Québec), Coïncidence/Jeunesse, 1992.

———. *La soucoupe affolante*. Illus. de Pierre Dagesse. Iberville (Québec), Coïncidence/Jeunesse, 1992.

Plante, Raymond. *Les Dents de la poule*. Illus. de Pierre Pratt. Montréal, Boréal, 1992.

Plourde, Josée. *Les Amours d'Hubert*. Illus. de Doris Barrette. Waterloo (Québec), M. Quintin, 1992.

Pouliot, Luc. *Le Voyage des chats*. Montréal, Éditions Paulines, 1992.

Poupart, Roger. *Pelouses bleus*. Montréal, Éditions P. Tisseyre, 1992.

Rivet, Brigitte. *Le mystère de la tuque*. Illus. de Pierre Dagesse. Iberville (Québec), Coïncidence/Jeunesse, 1992.

———. *Ne m'appelez pas Math*. Illus. de Diane L'Écuyer. Iberville (Québec), Coïncidence/Jeunesse, 1992.

———. *Le Virus de la bulle*. Illus. de Marc Auger. Iberville (Québec), Coïncidence/Jeunesse, 1992.

———. *Le Voeu d'Élodie*. Illus. de Marc Auger. Iberville (Québec), Coïncidence/Jeunesse, 1992.

Robert, Johanne. *En exil ... chez mon père*. Laval (Québec), HRW, 1992.

Rochette, Danielle. *Le Code perdu*. Illus. de Patricia Lapointe. Shawinigan-Sud (Québec), CERRDOC, 1992.

Rochon, Esther. *L'Ombre et le cheval*. Montréal, Éditions Paulines, 1992.

Sarfati, Sonia. *Tricot, piano et jeu vidéo*. Illus. de Pierre Durand. Montréal, La courte échelle, 1992.

———. *La Ville engloutie*. Illus. de Caroline Merola. Montréal, La courte échelle, 1992.

Sauriol, Louise-Michelle. *La Sirène des mers de glace*. Illus. de Georgetta Pusztaï. Saint-Lambert (Québec), Héritage, 1992.

Simard, Bertrand. *Exercice Papillon*. Moncton, Éditions d'Acadie, 1992.

Somain, Jean-François. *Le Baiser des étoiles*. Illus. de Stéphane Jorisch. LaSalle (Québec), Hurtubise, HMH, 1992.

———. *Parlez-moi d'un chat*. Illus. de Stéphane Turgeon. Montréal, Éditions Pierre Tisseyre, 1992.

Tousignant, André. *Josée l'imprévisible*. Laval (Québec), HRW, 1992.

———. *La Vengeance.* Laval (Québec), HRW, 1992.

Tremblay, Carole. *La Nuit de l'Halloween.* Illus. de Dominique Jolin. Montréal, Boréal, 1992.

Vacher, André. *L'Appel des rivières, 1 : Le pays de l'Iroquois.* Waterloo (Québec), Éditions Michel Quintin, 2000.

———. *L'Appel des rivières, 2 : Le caillou d'or.* Waterloo (Québec), Éditions Michel Quintin, 2000.

Vandal, André. *Les voiles de l'aventure.* Montréal, Éditions P. Tisseyre, 1992.

Secondary Works

Abu-Laban, Yasmeen, and Christian Gabriel. *Selling Diversity: Immigration, Multiculturalism, Employment Equity, and Globalisation.* Peterborough, ON: Broadview P, 2002.

Alcoff, Linda. "The Problem of Speaking for Others." *Cultural Critique* 20 (Winter 1991–92): 5–32.

Allen, Paula Gunn. Introduction. *Song of the Turtle: American Indian Literature 1974–1994.* Ed. Paula Gunn Allen. New York: One World-Ballantine Books, 1996. 3–17.

Anderson, Benedict. *Imagined Communities: Reflections on the Origin and Spread of Nationalism.* London and New York: Verso, 1994.

———. *L'Imaginaire national.* Trans. Pierre-Emmanuel Dauzat. Paris, La Découverte, 2002.

Anjou, Joseph d'. « Des livres de chez nous pour nos enfants ». *Pour mieux choisir ce que nos jeunes liront.* Montréal, Bellarmin, 1957. 21–28.

Appleyard, J.A. *Becoming a Reader: The Experience of Fiction from Childhood to Adulthood.* Cambridge: Cambridge UP, 1990.

Armstrong, Jeanette. "The Body of Our People." *Paragraph* 14.3 (1992): 9–12.

Armstrong, Nancy. *Desire and Domestic Fiction: A Political History of the Novel.* New York: Oxford UP, 1987.

———. "The Occidental Alice." *differences* 2.2 (1990): 3–34.

Ashcroft, Bill. *Post-Colonial Transformations.* London: Routledge, 2001.

Azim, Firdous. *The Colonial Rise of the Novel.* London: Routledge, 1993.

Bachelard, Gaston. *The Poetics of Space: The Classic Look at How We Experience Intimate Places.* Trans. Maria Jolas. Boston: Beacon Press, 1994.

———. *La Poétique de l'espace.* 1957. « Quadrige ». 7e Paris, Presses universitaires de France, 1998.

Bainbridge, Joyce, and Janet Fayjean. "Seeing Oneself in a Book: The Changing Face of Canadian Children's Literature." *English Quarterly* 32.1–2 (2000): 55–65. *Proquest.* 19 July 2004.

Bakhtin, M. *Speech Genres and Other Late Essays.* Austin, TX: U of Texas P, 1986.

Bannerji, Himani. *The Dark Side of the Nation: Essays on Multiculturalism, Nationalism, and Gender.* Toronto: Canadian Scholars' Press, 2000.

Barthes, Roland. *S/Z: An Essay.* Trans. R. Miller. New York: Hill and Wang/ Noonday Press, 1974.

Battiste, Marie, ed. "Introduction: Unfolding the Lessons of Colonization." *Reclaiming Indigenous Voice and Vision.* Vancouver: U of British Columbia P, 2000. xvi–xxx.

Batty, Nancy Ellen. "'We Are the World, We Are the Children': The Semiotics of Seduction in International Children's Relief Efforts." McGillis 17–38.

Beckett, Sandra L. « La littérature de jeunesse au Canada francophone : de la colonisation à la conquête du monde ». *La littérature de jeunesse au croisement des cultures.* éd. Jean Perrot et Pierre Bruno. CRDP de l'Académie de Créteil. « Collection Argos ». 1995. 121–140.

Belsey, Catherine. *Critical Practice.* New Accents. London: Routledge, 1980.

Benis, Toby. "Introduction: Homelessness Yesterday and Today: Repression or Relief?" *Romanticism on the Road: The Marginal Gains of Wordsworth's Homeless.* New York: St. Martin's P, 2000. 1–23.

Berger, John. *And Our Faces, My Heart as Brief as Photos.* New York: Vintage, 1991.

———. *The Shape of a Pocket.* London: Bloomsbury, 2001.

Bhabha, Homi. *The Location of Culture.* London and New York: Routledge, 1994.

———, ed. *Nation and Narration.* London: Routledge, 1990.

———. "The World and the Home." McClintock et al. 445–55.

Bissoondath, Neil. *Selling Illusions: The Cult of Multiculturalism in Canada.* Toronto: Penguin, 2002.

Blackwell, Jeannine. "An Island of Her Own: Heroines of the German Robinsonades from 1720 to 1800." *German Quarterly* 58:1 (1985): 5–26.

Blaim, Artur. "The English Robinsonade of the Eighteenth Century." *Studies on Voltaire and the Eighteenth Century* 275 (1990): 5–145.

Boulizon, Guy. « La littérature de jeunesse au Canada français ». *Vie française* 13, 5–6 (1959): 177–187.

Bourdieu, Pierre. *The Field of Cultural Production.* Ed. Randal Johnson. New York: Columbia UP, 1993.

———. *Language and Symbolic Power.* Ed. John B. Thompson. Trans. Gino Raymond and Matthew Adamson. Cambridge, MA: Harvard UP, 1994.

Bradford, Clare. *Reading Race: Aboriginality in Australian Children's Literature.* Melbourne: Melbourne UP, 2001.

———. "'To Hold Up Prisms': Australian and Canadian Indigenous Publishing for Children." *Bookbird* 42.2 (2004). *Proquest.* University of Winnipeg Library. 6 July 2004. N. pag.

———. "Transformative Fictions: Postcolonial Encounters in Australian Texts." *Children's Literature Association Quarterly* 28.4 (2003–2004): 195–202.

———, ed. *Writing the Australian Child: Texts and Contexts in Fictions for Children*. Nedlands, AU: U of Western Australia P, 1996.

Brah, Avtar, and Annie Coombes, ed. *Hybridity and Its Discontents: Politics, Science, Culture*. New York: Routledge, 2000.

Brennan, Timothy. "The National Longing for Form." Bhabha, *Nation* 44–70.

Bristow, Joseph. *Empire Boys: Adventures in a Man's World*. London: HarperCollins Academic, 1991.

Bronfen, Elisabeth. "Disavowal." *Feminism and Psychoanalysis: A Critical Dictionary*. Ed. Elizabeth Wright. Oxford: Blackwell, 1992. 70–71.

Brown, Laura. *Fables of Modernity: Literature and Culture in the English Eighteenth Century*. Ithaca, NY: Cornell UP, 2001.

Burton, Antoinette, ed. *After the Imperial Turn: Thinking With and Through the Nation*. Durham, NC: Duke UP, 2003.

Canada. Dept. of Indian and Northern Affairs Canada. *People to People, Nation to Nation: Highlights from the Report of the Royal Commission on Aboriginal Peoples*. Ottawa: Minister of Supply and Services, 1996.

Canclini, Néstor García. *Transforming Modernity: Popular Culture in Mexico*. Trans. Lidia Lozano. Austin: U of Texas P, 1993.

Chapman, Rosemary. *Siting the Quebec Novel: The Representation of Space in Francophone Writing in Quebec*. Oxford: Peter Lang, 2000.

Carpenter, Kevin. *Desert Islands and Pirate Islands: The Island Theme in Nineteenth-Century English Juvenile Fiction*. Frankfurt am Main and Bern: Peter Lang, 1984.

Chartrand, Gary. Telephone Interview. 25 May 2004.

Cheng, François. *Empty and Full: The Language of Chinese Painting*. Boston & London: Shambhala, 1994.

Child and Family Services Act. Chapter C80. *Continuing Consolidation of the Statutes of Manitoba*. 8 May 2006.

Chittenden, Edward A., Terry S. Salinger, and Anne M. Bussis. *Inquiry into Meaning: An Investigation of Learning to Read*. Rev. ed. New York: Teachers College P, 2001.

Clausen, Christopher. "Home and Away in Children's Fiction." *Children's Literature* 10 (1982): 141–52.

Coleman, Daniel. "Immigration, Nation, and the Canadian Allegory of Manly Maturation." *Essays on Canadian Writing* 61 (1997). Proquest. 17 Sept. 2004 <http://cybrary.uwinnipeg.ca/proxy.cfm?url=http://proquest.umi.com/pqdweb?did=15172213&sid=2&Fmt=3&clientId=38831&RQT=309&VName=PQD>.

Collits, Terry. "Theorizing Racism." Ed. C. Tiffin and A. Lawson. *Describing Empire, Postcolonialism and Textuality*. New York: Routledge, 1994. 61–69.

Conrad, Joseph. *Heart of Darkness: A Case Study in Contemporary Criticism.* Ed. Ross C. Murfin. New York: St. Martin's Press, 1989.

Convention on the Rights of the Child. United Nations. 25 May 2006 <http://unhchr.ch/html/menu3/b/k2crc.htm>.

Coombes, Annie E. "Translating the Past: Apartheid Monuments in Post-Apartheid South Africa." Brah and Coombes 173–79.

———, and Avtar Brah. "Introduction: The Conundrum of 'Mixing.'" Brah and Coombes 1–16.

Cooper, Clare. "The House as Symbol of the Self." *Designing for Human Behavior: Architecture and the Behavioral Sciences.* Ed. Jon Lang, Charles Burnette, Walter Moleski, and David Vachon. Stroudsburg, PA: Dowden, Hutchinson and Ross, 1974. 130–46.

Corriveau, Monique. "La littérature de jeunesse de langue française." *Canadian Library Association Bulletin.* 23.2 (1966): 122–24.

Daveluy, Paule. « Communication-Jeunesse ou l'union fait la force », *Review,* 7.3 (1973), 13–19.

Davidoff, Leonore, and Catherine Hall. *Family Fortunes: Men and Women of the English Middle Class, 1780–1850.* Chicago: U of Chicago P, 1987.

Davidson, Cathy N. "No More Separate Spheres!" *American Literature* 70.3 (1998): 443–63.

Dean, Misao. *Practising Femininity: Domestic Realism and the Performance of Gender in Early Canadian Fiction.* Toronto: U of Toronto P, 1998.

Delaronde-Falk, Deborah L. "Contexts for the Flour Sack Flora Series." E-mail to Deborah Schnitzer. 25 May 2004

———. "Contexts for the Flour Sack Flora Series." E-mail to Deborah Schnitzer. 29 June 2004.

———. "Contexts for the Flour Sack Flora Series." E-mail to Deborah Schnitzer. 25 July 2004.

Deleuze, Gilles, and Félix Guattari. *A Thousand Plateaus: Capitalism and Schizophrenia.* Minneapolis and London: U of Minnesota P, 1987.

Demers, Dominique, and Paul Bleton. *Du Petit Poucet au Dernier des raisins. Introduction à la littérature de jeunesse,* Boucherville, QC: Québec/Amérique jeunesse, 1994.

DePasquale, Paul. "Natives and Settlers Now and Then: Refractions of the Colonial Past in the Present." *Natives and Settlers Now and Then: Historical Contexts, Current Perspectives, with Harold Cardinal, Patricia Seed, Frank Tough, and Sharon Venne.* Ed. Paul DePasquale. Edmonton: U of Alberta P, forthcoming.

———, and Doris Wolf. "A Select Bibliography of Canadian Picture Books for Children by Aboriginal Writers." *Canadian Children's Literature* 115–16 (2004): 144–60.

Devereux, Cecily. "'Canadian Classic' and 'Community Export': The Nationalism of 'Our' *Anne of Green Gables*." *Journal of Canadian Studies/ Revue d'études canadiennes* 36.1 (2001): 11–28.

"domesticate, *v.*" *The Oxford English Dictionary.* 2nd ed. 1989. *OED Online.* Oxford University Press. 16 Nov. 2006 <http://dictionary.oed.com/cgi/ entry/50068487>.

Domino: The Shopping Magazine for Your Home. May 2006.

Doonan, Jane. *Looking at Pictures in Picture Books.* Stroud, Glos: Thimble Press, 1993.

Douglas, J. Yellowlees, and Andrew Hargadon. "The Pleasures of Immersion and Engagement: Schemas, Scripts, and the Fifth Business." *Digital Creativity* 12.3 (2001): 153–66.

Dresang, Eliza. *Radical Change: Books for Youth in a Digital Age.* New York: Wilson, 1999.

Dumont, Marilyn. "Popular Images of Nativeness." *Looking at the Words of Our People: First Nations Analysis of Literature.* Ed. Jeannette Armstrong. Penticton, BC: Theytus Books, 1993. 46–49.

Edgeworth, Maria, and Richard Edgeworth. *Practical Education.* 2 vols. London: J. Johnson, 1798.

Egoff, Sheila, and Judith Saltman. *The New Republic of Childhood.* Toronto: Oxford UP, 1990.

Eigenbrod, Renate. *Travelling Knowledges: Positioning the Im/migrant Reader of Aboriginal Literatures in Canada.* Winnipeg: U of Manitoba P, 2005.

Emberley, Julia V. "The Bourgeois Family, Aboriginal Women, and Colonial Governance in Canada: A Study in Feminist Historical and Cultural Materialism." *Signs* 27.1 (2001): 59–85.

Engelhart, Margaret. Additional Text. *They Sought a New World: The Story of European Immigration to North America.* By William Kurelek. Toronto: Tundra, 1985. 35.

Escarpit, Denise, et Mireille Vagné- Lebas. *La Littérature d'enfance et de jeunesse : État des lieux.* Paris: Hachette, 1988.

Fetterley, J. *The Resisting Reader: A Feminist Approach to American Fiction.* Bloomington: Indiana UP, 1978.

Findlay, Len. "Intent for a Nation." Readers' Forum: Always Indigenize! *English Studies in Canada* 30.2 (2004): 39–48.

Fleming, Robert. "Supplementing Self: A Postcolonial Quest(ion) for (of) National Essence and Indigenous Form in Catharine Parr Traill's Canadian Crusoes." *Essays on Canadian Writing* 56 (1995): 198–223.

Fleras, Augie, and Jean Leonard Elliott. *Engaging Diversity: Multiculturalism in Canada.* Toronto: Nelson Thomson Learning, 2002.

Gelder, Miranda. "Modern Traditions: A Three-Generation Mother's Day Feast with a Host of Vietnamese Family Recipes." *Martha Stewart Living.* May 2006: 151–57.

Gellert, James H. "'Circling the Square': The Role of Native Writers in Creating Native Literature for Children." *Cross-Culturalism in Children's Literature: Selected Papers from the 1987 International Conference of the Children's Literature Association.* May 14–17, 1987, Pace U. Ed. Susan R. Gannon and Ruth Anne Thompson. New York: Pace U, 1988. 79–82.

George, Rosemary Marangoly. *The Politics of Home: Postcolonial Relocations and Twentieth-Century Fiction.* Cambridge: Cambridge UP, 1996.

Gerson, Carole. "Nobler Savages: Representations of Native Women in the Writings of Susanna Moodie and Catharine Parr Traill." *Journal of Canadian Studies* 32.2 (1997): 5–21.

Gilroy, Paul. *The Black Atlantic: Modernity and Double Consciousness.* Cambridge: Harvard UP, 1993.

Gitlin, T. *Media Unlimited: How the Torrent of Images and Sounds Overwhelms Our Lives.* New York: Henry Holt, 2002.

Goldie, Terry. *Fear and Temptation: The Image of the Indigene in Canadian, Australian, and New Zealand Literatures.* Kingston, ON: McGill-Queen's UP, 1989.

Golombisky, Kim. "Ladies Home Erotica: Reading the Seams between Home-Making and House Beautiful." *Journal of Magazine and New Media Research* (Spring 1999). 15 May 2006 <http://nmc.loyola.edu/new mediajournal/current/article3/html>.

Grant, Agnes. "A Canadian Fairy Tale: What Is It?" *Canadian Children's Literature/Littérature canadienne pour la jeunesse* 22 (1981): 27–35.

———. "Contemporary Native Women's Voices in Literature." *Native Writers and Canadian Writing.* Ed. W.H. New. Vancouver: U of British Columbia P, 1990.

Green, Martin. *Dreams of Adventure, Deeds of Empire.* New York: Basic Books, 1979.

———. "The Robinson Crusoe Story." *Imperialism and Juvenile Literature.* Ed. Jeffrey Richards. New York: Manchester UP, 1989. 34–52.

Grewal, Inderpal. *Home and Harem: Nation, Gender, Empire, and the Cultures of Travel.* Durham: Duke UP, 1996.

Groening, Laura Smyth. *Listening to Old Woman Speak: Natives and Alter-Natives in Canadian Literature.* Montreal: McGill-Queen's UP, 2004.

Hage, Ghassan. *Against Paranoid Nationalism: Searching for Hope in a Shrinking Society.* Annandale, AU: Pluto Press, 2003.

———. *White Nation: Fantasies of White Supremacy in a Multicultural Society.* Annandale, AU: Pluto Press, 1998.

Hardt, Michael, and Antonio Negri. *Empire.* Cambridge, MA: Harvard UP, 2000.

Harrow, Sharon. *Adventures in Domesticity: Gender and Colonial Adulteration in Eighteenth-Century British Literature.* New York: AMS Press, 2004.

Haun, Beverly. "The Rise of the Aboriginal Voice in Canadian Adolescent Fiction." *Windows and Words: A Look at Canadian Children's Literature in English*. Ed. Aida Hudson and Susan-Ann Cooper. Ottawa: U of Ottawa P, 2003. 35–48.

Hawisher, Gail E., and Cynthia L. Selfe, eds. *Passions, Pedagogies, and 21st Century Technologies*. Logan: Utah State UP, 1999.

Hayward, D. Geoffrey. "Home as an Environmental and Psychological Concept." *Landscape* 20.1 (1975): 2–9.

Heilbron, Alexandra, ed. *The Lucy Maud Montgomery Album*. Comp. Kevin McCabe. Toronto: Fitzhenry & Whiteside, 1999.

Hermer, Joe, and Janet Mosher, eds. *Disorderly People: Law and the Politics of Exclusion in Ontario*. Halifax: Fernwood, 2002.

Higgitt, Nancy, Susan Wingert, and Janice Ristock. *Voices from the Margins: Experiences of Street-Involved Youth in Winnipeg*. Winnipeg: Winnipeg Inner-City Research Alliance and the Institute of Urban Studies, University of Winnipeg, 2003.

Higonnet, Margaret R., and Beverly Lyon Clark, eds. *Girls, Boys, Books, Toys: Gender in Children's Literature and Culture*. Baltimore: Johns Hopkins UP, 1999.

Hollindale, Peter. "Ideology and the Children's Book." 1988. *Literature for Children: Contemporary Criticism*. Ed. Peter Hunt. London: Routledge, 1992. 19–40.

Hoogland. Cornelia. "Constellations of Identity in Canadian Young Adult Novels." *Canadian Children's Literature/Littérature canadienne pour la jeunesse* 86 (1997): 27–42.

Hulme, Peter. *Colonial Encounters: Europe and the Native Caribbean, 1492–1797*. 1986. London: Routledge, 1992.

Hunt, Margaret R. *The Middling Sort: Commerce, Gender, and the Family in England, 1680–1780*. Berkeley: U of California P, 1996.

Hymer, Stephen. "Robinson Crusoe and the Secret of Primitive Accumulation." *Monthly Review* 23.4 (1971): 11–36.

« L'Institution littéraire au Québec », *Liberté*, 134, mars-avril 1981.

Iser, W. *The Implied Reader: Patterns of Communication in Prose Fiction from Bunyan to Beckett*. Baltimore: Johns Hopkins UP, 1974.

Jackson, Shelley. "Stitch Bitch: The Patchwork Girl." *Rethinking Media Change: The Aesthetics of Transition*. Ed. David Thorburn and Henry Jenkins. Associate Ed. Brad Sewell. Cambridge, MA: MIT P, 2003. 239–52.

James, Suzanne. "The 'Indians' of Catharine Parr Traill's *The Backwoods of Canada*." *The Rhetoric of Canadian Writing*. Ed. Conny Steenman-Marcusse. Amsterdam: Rodopi, 2002. 107–24.

Jenkinson, Dave. "Rachna Gilmore." *CM Magazine Profile*. Manitoba Library Association. 12 Jan. 2007 <http://www.umanitoba.ca/cm/profiles/gilmore.html>.

Johnston, Chris. "Children Need to Have Hard Fun." *Times Educational Supplement* 3 Sept. 1999: 12.

Johnston, Ingrid, and Jyoti Mangat. "Cultural Encounters in the Liminal Spaces of Canadian Picture Books." *Changing English* 10.2 (2003): 199–204.

Jones, Raymond E., and Jon C. Stott. *Canadian Children's Books: A Critical Guide to Authors and Illustrators.* Toronto: Oxford UP, 2000.

Jung, Carl. *Ma vie : souvenirs, rêves et pensées.* Folio, Paris, Gallimard, 1973.

Kamboureli, Smaro. *Scandalous Bodies: Diasporic Literature in English Canada.* Don Mills, ON: Oxford UP, 2000.

Kavanagh, James. "Ideology." Lentricchia 306–20.

Keahey, Deborah, *Making It Home: Place in Canadian Prairie Literature.* Winnipeg: U of Manitoba P, 1998.

Keeshig-Tobias, Lenore. "Not Just Entertainment." *Whole Earth Review* (Summer 1991): 64–66.

Kete, Kathleen. *The Beast in the Boudoir.* Berkeley: U of California P, 1994.

"Kids Can Press." 4 January 2007 <http://www.kidscanpress.com/ kidscanpress/ KidsCanPress_3/KCP/f_home.htm>.

King, Thomas. "Introduction: An Anthology of Canadian Native Fiction." *All My Relations: An Anthology of Contemporary Canadian Native Fiction.* Ed. Thomas King. Toronto: McClelland & Stewart, 1990. 4–10.

Klein, Lawrence. "Gender and the Public Private Distinction in the Eighteenth Century: Some Questions about Evidence and Analytical Procedure." *Eighteenth-Century Studies* 19.1 (1996): 97–106.

Kraniauskas, John. "Hybridity in a Transnational Frame: Latin-Americanist and Post-Colonial Perspectives on Cultural Studies." Brah and Coombes 235–56.

Krashen, Stephen D. *The Power of Reading: Insights from the Research.* 2nd ed. Westport, CT: Libraries Unlimited, 2004.

Kutzer, Daphne. *Empire's Children: Empire and Imperialism in Classic British Books.* New York: Garland, 2000.

LaRoque, Emma. "Preface or Here Are Our Voices—Who Will Hear?" *Writing the Circle: Native Women of Western Canada.* Ed. Jeanne Perreault and Sylvia Vance. Edmonton: NeWest Press, 1990. xv–xxx.

Lawson, Alan. "Proximities: From Asympote to Zeugma." Smith 19–37.

Leitch, Carolyn. "U.S. Housing Woes May Bode Ill for Canada." *Globe and Mail* [Toronto] 29 Apr. 2006: B8.

Lentricchia, Frank, and Thomas McLaughlin, eds. *Critical Terms for Literary Study.* 2nd ed. Chicago and London: U of Chicago P, 1995.

Lepage, Françoise. *Histoire de la littérature pour la jeunesse : Québec et francophonies du Canada.* Québec, Les éditions David, 2000.

Livingston, Robert Eric. "Global Knowledges: Agency and Place in Literary Studies." *PMLA* (January 2001): 145–57.

Locke, John. *Two Treatises of Government*. 1698. Ed. Peter Laslett. Cambridge: Cambridge UP, 1988.

Loxley, Diana. *Problematic Shores: The Literature of Islands*. London: Macmillan, 1990.

Lurie, Alison. « Le siècle de Babar. » *Le Nouvel Observateur*, 23 décembre 2004–2005, 132.

Macherey, Pierre. *A Theory of Literary Production*. 1966. Trans. Geoffrey Wall. London: Routledge and Kegan Paul, 1978.

Mackey, Eva. *The House of Difference: Cultural Politics and National Identity in Canada*. London: Routledge, 1999.

Mackey, Margaret. "Canadian Young People and Their Reading Worlds: Conditions of Literature in Contemporary Canada." *Canadian Children's Literature/Littérature canadienne pour la jeunesse* 31.1 (2005): 78–99.

———. "Imagining with Words: The Temporal Processes of Reading Fiction." Diss. U of Alberta, 1995.

———. "Good-Enough Reading: Momentum and Accuracy in the Reading of Complex Fiction." *Research in the Teaching of English* 31.4 (1997): 428–58.

Madore, Édith. *La littérature pour la jeunesse au Québec*. Montréal, Boréal, 1994.

Maher, Susan Naramore. "Recasting Crusoe: Frederick Marryat, R.M. Ballantyne and the Nineteenth-Century Robinsonade." *Children's Literature Association Quarterly* 13.4 (1988): 169–75.

———. "The Uses of Adventure: The Moral and Evangelical Robinsonades of Agnes Strickland, Barbara Hofland, and Ann Fraser Tytler." *Jane Austen and Mary Shelley and Their Sisters*. Ed. Laura Dabundo. Lanham, MD: UP of America, 2000. 147–58.

Manning, Erin. *Ephemeral Territories: Representing Nation, Home, and Identity in Canada*. Minneapolis: U of Minnesota P, 2003.

Marcotte, Gilles. « Institution et courants d'air ». *Liberté*, 134 (1981): 5–14.

Martin, Dianne. "Demonizing Youth, Marketing Fear: The New Politics of Crime." Hermer and Mosher 91–104.

Masschelein, Anneleen. "The Concept as Ghost: Conceptualization of the Uncanny in Late-Twentieth-Century Theory." *Mosaic* 35.1 (2002): 53–68.

Maynes, Mary Jo. "Class Cultures and Images of Proper Family Life." *The History of the European Family, Vol. II: Family Life in the Long Nineteenth Century, 1789–1913*. Ed. David I. Kertzer and Marzio Barbagli. New Haven: Yale UP, 2002. 195–228.

McCallum, Robyn. *Ideologies of Identity in Adolescent Fiction: The Dialogic Construction of Subjectivity*. New York: Garland, 1999.

McClintock, Anne, Aamir Mufti, and Ella Shohat, eds. *Dangerous Liaisons: Gender, Nation, and Postcolonial Perspectives.* Minneapolis: U of Minnesota P, 1997.

McGillis, Roderick. "'And the Celt Knew the Indian': Knowingness, Postcolonialism, Children's Literature." McGillis, ed. 223–35.

———, ed. *Voices of the Other: Children's Literature and the Postcolonial Context.* New York: Garland, 2000.

McGregor, Gaile. "A Case Study in the Construction of Place: Boundary Management as Theme and Strategy in Canadian Art and Life." *Invisible Culture: An Electronic Journal for Visual Culture* (2003). 1 Jan. 2003 <http://www.rochester.edu/in_visible_culture/ ivchome.html>.

McIlroy, Anne. "We Can Build Better Brains." *Globe and Mail* 10 Apr. 2004.

McKeon, Michael. "The Secret History of Domesticity: Private, Public, and the Division of Knowledge." *The Age of Cultural Revolutions, Britain and France, 1750–1820.* Ed. Colin Jones and Dror Wahrman. Berkeley: U of California P, 2002.

McLeod, Neal. "Coming through Stories." *(Ad)dressing Our Words: Aboriginal Perspectives on Aboriginal Literatures.* Ed. Armand Garnet Ruffo. Penticton, BC: Theytus, 2000. 17–36.

Media Awareness Network. Young Canadians in a Wired World. (2005) 5 Feb. 2006 <http://www.media-awareness.ca/english/research/YCWW/index .cfm>.

Micros, Marianne. "'My Books Are My Children': An Interview with Welwyn Wilton Katz." *Canadian Children's Literature/Littérature canadienne pour la jeunesse* 90 (1998): 51–65.

Moebius, William. "Introduction to Picturebook Codes." *Word & Image* 2.2 (1986): 141–58.

Mosher, Janet. "The Shrinking of the Public and Private Spaces of the Poor." Hermer and Mosher 41–53.

Moss, Anita. "The Spear and the Piccolo: Heroic and Pastoral Dimensions of William Steig's *Dominic* and *Abel's Island.*" *Children's Literature* 10 (1982): 124–40.

Mukherjee, Arun. *Postcolonialism: My Living.* Toronto: TSAR, 1998.

Myers, Mitizi. "Impeccable Governesses, Rational Dames, and Moral Mothers: Mary Wollstonecraft and the Female Tradition in Georgian Children's Books." *Children's Literature* 14 (1986): 31–59.

Naficy, Hamid, ed. *Home, Exile, Homeland: Film, Media, and the Politics of Place.* New York: Routledge, 1999.

———. "Introduction: Framing Exile: From Homeland to Homepage." Naficy 1–16.

Nahachewsky, J. "Expanding Notions: A Perspective on the Challenges Facing Contemporary Language Arts Teachers." *English Quarterly* 37.1 (2005): 22–26.

New, W.H. *Borderlands: How We Talk about Canada*. Vancouver: U of British Columbia P, 1998.

Niall, Brenda. *Seven Little Billabongs: The World of Ethel Turner and Mary Grant Bruce*. Ringwood, AU: Penguin, 1979.

Nikolajeva, Maria. *Children's Literature Comes of Age: Toward a New Aesthetic*. New York: Garland, 1996.

———, and Carole Scott. *How Picture Books Work*. New York: Garland, 2001.

Nodelman, Perry. "Little Red Riding Hood as a Canadian Fairy Tale." *Canadian Children's Literature/Littérature canadienne pour la jeunesse* 20 (1980): 17–27.

———. "A Monochromatic Mosaic: Class, Race and Culture in Double-Focalized Canadian Novels for Young People." *Canadian Children's Literature/Littérature canadienne pour la jeunesse* 116 (2004): 32–60.

———. "My Own False Face: A Response to Marianne Micros' Interview with Welwyn Wilton Katz." *Canadian Children's Literature/Littérature canadienne pour la jeunesse* 94 (1999): 81–93.

———. "Of Solitudes and Borders: Double-Focalized Canadian Books for Children." *Canadian Children's Literature/Littérature canadienne pour la jeunesse* 109–10 (2003): 58–86.

———. *The Pleasures of Children's Literature*. New York: Longman, 1992.

———. *The Pleasures of Children's Literature*. 2nd ed. New York: Longman, 1996.

———. *Words about Pictures: The Narrative Art of Children's Picture Books*. Athens: U of Georgia P, 1988.

———, and Mavis Reimer. *The Pleasures of Children's Literature*. 3rd ed. Boston: Allyn & Bacon, 2003.

———, and Mavis Reimer. "Teaching Children's Literature: Learning to Know More." *Canadian Children's Literature/Littérature canadienne pour la jeunesse* 98 (2000): 15–35.

Novac, Cylvia, Luba Serge, Margaret Eberle, and Joyce Brown. *On Her Own: Young Women and Homelessness in Canada*. Ottawa: Canadian Housing and Renewal Association, 2002.

Novak, Maximillian. *Economics and the Fiction of Daniel Defoe*. Berkeley: U of California P, 1962.

Nussbaum, Felicity A. *Torrid Zones: Maternity, Sexuality, and Empire in Eighteenth-Century English Narratives*. Baltimore, MD: Johns Hopkins UP, 1995.

O'Malley, Andrew. *The Making of the Modern Child: Children's Literature and Childhood in the Late Eighteenth Century*. New York: Routledge, 2003.

Official Site of Tourism British Columbia. Province of British Columbia. 25 May 2006 <http://www.hellobc.com/en-CA/default.htm>.

Ottevaere-van Praag, Ganna. *Le Roman pour la jeunesse*. Berlin, Peter Lang, 1987.

Oxford English Dictionary Online. U of Oxford P. U of Winnipeg. 17 May 2006 <http://dictionary.oed.com/entrance.dtl>.

Paré, François. "Histoire et narration dans l'œuvre de Monique Corriveau." *Canadian Children's Literature/Littérature canadienne pour la jeunesse* 23–24 (1981): 40–50.

———. *Les littératures de l'exiguïté*. Hearst, Le Nordir, 1992.

Perrault, Charles. *Histoires ou Contes du temps passé avec des Moralités*. Paris: Barbin, 1697.

Peters, John Durham. "Exile, Nomadism, and Diaspora: The Stakes of Mobility in the Western Canon." Naficy 17–41.

Philip, M. Nourbese. *Frontiers: Essays and Writings on Race and Culture*. Stratford, ON: Mercury, 1992.

Phillips, A.A. *The Australian Tradition: Studies in a Colonial Culture*. Melbourne, AU: F.W. Cheshire, 1958.

Pivato, Joseph. "Representation of Ethnicity as Problem: Essence or Construction." *Journal of Canadian Studies* 31 (1996): 48–58. *Proquest*. 5 Feb 2007 <http://cybrary.uwinnipeg.ca/proxy.cfm?url=http://proquest .umi.com/ pqdweb?did=11076695&sid=3&Fmt=3&clientId=38831 &RQT=309&VName=PQD>. N. pag.

Porteous, J. Douglas. "Home: The Territorial Core." *The Geographical Review* 66.4 (1976): 383–90.

Poslaniec, Christian. *L'Évolution de la littérature de jeunesse de 1850 à nos jours au travers de l'insistance narrative*. Lille, ANRT, 1997.

Potvin, Claude. « La littérature de jeunesse chez la minorité acadienne ». *Canadian Children's Literature/Littérature canadienne pour la jeunesse*. 38 (1985), 19–25.

Pouliot, Suzanne. *L'image de l'autre: une étude des romans parus au Québec de 1980 à 1990*. Sherbrooke, ED. du CRP, 1994.

Protherough, Robert. *Developing Response to Fiction*. Milton Keynes: Open UP, 1983.

Rabinowitz, Peter J. *Before Reading: Narrative Conventions and the Politics of Interpretation*. Ithaca, NY: Cornell UP, 1987.

Ramraj, Victor J. "The Merits and Demerits of the Postcolonial Approach to Writings in English." McGillis, ed. 253–67.

Rasporich, Beverly. "Native Women Writing: Tracing the Patterns." *Canadian Ethnic Studies* 28.1 (1996). *Proquest*. 3 May 2004 <http://cybrary .uwinnipeg.ca/proxy.cfm?url=http://proquest.umi.com/pqdweb?did= 418451621&sid=1&Fmt=3&clientId=38831&RQT=309&VName= PQD>. N. pag.

Razack, Sherene H. *Looking White People in the Eye: Gender, Race, and Culture in Courtrooms and Classrooms*. Toronto: U of Toronto P, 1998.

————. *Race, Space, and the Law: Unmapping a White Settler Society*. Toronto: Between the Lines, 2002.

Reimer, Mavis. "The Home Pages." E-mail to contributors. 4 April 2005.

————, and Anne Rusnak. "The Representation of Home in Canadian Children's Literature/La représéntation du chez-soi dans la littérature de jeunesse canadienne." *Canadian Children's Literature* 100/101 (2000–1): 9–46.

Richard, Jeffrey, ed. *Imperialism and Juvenile Literature*. Manchester: Manchester UP, 1989.

Robinson, Muriel, and Margaret Mackey. "Stages of a Cyber-Writing Partnership." *English in Education* 38.1 (2004): 64–79.

Rogers, Pat. "Crusoe's Home." *Essays in Criticism* 24 (1974): 375–90.

Romøren, Rolf, and John Stephens. "Representing Masculinities in Norwegian and Australian Young Adult Fiction: A Comparative Study." Stephens 216–33.

Roof, Judith, and Robyn Wiegman. "Part Two: Speaking Parts." *Who Can Speak? Authority and Critical Identity*. Ed. Judith Roof and Robyn Wiegman. Urbana: U of Chicago P, 1995. 93–95.

Rose, Jacqueline. *The Case of Peter Pan; or, The Impossibility of Children's Fiction*. 1984. Philadelphia: U of Pennsylvania P, 1992.

Rossiter, Richard. "The Return of Judy: Repression in Ethel Turner's Fiction." Bradford 55–75.

Ruddick, Sue. "Metamorphosis Revisited: Restricting Discourses of Citizenship." Hermer and Mosher 55–64.

Ruffo, Armand Garnet. "Why Native Literature?" *American Indian Quarterly* 21.4 (1997): 663–74. *Ebsco*. 3 May 2004 <http://web.ebscohost.com/ehost/detail?vid=5&hid=119&sid=bf2915b8–0ba1–4f39–92b7–56d3e 7fc89cb%40sessionmgr 103>. N. pag.

Rybczynski, Witold. *Home: A Short History of an Idea*. New York: Viking, 1986.

Said, Edward W. *Culture and Imperialism*. New York: Knopf, 1993.

————. *The World, the Text, and the Critic*. Cambridge, MA: Harvard UP, 1983.

Saldanha, Louise. "Bedtime Stories: Canadian Multiculturalism and Children's Literature." McGillis, ed. 165–76.

Saltman, Judith. *Modern Canadian Children's Books*. Toronto: Oxford UP, 1987.

Sánchez, Reuben. "Remembering Always to Come Back: The Child's Wished-For Escape and the Adult's Self-Empowered Return in Sandra Cisnero's *House on Mango Street*." *Children's Literature* 23 (1995): 221–41.

Seed, Patricia. *American Pentimento: The Invention of Indians and the Pursuit of Riches*. Minneapolis: U of Minnesota P, 2001.

Sefton-Green, Julian. "Cementing the Virtual Relationship: Children's TV Goes Online." *Small Screens: Television for Children*. Ed. David Buckingham. London: Leicester UP, 2002. 185–207.

Slapin, Beverly, Doris Seale, and Rosemary Gonzales. "How to Tell the Difference." *Through Indian Eyes: The Native Experience in Books for Children*. Ed. Beverly Slapin and Doris Seale. 1987. Phildadelphia, PA: New Society, 1992. 241–68.

Slemon, Stephen. "Climbing Mount Everest: Postcolonialism in the Culture of Ascent." Smith 51–73.

Smart, Patricia. *Écrire dans la maison du pére*. 2ᵉ éd., Montréal, Québec/Amérique, 1990.

Smith, Rowland, ed. *Postcolonizing the Commonwealth: Studies in Literature and Culture*. Waterloo, ON: Wilfrid Laurier UP, 2000.

Snyder, Gary. "The Rediscovery of Turtle Island." *At Home on the Earth*. Ed. David Landis Barnhill. Berkeley: U of California P, 1999. 297–306.

Sopher, David E. « The Landscape of Home: Myth, Experience, Social Meaning. » *The Interpretation of Ordinary Landscapes: Geographical Essays*. Ed. D.W. Meinig. New York: Oxford UP, 1979. 129–49.

Starobinski, Jean. « Je hais comme les portes d'Hadès ». Le dehors et le dedans, *Nouvelle revue de psychanalyse*, 9 (1974), 7–22.

Stephens, John. "Picture Books, Mimesis and the Competing Aesthetics of Kinesis and Stasis." Working Paper for Discussion Panel at the 16th IRSCL Congress. Kristiansand, Norway. 2003.

———, ed. *Ways of Being Male: Representing Masculinities in Children's Literature and Film*. New York and London: Routledge, 2002.

Stoicheff, R.P., ed. *The Sound and the Fury: A Hypertext*. 28 Sept. 2004 <http://www.usask.ca/english/faulkner>.

Stott, Jon C. "From Here to Eternity: Aspects of Pastoral in the Green Knowe Series." *Children's Literature* 11 (1983): 145–55.

———, and Christine Doyle Francis. "'Home' and 'Not Home' in Children's Stories: Getting There—and Being Worth It." *Children's Literature in Education* 24.3 (1993): 222–33.

Sugars, Cynthia, ed. *Unhomely States: Theorizing English-Canadian Postcolonialism*. Peterborough, ON: Broadview P, 2004.

———. *Home-Work: Postcolonialism, Pedagogy & Canadian Literature*. Ottawa: U of Ottawa P, 2004.

Taylor, Donald M., John E. Lydon, Évelyne Bougie, and Kiraz Johannsen. "'Street Kids': Towards an Understanding of Their Motivational Context." *Canadian Journal of Behavioural Science* 36.1 (2004): 1–16.

Thomson, Jack. *Understanding Teenagers' Reading: Reading Processes and the Teaching of Literature*. Melbourne, AU: Methuen Australia, 1987.

Traditional Home: Fresh and Fabulous May 2006.

Trinh T. Minh-Ha. *Framer Framed*. New York: Routledge, 1992.

Tuan, Yi-Fu. "Geography, Phenomenology, and the Study of Human Nature." *The Canadian Geographer/Le Géographe Canadien* 15.3 (1971): 181–92.

———. "Place: An Experiential Perspective." *The Geographical Review* 65.2 (1975): 151–65.

———. "Space and Place: Humanistic Perspective." *Progress in Geography* 6 (1974): 211–52.

———. *Space and Place: The Perspective of Experience*. Minneapolis, U of Minnesota P, 1977.

Universal Declaration of Human Rights. United Nations. 5 May 2006 <http://www.un.org/Overview/rights.html>.

Usher, Peter J. "Aboriginal Property Systems in Land and Resources." *Indigenous Land Rights in Commonwealth* Countries. Ed. Garth Cant, John Overton, and Eric Pawson. Christchurch, AU: Canterbury UP, 1993. 38–44.

Walcott, Rinaldo. *Black Like Who? Writing Black Canada*. Toronto: Insomniac, 1997.

Walters, William. "Secure Borders, Safe Haven, Domopolitics." *Citizenship Studies* 8.3 (Sept. 2004): 237–60.

Ward, Cynthia. "From the Suwanee to Egypt, There's No Place Like Home." *PMLA* 115.1 (January 2000): 75–88.

Ward, Stuart. "Transcending the Nation: A Global Imperial History?" Burton 44–56.

Watkins, Tony. "Cultural Studies, New Historicism and Children's Literature." *Literature for Children: Contemporary Criticism*. ed. Peter Hunt. London: Routledge, 1992. 173–95.

Watt, Ian. *The Rise of the Novel: Studies in Defoe, Richardson, and Fielding*. Berkeley: U of California P, 1957.

West, Alexandra. "English-Speaking Canada." *International Companion Encyclopedia of Children's Literature*. Ed. Peter Hunt. London: Routledge, 1996.

Wham, M.A., J. Barnhart, and G. Cook. "Enhancing Multicultural Awareness through Storybook Reading Experience." *Journal of Research and Development in Education* 30.1 (1996): 1–9.

White, Lucie. "Representing 'The Real Deal.'" *University of Miami Law Review* 45 (1990–91): 272–313.

Williams, Raymond. *Keywords: A Vocabulary of Culture and Society*. 1976. London: Fontana, 1983.

———. *Marxism and Literature*. Oxford: Oxford UP, 1977.

Wolf, Virginia L. "From the Myth to the Wake of Home: Literary Houses." *Children's Literature* 18 (1990): 53–67.

World Disasters Report 2003. International Federation of Red Cross and Red
  Crescent Societies. 19 May 2006 <http://www.ifrc.org/news/av.asp>.
Young-Ing, Greg. "An Overview of Aboriginal Literature and Publishing in
  Canada." *Australian-Canadian Studies.* 14.1–2 (1996): 157–71.

□ □ □

NOTES ON CONTRIBUTORS

NEIL BESNER is Professor of English and Associate Vice-President (International) at the University of Winnipeg. He writes mainly on Canadian literature, with books on Mavis Gallant and Alice Munro; his most recent books are a translation into English of a Brazilian biography of the poet Elizabeth Bishop (2002), an edited collection of essays on Carol Shields (2003), and a co-edited collection of essays on Canadian and Brazilian postcolonial theory (2003).

CLARE BRADFORD is Professor of Literary Studies at Deakin University in Melbourne, Australia, where she teaches literary studies and children's literature, and supervises students undertaking MA and PhD programmes. She has published widely on children's literature, with an emphasis on colonial and postcolonial texts and utopian discourses. Her most recent book is *Unsettling Narratives: Postcolonial Readings of Children's Literature* (2007).

PAUL DEPASQUALE is an Associate Professor of English at the University of Winnipeg, where he works in the area of Aboriginal cultural and literary studies. His publications include, as editor, *Native and Settlers Now and Then: Historical Issues and Current Perspectives on Treaties and Land Claims in Canada* (University of Alberta Press, 2007), and, as co-editor, Louis Bird's *Telling Our Stories: Omushkego Voices from Hudson Bay* (Broadview Press, 2005). He is also co-editor of *Contexts in Canadian Aboriginal and Native American Literatures* (Broadview Press, forthcoming 2008). DePasquale is of Mohawk and European backgrounds and is a member of the Six Nations of the Grand River Territory.

ALAIN JEAN-BART enseigne à Lille en France. Il s'intéresse à la littérature de jeunesse et aux arts plastiques. Il à été l'un des principaux collaborateurs de *Était-il une fois: Littérature de Jeunesse; panorama de la critique France-Canada* et co-auteur de *Les enjeux du roman pour adolescents*. Il entreprend actuellement des recherches sur les présupposés idéologiques de la fiction historique pour adolescents.

MARGARET MACKEY is a Professor in the School of Library and Information Studies at the University of Alberta. She has published widely in the area of young people's reading and media use. Her newest book is *Mapping Recreational Literacies* (Peter Lang, in press).

PERRY NODELMAN is a Professor Emeritus of English at the University of Winnipeg and the author of *Words about Pictures: The Narrative Art of Children's Picture Books*. In collaboration with Mavis Reimer he is the author of *The Pleasures of Children's Literature*. His latest novel for children is *Not a Nickel to Spare: The Great Depression Diary of Sally Cohen*, in Scholastic's Dear Canada series. He is currently finishing an academic book about the generic characteristics of texts of children's literature to be published by John Hopkins University Press and, in collaboration with Carol Matas, a young adult novel about ghost hunters to be published by Key Porter.

ANDREW O'MALLEY is an Associate Professor of English at Ryerson University. His book, *The Making of the Modern Child: Children's Literature and Childhood in the Late Eighteenth Century*, was published by Routledge in 2003. Currently, he is working on a larger study of robinsonades and of Robinson Crusoe in popular culture.

MAVIS REIMER is the Canada Research Chair in the Culture of Childhood and an Associate Professor in the Department of English at the University of Winnipeg. She is co-author of the third edition of *The Pleasures of Children's Literature* (2003), the editor of a collection of essays on *Anne of Green Gables*, entitled *Such a Simple Little Tale*, and Associate Editor of the journal *Canadian Children's Literature/Littérature canadienne pour la jeunesse*. At present, she is working on a book about the construction of the imperial child in Victorian children's literature.

ANNE RUSNAK est professeure d'études françaises à l'Université de Winnipeg, où elle enseigne un cours sur la littérature jeunesse francophone au Canada. Ses recherches et ses publications portent sur la littérature de jeunesse et, à présent, elle est la rédactrice associée (volet franco-phone) de la revue *Canadian Children's Literature/Littérature canadienne pour la jeunesse.*

LOUIS SALDANHA is an Assistant Professor in the Department of English at the University of Winnipeg, Manitoba. She is presently on leave and teaching at Grande Prairie College, Alberta. Her research and teaching interests are involved in the theory and practice of anti-oppression, especially concerning racialized and gendered identities. Her work is informed by critical theories of race, cultural studies, gender, diaspora and pedagogy, and has focused on children's literature and culture and Canadian literature and culture.

DEBORAH SCHNITZER is an educator, activist, editor and writer, most recently circulating in the speculative fiction *gertrude unmanageable.* She is honoured to be part of the conversation developed in this collection and the further exploration into words and pictures it encourages in her.

DANIELLE THALER enseigne au département de français de l'université de Victoria en Colombie-Britannique au Canada. Elle s'intéresse à la littérature de jeunesse depuis un nombre d'années et en particulier au roman historique, au roman-miroir et au roman d'aventures. Ses publications incluent : *Les enjeux du roman pour adolescents* en 2002 avec Alain Jean-Bart, L'Harmattan, Paris, et divers articles dont le plus récent, paru dans la collection éducation-recherche (Imaginaires métissés en littérature pour la jeunesse) aux Presses de l'Université du Québec en 2006, s'intitule *Métissage et acculturation : le regard de l'autre.* Elle travaille actuellement à une série d'essais mettant en lumière l'évolution de la représentation du personnage féminin dans la fiction historique contemporaine pour jeunes.

DORIS WOLF is an Assistant Professor of English and teaches and coordinates courses for the Community-Based Aboriginal Teacher Education Program at the University of Winnipeg. Her work on representations of Germans and Germany in Canadian literature has been published in *Studies in Canadian Literature* (2002), *Refractions of Germany in Canadian Literature and Culture* (Walter de Gruyter, 2003) and *Diaspora Experiences: German-speaking Immigrants and Their Descendants* (Wilfrid Laurier Press, forthcoming). She is currently working on representations of tribal nationalism in young adult novels by Aboriginal authors and literary celebrity in the field of Canadian publishing.

□ □ □

INDEX

Aboriginal literature, xii, 87–104, 104n3, 105n7, 105n8, 105n9, 108, 117–18, 165–68, 210, 227–28; myths, 88–90, 92–93, 104; protest, 91, 92

Aboriginal peoples, 88, 89, 94, 114, 177; Anishinabe/Ojibwa, 93; Beothuk, 120–25; community, 82, 93, 94, 96–100, 104, 111, 167–69; family, 94–96; Inuit, 94, 157; Iroquois, 88, 108, 109; Kootenay, 159; matrilineal, 95–96; Métis, 91, 93–95, 97–99, 100, 102, 117–18, 166, 167–69, 176n26; relationship with land, 91–92; self-determination, 92, 94, 99; Shawnee, 159; Sioux, 159; Tse-Shaht, 88; Tsimpshian, 90; Wyandote, 175n24

Aboriginal peoples, representations of, 5–7, 23n3, 70, 78–84, 103, 108, 116–20, 126–27, 158–60, 172n12, 176n26, 184–86, 192n1, 228; as children, 74–75, 79–80; community, 5; erasure, 5, 6, 14, 77, 78, 85n6, 120, 152, 177–78, 180; as other, 10; stereotypes, 82, 90–91, 92, 102, 118, 126. *See also* postcolonialism

Aboriginality, 112, 115, 116, 119–26, 212

Abu-Laban, Yasmeen, 130, 142n4

acculturation, 30, 41, 44

Achard, Eugène, 29, 30

adolescents : littérature destinée aux, 27, 45, 46, 53

adventure, xiv–xv, 67–68, 69–72, 73, 75, 89–90, 146, 158, 173n17; conquest and, 67, 78, 189; survival, 68, 72, 75, 82, 89

affiliation, 1, 2, 7–12, 13, 22, 123, 146, 155, 164, 181, 189, 230

Aker, Don, 8, 9, 10, 11, 12–13, 14, 18, 24n9

Alcoff, Linda, 111–12, 127–28

Alderson, Sue Ann, 172n10

Allen, Paula Gunn, 102, 105n8

altérité : Amérindiens comme incarnation de, 111; conception à partir du « home », 27-28, 31

Amérindiens : dans la littérature jeunesse de la France, 39; évolution de l'image dans la littérature jeunesse québécoise, 37-38; images des, 35-36; incarnation de l'altérité, 30-31, 34

Anderson, Benedict, xv–xvi, 51, 173n16

Anderson, Grant, 100–101, 103

Andrews, Jan, 172n11

Anfousse, Ginette : *Barricades d'Arthur, Les,* 60; *Grand rêve de Rosalie, Le,* 60

Books in the Studies in Childhood and Family in Canada Series
Published by Wilfrid Laurier University Press

Making Do:Women, Family, and Home in Montreal during the Great Depression by Denyse Baillargeon, translated by Yvonne Klein • 1999 / xii + 232 pp. / ISBN: 0-88920-326-1 / ISBN-13: 978-0-88920-326-6

Children in English-Canadian Society: Framing the Twentieth-Century Consensus by Neil Sutherland with a new foreword by Cynthia Comacchio • 2000 / xxiv + 336 pp. / illus. / ISBN: 0-88920-351-2 / ISBN-13: 978-0-88920-351-8

Love Strong as Death: Lucy Peel's Canadian Journal, 1833–1836 edited by J.I. Little • 2001 / x + 229 pp. / illus. / ISBN: 0-88920-389-X / ISBN-13: 978-0-88920-389-230-X

The Challenge of Children's Rights for Canada by Katherine Covell and R. Brian Howe • 2001 / viii + 244 pp. / ISBN: 0-88920-380-6 / ISBN-13: 978-0-88920-380-8

NFB Kids: Portrayals of Children by the National Film Board of Canada, 1939–1989 by Brian J. Low • 2002 / vi + 288 pp. / illus. / ISBN: 0-88920-386-5 / ISBN-13: 978-0-88920-386-0

Something to Cry About: An Argument against Corporal Punishment of Children in Canada by Susan M. Turner • 2002 / xx + 317 pp. / ISBN: 0-88920-382-2 / ISBN-13: 978-0-88920-382-2

Freedom to Play:We Made Our Own Fun edited by Norah L. Lewis • 2002 / xiv + 210 pp. / ISBN: 0-88920-406-3 / ISBN-13: 978-0-88920-406-5

The Dominion of Youth: Adolescence and the Making of Modern Canada, 1920–1950 by Cynthia Comacchio • 2006 / x + 302 pp. / illus. / ISBN: 0-88920-488-8 / ISBN-13: 978-0-88920-488-1

Evangelical Balance Sheet: Character, Family, and Business in Mid-Victorian Nova Scotia by B. Anne Wood • 2006 / xxx + 198 pp. / illus. / ISBN: 0-88920-500-0 / ISBN-13: 978-0-88920-500-0

A Question of Commitment: Children's Rights in Canada edited by R. Brian Howe and Katherine Covell • 2007 / xiv + 442 pp. / ISBN: 978-1-55458-003-3

Taking Responsibility for Children edited by Samantha Brennan and Robert Noggle • 2007 / xxii + 188 pp. / ISBN: 978-1-55458-015-6

Home Words: Discourses of Children's Literature in Canada edited by Mavis Reimer • 2008 / xx + 280 pp. / ISBN: 978-1-55458-016-3